Communal Violence in the British Empire

Disturbing the Pax

Mark Doyle

Bloomsbury Academic
An imprint of Bloomsbury Publishing Plc
BLOOMSBURY
LONDON • OXFORD • NEW YORK • NEW DELHI • SYDNEY

Bloomsbury Academic
An imprint of Bloomsbury Publishing Plc

50 Bedford Square
London
WC1B 3DP
UK

1385 Broadway
New York
NY 10018
USA

www.bloomsbury.com

BLOOMSBURY and the Diana logo are trademarks of Bloomsbury Publishing Plc

First published 2016

British Library Cataloguing-in-Publication Data
A catalogue record for this book is available from the British Library.

ISBN:HB: 978-1-4742-6-825-7
ePDF: 978-1-4742-6-827-1
ePub: 978-1-4742-6-826-4

Library of Congress Cataloging-in-Publication Data
A catalog record for this book is available from the Library of Congress.

Cover design: Sharon Mah
Cover image: The Bombay Religious Riots (engraving), Prior, Melton © Look and Learn / Illustrated Papers Collection / Bridgeman Images

Typeset by Newgen Knowledge Works (P) Ltd., Chennai, India.
Printed and bound in Great Britain

For Kate.

Contents

Acknowledgments

It has become common in historical scholarship to faintly praise bold or unconventional books as "ambitious"—the implication usually being that the author has bitten off more than she or he can chew, or, more prosaically, has offered stronger arguments than the evidence can support. I happen to prefer "ambitious" books, not because I place little value on evidence, but because I recognize that all historical knowledge is provisional. The most valuable works of historical scholarship, to my mind, are those that are led by their sources to ask more questions or suggest more possibilities than they can satisfactorily resolve. They are also those that manage to capture the complexity and ultimate unknowability of the past not by setting out to prove just how complex things were, but by constructing narratives that uncover new mysteries even as they dispel others—or by making it clear that every story about the past intersects with many other, sometimes contradictory, often irrecoverable stories. It is in the asking, not the answering, that we discover new ways of thinking about the past, and, while I have certainly tried to answer some important questions about the form, function, and legacy of the British Empire in this book, I hope that the questions I ask, or the stories I hint at but cannot tell, prove to be just as stimulating as the answers.

This book and I have been companions for nearly eight years. We have traveled together from Massachusetts to Tennessee, made journeys of varying lengths to Ireland, the United Kingdom, France, Belgium, and India, watched our circumstances progress from postdoctoral limbo to tenured stability, and tested our ideas with any number of students, colleagues, friends, and strangers. The arguments I present here, and the stories I tell, are undoubtedly incomplete, and they are certainly shaped by my own assumptions and preoccupations. A different historian would probably approach this material with a different set of questions and arrive, perhaps, at different conclusions. In fact, I sincerely hope that this book will challenge somebody (better, a modest parade of somebodies) to do just that. This book is the culmination of a long process of research, reflection, and discussion, but it is also part of an ongoing historical investigation into the meanings and legacies of the British Empire that is much bigger than myself. Not only would this book never have seen the light of day without the assistance of the people and institutions I am about to mention, but it would also have served very little purpose in the world, once it did appear, were it not for the inquisitive and dedicated community of scholars whose ideas have helped guide my own.

This book began during my year at Amherst College as a Copeland Colloquium Fellow in 2008–9. I would like to thank the participants in the colloquium, Carleen Basler, Thomas Dumm, Amy Huber, Laure Katsaros, Theresa Laizer, Maple Rasza, Austin Sarat, and Leo Zaibert, for helping me think in a focused way about the meaning and nature of violence in modern societies. Special thanks go to Catherine Epstein, not only for looking after me during my time at Amherst, but also for her continued friendship and support in the years since.

The History Department at Middle Tennessee State University has been my home for the past seven years, and I could not have asked for a more welcoming and supportive environment in which to pursue my passion. Nearly all members of this (quite large) department have helped this project along in one way or another, sometimes by contributing ideas and suggestions about the project itself and sometimes through their companionship and encouragement; I will refrain from listing them all by name. However, I do want to acknowledge the particular support of Amy Sayward, Robert Hunt, and James Beeby, the three department chairs at various periods during the past seven years, as well as Sean Foley, Pippa Holloway, and Brian Ingrassia, who have read and commented on some facets of this project. The provost Brad Bartel and the dean of the College of Liberal Arts Mark Byrnes have generously provided funding to pursue research and attend conferences. Much of the archival research in Ireland and the United Kingdom was funded by a grant from the Faculty Research and Creative Activity Committee and an Access and Diversity Grant. I would also like to thank the many students who, wittingly or not, have served as sounding boards for my ideas about violence and empire. I would especially like to thank Mason Christensen and Jennie Epp, who transcribed some of the source material, and Katie McClurkin, who assisted with the preparation of the manuscript for publication.

In 2013 I participated in a summer institute in New Delhi funded by the National Endowment for the Humanities, called "India: Past and Present." This allowed me to undertake archival research at the Indian National Archives and, perhaps more importantly, helped me come to grips with the complex history and culture of Britain's most important imperial possession. My excursions with Steven Patterson to Amritsar, Wagah, and the Nicholson Cemetery in

Delhi were especially eye opening, and I have highly valued Steven's input on this project ever since. My deepest thanks to Beverly Blois, Daniel Ehnbom, and Meena Nayak for organizing the institute—it must have taken nerves of steel to pull it off—and to my fellow participants for making it such an unforgettable experience.

I must also acknowledge the assistance of the staffs of numerous archives and libraries around the world: the Bodleian Library, Oxford University; the Borthwick Institute of Historical Research, University of York; Public Record Office of Northern Ireland, Belfast; Linen Hall Library, Belfast; British Library (especially the Asian & African Reading Room); National Archives of Great Britain, Kew; National Archives of Ireland; National Library of Ireland; National Archives of India; National Archives of Scotland; James E. Walker Library, Middle Tennessee State University; and Robert Frost Library, Amherst College.

Many of the ideas in this book first took shape during academic conferences and colloquia, and I would like to thank the organizers and participants of the following: Amherst College Copeland Conference on "Performing Violence," Amherst, 2008; CIRSAP Workshop on "Police and Colonial Empires, 18th–20th Centuries," Paris, 2009; Southern Conference on British Studies, Charlotte, 2010; British Scholar Conference, Austin, 2011; American Conference on Irish Studies, New Orleans, 2012; Northeast Victorian Studies Association Conference, Boston, 2013; Policing Empires Conference, Brussels, 2013; and Midwest Victorian Studies Association Conference, April 2014.

I would also like to thank Jill Bender and Ely Janis for helping this project find a home; Claire Lipscomb and the editorial staff at Bloomsbury, as well as the anonymous peer reviewers; and the innumerable friends and acquaintances on both sides of the Atlantic who have taken an interest, cheered me on, or simply nodded politely whenever the subject of my research has come up. My most emphatic thanks go to my wife, Kate, who took a chance seven years ago on a new life in an unfamiliar place with a guy who spends his time contemplating mass violence. I am incapable of expressing just how glad I am that she took that chance—and I'm sure our two daughters are equally grateful. This book, like so much else in my life, is dedicated to her.

List of Abbreviations

BL	British Library
CSORP	Chief Secretary's Office Registered Papers (in the National Archives of Ireland)
HC Deb	House of Commons Debates (Hansard)
HL Deb	House of Lords Debates (Hansard)
IOR	India Office Records (in the British Library)
NAGB	National Archives of Great Britain, Kew
NAIn	National Archives of India, New Delhi
NAIr	National Archives of Ireland, Dublin
NLI	National Library of Ireland, Dublin
PRONI	Public Record Office of Northern Ireland, Belfast
RNN	Reports on Native Newspapers (in the National Archives of India)

Introduction

Few people in Victorian Britain would have thought to contradict Sir John Strachey on the subject of India. Strachey had spent nearly forty years in India, working as everything from a cholera inspector to an interim Viceroy, as a servant first of the East India Company and then, after 1858, of the Queen-Empress Victoria. Few could match his knowledge of the intricate web Britain had spun across the subcontinent, its faults and gaps, its areas of strength and support. Certainly, few who heard his lectures at Cambridge University in 1884, four years after his return from India, would have known enough about that distant land to gainsay his encomium to Britain's benevolent regime there, the prosperity and enlightenment it was spreading, the morality it was inculcating, and the peace it was securing. Few would have quarreled with his assertion that India was not a nation in any proper sense, that the only thing giving it coherence was the fact of British rule, or that only Britain's impartial regime was capable of holding together such an unruly swarm of humanity. In fact, so authoritative were Strachey's pronouncements on these and other topics that when he expanded his Cambridge lectures into a book in 1888 it quickly became the standard text about Britain's Indian administration, going through four editions by 1911, the year of George V's Coronation Durbar in Delhi, arguably the high tide of Britain's imperial career. Like the countless students and armchair imperialists who pored over its pages, Strachey's book was splendidly self-assured, confident in the judiciousness and humanity of the British race, and fully convinced of the selfless virtue of British imperialism—except, that is, for a strange, and by most people probably unnoticed, caveat toward the book's end.

After laying out the history of India and the current character of the British administration there, Strachey closed his book with an evaluation of the benefits and prospects of British rule, starting with the (wholly conventional) observation that Britain had brought peace to a disordered land. The first edition began its reckoning as follows:

> The first great and obvious fact is this, that in place of a condition of society given up, as it was immediately before our time, to anarchy and to the liability to every conceivable form of violence and oppression, we now have absolute peace. Let not this unspeakable blessing of the Pax Britannica be forgotten. There are not many European countries where protection to life and property is so complete. … Except when sometimes for a moment the fanaticism and intolerance of rival sects of Mohammadans and Hindus burst into violent conflict, and show what would instantly follow if the strong hand of our Government were withdrawn, unbroken tranquility prevails.[1]

Internal peace was the *sine qua non* of Britain's civilizing mission, the condition that had to be achieved before all the other blessings of civilization could take hold, and in 1888 Strachey believed that this condition had, for the most part, been met. He went on to say that Indians did not yet fully appreciate the changes Britain had wrought, but that Britain must nevertheless continue "to govern India on the principles which our superior knowledge tells us are right," even if such principles were unpopular.[2] The next three editions of the book made the same argument, but with one slight alteration. Instead of bursting into conflict "sometimes for a moment," by the second edition (1894) the "rival sects" of Hindus and Muslims were said to be clashing with one another "not unfrequently."[3] It was a subtle but significant change, rendering Strachey's pronouncement not only ungrammatical but slightly unintelligible. "Absolute peace" except for "not unfrequent" outbursts of "fanaticism and intolerance"? Frequent communal violence under British rule as a sign of what would happen if Britain ceased to rule? Just what kind of a "Pax" was this?

The immediate reason for this strange revision—let us call it Strachey's Caveat—was undoubtedly the wave of rioting that swept through India in 1893, an outbreak whose course we will examine in due time, but it points to a larger truth, and one that was not confined to India. Unlike the great empires of earlier times, the British Empire of the Victorian period staked its legitimacy not primarily on the right of conquest but on the moral benefits that the conquered people would derive from foreign rule. This civilizing mission may have been an illusion, a fig leaf hiding (just barely) the avarice of plunderers and businessmen, but as fictions go, it was utterly necessary, for it enabled Britain's empire builders to justify their project before the British public, their colonial subjects, foreign powers, and (not least) themselves in moral, rather than self-interested, terms. In a world, or anyway a Europe, that was beginning to insist that governments draw their legitimacy from their ability to promote the interests of their people (whoever their people might be, and however their interests might be defined), European empires had to demonstrate that there was some moral purpose, some fundamental beneficence, underlying their claims to rule over distant strangers.[4] And for that civilizing mission to take hold—indeed, even for the empire's less altruistic motives to be realized—a certain level of internal peace had to be maintained.

Yet, there was no "unbroken tranquility" in Britain's empire, either in India or in many other places. There were riots between rival communities (or elements within those communities), as well as clashes between communities and the state, right across the globe, from South Asia to the West Indies to the United Kingdom itself. These outbreaks were not exactly frequent, but neither were they "unfrequent," and in some areas they were positively endemic. They were also quite damaging, not only to lives and property but also to the imperial state's prestige, its reputation for fairness and impartiality, and even its ability to perform the fundamental duties of a state. Strachey's Caveat, in short, was wide enough to steer a gunboat through. What might we find if we step inside and examine its contents?

This book does not argue that the *Pax Britannica* was a lie or an enigma—apart from the wars of conquest on the frontiers, most places under the Union Jack in the Victorian period were indeed peaceful most of the time—but it does argue that internal violence was more important to the theory and practice of British imperialism than either the Victorians or historians of our own time have recognized. Of course, few modern historians share Strachey's complacency about the benevolence of the British Empire (although there are exceptions[5]); the perfidies and brutalities of British imperialism are so well known as to have formed their own sort of academic orthodoxy, and even scholars who admire some aspects of the empire recognize that it rested on a foundation of racial arrogance and self-serving paternalism. Nevertheless, the notion of a Victorian *Pax Britannica*, of a red-tinted force field sheltering large parts of the globe from internal and external threat, remains curiously intact.[6] It is not that scholars are unaware of the many riots and disturbances that took place during the Victorian era, but there has been little effort to investigate what these outbreaks meant for the empire as a whole: for its self-image, for its reputation among its subjects, for its coherence or incoherence as a world system, or for the mundane tasks of governance. This book focuses on one kind of internal violence, riots that took place between different subject communities (or elements within those communities), which I will broadly categorize as communal, in order to show how violence that was not a direct threat to the British state nevertheless became central to the ideology, practice, and long-term survival of the British Empire. I propose, in other words, to treat communal violence, and the state's response to it, not as an anomaly but as fundamental to the imperial experience. Itself an outgrowth of empire, communal violence helped Britons justify their empire, influenced how they controlled their empire, and ultimately helped to undermine their authority in large parts of the empire. To accept Strachey's vision of a *Pax Britannica*, unamended, is to miss one of the vital forces that made the Victorian Empire what it was.

This book makes four major arguments and rests on three core assumptions. First, I argue that British imperialism, through the mechanisms of modernity and liberalism, helped to cause the very violence it purported to extirpate. This is not to deny that there were other causes, both deep and immediate, for each outbreak, but it is to suggest that there was something peculiar about being on the receiving end of British imperial expansion that made some places vulnerable to internal violence. Second, I argue that British officials and observers were largely blind to the way their imperium contributed to communal violence, choosing instead to see these outbreaks as evidence that turbulent locales needed more, not less, British intervention. Third, I argue that British prejudices and cultural assumptions informed the policing of communal riots and show how these practices changed over time. Fourth, I argue that episodes of communal violence, while not exactly fatal to British authority, nevertheless helped to erode the legitimacy of the imperial state and contributed to the various crises that afflicted the empire in the first decades of the twentieth century. I have devoted one chapter to proving each of these arguments, so I will not develop them further here; my three core assumptions, however, need some explanation at the outset.

My first assumption is that areas of the empire as radically different from one another as Ireland, South Asia, and the West Indies—my main areas of analysis—are, in fact, comparable, and that such a comparison can tell us something valuable about how the British Empire operated. The rest of the empire, especially the settler colonies of Canada, Australia, New Zealand, and southern Africa, also experienced communal tensions, and occasional violence, but I have omitted them for a couple of reasons. For one thing, their power dynamics were very different from colonies answerable directly to London: settler elites often had very different conceptions of the purpose of empire than their metropolitan counterparts, and they rarely felt the need to justify their conduct to anyone other than themselves. For another thing, communal violence in these colonies often involved rival settler groups (e.g., Protestant Orangemen and Irish Catholics in

Canada), rather than indigenous groups; they therefore raise a somewhat different set of questions—in part because they evoked a different set of official responses—than clashes between, say, Hindus and Muslims in India. Other colonies that might have been added to this study, for instance the old slave ports of western Africa or the new African colonies acquired in the late nineteenth century, have been omitted largely because they did not experience significant outbreaks of internal violence during the Victorian period. Many, perhaps most, of these colonies experienced violence between whites and indigenous people, but these clashes usually occurred within the context of colonial conquest and were not therefore a problem of colonial governance as such. Moreover, in many of the newer African and Asian colonies, effective authority rested with chartered companies rather than the British state, making them even less directly comparable to colonies ruled directly from Whitehall.

None of these are unassailable reasons for omitting huge swathes of the empire, of course, and I hope my study will lead others to apply, test, or challenge my arguments in any relevant parts of the empire that I have left out. I believe my arguments are generally applicable to the empire as a whole, but we will not know for certain until they are tested against more evidence. The fact is that with a mammoth topic such as the British Empire, one must draw the line somewhere, and I have chosen to draw my line around a limited but diverse collection of colonies whose vastly different circumstances nevertheless gave rise to very similar discussions and practices. The primary sites we will visit are India, Ceylon, British Guiana, and Ireland, with short excursions into other areas. The inclusion of India needs little justification: as the largest and most important British possession, India's complexity, ethnic and otherwise, was the topic of limitless comment and accommodation among the Victorians, especially during the "not unfrequent" clashes between its various communities. My analysis of India concentrates on the post-1857 period, when the crown assumed sovereignty from the East India Company (following the massive revolt of that year) and publicly committed itself to a policy of religious neutrality. I focus especially on Bombay, which saw major riots every couple of decades, and on northern India, where disputes between Muslims and Hindus became increasingly common as the century drew to a close.

Ceylon is also an illuminating site of analysis, for, while it was much more peaceful than some other parts of South Asia, it did experience a handful of riots in the late nineteenth and early twentieth centuries, which shed considerable light on the evolution of state responses to communal violence. While I have not given it a chapter of its own, Ceylon (with its mix of Buddhist, Catholic, and

Muslim inhabitants) appears in several of the thematic chapters to show that the challenges of ruling heterogeneous Asian populations were not limited to India. The West Indies, which also appear with some frequency in what follows, were also comparatively peaceful, but they experienced just enough communal conflict (and other disturbances) during our period to show that the tendencies and trends of the East were also evident in the West.

The prominence of Ireland in this study requires a bit more explanation, since Ireland was not a colony in a formal sense but rather a constituent member of the United Kingdom. The Irish sent representatives to Parliament, were subject to the same common law (and some statutory laws) as Britain, and were, moreover, responsible for peopling the empire with thousands of soldiers, settlers, and administrators. Partly for these reasons, some scholars have begun to doubt whether Ireland in this period should be considered a colony at all.[7] Most would agree that through the early seventeenth century, when the last explicit colonization scheme occurred, Ireland was indeed a colony of sorts, but by the Victorian period the picture is less clear. Since being absorbed into the United Kingdom in 1801, Ireland had retained certain colonial remnants, such as a viceroy acting as the monarch's representative and a separate administration based in Dublin Castle, and it was often spoken about and treated as if its people were fundamentally different from "real" Britons, but it was also heavily Anglicized in many respects and enjoyed formal legal equality with Scotland, England, and Wales. My position is that, whatever Ireland's ontological status, examining the country *as if* it was a colony is analytically useful, both for understanding Ireland's relationship with Britain and for understanding the empire as a whole. Communal violence in Ireland—or sectarian violence, as it is usually called there—elicited many of the same policies, prejudices, and paradoxes that governed British behavior in South Asia and the West Indies. Historians and literary theorists have begun to explore some of the ways the Irish experience of British rule resembled that of South Asia, but so far there has been relatively little attention to the shared history of communal violence in these two regions, and there has been even less attention to Ireland's similarities with other parts of the empire.[8] This book will demonstrate that although Ireland's internal violence grew out of the island's unique historical circumstances, Irish violence also bore striking resemblances to violence elsewhere in the empire, both in its causes and in its character. These resemblances allowed the British imperial imagination to see the "fighting Irish" as part of a larger mass of irrational and incomprehensible subjects beyond Britain's shores, a sort of worldwide mob of fanatics upon whom the sun never set. Because it is analytically useful to do so, then, I will be referring to Ireland as a "colony" throughout this book, but we should bear in mind that Ireland's place in the empire was much more ambiguous than that of many other colonies.

My second assumption is that there was (and is) a type of violent behavior that can be analyzed under the heading "communal violence." I have chosen this term, which is most commonly applied to Hindu-Muslim violence in India, not because it is especially elegant or accurate but because it is the best of a limited set of choices. Other terms—such as religious violence, sectarian violence, or ethnic violence—are either too reductive or too closely tied to causative explanations to be helpful.[9] To call a conflict religious, for instance, is to imply that the belligerents are somehow fighting "about" religion, rather than being motivated by economic tensions, political disagreements, or other secular forces. In fact, while most of the disturbances I examine here involved adherents of antagonistic religious groups, their quarrels centered much more often upon access to public space, incompatible political aspirations, and economic resentments than upon religious disagreements per se. Of course, the term communal has its own shortcomings, largely because it implies a set of discreet, more or less homogeneous "communities" whose members share similar priorities and outlooks; to call a violent episode communal, without further elaboration, risks implying that entire communities were out on the streets fighting against one another. In reality this was never, or almost never, the case. Normally it was a body of extremists—self-appointed communal champions or defenders, people whom social scientists call "ethnic entrepreneurs"—who provoked and maintained these conflicts, while the more peaceably inclined inhabitants stepped aside, fled, sought shelter, worked to stop the violence, or (at most) gravitated toward the extremists of their "own side" for self-defense. Each riot and demonstration that I examine here was merely the most visible manifestation of an infinitely more complicated set of group dynamics that no label can adequately convey, but if we must choose a label, then "communal" is the most capacious term that still manages to distinguish these events from other forms of mass violence, such as rebellions or warfare.[10]

The problem of labeling mass violence is not confined to adjectives, however. The term "riot" also appears frequently in this book, and here, too, it is a case of choosing the least-bad option. Scholars have frequently noted how this term tends to reproduce the perspective of the powerful: to call an event a riot is often to delegitimize it, to emphasize its illegality, and to imply that its protagonists are motivated by passion rather than reason. Charles Tilly has suggested several more precise terms for describing mass violence – among them are scattered attacks, brawls, violent rituals, and coordinated destruction—each term distinguished from the others by the extent to which the violence is coordinated among different actors and by the frequency of violent encounters within a larger set of confrontations.[11] These terms are indeed useful for explaining, as Tilly wants us to do, how outbreaks of mass violence ebb and flow from one stage to another, for example, how they escalate from scattered attacks into campaigns of coordinated destruction before degenerating into brawls. However (and Tilly recognizes that this is the case), these forms of violence often occur simultaneously, as part of a larger outbreak of mass violence. What do we call an episode in which scattered attacks coincide with opportunism (another of Tilly's categories) along the fringes of some violent ritual? It seems to me that riot is the only term that will do.[12]

Used with caution, the term riot can, I believe, be used without reproducing the value judgments of the authority figures who were most likely to use the word. A guide to Irish constables published in 1895 offers the standard, legal definition of a misdemeanor riot:

> A riot is a tumultuous disturbance of the peace by *three persons or more* [twelve or more constituted a felony], assembling together of their own authority, with an intent mutually to assist one another against any one who shall oppose them in the execution of some enterprise of a private nature, and afterwards actually executing the same, in a violent and turbulent manner, to the terror of the people, whether the act intended were of itself lawful or unlawful.[13]

This is how the authorities defined a riot, and, since it is the authorities with whom we will primarily be concerned in this book, it is well to have this definition in mind as we proceed. However, let us push back against the official view by observing that a riot also entails a temporary *breakdown of authority*. It is a momentary lifting of the usual rules governing social interaction in a society, one in which the power structure loses its ability to enforce "law and order," while, at the same time, some individuals abandon the tacit restraint with which members of a society normally act toward one another (and toward one another's property) and begin performing acts of violent aggression. A riot, in other words, is not only an episode of momentary, large-scale criminality, but also a temporary overturning or rearranging of power structures and social relations. This, as we will see, is one of the reasons communal riots were so threatening to British imperial prestige.

My third assumption is that there is some value in speaking of the attitudes and practices of British officials in general, rather than merely individual, terms. Although I am careful to identify differences of opinion among British officials (and other observers), and I also carefully scrutinize the motivations and predispositions of certain key individuals, it is also possible (and necessary) to examine those attitudes that were common to most, if not quite all, British observers. Peter Robb has made a similar point about British officials in India:

> It is possible to talk of British attitudes, not because they were uniform or consistent but because of certain repeated assumptions and tendencies. … Attitudes were readily enforced by the smallness of the ICS [Indian Civil Service], by shared or parallel educational experience among the recruits, by periods of training almost as apprentice to established officers, and by frequent points of contact, at the club or hill-station, in constant reports and letters, and through frequent changes of job.[14]

Most of these observations can apply to British officials elsewhere in the empire. Britons were certainly no more monolithic than the people they ruled, but the small subset of Britons who worked as professional empire builders (and here I include journalists who helped construct and promote the idea of empire) did share a certain set of assumptions that became, in effect, the "common sense" of British imperialism, and these assumptions closely guided Britons' interpretations of, and behavior toward, communal disturbances.

One of the most important components of this imperial "common sense" was liberalism, a concept that will appear with some frequency in the coming chapters. By liberalism I mean not a formal political doctrine but a general habit of mind that Theodore Koditschek defines as "a loose constellation, encompassing free trade, free labor, free association, free press, and formal equality."[15] By the beginning of the Victorian period the British mainland was well on its way to becoming a predominately liberal society, and British empire builders (even those who called themselves Conservatives) increasingly invoked liberal principles to justify the maintenance and expansion of the empire. Progress—that is, progress toward the sort of liberal society supposedly embodied by Britain itself—was, for many of these men, the principal measure of Britain's success overseas, however much their actual behavior contradicted these principles.

A central preoccupation of the liberal imagination was the idea that the state, no less than the people, must be bound by the rule of law. R. W. Kostal has noted the "extraordinary legal-mindedness of British imperial and domestic politics" in the middle of the nineteenth century, citing British responses to uprisings in Ceylon (1848) and Jamaica (1865) as evidence that the "British political class took pride—derived a keen sense of moral superiority—in its conviction that its power was not absolute, that it was constrained by and accountable to law."[16]

Nasser Hussain has similarly noted how, "Government by rules became the basis for the conceptualization of the 'moral legitimacy' of British colonial rule. The applicability of rules to all was understood as the distinguishing feature of British rule, and counterpoint to the 'personal discretion' found in a theory of precolonial sovereignty known as Oriental Despotism."[17] If Britain's was a liberal empire, and most historians agree that it was (at least in principle), and if, as Charles Townshend says, "[t]he essence of liberalism was the insistence that government must be under the law, and that the law must be the same for every citizen," then there would appear to have been a profound paradox at the heart of the empire.[18] How could a liberal, rule-bound regime uphold a system that was inherently unequal, authoritarian, and exploitative?

The tension between the ideals of British liberalism and the realities of colonial rule was the fundamental tension of the Victorian British Empire.[19] Indeed, tension may be too mild a word for what would become, in time, an irresolvable contradiction that first undermined the empire's moral legitimacy and then threatened its very existence. While we must avoid viewing the nineteenth century solely through the lens of the twentieth, it is surely significant that three of the colonies studied here—Ireland, India, and Ceylon—were among the first to achieve independence when the empire began its great unraveling. They were also (again, not quite coincidentally) the sites of some of the worst communal violence among former British colonies after independence. I am reluctant to suggest too close a connection between the communal violence of the Victorian period and the independence struggles of the twentieth century (to say nothing of the communal conflicts at the tail end of that century), for there were too many intervening steps—too many new historical forces—between the Victorian era and these later episodes to chart a clear causal connection. Nevertheless, this tension between imperial ideology and imperial reality, this design flaw in the very foundations of empire, grew stronger and more apparent as the Victorian period advanced, thanks in part to the outbreaks of communal violence that we will examine here. While they did not kill the empire, these disturbances exposed (and sometimes introduced) some of the weaknesses to which the empire would eventually succumb.

Much of the research for this book comes from official and unofficial archives in London, Oxford, Dublin, Belfast, and New Delhi, where I have examined the correspondence of British administrators, police reports, statistical returns, judicial records, and other state-generated or state-centered documents. I have also made extensive use of parliamentary papers containing either the reports and minutes of official inquiries or collections of correspondence relating to riots. Although these sources are not without their problems—being state-generated, they often obfuscate or exculpate the behavior of officials and do not adequately address the motives or complexities of "native" society—they are among the most reliable gauges of state perceptions, assumptions, and actions. Newspapers—from Britain as well as the colonies, and from the colonizers as well as the colonized—have allowed me to evaluate nonofficial opinion and to reconstruct events, as have numerous memoirs, travelogues, and other printed sources.[20] The advent of digital, keyword-searchable databases, newspapers, and books has enabled me to consult many more printed sources than would have been possible just a few years ago. These new research tools have made the broad scope of this book possible, setting it apart from earlier (primarily local) studies that rely on a much smaller source base.

Normally when historians write about communal riots, they are trying to understand the underlying economic, cultural, and social tensions of particular localities. In such studies (many of which I have used in my own analyses) the state's role is only part of the equation, and rightly so: if the aim is to understand why a riot happened or what it reveals about a specific locality, then there are many more factors to consider beside the state. The drawback of such studies, however, is that they often downplay the role of the state, which, among other things, normally set the parameters within which local power relations played out. One great exception to this trend is the vast and sophisticated body of scholarship relating to Britain's role in shaping communal relations in South Asia. Gyanendra Pandey, Bernard Cohn, and Nicholas Dirks, among others, have all offered good reasons for seeing Britain as an active force in the construction (or, at the very least, the ossification) of communal identities in nineteenth-century India.[21] Historians such as Patricia Gossman and Sandria Freitag, meanwhile, have shown how state officials, far from being neutral bystanders in India's communal disputes, played a crucial role in fostering, shaping, and sometimes exacerbating violence.[22] Studies focusing on the state's role in communal violence are rare for Ireland and the West Indies, but, as we will see, the lessons of South Asian historiography can profitably be applied to these places as well.[23] Indeed, one of the benefits of a comparative study like this is that it allows us not only to place different regions' histories side by side, but also to bring together ideas from different scholarly traditions and to see whether they work for the empire as a whole.

Of course, a transcolonial project of this sort also requires us to come to grips with the complex interaction between the universal and the particular aspects of empire, or, put another way, the relationship between the center and the periphery. Is the British Empire best understood as a single unit controlled by a dominant metropolitan center, or as a collection of loosely connected, heterogeneous territories whose histories were driven primarily by local, rather than central, concerns? In recent years historians have begun to embrace the notion of a decentered (or multicentered) empire, seeing it as a single field of force in which people, goods, ideas, and discourses flowed in multiple directions. This notion, usually associated with the movement known (with diminishing accuracy) as the "new imperial history," has produced many fine studies, and it is certainly preferable to a model of empire in which all-powerful Europeans rule over passive and powerless natives.[24] However, as Richard Price has pointed out, many of these newer works, shaped as they are by the concerns of post-linguistic-turn discourse analysis, have little time for unfashionable, but still relevant, categories of analysis like great power rivalries, mercantile and industrial capitalism, technological and military developments, party politics, and the state.[25] Yet these categories are still relevant to any understanding of British imperialism, because they force us to consider the disparate power relations upon which the empire depended. Viewed from the top (say, the Colonial Office in Whitehall), the British Empire was not a level field upon which matter and spirit flowed freely, but a hierarchical system where power was concentrated in a limited number of persons and locations. Seen from the bottom (say, a village in rural British Guiana), the system was also hierarchical, even if local realities occupied much more official attention than the global priorities of Whitehall. However much people around the empire might challenge, resist, alter, refract, co-opt, mimic, accept, or ignore the imperatives of the center, the empire remained a system in which Britons had more power than non-Britons and the center normally had more power—military, economic, and political—than the periphery. When conflicts occurred between center and periphery, it was usually because the universal objectives of the center clashed with the particular realities and priorities of people on the ground. This tension was not incidental to, but actually constitutive of, the entire imperial project.

Rather than obscuring, or attempting to resolve, this tension, I have chosen to embody it within the structure of this book. Half of the chapters that follow are detailed narratives of significant communal disturbances in British Guiana (1856), Belfast (1872), Bombay (1874), and different spots across northern and western India (1893). These narrative chapters detail the personalities, decisions, and discussions that made each riot unique, but taken together they also reveal patterns of British thought and behavior that remained remarkably consistent across time and space. Interleaved among the narrative chapters are four thematic essays that explore those larger patterns. Drawing upon evidence from many outbreaks, large and small, these chapters present arguments about Britain's role in causing, interpreting, and policing communal violence, and about the consequences of this violence for the British Empire generally. These thematic chapters do not ignore the unique circumstances that produced violence in different places, but they do present arguments that are applicable to the Victorian empire as a whole.

The model of Victorian imperialism that I am proposing here is one in which there was a universal, and fairly consistent, body of ideas and practices that expressed themselves in unique ways across the world. Each local outbreak was a variation on a theme, a product of an underlying logic that both local belligerents and British officials tended to adhere to. There are undoubtedly numerous exceptions to the arguments I put forward in my thematic chapters, especially in parts of the empire that I have not examined for this study, but I believe the overall patterns I identify were valid for most of the empire, most of the time. We will not know for sure, however, until more research is done in those areas that I have not considered here. I hope this book will stimulate such research.

One final word about the parameters of this study: this book focuses on the Victorian period (bleeding over the edges into the early twentieth century) in order to understand how communal violence interacted with British imperialism in its most self-assured and benevolent guise. Prior to this period the civilizing mission, if articulated at all, was usually accompanied by frank acknowledgments of the colonizers' self-interest, whether commercial, military, or religious; a sense of moral purpose, apart from spreading Christianity, was not yet integral to the enterprise, nor was there any talk of a *Pax Britannica* until quite late in the nineteenth century.[26] Looking at the period from the other direction, it is certainly true that the civilizing mission lived on well into the twentieth century, but in later decades—especially after the First World War—popular nationalist movements, many of them violent and insurrectionary, would coax Britain into much more aggressive behavior toward colonized peoples. As periodic crises flared up around the globe, and as these met with ever more violent repression, the existence of a "British peace" became harder and harder to discern, much less discuss. The Victorian period represents not exactly a lull (for new territories were violently acquired then, and militant nationalist movements did exist), but a sort of plateau, a moment when, in most parts of the empire, what concerned British officials was not how to claim new territory or to suppress insurrection (the Indian revolt of 1857 was the great exception), but rather how to govern all those foreign peoples over whom the Union Jack flew. Toward the end of the Victorian period there was a definite shift, both in the nature of communal violence and in the state's responses to it, which marked the beginning of a new paradigm, closing off one period and setting the stage for the much more turbulent decades ahead. Understanding why this shift happened will be one of the major concerns of this book, but not before we explore the plateau that preceded it.

1

The Angel Gabriel in the Tropics: British Guiana, 1856

If ever a man knew how to start a fire using only words for tinder, it was John Sayers Orr. In the five years before he set the colony of British Guiana aflame, in February 1856, he blazed a trail of destruction from Scotland to Quebec and along the northeastern seaboard of the United States with a powerful kind of street oratory that blended apocalyptic anti-Catholicism with bread-and-butter xenophobia. He was not the only street corner preacher of his time, but he was among the more successful—if success is measured in the amount of territory covered and property damaged—and also among the more colorful, his practice of blowing a trumpet to attract an audience earning him the nickname "Angel Gabriel," a sobriquet that he may or may not have appreciated.[1] He was also among the more practiced: we find him in the newspapers as early as 1832, appearing before a London magistrate after addressing a "motley assembly" in Leicester Square, proudly announcing that he had been arrested twenty times already and had, on this occasion, been out of jail for scarcely a month.[2] In the Chartist year of 1848 he was again arrested in London, this time while telling a crowd in Clerkenwell Green about the benefits of republican institutions and asking them, "if a man saw another with two coats, have you not a right to take one of them?"[3]

But it was not until 1851 that Orr's career really took off. In that year he began preaching regular sermons at the custom house in Greenock, Scotland, once the home of his merchant father (dead since 1804) and now home to a growing number of refugees from famine-stricken Ireland. Sometimes he could not get more than a few words out before being attacked by Irish navvies,[4] but other times he managed to decry the wickedness of priests and popery at greater length.[5] The year 1851 was a tense one for Protestant–Catholic relations in Britain, not only because of the massive influx of Irish Catholics over the previous five years, but also because of the so-called papal aggression of Pope Pius IX, who had just proclaimed the restoration of the ancient Catholic hierarchy in England, a move that sent evangelical Protestants into an indignant frenzy of antipapal campaigning. Orr's timing was inauspicious in another way as well, for he chose to give one of his addresses on the evening of July 12, the day Orangemen throughout Britain and Ireland celebrated the defeat of the Catholic king James II by William III at the 1690 Battle of the Boyne, and usually a day of much sectarian rioting across the country. That night, as he probably expected, a gang of Irish navvies interrupted Orr's address on the Greenock quays and chased him into a police station. Two days later, when rumors circulated that Orr was planning to preach again, a regular melee broke out between the navvies and a group of Protestant locals. Some of the latter broke away and damaged several Catholic homes as well as the Catholic chapel, forcing some families to flee to the hills, but that night Orr was nowhere to be seen.[6]

Three years later he surfaced in North America, where he helped start anti-Irish riots in Boston, New York, Montreal, Philadelphia, and elsewhere. We get an interesting, if not entirely accurate, picture of Orr during this tour from a senior policeman in Boston, who described him as a

> poor, illiterate, half-breed Scotchman with more impudence than brains, who, with a three-cornered hat and a cockade on his head, and an old brass horn in his bosom, took advantage of the political excitement then existing, and travelled about the city and suburbs from place to place tooting his horn, collecting crowds in the streets, delivering what he called Political Lectures, and passing round the hat for contributions.[7]

This was somewhat at odds with other witnesses who stressed Orr's respectability, and there is plenty of evidence that Orr was not illiterate, but it does accurately portray his modus operandi. After sparking a few disturbances in and around Boston he moved in June 1854 to New York City, where he preached on the steps of the City Hall, protected by a youth auxiliary of the Know-Nothing Order (known as the "Wide Awakes") and accompanied by an accordion-playing preacher named Samuel C. Moses.[8] When things got too hot in New York he went north to Manchester, New Hampshire, where in early July he inspired locals to attack Irish homes and the town's new Catholic church.[9] Immediately thereafter he was reportedly preaching in Bath, Maine, where his followers burned down the Old South Church, which was being used by Catholics for worship. He was arrested again in Boston on August 14, and in late September he went to jail for blowing his horn and collecting a dangerous crowd in Philadelphia's

Independence Square.[10] The precise contents of his lectures are unclear, but a poster from his North American tour suggests a unique blend of egalitarianism, anti-Catholicism, and British imperialism:

> Scorn be on those who rob us of our rights,
> Purgatory for Popery and the Pope,
> Freedom to man be he black or white,
> Rule Britannia![11]

These themes would form the core of his message when Orr arrived in British Guiana a short time later.

British Guiana, a struggling sugar colony carved into the northeast coast of South America, might seem a strange place for Orr to venture after the hurly-burly of Britain and North America, but in fact it was his birthplace. Orr's father had been not only a Greenock merchant but also the coproprietor of a Guiana sugar plantation worked by slaves, where he had once served as the colony's paymaster general. Orr's mother was a black woman from the colony, named Mary Ann, and in all likelihood she was a slave (perhaps even a slave of Orr's father) before slavery was abolished in the British West Indies in the 1830s.[12] John Sayers Orr, then, was a mulatto—a "half-breed," in the demotic lingo of the Boston policeman—with a keen sense of the racial politics of the British and Atlantic worlds. Why he had left the colony in his youth is unclear, as are his reasons for returning in December 1855, but his mother, still living in Guiana all these years after his father's death, may have had something to do with it.

Whatever the cause, when he finally stepped ashore in Georgetown, Guiana's capital, for his greatest and final act of evangelical incendiarism, Orr clearly intended to continue the work he had begun in Britain. Shortly after arriving he wrote a letter to the governor, Philip Wodehouse, asking for his protection.[13] His purpose in Guiana, Orr explained, was "in every way possible, to get at the masses of the poor, the ignorant, and despised, and to publish to them the truth of my God." Claiming the "right of speech" to which every subject of the British Empire was entitled, Orr said he understood that the right did not encompass "sedition" or the interruption of thoroughfares. He also sent Wodehouse several "papers" (probably pamphlets) with titles such as "The Glorious Majesty of the Approaching Kingdom and Its King" and "Victoria Reigns Our Anointed Queen," which he claimed would demonstrate his loyalty, his doctrines, and the unacceptable behavior of government officers who had interfered with his addresses heretofore.[14] To this, Wodehouse sent a curt reply stating that he was "not aware of your having any reason to apprehend insult or ill treatment so long as you conduct yourself in a legal and peaceable manner."[15] This was all the permission that Orr needed.

The Portuguese in Guiana

When Orr sailed into Georgetown Harbor at the end of 1855 he was like a foreign body thrust into a diseased organism: he did not bring the disease, but he did inflame it. The world that Orr left behind was the world of paranoid transatlantic anti-Catholicism, a world peopled not only by street corner ranters but also by clerics and statesmen, and one that was growing larger and crueler with each new boatload of Irish refugees docking in Boston or Liverpool.[16] The world he intruded upon was very different. British Guiana, like most other West Indian sugar colonies, was still trying to find its feet after the abolition of slavery two decades earlier. Free blacks now worked the plantations their parents had worked as slaves, but their wages were low, production was unsatisfactory, and many of them, naturally enough, preferred other kinds of employment, leaving the plantations (and the economy they sustained) to languish.[17] To cope with the crisis, Guiana's plantocracy had begun encouraging immigration from elsewhere: by the mid-1850s, some indentured workers had begun to arrive from India, but much more prominent were immigrants of Portuguese descent who came mostly from Madeira but also from the Azores, Cape Verde, and even Brazil. The Portuguese (as they were uniformly called) acted as a sort of buffer between blacks (or Creoles, as they were locally known) and whites in the colony, filling the niches that blacks were not filling, both on and off the plantations, and drawing some of the underclass's resentment away from the white elite.[18] What made their story intersect with Orr's, of course, was the fact that nearly all of Guiana's Portuguese were Catholic.

Unlike the Irish Catholics Orr encountered in Britain and North America, the Portuguese of Guiana were not despised for their poverty, but for their wealth. Observing high mortality rates of Portuguese plantation workers, many officials and planters had begun to ignore, or only lightly enforce, the terms of their indenture, allowing them to move into retail and other sectors.[19] Within a short time, the Portuguese had become a sort of business elite in the colony, displacing, in the process, those few blacks who had managed to overcome the financial hurdles erected between them and nonwage labor. Rare was the Guianese village or plantation without at least one Portuguese shop. These shops sold all sorts of things, but they were primarily rum shops, small bars whose customers were mostly black laborers: by 1852, 70 percent of the colony's rum shop licenses were in Portuguese hands, and in some localities they essentially monopolized the trade.[20] Although their numbers were quite small (nearly 8,000 in 1851, or 6 percent of the population), the Portuguese were more numerous than other whites (3,630, or 2.8 percent), and their retail activities made them both more visible and more powerful than their meager numbers implied.[21] While the British elite did not accept them as full Europeans, they generally held them in higher esteem than they did blacks, and this fact, along with their economic strength, made them objects of envy and irritation among Creoles, who called them "white niggers" and "yellow buckras."[22] Whites, on the other hand, praised them (in the words of Anthony Trollope, who visited Guiana in 1859) as "a steady, industrious class, [who] have proved themselves to be good citizens."[23] In British eyes they contrasted favorably with the supposedly indolent blacks, of whom one longtime civil servant observed, "Quashie lives only for the day; he never saves any money, and never looks for a day ahead."[24] In fact, British planters and officials, Governor Wodehouse included, felt that the Portuguese could serve not only an economic function but also a moral function in Guiana: by their industrious example, it was hoped, they might prevent the blacks from reverting fully to barbarism.[25]

In Georgetown, where Orr was shortly to hold forth, Portuguese shops were everywhere. The Portuguese owned most of the drug stores and butcher shops, ran the best carts and carriages, and, of course, operated most of the rum shops. In some sectors they acted as a sort of retail cartel, fixing prices among themselves and exacerbating the hostility of blacks, who sometimes assaulted the more flagrantly fraudulent or rapacious Portuguese shopkeepers. A few years before Orr arrived, in fact, there had been trouble between blacks and Portuguese outside the city when some Portuguese had worked as blackleg labor on the plantations during a series of strikes. During the unrest, which coincided with a worldwide economic downturn in 1847–8, Portuguese retailers had also refused credit to black strikers and kept prices high, provoking isolated attacks in a few places.[26] Tensions had been building up since then, and it took very little to snap the cord.[27]

Orr lights the fire

Orr's method was the same in Georgetown as elsewhere: he found a busy spot—in this case the Stabroek Market, where many Portuguese had stalls—and began delivering regular Sunday addresses to mostly black crowds. Most other days he could be seen walking the palm-shaded streets, wearing a badge and waving a flag, periodically blowing his horn to advertise his Sunday services.[28] He also delivered shorter addresses at different places around town, including near the town's new Catholic convent, a spot probably chosen for its provocative potential. His performances combined theatrical no-Popery rhetoric, including lurid descriptions of the sexual immorality of priests and nuns, with a xenophobic political message that he had perfected during his sojourns in Britain and North America. We know a fair amount about what Orr said in Guiana because on February 10 the police, acting on a complaint from the Catholics, sent a shorthand writer to record that Sunday's address at the Stabroek Market to ascertain whether what Orr was doing constituted an illegal assembly.

By that time, Orr had already made many Catholic enemies. An Irishman named John Taggart, supervisor of customs and consul for Portugal (and under investigation for smuggling Portuguese indentured laborers into Brazil), led the Catholic opposition. Having gone to the police for action against Orr, and having been told that he needed witnesses to bring charges against him, Taggart and his daughter went to Mass at the convent on Saturday, February 9, along with a large crowd of Portuguese to act as "witnesses" in case Orr showed up. The Catholics were armed with whips and sticks, doubtless hoping for a confrontation, but there was no sign of Orr, just a number of blacks who showed up shouting "Down with the Pope," "Hang Taggart," and so forth.[29] Like most of his ilk, Orr thrived on this sort of opposition, so it was with a theatrical flourish that he came to the Stabroek Market the next day for his Sunday service, armed with a dagger in his belt and a life preserver (a sort of weighted stick) strapped to his wrist.[30] Mounting the pump platform outside the market, within sight of the courtroom from which he would subsequently be tried, Orr threatened to strike down at least two of his enemies if they attacked him, and if he did not do it, he knew "there are plenty of black and yellow faces around" to do it for him.[31] As he flourished his life preserver like a warrior attacking his foes, he called upon his audience—"upwards of a thousand people," according to the police observer—to show the same courage as the British soldiers who were currently facing the Russians in the Crimea.[32]

Then Orr got down to business. He accused the Portuguese of coming to Guiana to drive poor Creoles out of business, and he read a letter from a supporter who described the immigrants as a "dog-barking, pig-grunting, perfidious crew." Orr let those insults perfume the air while he went on to insist that his hearers "respect the laws" of the colony. He had not come "to pull down the Governor," he told them, "or to pull down Queen Victoria, and to lift up the Pope." He had not come to preach "sedition." He had, he said, merely come to defend the people of Guiana from their enemies. He then read a letter from another supporter—read it and distributed printed copies—that laid out the blacks' main complaints against the Portuguese:

> We have been taxed to pay their passage here; we have received them kindly; we have purchased from their stores and shops, and we have given them our monies, by which means they have accumulated large profits and wealth. Had it not been for us creoles, how could they get rich and become possessed of property. I say it is our support, it is our good feeling, it is our monies, it is our patronage that made them what they are; and if they are ignorant enough to forget themselves and insult and annoy you, the laws of your country must protect you.

In his written reply, copies of which he circulated along with the original letter, Orr attached the Creoles' local grievances to a larger, global struggle:

> The bloody Papists have the wrong man to show forth their blood-thirsty spirit towards, as long as that man has, under God and the laws of a country wherein he is engaged, for an arm of defence, as he had the Highlanders in Scotland, John Bull in England, the Irish Orangemen in the Canadas, Nova Scotia, and New Brunswick, the Americans in America, and as he believes he now has, the negroes, mulattoes, mustees, and creoles on his side here, in his present contest with the armies of the Pope, and the Devil at their head.

Orr's portion of the letter ended with the following cry:

> America for the Americans! the West Indies for the West Indians! purgatory for Popery and the Pope! Scorn be on those who would rob us of our rights! Rule Britannia, and God save the Queen!

Orr then came to the ostensible subject of the day's sermon: the town's new convent. Referring to a North American anti-nunnery tract that purported to expose the sordid activities of a convent in Montreal, he hinted that Georgetown's convent was nothing more than a brothel for priests and bishops, linked by an underground passage to the monastery, and that the offspring that issued from these unholy unions were secretly murdered. Four nuns, he said, had recently become pregnant in Rome; might the same thing be happening in Georgetown? "But if you see a nunnery, with young women, in the town, and you see a bachelor priest going from the Brick-dam to the nunnery whenever he likes, it looks very queer—doesn't it?"[33]

At the end of his address Orr pulled several pamphlets out of a tin cylinder and offered them for sale. One told of the official persecution he had endured in Philadelphia. It described his trumpet as, first, an instrument to call people to his service, and second, a weapon "to strike terror into all those who are rotten hearted." It also called upon all right-hearted people to "break a lance at or have a shy at" all powers "who are oppressing and desolating the heritage of God, either civilly or ecclesiastically." Another pamphlet described his mistreatment at the hands of the authorities in Providence, Rhode Island. This one contained a song, set to the tune of "T'other side of Jordan," that began:

We went to Bunker Hill for to hear Gabriel,
And the Romanists were there accordin';
They swore they'd kill him dead, if a single word was said
'Gainst the Pope or t'other side of Jordan.[34]

It was a bravura performance, full of swaggering belligerence and outraged righteousness, high principle and low comedy, and maybe just a hint of commercial calculation.

But just how much of this did the people in the crowd understand? Did they see their own resentment of Portuguese retailers as part of a cosmic struggle against the forces of evil? Probably many blacks would have been open to the idea that their economic and religious grievances were intertwined, since many of them had been educated by Protestant missionaries who were themselves hostile to Catholicism, but we cannot know this for sure.[35] In any case, here was a man—well spoken, worldly, by most measures respectable—who was telling them that their problems were due to the greedy aliens in their midst, and it was a message that many seem to have had little trouble accepting. Throughout early February, while Orr continued to preach, violence against the Portuguese increased: "unoffending Portuguese men, women and children were insulted, pelted, and beaten in different parts of the town," as Wodehouse reported to London.[36] On February 15 the local Catholic bishop wrote a letter to Wodehouse complaining of the harassment that he and his parishioners were enduring.[37] This was the first formal complaint the government had received, and, evaluating it alongside the simultaneous determination of the attorney general that Orr's February 10 address contained illegal incitements, the police decided to arrest Orr on February 16.[38]

On the day of Orr's hearing before the magistrate, two days after his arrest, the wide streets around the public buildings were filled with agitated women and men.[39] Prior to Orr's hearing, Wodehouse had convened the Court of Policy, a legislative body controlled by the planters and the governor's office, to ask for stronger policing power, which they obligingly granted. Up until this time the police had been inclined to tolerate a little rough-and-tumble in the streets, provided it stayed within certain bounds, and the most a magistrate could do was to punish such behavior with six days' imprisonment and a fine of $24.[40] Now it became a serious crime, within Georgetown and its environs, for someone to assault "a person not of the same race as himself," to forcibly enter or attack another's property, to carry weapons in the streets, to publicly "make use of any abusive or insulting or provoking language," or to incite anyone else to do the same. Violators could now be fined up to $100, imprisoned with hard labor for up to six months, flogged with up to thirty-nine lashes, or subjected to any two of these penalties in combination (the flogging order was slightly tempered by the requirement that all floggings had to be approved by the governor). Repeat offenders could be subject to transportation for seven years or imprisonment with hard labor for three years. Police now also had the right to disperse any "disorderly" gathering of five or more people, to arrest anyone tampering with official placards, and to enter any home or business to arrest known offenders.[41] These measures, enacted by a body that was more Privy Council than legislature, enabled Wodehouse to avoid declaring martial law—which he felt would "shake public confidence"—while ensuring that he, the supreme civil power, retained control over the state's response.[42] Martial law or no, summary judgments and floggings were soon to be the order of the day.

The announcement of these new police powers angered Orr's black supporters, and his hearing on February 18 did little to placate them. In stating his case against Orr the Crown Prosecutor made no reference to the illegal threat upon his life by Taggart and his Portuguese friends, which many regarded an important mitigating factor. To make matters worse, the magistrate sent Orr for trial to the Supreme Criminal Court and set bail at the substantial sum of £500, plus two additional sureties of £250 each, making it virtually impossible for him to avoid going to jail prior to his trial.[43] Upon learning of Orr's indictment, crowds of his supporters began attacking Portuguese shops and homes in Georgetown and beyond. Adopting language more appropriate to a rebellion than a communal pogrom, Wodehouse reported that Georgetown was now "in open insurrection."

> The pope, the bishop, the nuns were clean forgotten. Nothing remained in the minds of the actors but the long subsisting hatred and jealousy of the Portuguese immigrants from Madeira, the love of plunder, aggravated by the gross and brutal character of the female population, who have throughout

the colony taken a most active part in the riots, and who are of course the most difficult to punish.[44]

In the Charlestown neighborhood, where Orr was imprisoned, a policeman was fatally injured during a brawl with blacks who gathered to raid and loot Portuguese shops, and it took several soldiers of the West India Regiment to protect the police station and jail, where the authorities feared a rescue attempt might be made.[45] Also in Charlestown a black woman reportedly died of fright after special constables charged a crowd.[46] Throughout the region the police, soldiers, and hastily enrolled special constables struggled to control the crowds, but, acting with the new powers granted them that morning (especially the power to arrest people hidden in private houses and yards, which closed off a legal loophole frequently exploited by criminals), they managed to contain the unrest, a success that Wodehouse significantly called the "speedy defeat of the town."[47]

The fire spreads

A traveler to British Guiana, beholding the coastal flatness around Georgetown for the first time, once imagined "that a wave of moderate proportions would submerge the country."[48] Something like that imagined wave rushed out of Georgetown the day of Orr's indictment as emissaries sped off in all directions to urge their countrymen to rise up against the Portuguese. Orr had arrived at a particularly hard time in Guiana. A prolonged drought had left farmers, especially those west of Georgetown, struggling to feed their families: they had only muddy water for drinking and washing, and sugar work was scarce.[49] The combination of low wages and rising prices naturally increased these people's resentment of Portuguese shop owners, and they were perfectly ready to heed the call to arms. Within a few days, all three counties of Guiana—Demerara, Berbice, and Essequibo—were awash with anti-Portuguese violence. According to Wodehouse there was hardly a Portuguese shop that escaped the attention of rioters.[50] Everywhere the pattern was the same. Creoles, sometimes accompanied by East Indians and African immigrants, broke the windows and doors of shops, consumed or dumped barrels of liquor, and made off with whatever they could carry. One British missionary described men and women walking past his house with "unskinned pieces of cows and hogs on their backs … the blood dripping down their bodies."[51] Women and children were especially prominent in these raids, a fact that both scandalized the magistrates and convinced them not to employ overwhelming violence against the rioters lest they be accused of behaving recklessly. When the police did intervene, they were often pelted with bottles and bricks.

In many outlying districts, agitators claimed that they had been sent by the government to make sure that all Portuguese shops were destroyed. In Essequibo, according to a police official, rumors went around that "the Governor wished them [the Creoles] to drive the Portuguese out of the country, because they wanted all to be shopkeepers, and none peasants; and to do it the governor permitted them to sack the shops, but enjoined all to shed no blood."[52] Other officials sent similar reports, noting that some of the agitators read from a false government ordinance to this effect. Whether the people believed these assertions is unclear, but according to the *Demerara Royal Gazette*, at least some rioters "were completely surprised" when soldiers arrived to suppress them, since they believed they were acting on the orders of the government.[53] Wodehouse found it "scarcely possible to suppose that a race of people living under our rule should be so ignorant as to believe" that the government endorsed these pogroms, but believe them they evidently did, sometimes on the semi-patriotic grounds that, since the Portuguese had allegedly refused to contribute to a Patriotic Fund in support of British troops in the Crimea, they were a disloyal people who had "joined the Russians."[54] At the same time, some rioters apparently believed just the opposite—that is, that they were acting *against* the government. During the riots one Creole reportedly told the chief justice, "the Governor was the Governor of the Portuguese and kept the black people down," and, as we will see, postriot denunciations of Wodehouse and the government revealed similar sentiments.[55] These currents of rumor and counter-rumor make it hard to generalize about the rioters' perceptions of the state's position, but they do nicely illustrate a point that I will develop in later chapters: that is, despite the state's (usually genuine) attempts to remain impartial during communal disputes, it was difficult in the excitement of a riot for it to remain so in the eyes of belligerents. Even when actual evidence of state partisanship was lacking, the cynical and the imaginative could still find a way to enlist the British as a party to their dispute.

In fact, over the ensuing days people could be forgiven for thinking the state had taken the side of the Portuguese, since the one-sided nature of the popular violence led the state to aim its repressive measures at Creoles, rather than Portuguese acting in self-defense. On Tuesday, February 19, Wodehouse expanded the initial emergency measures to include the entire colony, dispatching bands of policemen and soldiers to the trouble spots, calling upon all householders to enroll themselves as special constables, and offering rewards for information about ringleaders or other rioters.[56] Compared to similar episodes elsewhere in the empire (including Wodehouse's subsequent handling of the Bombay riots of 1874, as we will see), the Guiana government's response was swift, decisive, and even somewhat creative. The biggest problem was lack of manpower—most reports coming into Georgetown spoke of the sparse police presence and begged for more policemen and soldiers—so in outlying districts there was a heavy reliance on "specials" culled from the tiny but well-armed white population, as well as "loyal" laborers of East Asian or even African descent. In some places the authorities trusted these irregulars more than they did the police. At Plantation Blankenburg the magistrate, finding the black rural constables unreliable, enlisted East Indian "coolies" as special constables.[57] Another magistrate enlisted "managers, overseers, headmen, and a number of immigrants belonging to their respective estates" rather than rely on black policemen.[58] In remote Essequibo, where the military was slow to arrive, the government even mobilized troops of Arawak and Carib Indians.[59] These special constables performed all sorts of duties—dispersing crowds, guarding property, protecting the jails—but in some cases their utility was limited. At Essequibo the Inspector of Police complained that many special constables, principally the Creoles, were "doubtful fellows" who could not fire a gun; and at Queenstown they either joined the rioters or refused to stop them. "I shall do all in my power," wrote this magistrate, "but have no faith in any black man."[60]

On Thursday, February 21, with the country still in an uproar, the Court of Policy enacted yet more emergency measures. It authorized Wodehouse to empower certain magistrates to flog prisoners without prior approval, permission that he swiftly granted to five magistrates (with the proviso that they "flog only the most daring and active offenders"). Responding to the large number of women arrested during the riots, the Court of Policy also authorized the employment of female prisoners in labor outside the prisons—there being, as Wodehouse explained, insufficient hard labor within the jails, and the women arrested belonging largely to "the most vicious and savage class of the community." It also re-embodied the Colonial Militia, in which all men holding a certain amount of property were required to serve when called. At the same time, the authorities also began looking for outside help. They sent to Barbados for reinforcements of troops and ammunition. Then, in an act of solidarity possibly inspired by the Anglo-French alliance in the Crimea—and certainly driven by a fear that the disturbances would spread into French territory—the French man-of-war *Voyageur* arrived from French Guiana and landed troops to help with the disturbances in the west. Later, Dutch Suriname also sent a ship to assist in transporting Barbadian troops to Berbice.[61]

Considering the scale of the unrest and the uneven quality of state forces, there was remarkably little lethal state violence during the riots. Wodehouse reported that wherever the military went, they met little resistance and did not find it necessary to fire upon any crowds, although he did acknowledge that the police had had a few serious scrapes.[62] The one place the police undoubtedly opened fire was at Canal No. 1, just west of Georgetown, where the drought was particularly bad and measles and dysentery were raging.[63] Here police shot two rioters, and the frantic magistrate subsequently implored the governor for more armed men "at whatever cost."[64] Nonofficial Europeans also opened fire on occasion. In Essequibo a plantation manager fired on a crowd of blacks, but it is unclear what effect this had, apart from persuading some of the blacks to arm themselves with sharpened cutlasses.[65] In Mahaica, a village along the railroad east of Georgetown, a Portuguese shop owner named Jose de Costa shot at his attackers, hitting one and infuriating the remainder. There were only eight soldiers in this district, and the magistrate, distrusting his black policemen, wrote to Georgetown asking for permission to open fire if things got any worse, but it is unclear if he ever did so.[66]

The reasons for this relative restraint are not immediately apparent. Certainly it was due neither to the humanitarianism of the men running the country nor to an underestimation of the dangers they faced. The official correspondence is full of sentiments such as those expressed by a magistrate at Canal No. 2, who felt that only a force equipped with firearms was capable of quelling "such a host of savages, intoxicated with all kinds of plundered spirits, and bent upon destruction."[67] Indeed, the authorities' greatest fear was not so much for the fate of the Portuguese, although they were troubled by such wanton attacks on (as they saw it) such peaceable and industrious people; rather, they worried about what the riots might mean for the white elite. "What has taken place," wrote one worried magistrate, "may well open our eyes to our defenceless position …"[68] One panicked plantation manager reported that the Creoles were saying "when we have done with the Portuguese we will attack the whites."[69] The Police Inspector of Essequibo, L. G. Tucker, seemed incapable of speaking of the riots in anything but military terms; some of his dispatches, speaking as they do of "retreats," "rebels," and "salients," read like reports from a general in the field (or, indeed, from a slave uprising such as had convulsed Demerara in 1823).[70] Wodehouse, whom we have already observed speaking in a similar fashion, likewise described the riots as a "most general rising" that was only suppressed once large numbers of soldiers were on hand.[71] In reality, it seems as if damage to fields and other plantation property not belonging to the Portuguese was quite limited. Nevertheless, especially in remote Essequibo where government forces were few, there was great official fear that the sacking of the plantations would inevitably follow the sacking of Portuguese shops.[72]

The most likely explanations for the relative scarcity of state shootings are, first, the fact that Guiana's constabulary was sparse and poorly armed, and, second, the readiness of officials to resort to another form of violent punishment: flogging. A standard punishment of the slavery period, flogging had remained an important, if now less commonly used, tool in the state's repertoire that was generally reserved for the worst criminals.[73] Now it became an instrument of exemplary justice, meant not only to punish the worst rioters but also to frighten the population at large. In the village of Mahaicony, for instance, a magistrate named James Roney summarily tried twenty-seven prisoners, sentencing seventeen to immediate flogging (thirteen with thirty-nine lashes, four with twenty-nine lashes) and distributing jail sentences of six months with hard labor to a total of nineteen convicts (six of the convicted were women, for, as Roney said, "their conduct in this quarter was the most violent"). To make the punishment as visible as possible, Roney had the prisoners flogged at halberts constructed opposite the village's main Portuguese shop, which had been looted and heavily damaged, and not far from the Scotch Church, which Roney had converted into a makeshift jail. The effect of the floggings on the public, Roney reported, "was immediate and most marked, and several applications for mercy were made to me." Addressing the crowd from the pulpit of the church, Roney warned the people against any further mischief, and he let a few prisoners go with a warning.[74] Thus did Roney advertise both the terrible vengeance and the merciful justice of the outraged state.

Not all Europeans approved of the floggings, however. Another flogging magistrate, accompanying the French force in the west, reported that the French doctor in his party was "so frightened at this kind of punishment (unknown in the French service), that, although the flogging was not at all severe, he said he could not, as a medical man, allow more than nine or ten blows to be inflicted on each man." It took the arrival of a British doctor for the flogging to reach its full ferocity, and altogether the magistrate reported that it had "a very salutary effect" on the people.[75] Wodehouse, aware of "the jealousy with which it is regarded in England," defended the floggings to the Colonial Office by explaining that they were used very sparingly—only ten floggings in Georgetown, and only two of them in public—and insisting that the choice was either to flog miscreants or to order the troops to fire. The latter option, he said, was undesirable because many of the rioters were women; flogging, carried out in a limited and carefully controlled fashion, was the more merciful policy in his eyes.[76]

Six days after Orr's arrest the riots began to ebb, and, true to what he saw as a policy of restraint, Wodehouse soon rescinded the extraordinary powers of the magistrates, leaving 200 Barbadian troops to patrol the trouble spots.[77] The difficulty now was figuring out what to do with all the prisoners. Hundreds had been arrested, and the jails were so full that the government had to improvise a prison ship to handle the excess. Wodehouse eventually managed the situation by ordering his men to arrest only the ringleaders. Three hundred people had been summarily convicted under the emergency legislation—most eventually ending up at the penal settlement at Massaruni (or Mazaruni), "[o]ne of the prettiest places in the colony," according to a former sheriff who delighted in its riverside vistas[78]—while 114 were sent to trial before the Supreme Criminal Court, which convicted 103 people, doling out fines, floggings, and/or prison sentences ranging from two to ten years.[79] During his trial in April, John Sayers Orr pleaded not guilty to four charges relating to unlawful assembly and provoking animosity against the Portuguese.[80] Despite being represented by a famous attorney named Gilbert (whom his supporters had paid for) who argued that Orr's actions may have been unwise but were not actually illegal, Orr was found guilty and sentenced to three years at the Massaruni penal settlement. In a show of impartiality, the court also tried four Portuguese who had tried to attack Orr, convicting three and sentencing them to be fined $250 and be imprisoned (without hard labor) for six months.[81] These were much lighter sentences than those handed out to Creoles.

The trials engendered renewed tensions—someone tried to burn down the house of the Attorney General while the trials were under way[82]—but they also provided a novel way for the government to help out the struggling planters. Instead of serving time or paying fines they could not afford, some convicts were given the option of performing labor services on plantations.[83] In explaining the policy to the Colonial Office (he worried that it might appear too lenient), Wodehouse wrote that "the great causes of all crime and vice here, are idleness and habits of self-indulgence of the lowest order," not a "positive desire to do evil." The people simply did not know any better—they suffered from "an absence of all moral apprehension of a necessity for doing good"—and it was therefore better to compel them to do honest and useful labor than to inflict more forceful punishments.[84] "The fact is," Wodehouse wrote, echoing the slave drivers of old, "that a negro requires to be under a necessity to do right; as long as that necessity exists, he not only obeys, but appears to have no wish to avoid. Remove the necessity, and the spirit of license comes into operation at once."[85] Far from being a reversion to the conditions of slavery, however, Wodehouse pointed out that these convict laborers would live at home, make good wages, and perform only a moderate amount of work. These were, he said, conditions "in which any English labourer would be too happy to find himself."[86]

Altogether the Portuguese claimed nearly $300,000 in damages, subsequently reduced by the Combined Court to $250,000, which was to be paid via a new, universal poll tax ($2 for a man, $1 for a woman), a measure that placed the burden of reparations on the lower classes of blacks—those, that is, whom the government blamed for the violence. Outraged blacks alleged (rightly) that the tax was intended to punish the entire Creole community, and the local Anti-Slavery Society sent a deputation to Wodehouse to ask for its repeal, but it was not until June 1858, after serious difficulties in collecting the tax, that the government relented and abolished the tax.[87] In addition to punitive taxation, Wodehouse also enhanced the repressive powers of the white community, sending arms and ammunition to plantation managers and providing the police force with regular arms. Now, instead of rushing to armories to obtain weapons, both police and estate officials would carry guns as a matter of course.[88] The steady militarization of the Guianese police force, which would become ever more evident in the coming decades, had begun.

Back in London the Colonial Secretary, Henry Labouchere, approved of Wodehouse's handling of the (as he put it) "barbarous and disgraceful outrages directed against a class of unoffending and industrious inhabitants of the colony."[89] He did, however, instruct Wodehouse to confine the floggings to men (which Wodehouse was already doing) and not to make it a punishment reserved only for blacks.[90] He also endorsed Wodehouse's labor scheme and suggested that Guiana introduce some stricter laws regulating public assemblies, so that no future agitator would have as much freedom as Orr had.[91] Otherwise, apart from a parliamentary order for copies of the official correspondence about the riots, and brief notices in a few British papers, the outbreak received little attention in Britain.

Aftermath

What had caused the riots? Wodehouse put them down to blacks' jealousy of a manifestly superior people. "Idle, irregular, and extravagant in their own habits, they [the Creoles] have from the commencement regarded with an unfriendly eye the Portuguese immigrants, who were, like other immigrants, introduced to fill the vacuum caused by the deficiencies of the Creoles." As often happened with outbreaks of this sort, Wodehouse and his deputies suspected that the riots were the product of a conspiracy, based in Georgetown and organized by Orr and "other designing characters," to destroy Portuguese shops and establish Creole shops upon their "ruins."[92] Wodehouse chiefly suspected the Mutual Aid Society, a group set up by several Creoles as a sort of cooperative trading society to give them a stronger position in the retail sector.[93] Whatever the culpability of this single group, there does seem to have been an organized effort to spread the riots beyond Georgetown by telling people that the government had ordered Portuguese businesses destroyed, so perhaps there was a grain of truth to this conspiracy theory. Less certain is Wodehouse's characterization of the people in the outlying districts, whose debased character, he believed, made them uniquely vulnerable to the designs of the conspirators: in many villages, he said, the Creoles lived in idleness and degradation, while in the most remote areas people who had recently arrived from Africa were living "a life little less savage than that of the beasts of the field." In these places men and women went about naked, "utterly useless for any good purpose" and serving as "ready instruments for all acts of violence."[94]

Other whites agreed with this analysis. The head of the colony's Wesleyan Missions, William Hudson, conducted an internal investigation that found only eight of the Wesleyans' several thousand congregants had been convicted of rioting. After assuring the government that his ministers had worked diligently to instill morality in their people and had tried to quell the riots in their locales, Hudson said what was really needed was greater control over the "worthless and vile" elements in the population: in the villages, "more efficient government;" for the "wild, vicious, and untaught children," compulsory education and employment; and among the "heathen population" of the remotest areas, more missions.[95] Some nonofficial whites went even further. In March, the *Liverpool Daily Post* published a letter from an unnamed gentleman in Georgetown who vented his disgust—and, no doubt, those of many of his colleagues—with unmitigated fury. "I am most thoroughly disgusted with niggers," he wrote. Observing that "we have only killed some sixteen this time" (most official reports mentioned only one death), he warned that next time it might be even worse. "The romance of 'Uncle Tom's Cabin' is gone, Wilberforce is forgotten; and although not actually, still virtually niggers must be slaves." For this reason, the writer said, he had told the governor himself that "we must take care to keep the string tight, and give them no play at all." In a spirit of impartial contempt, however, the author did also note that the Portuguese "showed no courage at all" during the riots, but rather "the most pitiable cowardice."[96]

Blacks were not oblivious to the ways these racial attitudes were shaping the government's actions. According to the black-run newspaper *The Creole*, the floggings and the introduction of the poll tax were both traceable to the whites' "hatred" of black and mixed-race people. The real aim of the poll tax, the paper maintained, was to goad Creoles into defiance so that the government could justify even more repression.

> The law makers have not disguised the hostile feelings they entertain towards the people, and it is not to be surprised at that every political dodge is resorted to to annoy, harass, and punish, the hated race—among them a poll tax ordinance is now to be thrust down their throats, which, if they do not swallow, the sea-walls, the hulk, the prison, the cat-o'-nine tails, the penal settlement, of course, will restore their orderly submission to the same.

In order to forestall such designs, *The Creole* advised its readers to pay the tax and hope that London would eventually overrule it.[97] Indeed, *The Creole* generally placed much more faith in the "justice and impartiality" of the London government than it did in the "class government" of Georgetown, by which it meant government carried on for the benefit of the planters and to the detriment of the black poor.[98]

It was not just the poll tax that rankled blacks, however, or the re-embodiment of the militia, or the racist language with which prominent officials and clerics discussed the riots, or even the government agents sent around after the riots to listen for murmurs of disaffection. It was also the significant postriot display of military force at Georgetown's docks, Portuguese shops, the Court of Justice, the racetrack, and other potential flash points in the months that followed. Such measures, *The Creole* maintained, "shook the confidence of the public in the wisdom and courage of our rulers, at the same time they produced irritation in the minds of well-disposed people."[99] That many ordinary blacks felt as the editors of *The Creole* did was eloquently demonstrated in July 1857 when Wodehouse and his wife departed Georgetown for a ten-month furlough. As they boarded the ship, a jeering crowd some two or three thousand strong gathered at the wharf to throw stones, plantain stalks, and offal at the governor's party, striking Mrs. Wodehouse on the forehead, slicing open the ear of the chief justice, and wounding a bishop. It was, said one English paper on receiving the news, "a pelting and a riot upon the most approved Belfast fashion."[100] Nobody was seriously hurt as the police and soldiers charged the crowd, but a Lieutenant Herrick did strike a man on the head with the flat of his sword, breaking the sword and subsequently earning a reprimand for having drawn his weapon without orders. Herrick's humiliation was short-lived, however, as before long the European colony presented him with not one but two new swords (one from the men and one from the ladies) in recognition of his gallantry.[101] Wodehouse, meanwhile, had acquired the dubious distinction of being "the only Governor ever to be stoned in British Guiana,"[102] and four years later, when he departed the colony for good, he made sure to leave by an early-morning packet.[103]

John Sayers Orr made no such escape. Details of his imprisonment are scanty, but at the insalubrious and overcrowded Massaruni penal settlement he would probably have done what most other prisoners did: quarrying granite by day and attending (perhaps leading) evangelical chapel services in the evening. It is possible, however, given Orr's status as an educated man of mixed race, that he performed lighter tasks such as tending livestock, making billiards, or bookkeeping.[104] We do know that his mother tried to get the home government to intervene on his behalf, reaching out to a Glasgow newspaper to help publicize her son's plight, but to no avail.[105] By the end of the year, Orr was dead, reportedly of dysentery, although he may have been a victim of the cholera epidemic that swept the colony that winter.[106] Meanwhile, tensions between Portuguese and Creoles persisted, and there would be at least one more serious outbreak of anti-Portuguese violence (also triggered by a clash at the Stabroek Market) in 1889, more than three decades after the Angel Gabriel was called home to the Lord.[107]

2

Causes: How British Imperialism Conjured the Very Violence It Sought to Suppress

Every riot has at least three layers of causation. The proximate causes are usually the easiest to identify and the most context-specific: processions, sermons, elections, demonstrations, court cases, sporting events, accidents, brawls, and any number of trifling or not so trifling events can set off a riot if the ground has been well prepared—as it was when John Sayers Orr began attacking Catholicism in front of Georgetown's Stabroek Market.[1] Proximate causes are usually the most susceptible to policies of quick amelioration. If public sermons are causing riots, then perhaps they need to be banned or regulated; if football matches are turning violent, then perhaps they need to be more carefully policed. The second layer of causation, individual motivation, is much harder to pin down. Political beliefs, religious passions, personal grudges, bigotry, opportunism, fear, sadism, boredom, greed, intoxication, hunger, the anonymity and impunity of the crowd—each person in a riot might be animated by any, all, or none of these things, and no two people will have the same constellation of motivations. Individual causes are nearly impossible to pinpoint, and they do not usually fall within the historian's purview, although it is sometimes necessary to push back against character-based explanations of rioters' behavior (e.g., Philip Wodehouse's contention that Guiana's blacks had rioted in 1856 because they were improvident, greedy, and savage) by identifying a set of more rational or circumstantial motives (e.g., economic depression, feelings of political powerlessness, opportunism). The third layer of causation is structural. Identifying the structural causes riots—the underlying economic, social, cultural, institutional, political, ideological, or religious forces that fostered the violence—is the usual approach of journalists and historians looking for the larger significance of a particular outbreak. Journalists writing in the immediate aftermath of a riot will often undertake structural analyses as a springboard for a broader social or political critique, pointing to the riot as evidence of unjust police practices, a reprehensible failure to integrate immigrants, the government's failed economic policies, or any of a hundred other structural failings. Historians and other scholars also look to structural causes as a way of understanding a riot's larger significance, usually guided by the notion that a violent episode like a riot can tell us something unique about the social relations, tensions, or contradictions that shaped the society in which it took place. For both scholars and journalists the usual procedure is to start with the violent episode and work one's way backward to the underlying causes, and then, having identified and weighed the main causes, to move outward and upward to a broader set of conclusions about the society in question.

This chapter is concerned primarily with this third, structural layer of causation, but its method is slightly different than what I have just outlined. Rather than beginning with the single episode and working my way backward to find underlying causes, I have examined a large number of episodes in search of patterns that unite them. Within these patterns, I have identified a small number of superstructural forces that seem to have contributed to communal violence in different spots across the British Empire. I have organized the chapter around these forces, rather than around particular violent episodes; when I discuss a violent episode, it is to demonstrate how these forces operated in different parts of the empire, not to prove that the superstructural force in question was the sole or primary cause of each specific episode. Because this analysis spans half a century and covers a large portion of the globe, it is impossible to go into the proximate causes of each riot at any length; this layer of causation is relevant here only insofar as the structural *causes* I identify made the proximate *occasions* for violence more likely. Nor will I look closely at the different kinds of individual motivations that drove people to participate in riots. Let us allow that most societies, most of the time, have individuals who are predisposed to take part in a riot, for whatever combination of reasons; the task of this chapter is to identify what it was about British imperialism in the Victorian period that enabled them to do so.

What follows is neither a vindication nor a vilification of British imperialism, but merely an examination of how British imperialism—that is, imperialism as practiced specifically by the British (and, even more specifically, by the Victorian British)—helped to conjure with one hand the very violence that it sought to suppress with the other. I will argue that British imperialism introduced at least two superstructural forces, colonial modernity and rights-based liberalism, that made communal violence more likely in certain colonial settings. These were not the only causes of communal violence: complex, highly specific forces of a social, economic, and cultural variety were also at work in each instance, and sometimes the ruling power played only an indirect, seemingly negligible part in fostering particular outbreaks. Nevertheless, even the most parochial conflicts played out within parameters that were set in large part by the British state and its non-state adjuncts, and belligerent parties often used tools and pursued goals that were only available because they were living within a British imperial context. Before explaining what this looked like, however, I first want to explain why these riots cannot be blamed solely on British policies of "divide and rule," a term that implies much more devious intentionality on the part of British officials than the evidence can support.

Divide, riot, and rule

It has long been argued by critics of imperialism, in the Victorian period and ever after, that Britain deliberately pursued a strategy of "divide and rule" to maintain its empire. Protestants and Catholics in Ireland, Hindus and Muslims in India, Chinese and Malays in Malaya, immigrants and Creoles in the West Indies, myriad rival ethnicities in Africa: such groups, the theory goes, were deliberately kept at each other's throats by cynical rulers who preferred them to fight each other rather than combine together against the British. There is no doubt that such calculations did inform British imperial policy in a number of areas; in our period, perhaps the most visible sign of this was the enlistment of the "martial races" of Sikhs, Pathans, and Gurkhas to keep the peace among less demonstrably "loyal" communities of post-Mutiny India.[2] In the West Indies the post-emancipation drive to recruit Portuguese and East Indian indentured labor was also meant, in part, to provide a racial and social buffer between whites and blacks.[3] In many Asian cities the local police were drawn largely from minority communities—for example, Muslim policemen in Penang—for the same purpose. But did this encouragement of communal divisions extend to the active promotion of violence?

Some colonized people certainly believed that it did. When violence swept through northern India in the summer and fall of 1893 (see Chapter 7), the vernacular and nationalist press was livid with such accusations. As one Bengali journal put it, "The authorities seem to have taken a determination to weaken the people by creating quarrels among them and by setting class against class."[4]

This was a recurring theme during Irish riots as well; nationalists, particularly those of a socialist bent, frequently argued that the authorities were setting Protestant and Catholic workers against one another (e.g., by patronizing the ultra-Protestant Orange Order) to prevent Irish unity.[5] Few modern scholars would take things quite this far; at most they might, like Gyanendra Pandey, hold the British state responsible for "constructing" communalism by treating the colonized—in gazetteers, history books, schools, legislative assemblies, and so on—as if they were a set of internally homogeneous blocs with irreconcilable differences among each other, a construct that actually helped to bring their rivalries into being.[6] There is a considerable amount of truth in this argument, but to say that British officials and other colonial experts helped to construct communal identities, or that they exploited communal divisions that were already in place, is not quite the same as maintaining that they purposely started riots, much less enjoyed riots once they began. Occasionally one does encounter a colonial official who saw a silver lining in communal conflict, as Lord George Hamilton, secretary of state for India, did in a letter to the viceroy during the India riots in the 1890s:

> These outbreaks are, from an administrative point of view, regrettable, but they do seem to me to strengthen our position generally, as reminders of what was the condition of India before our authority was there established, and what it would be if abolished.[7]

These views were in the minority during the Victorian period, however, and were generally more common among officials in London (as Hamilton was) than among officials on the ground.[8] In reality most British authorities, especially those concerned with policing the colonies, expended tremendous energy and resources to prevent and quell violence rather than encouraging it.

There was a simple reason for this. As David Arnold has said of India, British officials had "a persistent fear that unless the government acted promptly and forcefully to quell even minor outbreaks of violence, [the state's] authority would suffer. Violence unchecked in one place would be a signal for wider defiance of colonial rule."[9] Not only might sustained violence expose the limits of the state's repressive capability, but it could also undermine one of its fundamental claims to legitimacy—that is, its ability to preserve the peace. This image of the British state as a fully competent, disinterested force committed to maintaining social peace was central not only to the way Britain presented itself to the people of the empire—this was, after all, the very essence of the *Pax Britannica*—but also to the self-image of the men who served the empire. One former policeman remembering his time in India explained how he understood his duty at the time:

> The allegation so often repeated that the British Govt. pursue in India a policy of *divide et impera*, as between Hindus and Muhammadans, is very far from the truth. The British officials in India are on the contrary continually endeavouring to keep the peace between these two communities and, were it not for the elaborate police precautions which are taken throughout India on the occasion of annual festivals of both communities, the tale of bloodshed and riot would be very much more serious.[10]

We will see much more of this sort of talk when we examine British interpretations of communal riots in Chapter 4. The important point here is that, quite apart from their fear that unchecked violence might overflow the "native" quarters and endanger British lives and treasure, there was a strong sense among British officials that defeating such outbursts of "fanaticism" was part of the state's *raison d'etre*. Given such considerations, and given the abundant evidence, which we will encounter throughout this book, of police officials working to prevent or contain communal riots, it is far too simplistic to claim that the British state desired, provoked, or deliberately encouraged these riots. Moreover, it is also erroneous to see British communal policy as proceeding solely in a top-down manner. As G. R. Thursby points out, there were no master strategists pulling the strings of communal division; rather, "communal separatism seems to have been more nearly the result of a complex process of interaction between the government and the communities than of a simple policy of divide and rule handed down from on high."[11] Most of those complex interactions took place within the parameters of colonial modernity.

Colonial modernity

Apart from securing the peace, one of the other putative benefits of British imperialism was that it brought modernity to primitive people around the world. By modernity we should understand not just technologies like railroads and factories, but a whole bundle of intellectual, political, cultural, and economic changes intended to bring non-Western areas more in line with Western norms. Commercial and industrial capitalism, constitutionalism and the rule of law, the securing of individual liberties, preserving the rights of women, secularism, security of persons and property, sexual restraint and the eradication of vice: all these markers of material and moral progress (and many more) would, imperial enthusiasts insisted, eventually flow from British rule overseas. A decline in everyday violence was just one of the benefits that was supposed to ensue. Yet it was one of the great paradoxes of British imperialism—one that was not lost on those who watched it operate—that those places that seemed to have benefitted the most from British modernity were often those that were the most troubled by communal violence. Belfast, the only industrial city in Ireland (and therefore its most "British"), was one of those places. A typical observation on the seeming paradox of Belfast's increasingly deadly sectarian violence was the *Saturday Review's* disappointment, after a riot in 1864, that Belfast—"opulent, self-governed, enterprising," and enjoying "no pretence of poverty as an excuse for crime"—should be "for eleven days at the mercy of a mob."[12] Another such place was Bombay, one of the most apparently modern, yet one of the most disturbed, places in India. When riots erupted there in 1874 the *Glasgow Herald*, noting the city's commercial and political sophistication, observed, "[f]rom the standpoint of Western civilisation Bombay is . . . the last place in India we should look to for one of these mad outbursts of fanaticism."[13] What was so perplexing was that violence of this sort was, in British eyes, the product of a primitive atavism that modernity (particularly capitalist modernity) was supposed to wash away, just as it had allegedly done in Britain itself.[14] That violence was persisting (and even worsening) in these places called into question the very premise of Britain's civilizing mission. Was it possible that colonial modernity was encouraging, rather than obviating, communal violence?

There are several ways that it clearly was. To begin at the most general level, let us consider the impact of capitalism, industrialization, and the commercialization of rural economies. Areas drawn into Britain's commercial orbit often experienced an upsetting of existing communal equilibriums and intensified competition for new or scarce resources, and the ensuing social tensions often found expression in violent conflict. It is therefore no coincidence that some of the bloodiest sectarian battlegrounds in Ireland were those that were most closely tied to British markets. South Armagh, where the ultra-Protestant Orange Order was born, was one such battleground. In the late eighteenth and early nineteenth centuries local squabbles between that region's rival communities of linen weavers, who were serving mostly British markets, hardened into some of the most entrenched communal rivalries in the entire British world.[15] Likewise Belfast, a major supplier of linens, ships, and other goods to the empire, also became Ireland's most divided city thanks to its involvement with the imperial economy. A mid-nineteenth century linen boom, coupled with a collapsing rural economy and the famine of the 1840s, sent wave upon wave of poor Catholics into what had been a self-consciously Protestant city, setting the stage for a series of violent battles over civic space and the politics of Irish self-rule from the 1850s until well into the twentieth century.[16] This pattern repeated itself in countless industrial communities in Britain as well: wherever Irish Catholic economic migrants settled in Britain, they tended to encounter (at least initially) resentment among local Protestants with whom they competed for jobs or for access to urban space, often with violent results.[17]

Similar dynamics developed elsewhere. In India, commercial and industrial developments prompted migration into, and economic competition within, provinces like Bombay and Bengal, bringing into contact groups who had previously had little opportunity or reason to oppose one another. Severe riots among Bengal jute hands, which began in the 1890s and persisted for over a decade, were one manifestation of this.[18] Communal clashes were also common in Bombay, a city that owed its very existence to European commercial expansion and where Hindus, Parsis, and Muslims from many different regions of India coexisted in an uneasy balance that could easily be upset. Moreover, many of India's outbreaks involved communities that were not just migratory but actually transient—Arab and Sidi seamen who plied the Bombay to Arabia trade, Bengali peasants-turned-millworkers—much as many riots in Ireland and Britain involved migrant bands of (usually Catholic, usually male) laborers who traveled from place to place building railroads, docks, and canals.[19] Indeed, right across the empire there were riots between communities who had been driven by economic necessity to settle, or sojourn, somewhere new: one thinks not only of the Irish in Britain (and, indeed, in North America and Australia), but also of South Asian "coolies" in the West Indies, Muslim traders in Ceylon, and (as we have seen) Portuguese immigrants in British Guiana. Usually this violence was between immigrants and their host communities, but sometimes riots could erupt between immigrant communities, as during the 1893 riots in Rangoon, Burma, which pitted Indian Hindus against Indian Muslims, or the many riots in Britain and North America between Catholic and Protestant Irish.[20] Whatever their immediate causes, these riots were essentially products of the market economy into which British imperialism had pulled people, and of the population movements that often ensued.

Frequently it was the demand for cheap labor on the part of capitalists, and the desire for employment on the part of migrants (usually against a backdrop of a collapsing rural labor market, also the product of a commercializing imperialism) that threw disparate groups together, destabilized communal balances, and set one group of economically marginalized people against another. But there was an equal—and, in some ways, opposite—tendency that was similarly destabilizing. This was the tendency of British policy, particularly in rural India, to ossify communal relations that had previously been fluid. From the mid-eighteenth century, Britain adopted a policy of sedentarization in India, reducing labor mobility, encroaching on the lands and customs of tribal peoples, and creating newly rigid social hierarchies in order to speed the work of the colonial tax collector (among other things). The consequences for India—and, later, for other parts of the world—were profound: caste and tribal identities became more pronounced as rural economies became more stratified; local elites became more powerful and better able to mobilize their dependents on the basis of a putative shared identity; the poor became even more vulnerable to exploitation and economic competition; and a complex and overlapping network of precolonial social relations gradually coalesced into discreet blocs—"carving blocs," as one historian calls them[21]—with their own identities, organizations, and agendas.[22] Once those conditions were in place, clashes between competing communities were only a matter of time.

There were other ways that colonial modernity created the conditions for conflict. "Wherever Englishmen govern they will make roads and bridges," Bombay policeman Edmund C. Cox boasted in his 1887 history of Bombay.[23] The same was true of railroads and telegraph lines, all signs of progress that imperial enthusiasts like Cox celebrated as among the unmitigated benefits of British rule. Historian Deep Kanta Lahiri Choudhury describes the telegraph as "the supreme celebration of the scientific empire that Britain promised," and Martin Wainwright has also shown how the imperial press celebrated innovations such as the telegraph and railway as among the key benefits of British rule.[24] Like the Romans before them, the British saw such feats of engineering both as signs of their intellectual superiority and as practical measures for joining their diverse territories together into a unified whole. Speaking in Benares in 1895, Antony MacDonnell, lieutenant governor of the North-West Provinces, described the new Dufferin Bridge across the Ganges as

> the latest product of material civilization, which, by abridging distances, seeks to weld together the various parts of a heterogeneous empire into a solid whole; and the seal of a polity which abjures intrusion on the domain of conscience, and guarantees to every creed the full exercise of its religious beliefs. The effect of this newer civilization is to mitigate animosities, to make one sect tolerant towards another, and to stimulate all in the direction of material prosperity.[25]

MacDonnell surely knew better than this, however: just two years earlier, as lieutenant governor of Bengal during the cow-protection riots of 1893, he had seen communal agitators use just such "products of material civilization" as telegraphs, railroads, and newspapers not to spread peace and understanding but to incite hatred across the subcontinent. Daniel Headrick has called new communications technology a "double-edged sword" for the British Raj, since, while it did allow Britain to more effectively control India, it also helped Indian nationalists to stitch together a nationalist movement and the beginnings of a shared national identity.[26] In fact, Headrick's sword was available to anybody with an idea to spread or a community to build: communalists, no less than nationalists, could bend this technology to their will.

Communication and transportation technologies fostered communal violence in many ways. They aided the work of religious revivalists. They spread news of communal riots and thus spawned copycat riots elsewhere. They enabled the violently disposed to travel somewhere in order to riot (by 1880 some 80 million people were riding the low-fare Indian rails[27]). They allowed people to take vicarious pleasure in the victories of "their side," or to feel aggrieved when some of "their own" were wronged. We will see detailed evidence of these processes in later chapters, especially Chapter 7 on the 1893 riots in India, but for now we might glance at a report prepared by MacDonnell's Bengal government in 1893, which explained how these technologies contributed to the violence of that year:

> In former years, … before we had by improvements in the means of communication and locomotion bridged distances and made intercourse between remote places easy, the old Hindu feeling used to display itself in isolated outbreaks with no concerted plan of action. But times have now changed, and the change has by no means reached its limit. A religious enthusiast or political agitator, whose operations but a few years ago would have been restricted to say a corner of Punjab, lectures in North-East Bengal in one week, at Allahabad in the next, and at Nagpur, Poonah, or Madras in the week after; and he leaves behind him disciples who are eager to work on the lines of an organization which, if not identical, are everywhere more or less directed to the same ends.[28]

Moreover, as Choudhury has shown, technologies like the telegraph not only assisted communal organizers and nationalists, they also served to spread panic among administrators by transmitting false information, raising the specter of widespread revolt, and (as during an Indian telegraph strike of 1908) making the state dependent on the cooperation of local, and potentially unsympathetic, telegraph operators.[29]

The double-edged nature of modern technology was not just an Indian phenomenon, of course. In the north of Ireland in the 1860s, for instance, railway companies began running special excursion trains for Protestants traveling to Derry, a mostly Catholic city, to take part in controversial public marches; some Catholics saw such demonstrations as an invasion of their territory, and the result was serious violence in that city in 1868 and 1869.[30] Similar things happened in Belfast. In 1864, local Catholics returning by special train from a nationalist demonstration in Dublin were greeted by a burning effigy of a Catholic hero as their train steamed through a Protestant district. The resulting riots lasted nearly two weeks.[31]

The most important communications technology for creating and sustaining communal rivalries was undoubtedly the printing press, often in alliance with the telegraph. By the end of the nineteenth century nearly every faction and subfaction within every British colony had at least one newspaper to its name.[32] In addition to English-language papers, by the end of the century most colonies had any number of vernacular papers that, as Su Lin Lewis has said of Malaya, "solidified communal bonds by standardising shared vernacular languages in print."[33] This did not mean that they always promoted intercommunal hatred, but they certainly could. As we will see in several upcoming chapters, the more spirited newspapers had no compunction about fanning the flames of communal rivalry into full-blown riots, sometimes by publicizing or sensationalizing communal controversies, sometimes by publishing exaggerated (or entirely accurate) reports of insults or atrocities committed by the other side, sometimes by advertising gatherings for communal "self-defense" or other vigilante initiatives, and always by sounding a steady drumbeat of innuendo, grievance, rumor, and accusation.

Officials often complained about what they saw as the press's irresponsible behavior. In 1864 the undersecretary at Dublin Castle told Queen Victoria that the newspapers were "the greatest enemies to peace & order in Ireland."[34] In 1893 India's home secretary made the same point at greater length.

> The main and chief cause [of communal riots], I believe, is the existence of the public press and the rapid spread throughout India of information of what takes place in any particular locality. Nowadays news is conveyed everywhere by telegraph … in a day or two. A riot at Rangoon is heard of at Delhi in two days, and immediately Hindus and Muhammadans begin to look at one another with suspicion.[35]

Why not quash troublesome newspapers, then? Certainly some men in the field would have favored such a step, men like Edmund C. Cox, the Bombay policeman who argued (in his history of that city) that Indians were incapable of enjoying "liberty of the press" without "descend[ing] into license."[36] There were some limits on press freedom in the empire, of course—as, indeed, there were in Britain itself. Outright sedition (usually defined more broadly overseas than at home) was illegal, as was obscenity, and some colonial governments also tried to influence the content of newspapers by supplying them with money and information. Nevertheless, in most places the authorities' desire to control the press existed in uneasy tension (and sometimes open conflict) with a widespread philosophical belief, held by the rulers as well as the ruled, that press freedom was a fundamental principle of Britain's liberal imperium—one of those liberties, as Simon Potter observes, that made the empire distinctly British.[37] Not only did a free press set Britain's empire apart from the "Oriental despotisms" against which it positioned itself, it also had several practical benefits. In India, during a period of liberalization in the 1830s, important officials came to believe that a vibrant local press could serve an educational purpose by contributing to what Sir Charles Metcalfe (India's governor-general in 1835) called an "increase in knowledge" that would "strengthen our empire; … remove prejudices, soften asperities, and substitute a rational conviction of the benefits of our government."[38] As C. A. Bayly has shown, British administrators also saw the local press as a valuable gauge of "native" opinion, an attitude institutionalized in India with the reporters on the native press who provided British officials with translated précis of articles in the vernacular press.[39]

Because of such attitudes, following an early period of close censorship during the French Revolution and Napoleonic Wars, by the middle of the nineteenth century most parts of the British world (both within and beyond the United Kingdom) began to enjoy press freedom to a greater or lesser extent.[40] Often it was British colonists, concerned not only with the free flow of news but also with dispersing information in the commercial, financial, scientific, and missionary spheres, who pushed for these changes.[41] As more and more locals began publishing newspapers, they likewise claimed the right to journalistic freedom, and usually received it. By the end of the century many British officials had begun to detest the "license" with which some local newspapers behaved, but most efforts to reintroduce strict censorship failed. In Ireland, as Myles Dungan has shown, both free-speech advocates and the judiciary frequently frustrated the efforts of late-Victorian governments to suppress "seditious" nationalist papers with so-called Coercion Acts; although individual papers and journalists might be silenced, the Irish press (including those papers with a communal, rather than strictly nationalist, orientation) remained functionally free.[42] India likewise underwent a failed experiment in press censorship with the Vernacular Press Act of 1878, which was modeled on the Irish Coercion Act of 1870. After allowing the vernacular press to publish without significant legal restriction since 1835 (apart from a brief period following the 1857 revolt), Britain introduced this new law to suppress criticism of government action in the Second Anglo-Afghan War. The law required native-language newspapers to submit proof sheets to the police before publication, and it inevitably led to censorship of much more than just the newspapers' war coverage. The Act caused such outrage, however—not only in India but also in Parliament, where MPs objected to it largely on the grounds of its violation of liberal principles—that the Liberal viceroy, Lord Ripon, repealed it in 1882, and the experiment was not repeated until the twentieth century.[43] Indeed, when some officials toyed with renewing press censorship during the Indian cow-protection riots of 1893, the secretary of state flatly rejected the idea, telling the viceroy, "I have no doubt [the press] does a world of harm in India; it also does, you may rely on it, some good, as a safety valve for explosive opinions."[44] He also pointed out that such a move would cause "a great outcry" at home; the viceroy agreed, and nothing more was said of the matter.[45]

For the most part, even when governments did try to suppress "seditious" nationalist newspapers, such censorship had little impact on religious or other kinds of communal publications, except, perhaps, for helping to channel nationalist energies into communal forms.[46] As several historians of India have noted, many late-Victorian movements for religious revival or reform acted as a sort of proxy for nationalist activity or for the local political power that nationalists were seeking.[47] In India this revivalism took the form of Wahhabism among Muslims (in the 1860s and 1870s) and the cow-protection movement among Hindus (in the 1880s and 1890s), movements that exploited the communications technologies fostered by British rule and in some cases (as we will see) presented serious threats to the peace.[48] In Ceylon Buddhist revivalists, using printing technology introduced by British missionaries, became increasingly assertive in the 1870s and 1880s, leading to clashes with native Catholics in and around Colombo.[49] Meanwhile Irish Catholics went through a profound, demi-nationalist, technology-enabled "devotional revolution" in the second half of the century that simultaneously boosted their self-confidence and worsened relations with Protestants, especially in the north.[50] In all of these cases, and in many more across the empire, revivalists used the tools of colonial modernity—printing presses, telegraphs, monster meetings, railways—to spread their messages, often creating national and, indeed, international movements that both promoted a distinctive communal identity and created friction with their ethnic, caste, or religious rivals long into the twentieth century.

The perils of liberalism

As the issue of press freedom suggests, for much of this period the state's very liberalism was part of its problem, at least from a public order perspective. In the accompanying case studies we will see ample evidence that the state did adhere to its liberal principles in most places, most of the time, even during periods of panic and emergency. Indeed, we have already seen how the government of British Guiana was careful to record the sermons of John Sayers Orr and submit them for legal review before deciding to arrest the preacher, steps that a less liberal state would have scarcely bothered with. On the whole, apart from a few extraordinary incidents—usually involving existential threats to the state itself—liberal principles like the rule of law, due process, and freedom of expression were fairly secure in the Victorian Empire. This did not preclude authoritarianism, of course, for in most places colonized "natives" (that is, non-settlers) had no real political rights; however, if we can accept that there can be such a thing as liberal authoritarianism (as Howard Brown has recently characterized Bonaparte's France) or enlightened despotism (as the Victorians preferred to call it), then we can begin to appreciate one of the great internal contradictions of the British Empire.[51]

As an emblem of this contradiction let us examine the issue of religious freedom, one of the pole stars of British policy across the Victorian Empire.[52] Wherever the Union Jack flew, the ideal posture of the state—repeated again and again in official pronouncements, police reports, private correspondence, and the English-language press—was that of an impartial referee standing outside of, but often regulating, local religious squabbles.[53] This principle was most explicitly articulated in India, where the Queen's Proclamation of 1858 promised "that none be in anywise favoured, none molested or disquieted, by reason of their religious faith or observances, but that all shall alike enjoy the equal and impartial protection of the law."[54] A more detailed, but entirely consistent, statement of principle came from Antony MacDonnell in the Indian Viceroy's Council in 1895: "The duty of the Government is to preserve the peace, to extend impartial toleration to all creeds, to maintain the lawful liberties of all its subjects, and repress all persons or classes of persons who infringe such liberties or insult the religion or wound the religious feelings of others."[55] Although designed for India, these declarations of religious liberty and state neutrality generally applied to all of Britain's territories in "the East," a notion that several governors in Ceylon, for instance, publicly affirmed and sought to enforce.[56] In the West Indies the post-Emancipation arrival of Portuguese, East Indian, and Chinese laborers likewise brought the question of the state's religious orientation to the forefront, and here, too, with a few exceptions, officials adopted a policy of broad religious toleration (while retaining a moderate official preference for Christianity). In 1868 the Church of England was disestablished in most of the West Indies, and, although this measure was the result of economic as well as philosophical considerations, it was generally in line with the stance of religious neutrality that Britain was adopting elsewhere.[57] In Ireland the situation was more complicated—historic state support for Protestantism meant that many Irish Protestants expected the state to look after their interests—but the general trend toward religious neutrality was the same, as shown by the disestablishment of the Anglican Church of Ireland (also in 1868). In any event, officials in Ireland generally understood that to rule the country effectively they must appear to be impartial; as one former lord lieutenant told the House of Lords in 1853, "There was no people in the world on whom it was so necessary to impress the idea that they are governed equitably as the Irish."[58]

In Chapter 8 we will explore how the impartiality doctrine—or, more accurately, the inherent impossibility of adhering to that doctrine—could undermine the colonial state's prestige. Here we will simply consider how this undeniably liberal determination to allow the free exercise of religion served, at times, to foster violence. The 1882 riots in Salem, Madras, are a good example of this. The dispute between Salem's Hindus and Muslims was complex and of long standing, but it largely took the form (as so many did) of an argument over religious processions. In 1874, following a riot in the town of Gooty, the Madras government had ordered district collectors to issue a blanket ban on the playing of music while processions passed any place of worship.[59] The following year construction began on a new mosque in the town of Salem, which was 90 percent Hindu and 6–7 percent Muslim.[60] The mosque was built near three Hindu temples, which, according to the Madras government's order, meant that Hindu processions going in and out of the temples could not play music in their own neighborhood, an arrangement that the Hindus felt conflicted with established custom and thus violated their religious rights. The case found its way to the Madras High Court, which ruled that the Madras government had been in error: there could be no blanket ban on musical processions, the court held, but instead each situation had to be judged on its own merits. In the words of historian R. Suntharalingam, the High Court's judgment "threatened to undermine what had been one of the main props of sustaining the fabric of communal peace in South India."[61] Across Madras, Hindus realized they could use the ruling to restore their right to play music in their processions, and Muslims foresaw endless streams of obnoxious music disturbing their prayers. They also worried that they would be required to fix specific hours for worship, which would contradict *their* established custom. Moreover (again in Suntharalingam's words), the High Court order "demanded from district officials tact, patience, and strict impartiality, as well as an ability to discern whether their decision would precipitate a disturbance. Where officials failed to display such virtuosity, trouble was not far away."[62]

In 1881, after trying and failing to get the Muslims to abide by special prayer times, the Salem magistrates allowed Hindus to hold their musical processions under police escort. Meanwhile the Madras government, ignoring the High Court's ruling, called for legislation banning music in front of religious buildings, but the central government in Calcutta refused. This tangle of orders and cross-orders sapped the government's credibility and led both sides in the dispute to question the state's ability to act impartially. In early July 1882 even the Anglophone, generally pro-state *Madras Times* pointed to "an inconsistency of principle" and the appearance of "a partiality of practice" in the government's behavior. "Surely it would be better," it wrote in a leader (which Salem Muslims subsequently forwarded to the viceroy), "to make the law universal and forbid the use of music in religious processions whenever they pass a place that is used for public worship." The High Court's decision may have been just, the *Madras Times* continued, and the law may be "right and good, but the people are not sufficiently civilized or philosophical to be benefitted by it."[63] Upholding freedom of religious expression was certainly praiseworthy, the newspaper seemed to suggest, but it was folly to do so among people who were incapable of acting like free and rational individuals.

With the High Court's blessing, then, Hindu processions continued to go past the new mosque until July 28, 1882, when one such procession was finally attacked. During the affray a Muslim constable killed a Hindu woman, leading many Hindus to allege that the police were siding with their enemies. This suspicion was strengthened by the subsequent decision of Dr. Macleane, the district collector, to prohibit a subsequent Hindu procession planned for September.[64] Rumors began to circulate among the Hindus that the only reason the mosque had been built in the first place was that the previous district collector had had a

Muslim butler who convinced him to permit the new construction. "The secret may be a gross exaggeration," wrote a correspondent to the *Madras Times*, "but if Hindus believe it, it is none the less mischievous."[65] Matters finally came to a head in mid-August when a Hindu crowd raided the mosque, knocked down the walls, and set it on fire. They also attacked several Muslims and burned their homes. When the police arrived they fired on the Hindus, which only confirmed in many Hindu minds that the state was their enemy. By the time the military arrived, some sixty-nine houses had been gutted, forty people had been wounded, and ten people (seven Hindus and three Muslims) had died.[66] Further complicating the state's position were reports of a Hindu police officer who, during the Hindu assault on the mosque, "was seen on his housetop, waving a flag and encouraging the mob in their work of destruction."[67] If the Hindus had suspected state antipathy before, now the Muslims had reason to believe that some agents of the state opposed them, too.

The government of Madras alleged that the riots were the result of a Hindu conspiracy, but the courts chose to blame the local officials who had failed to effectively mediate the dispute.[68] According to Bombay's *Times of India* the fracas was an inevitable consequence of the religious liberty that British rule guaranteed to India.

> Men in responsible positions are bound, in the interests of law and order, to interfere in matters which they would very gladly let alone, and until all classes and creeds recognise the propriety of respecting the religious susceptibilities of others as they would have their own respected, magistrates will frequently be placed in the position of seeming to interfere with the rights and privileges of some section or other of the population.[69]

The liberal regime that Britain was enforcing in India relied, in this analysis (and this was something the *Madras Times* had also argued), on the ability of the people to respect one another's rights—to be, as the *Madras Times* had said, "sufficiently civilized or philosophical" to act as good liberal subjects should—but in Salem the people had shown that they could not do this. In reality, the main problem was probably the "vacillation and inconsistency" (as Suntharalingam puts it) of state agents at all levels, whose conflicting signals, shifting orders, and occasionally partisan behavior undermined people's confidence in the state and provided opportunities for communal activists to press their advantage.[70]

While much of the chaos in Salem, then, was due to official bungling and dysfunction, it was also a consequence of the determination of both Hindus and Muslims to claim the religious liberty due to them as British subjects, as well as the efforts of British officials (inconsistent though they may have been) to preserve that liberty. A more authoritarian state would simply have suppressed all public religious displays, but this was not the British way. Across the empire the pattern was the same: religious liberty, far from being a mere liberal abstraction, was something that colonial subjects highly valued and that state officials sought to uphold. In Ireland the cry of "civil and religious liberty" was never far from the lips of evangelical Protestants determined to resist the "intolerance" and "bigotry" of Catholics, and it was a cry that most officials took quite seriously. In Ceylon, after a clash with Catholics in Colombo, Buddhist leaders sent an emissary to London to seek assurances from the colonial secretary himself that the state would preserve their religious freedom, assurances that they duly received. In Trinidad in 1884, East Indian plantation workers used the language of religious liberty in a petition begging the government not to restrict their annual Muharram festival; although in this case their request was denied, it was largely on the (inaccurate) grounds that the festival had no real religious meaning, not that the state had no duty to protect free religious expression.[71]

And on and on it goes, in countless instances across the globe. Perhaps the most striking example of this popular appetite for religious freedom was the response in India to a decision by the Bombay government in 1882 to ban Salvation Army processions in that city. The Salvationists were four white British missionaries who, having set up the organization's first Indian mission in Bombay, had begun holding musical processions in "native" garb through the streets. Fearing disorder, the authorities prohibited the processions and arrested some of the missionaries. This prompted protests across India from Christians and non-Christians alike, including many vernacular newspapers that were not otherwise especially sympathetic toward evangelical Christianity. In Calcutta a meeting of thousands of Hindus (along with a few Christians) drafted a memorial to the governor that clearly explained their apprehensions. While disavowing any particular sympathy with the doctrines or methods of the Salvation Army, the memorialists were

> deeply concerned and grieved whenever any attempts are made by any local executive authorities to the detriment of that religious liberty and toleration which it has been their great privilege to enjoy under the British Government; for if once the well-established principle of religious liberty and toleration be departed from in the case of even a single individual, be his creed or race what it may, your memorialists believe that their common liberty is endangered, and there is no guarantee that the same may not be repeated in the case of others.[72]

After a series of trials and appeals, the Indian courts eventually ordered the Salvationists to stop playing music in Muslim quarters, where they were most likely to cause disturbance, but otherwise permitted them to continue their public displays in Bombay.[73]

India was probably the place where the principle of religious liberty was most frequently invoked, partly because of the country's complex religious geography, and partly because partisans of all faiths could point to a specific document (the Queen's Declaration of 1858) to press their claims. In much of India, even-handed protection of religious liberty was a new phenomenon—indeed, in those areas still nominally ruled by Indian princes, religious policies normally favored the religion of the prince—and so forms of religious expression that might have been repressed under Indian rulers became increasingly common under British ones.[74] When competing religious claims threatened the peace, the state's usual practice was to consult "ancient custom" to establish a rule of precedence. There were serious problems with this approach, however. As the Indian government's report on the 1893 riots explained, "such custom may have been violently interrupted; or circumstances may have entirely changed since it was established; or the evidence as to the custom may (as is not unfrequently the case) be so conflicting that certainty is unattainable; or the repression which was formerly acquiesced in may be held to be inconsistent with reasonable religious liberty."[75] In such circumstances it was impossible for the state to maintain its detachment from the quarrel. A letter to the *Times of India* after a riot in 1894 explained the dilemma:

> A departure from old usage on the part of a British officer is always ascribed, naturally, by the community against whose claims it is made, to a desire in that officer to please the community in whose favour it is made; while the latter community always account for it as being due either to special favour for them or to fear of them. In this manner a mistaken step is calculated to produce a double evil. It fills one community with discontent, while it stimulates the other community to demand greater concessions.[76]

By taking on the role of mediator, officials inevitably became a party to these conflicts, whether they wanted to or not.

The fundamental problem was that the state's liberal determination to preserve free religious expression ensured that free religious expression did, in fact, take place—and this, in turn, created opportunities for those who opposed a particular form of religious expression to behave violently.[77] This was the point made by the Indian government's report of the 1893 riots. Unlike in the princely states, where religious expression was restricted by Hindu or Muslim rulers, under the impartial administration of the British, "there has been a general tendency towards assertion of religious privileges on both sides … and this has naturally been greatest in those localities where during previous administrations one party possessed an ascendency which has now ceased." One of the great difficulties of British rule in India, the report continued, "is to reconcile the impartial administration of justice and equal treatment of all creeds with the necessity of keeping the peace."[78] This was the problem of liberal imperialism in a nutshell.

In a leader on the 1893 Indian riots, the *Glasgow Herald* expressed the frustration that many Britons felt about the fruits of these liberal policies. Before Britain ruled India, the writer maintained, Muslim rulers had managed to keep Brahman bigotry in check. "Then came the British *Raj* with its steady maintenance of the principle of religious toleration, and the worshippers of Brahma and Siva suddenly found themselves placed on a level of unaccustomed equality and religious freedom with their erstwhile Mohammedan oppressors. It is not surprising that they should have abused the tolerance and liberty thus secured to them." What it came down to for the *Herald*—echoing sentiments in the Anglophone press following the Salem riot of 1882—was that Indians were not mature enough to act as good liberal subjects.[79] The fault lay not with British liberalism, but with a people who were not capable of exercising their liberty in a responsible manner. As we will see in the Chapter 4, this idea was frequently applied to populations across the empire.

Conclusion

In response to what I have been arguing, it might be objected that modernity—especially capitalist modernity—was going to come to India, Ireland, Ceylon, the Caribbean, and other parts of the world, whether they were ruled by Britain or not, and that British imperialism, as such, ought not to be blamed for creating the conditions in which communal violence took place. I am inclined to agree with this, but only because what I am trying to do here is not to assign blame but merely to identify the parameters within which communal violence played out. Railroads, the telegraph, newspapers, transformations in rural and urban economies, and other products of modernity would certainly have appeared in these places without British encouragement, but the fact is that it *was* the British—British governments, British investors, British missionaries, British settlers—sometimes working together, sometimes independently, and sometimes in cooperation with local elites—who brought about these changes. Insofar as these groups were the agents of empire, then it was the British Empire that helped to create the conditions for communal violence.[80]

One feature of the colonial encounter that was distinctly British, however—and one that would not have been the same if these places had been colonized by someone else, or if they had not been colonized at all—was Britain's commitment to liberal imperialism. Though not universally enforced, liberal principles like the rule of law, due process, freedom of religion, and freedom of expression were enforced most of the time in most of the empire, if not by individuals then at least by institutions (the glaring exception, in most places, being the absence of representative political institutions). These principles were certainly honored often enough to create the conditions for communal competition, and they were proclaimed loudly enough to create high expectations among the colonized about the state's integrity and disinterestedness—expectations that were not always fulfilled. What state officials did not deliberately do was to pit one community violently against another. British rulers did pursue policies of divide and rule, especially when it came to staffing armies, police forces, and local political institutions, but outright rioting was almost never in British interests. All riots, no matter how localized, are costly and time consuming (tying up not only soldiers and policemen but also the courts and jails), physically dangerous, bad for business, fodder for a hostile press, and, not least, tremendously embarrassing. Riots not only endangered the British state's reputation for impartiality and eroded its legitimacy, they also called into question its very competence to rule. The strategies by which British observers tried to overcome this embarrassment, and even turn it to their own rhetorical ends, form the subject of Chapter 4; but first we will make an excursion to the Irish city of Belfast, where we will see many of the forces we have examined in this chapter at work.

3

Trouble on the Queen's Highways: Belfast, 1872

They called him the Red Earl—this shy, grave man who traveled to Belfast in the summer of 1872, his beard leaping from his face in a great tangle of ginger—partly in jest and partly out of affection. Unlike his namesake, a seventeenth-century Ulster lord who had resisted English power in Ireland, John Poyntz Spencer—the fifth Earl Spencer, former groom to the royal household, master of the Pytchley hounds, bestower of Wimbledon Common upon a grateful nation—was certainly no rebel. Indeed, as lord lieutenant of Ireland (some still said viceroy) he was the queen's own representative in this troubled land that both was and was not a full member of the United Kingdom. Yet Spencer was something of a reformer, a Liberal in the Gladstonian mold who supported sensible reforms such as disestablishing Ireland's unrepresentative Protestant Church (a task completed in 1868), limiting the power of the country's Protestant landlords (via a modest Land Act in 1870), and expanding the franchise to some (but certainly not all) of the working classes. Like most British Liberals, Spencer felt that Ireland's woes could best be solved by an impartial and enlightened British regime, one that was beholden neither to Popery nor Property, and he did not flinch from adopting harsh measures against those who would liberate Ireland by force. Had he confronted the original Red Earl, one of Queen Elizabeth's most fearsome foes, he would probably have had him hauled away in chains.[1]

Spencer had come to Belfast that August at the invitation of the city's industrialists and merchants who, in their ongoing efforts to expand their city's commercial might, had just opened two new docks in the harbor. One of these docks they had loyally named after Spencer, and the other they had named for Spencer's friend Lord Dufferin, an Ulster lord who had just become governor-general of Canada ("Our names," Spencer wrote to Dufferin after the visit, "are thus linked together in the middle of the ships of Belfast"[2]). Belfast was booming, and had been so for decades, and the new docks were to usher in an age of iron shipbuilding that would make Belfast one of the empire's great shipbuilding powerhouses. These new docks were just the sort of thing for which Belfast was known—in a country of crumbling farms and ill-fed peasants, the industries of northeast Ulster glimmered like a shaft of sunlight on a boggy plain—and it was for just such occasions that the office of the lord lieutenant remained useful, for, like any lord lieutenant, Spencer was more a figurehead than fountainhead. The real sources of Irish policy these days were the cabinet in London, the chief secretary in Dublin, and the bureaucratic paper shufflers in Dublin Castle. Although he retained some executive powers, Spencer's principal duty was to embody the majesty of the British Crown by doing things like hosting fancy balls and opening new docks. On occasions like the present one, Spencer normally hid his natural nervousness behind a tone of aloof, viceregal dignity, much as he hid his face behind that great puff of red hair, staying safely on script and avoiding controversy.

On this occasion he was largely successful. After surveying the new docks, Spencer bestowed knighthoods on the mayor and the chairman of the harbor commissioners, lunched aboard a ship in Belfast Lough (where, as he told Dufferin, he listened to innumerable speeches relating "the hackneyed tale of Belfast's prosperity"), and attended a fine but sparsely attended banquet at the Ulster Hall. There he gave a very long and rather dull speech about the state of the country, citing recent agricultural data and crime returns to show how much Ireland was improving under the present Liberal government, and he praised Belfast for the industrious example it was setting for the rest of Ireland. He drew a few heckles when he mentioned the government's recent introduction of the secret ballot (a measure that undermined the power of many Ulster landlords), but this was not unexpected for a Liberal viceroy speaking to a largely Conservative audience—for Belfast was, despite its industrial prowess, a predominately Tory town. Once he had finished with the agricultural and crime statistics, Spencer turned to Parliament's recent decision to repeal the Party Processions Act, an 1850 law that prohibited the sorts of sectarian marches and demonstrations that frequently provoked riots in the north of Ireland. The repeal had come after a long campaign by members of the Orange Order, the chief Protestant fraternal organization in Ireland, who argued that the law was being enforced more rigorously against them than against their Catholic rivals. In celebration of their triumph the Orangemen had held several grand marches that July, the first legal Orange marches in over twenty years, and most of them had ended peacefully. This made Spencer cautiously optimistic:

> I do not know whether party processions or demonstrations will altogether cease or assume a character which will not offend any party in the community. It would be very unwise of me were I to predict what will occur; but I cannot help thinking that the independence and principles of one party might well, in future, lead them to give up some of those demonstrations, if they are of a character to hurt the feelings of any of their neighbours; and, on the other hand, I believe that the other party, equally strong in the view they may take of their principles, will be able to bear patiently any such demonstrations which the others may choose to have.

Spencer knew that some Catholics were planning their own demonstrations on August 15, just a week after his visit, and he expressed an earnest hope that these would end as peacefully as the Orange ones. Come what may, Spencer assured his audience, the duty of Her Majesty's Government was "most cordially to apply with impartiality the laws of the land in every part of Ireland … to respect no person or power whatever … but, wherever the law is resisted, to rigidly put it in force, and to maintain the dignity and independence of our Constitution."[3] Should any trouble erupt, Spencer's address implied, the state would be both Solomon and Zeus, dispensing justice and lightning bolts with cordial disinterestedness.

After the banquet, as Spencer told Dufferin, "I as usual felt that I had missed a good opportunity and never in retrospect groaned so much over a speech." It is unclear whether he meant that he had missed an opportunity to sell the ballot initiative to the crowd, or if he felt he had made some graver error that night in the Ulster Hall. It may be that Spencer groaned so much because his speech failed to prevent what happened next in Belfast. "But now," he wrote Dufferin, "what am I to say as to the second chapter of Belfast history of August '72?" The Catholics had gone ahead with their planned demonstration, the Protestants had opposed it, riots had broken out, and Spencer had had "to pour in police and soldiers" to put them down.[4] The Red Earl was stunned by the violence that followed his visit (he told Lord Halifax, the lord privy seal who would relate these matters to the queen, that when he was in Belfast, "nothing could exceed the loyalty & apparent peacefulness of the people, but a spark blew all this up."[5]). Still struggling to be Solomonic, however, he told Dufferin that it was of course "very wrong" of the Catholics to hold their processions, but it was "still more ungenerous and wicked" of the Protestants to interfere with them. "It is," he concluded, "very disheartening."[6]

The Belfast riots of 1872 would indeed have been disheartening to anyone expecting the historic antagonism between Irish Protestants and Catholics to dissipate under the evenhanded benevolence of British rule. The mid-Victorian British Empire—liberal, progressive, confident of its ability to reshape foreign lands in its own image—was founded on just the sort of optimism that Spencer had shown that evening in the Ulster Hall. Like most members of the ruling caste, Spencer believed that Ireland's troubles could be solved by a patient hand steadily applied—by a state headed by firm and clear-eyed men who harbored no prejudices and favored no parties. Of course the state had also to be strong, its laws respected: disorder not only endangered lives and property, it endangered the law itself, for it revealed the limits of the state's authority, exposing the terror beneath the mask of omnipotence. For that reason Spencer, again like most men of his caste, could be quick to resort to violence when state-fostered reconciliation failed. A few years before the Belfast riots, he had demanded emergency coercive powers to deal with an upsurge in agrarian crime, and he had nearly resigned when the cabinet acted more sluggishly than he required. During his second stint as lord lieutenant, in the 1880s, he would show a similar proclivity for overwhelming displays of force, traveling the country with an armed entourage of nearly two dozen men to protect him from assassination. And in the present instance, after the riots in Belfast had begun, he would postpone his interest in reconciliation and side with those who felt that a few salutary shootings at the outset of the riot might have stifled the whole thing in its infancy. Optimism, it turned out, was not incompatible with authoritarianism; the justice of Solomon had sometimes to be enforced with the lightning of Zeus.

Like the 1856 riots in British Guiana, the 1872 Belfast riots raised the question of how much freedom of expression should be granted to subject peoples and how far such freedom should be curtailed for the sake of order. They also showed just how difficult it could be, in the heat of battle, for the state to maintain its commitment to impartiality: at such moments one or the other rival faction (or, indeed, both factions) tended to see the state as siding with their enemies, and this belief often prompted people to take the law into their own hands. Even more than during the Guiana riots, moreover, the prolonged nature of the Belfast disturbances made the forces of law and order appear not just partisan but actually incompetent. This was deeply damaging to the state's prestige, and, in a society where the state's legitimacy was already shaky, prestige was something the state could ill-afford to squander. Like other Belfast riots before and after them—and the city endured a regular deluge of these outbreaks during the Victorian period—the 1872 Belfast riots not only exacerbated the unhappy relationship between the people and the state, but they also made future outbreaks more likely by enforcing a rigid code of communal segregation that forced each group into their own solipsistic urban enclaves. Perhaps this was why the Red Earl had groaned so much over his Ulster Hall speech: his well-meant, if platitudinous, words of hope and reconciliation had been no match for the powerful forces fueling communal conflict in Belfast.

Evenhanded suppression

When Parliament repealed the Party Processions Act in June 1872 they were taking a leap in the dark. The 1850 Act banning sectarian processions, along with a supplementary Act in 1860 prohibiting the display of "party emblems," had been rare legislative interventions in Ireland's communal troubles. The original Act had been passed in response to a horrific riot in 1849 at Dolly's Brae, in rural County Down, where a dispute about an Orange parade had culminated in a pogrom against Catholic homes along the procession route in which some thirty Catholics died. In the ensuing investigation it emerged that the Orange marchers had been led by several justices of the peace who were members of the Orange Order; these men were subsequently censured for their naked partisanship and stripped of their commissions. Parliament intended the ensuing ban on party processions to apply to both Protestants and Catholics, but it naturally fell harder on Protestants, for whom Orange processions were a vital yearly event—an expression of group solidarity and a reminder of historic triumphs—whereas Catholic political processions were much less frequent or important.

Moreover, Catholics often found ways to hold "party" processions in all but name by cloaking their political or sectarian displays in the garb of religious or civic celebrations. This happened in 1864, when Dublin Catholics organized a massive procession to mark the construction of a statue of Daniel O'Connell, the so-called Liberator who had waged campaigns for Catholic political rights and repeal of the Act of Union that joined Ireland to the United Kingdom. Hailed as a hero by Catholics but detested by many Protestants, O'Connell (who had died in 1847) was a divisive figure even in death, but the Dublin parade did not fit Parliament's definition of a "party" procession, so it was allowed to proceed. Angry at what they saw as official double standards, some working-class Belfast Protestants decided to have a procession of their own, and what began with a defiant effigy-burning and mock funeral procession for O'Connell on the evening of the Dublin procession quickly spiraled into a massive riot that lasted ten days and killed at least eleven people. At the height of the conflict thousands of Protestants marched in a funeral procession to honor an Orangeman killed by the police, an event intended as a riposte not just to the Catholic marchers of Dublin but also to the British administration, which seemed to be allowing Catholics to march with impunity while suppressing the rights of Protestants to "march the Queen's highways."[7]

In the years after 1864 the great champion of the Orange cause was the Protestant landowner and sometime novelist William Johnston, the penurious patriarch of an old Anglican family based at Ballykilbeg, County Down, who used his considerable rhetorical skills to launch a populist campaign to overturn the processions ban. In 1867 he led a gathering of 9,000 Orangemen in an illegal, five-mile procession from Newtownards to Bangor; when the authorities unwisely threw him in jail, they made him an instant martyr to the cause. The following year Johnston defied the Conservative establishment in Belfast and won election to Parliament as an independent candidate pledging to repeal the Party Processions Act. His running mate in that election was a Presbyterian Liberal named Thomas McClure, who also won a seat that year and thereby became Belfast's last ever Liberal MP. Remarkably, both Johnston and McClure captured a large share of the Catholic vote that year, partly because their election promised to loosen the grip of the Conservative Party on Ulster, and partly because they both pledged not to oppose a proposal to disestablish the (Anglican) Church of Ireland.[8]

This unexpected Protestant–Catholic cooperation created a buzz of optimism among the Liberals of Belfast, who hoped their city might finally be moving beyond the sectarian politics of the past. Reflecting on the buoyant mood, the Liberal Protestant James Kennedy wrote in 1870, "party animosity is in course of rapid extinguishment, the hatchet buried, & little likelihood of its being exhumed. For the first time for many years Catholic & Protestant meet like Christian men, interchange ideas, & unite for the common good."[9] But such friendly feelings, if they ever really existed, would not last long. In 1872 Johnston finally managed to get Parliament to repeal the Party Processions Act, and that July the Orange Order planned its first legal processions in over twenty years. The failed experiment in evenhanded suppression had come to an end, and Ulster braced for what this new era of liberty might bring.

The Twelfth

Most people expected that any violence in the summer of 1872 would occur on the Twelfth of July. This was the day Orangemen celebrated the anniversary of the 1690 Battle of the Boyne, when the armies of the Protestant king William III (of the House of Orange) delivered a crippling blow to the deposed Catholic king James II in the war that followed England's "Glorious Revolution," an event that secured Protestant dominance in the British Isles once and for all. This was traditionally the day of the biggest Orange marches and one that had been rambunctious enough even when the Party Processions Act was in force, so what might happen after the ban was revoked was anybody's guess.

In the days prior to the Twelfth, Belfast was astir with rumor and suspicion. Inside the mill of the Ulster Spinning Company, in the Catholic district of Falls Road, Protestant women decorated their machines with orange lilies and erected an orange arch under which their Catholic coworkers had to pass. When management refused to intervene, upward of a dozen Catholic women quit their jobs in protest. News of the dispute quickly spread along the Falls, and before long a crowd of angry Catholics had gone racing toward the mill, only to be intercepted and dispersed by a force of constabulary.[10] Nothing much came of this or similar episodes in early July, but the atmosphere had grown quite tense by the time the Twelfth arrived.

The usual pattern for Twelfth of July processions in Belfast was (and is) for Orangemen to form feeder processions in different parts of Belfast, converging in the center of town into one grand river of banners and bowlers flowing south to a rally outside the city. Out in "the field" they listened to speeches, socialized, and frequently drank to excess (albeit under the disapproving gazes of the temperance lodges) before marching back, weary and a little unsteady, to their respective lodges and homes. This was the pattern in 1872, and it was, overall, a surprisingly peaceful affair. The Royal Irish Constabulary (RIC)—an Ireland-wide force assigned to the town after the local Belfast police were disbanded in 1865—were out in force, many posted near barricades at the usual trouble spots. On the morning of the Twelfth they kept themselves busy turning back the few stray Orangemen who tried to get into the Catholic neighborhoods, but no Catholics interfered with the outward march.[11] During the day, while the Orangemen gathered outside of town, a reporter for the *Northern Star and Ulster Observer*, the city's secular Catholic paper, wandered from neighborhood to neighborhood taking Belfast's temperature. On Hercules Street, the butcher district and a famous Catholic stronghold, he saw a large green-and-gold flag fluttering from the home of Catherine Moore, "while the patriotic owner sits opposite on a windowsill, pointing it out with just pride to her friends, and declaring that she is neither afraid nor ashamed to show her colours." Further west, up the Protestant Shankill Road, he saw a very different scene: orange arches soared above the streets bearing the insignia of the Orange Order and images of King William, coaches festooned with orange ribbons careened through the streets, and children in miniature drumming parties marched up and down in their own juvenile processions. While the reporter stood gazing at a "remarkable" orange arch across Broadbent Street a woman approached him and asked if he had seen anything that day to equal it. Receiving no reply, the "sallow-faced virago" told the Catholic reporter, "You may stick your paper and pencil up your—" and walked away.[12]

There were a few clashes when the processionists returned that night, but by Belfast standards these were rather mild. In the center of town, near Hercules Street, stone-throwing crowds injured a few people and provided the constables with a few prisoners. More stones were hurled further north, at Carrick Hill, and there was another scuffle along the quays. By the next day some seventy-two people were lodged in the police office, most of them for Twelfth-related offenses, but this was hardly an astronomical total. A month later, once the real rioting started, Catholics would attribute the relative tranquility of the Twelfth to their own high-minded forbearance, but the real reason appears to have been a massive thunderstorm that drenched the town around 9:00 p.m. ("the fiercest storm ever witnessed in Belfast," according to the *Daily Examiner*), which drove the crowds inside and kept them there all night.[13]

The riots

In the days after the Twelfth, some Catholics began planning their own procession for mid-August. The ostensible purposes of the procession were to petition the government to release nationalist political prisoners and to press for Home Rule (that is, internal legislative autonomy for Ireland), but it was also undoubtedly meant as a response to the Orange processions of the Twelfth. Two groups were behind the demonstration: the Belfast branch of the Home Rule Association, a small club headed by the rising Presbyterian politician, Joseph Biggar; and the Catholic butchers of Hercules Street, who ran advertisements in the *Daily Examiner* that described the procession as a nonsectarian event and urged participants to show "respect for the opinions of those who differ from them." A leader in the *Daily Examiner*, a Catholic paper run by the bishops and espousing a fairly aggressive, if orthodox, constitutional nationalism, went along with the spirit of this ad, expressing a hope that Protestants would participate alongside Catholics, but it is unlikely anyone really expected this to happen.[14]

August 15, the day fixed for the demonstration, was the Feast of the Assumption, commonly known as Lady Day, an important Catholic holiday that had seen violence at least once before. During the Belfast riots of 1864 a group of Catholic navvies had attacked Protestant homes and a school on Lady Day, provoking violent retaliation from the Protestant shipyard workers a few days later in a harborside battle that became part of the city's growing folk memory of communal violence. It is unlikely that many Protestants living in Belfast in 1872 had not heard the story of the navvies' Lady Day assault, or of the subsequent retaliatory drubbing by the burly men of the shipyards—known as the Islandmen, for the Queen's Island on which they worked—and it was the rare Protestant indeed (such as Biggar, who would in fact convert to Catholicism a few years later) who would have been seen in a nationalist procession on that day.

The plan was for marchers to convene at Carlisle Circus, in the northwest part of town, and then to proceed west to the village of Hannahstown, where they would hold a rally and assemble for the march back to Belfast. Carlisle Circus was a popular spot for demonstrations to gather, but it was also a dangerous spot for a demonstration of this sort: not only was it near the heavily Protestant Shankill and New Lodge Roads, but it was also the site of a new Presbyterian church, St. Enoch's, which was the headquarters of the redoubtable Hugh Hanna. Hanna, a blood-and-thunder preacher with a penchant for public controversy, had been at the center of several earlier disputes in Belfast, most famously in September 1857, when he had held an open-air sermon near the Custom House that sparked the worst riots Belfast had yet seen. A powerful speaker with an ear for the rough cadences of the working classes (he was of humble origins himself, having worked as a draper's assistant in his youth), Hanna had begun his clerical career at a small meeting house in a poor district in the center of town, preaching mostly to millworkers and trying to coax churchless Catholics into the light. As his notoriety grew, so did his congregation, and in the spring of 1872 Hanna had moved into St. Enoch's, a towering new church with space for more than 2,000 people. It was one of the largest churches in Ulster and a source of great pride for Hanna and his flock; the idea of a Catholic demonstration gathering outside its doors was a serious affront—as, perhaps, it was intended to be.

Prior to the demonstration, Hanna gave a sworn statement to the magistrates that he anticipated a disturbance if Catholics gathered in front of his church. This was somewhat disingenuous, since he had also virtually ensured a disturbance by asking neighborhood Protestants to come out and defend his church, but it was enough to ensure a police presence at Carlisle Circus that day. When the Catholics, adorned with green sashes and holding banners with nationalist political slogans, began gathering at the assigned spot on the morning of August 15, they came under attack from a stone-throwing Protestant guard stationed near St. Enoch's. A force of constabulary, with bayonets fixed, just managed to keep the two groups apart. The Catholics then decided that rather than marching west, through hostile Protestant territory, they would go south to the center of town, then turn west along the mostly Catholic Falls Road. Even on the Falls, they endured some moderate stone throwing, but after retaliating in kind they were able to march unimpeded along the road to Hannahstown, silk banners billowing and pistols loaded.[15]

Hannahstown was a scattering of six or seven houses on a hillside five miles west of Belfast; the swiftest marchers would have reached it within two hours. Estimates varied as to the size of the procession: the Catholic *Daily Examiner*, the chief promoter of the procession, said there were more than 100,000 people, but a magistrate put the number closer to 20,000.[16] Even the smaller figure would have made for quite a large gathering, and once assembled they listened as Joseph Biggar offered a spirited attack on the Orangemen, "whose religious creed is to hate their fellow co-religionists and whose political creed is to hate their country," before calling for the release of nationalist prisoners and urging the crowd to vote for Home Rule candidates. Several other speakers likewise came forward to make the case for Home Rule, and the addresses ended amid much cheering and cap waving.[17] Although some in the crowd did fire their guns into the air, this portion of the day was largely peaceful; the only casualty was one William Millen who was accidentally shot at the village pub where many marchers gathered after the rally. He later died of his wounds.[18]

Back in Belfast, meanwhile, groups of Protestants had begun causing trouble. The next day the Catholic press would report that the marauders had been shipbuilders, but it subsequently emerged (after a vigorous denial by the Islandmen themselves) that these men were, as the *Daily Examiner* put it in its retraction, "mere rivet drivers, or handy labourers of some description or other, with no respectability to forfeit, and little or no character to lose."[19] Whoever they were, the men broke the windows of several Catholic businesses in the center of town—including those of the drapers Maguire and McGill, where some of the marchers had bought their green sashes—before trying to invade Hercules Street, where they were repulsed by those Catholic butchers who had stayed behind during the day's procession.[20]

The Hannahstown party, ignorant of the tumult back in town, headed for home about five o'clock. Several marchers stopped along the way to pick up thorny branches to serve as bludgeons, should any be needed. When they arrived in Belfast, some marchers tried to enter Carlisle Circus, where Protestant crowds still gathered, but they were repeatedly repulsed by the police; at about the same time, other marchers got into fights with Protestants in College Square and Great Victoria Street, while on the largely Protestant Shankill Road gangs rushed up and down attacking Catholic pubs. Then Hugh Hanna appeared on the Shankill carried on the shoulders of admirers who eventually set him down near Dover Street (the scene of some stone-throwing that morning), where he thanked the Shankill Protestants for keeping the Catholics away from St. Enoch's. A little while later a crowd gathered in the Protestant neighborhood of Brown Square to watch a group of women sing Orange songs deep into the night.[21] Across town, as men paced at doorways and women gossiped from windows, rumors circulated wildly. Each side expected an invasion at any minute, and the hard men (and women) of the neighborhoods began preparing for battle, although nothing more happened that night.

As often happened in Belfast, the first day of rioting was mild compared with what came after. The next day was a Friday, a day when most people had to go to work, so it was not until that evening that the fighting resumed in earnest. At about 8:00 p.m. a crowd of some 5,000 bludgeon-wielding men, women, and boys from the Shankill tried to invade the Falls, only to be repulsed by the police. After that they returned to the Shankill and began attacking the few Catholic homes there. At about 10:00 p.m. the sexton of the Protestant Trinity Church tolled the bells to warn the neighborhood of an impending attack. Thousands of people from the Old Lodge Road and the Shankill converged on the church. In fact there was no attack under way, but someone fired shots at the Protestant crowd from the home of a Catholic named Gavin (said to have taken a prominent role in the Hannahstown procession), and in retaliation some Protestants invaded Gavin's home, stole his furniture, and tore his large green flag to shreds.[22] Also that night a constable killed a Catholic, James McSorley, as he and some other Catholics were attacking the home of a man named Lappin in Lincoln Street. One witness reported hearing the constables say, just before they charged the crowd with their bayonets, "Go into them and cut them up."[23]

The riots reached their climax that weekend—the second and third days after the Hannahstown procession—although the fighting would continue well into the following week. Saturday was the famous Battle of the Brickfield, when combatants from the Falls and Shankill squared off across the grounds of a brickworks spanning their two districts. The newspapers reported it like a regular military engagement. "The Catholics were at one time driven back," said the *Northern Whig*, "and the Protestants the next. The realization of a battle scene was perfect—shots were fired, stones thrown, bludgeons used, the *melee* was terrific—and all this happening in one of the most respectable quarters of the town, produced an amount of excitement and terror which it is not possible to describe."[24] The battle lasted little more than fifteen minutes before the constabulary rushed into the field and separated the combatants without firing a shot.[25]

One of the major goals of communal activists on both sides during the riots was to create communally "pure" spaces in those areas of town where Protestants and Catholics still lived side by side. Earlier riots had made some neighborhoods almost wholly homogeneous—Sandy Row was the undoubted preserve of Protestants, for instance, while the Pound belonged to Catholics—but it had been eight years since the last major riot, and newly built areas, especially along the Shankill and Falls Roads, had not yet gone through the fires of communal purification. Gangs therefore attacked homes and businesses belonging to people of the "wrong" persuasion (i.e., Catholics on the Shankill and Protestants on the Falls), and among the most prominent targets were the handful of Catholic-owned pubs along the Shankill. These attacks inevitably entailed a good deal of plundered liquor, giving rise to scenes that inspired a writer for the *Daily Examiner*, the Catholic paper owned by the bishops, to describe scenes of debauchery that were positively Hogarthian:

> Those portions of the rabble in the immediate vicinity of the dismantled spirit-stores, now became delirious, rolling about the ground in the height of their drunken frenzy. Liquor flowed into the streets, and trickled down to the gutters, and hideous creatures with almost the vestiges of their humanity obliterated from their faces, wallowed in it, and only rose to fight with one another, finding nothing better, and uttering the most horrid threats and curses against the inhabitants of the opposing districts. In several instances they offered drink to the soldiers on duty, and in some, we are sorry to record, it was accepted. Whenever this occurred, they tossed their hats in the air, and declared, with drunken howls of delight, that the "Kilties" were "brave fellows," and would never turn against their own.[26]

This last detail, about rioters fraternizing with soldiers, was echoed in the *Northern Star and Ulster Observer*, the other Catholic paper.[27] Indeed, both the *Examiner* and the *Observer* tended to deride the military—whom the magistrates called out on Saturday evening—but to praise the RIC, and they noted similar sentiments among Catholics generally. In the Pound, according to the *Examiner*, the constables "are treated with every kindness, and young and old evince the strongest friendship for them—an evidence, we should say, which goes far to prove that respect for authority has a deep hold upon our people."[28] The *Observer* reported, "Since the beginning of the riots great dissatisfaction has been felt and shown towards this regiment [the 78th Highlanders] by the Catholic people of the town."[29] None of their readers needed reminding that the constables, with their bottle-green uniforms, were mostly Catholic Irishmen from the south (as in the rest of Ireland, constables rotated through Belfast on a regular basis, so as to avoid forming "local attachments"), while the khaki-clad soldiers were mostly Scottish Protestants.

It was always a difficult decision for the civil power to call out the military in circumstances like this; when the Belfast magistrates brought in the troops that Saturday they were essentially admitting that they were unable to control the city with the 450 armed constables at their command. They were also sending a signal to the rioters that the police were outmanned. There was a tactical risk in this as well: heavily armed soldiers, sometimes on horseback or dragging cannons, were not as maneuverable as small groups of constables, and they also tended not to know the city very well. Many of the soldiers who arrived on Saturday evening were stationed on the Shankill, where the worst of the violence was taking place, and, whatever the feelings of the Catholics about the troops, it was quite clear that the people of the Shankill were not happy to see them, either. About 9:00 p.m. on Saturday Hugh Hanna approached the magistrates and gave them his word that there would be no more rioting on the Shankill if they would only remove the soldiers, but the magistrates declined.[30] Hanna then addressed the Shankill crowd, telling them "that such deeds [as attacking Catholic homes and property] would never accomplish a neighbour's conversion" and counseling "a spirit of charity towards those who differed from us in religious convictions."[31] Hanna was never one to underestimate his own powers of persuasion, but even he must have known that on this occasion the fire he had helped to light would not be so easily doused.

By Sunday the authorities were taking even stronger measures. In addition to the soldiers (who numbered some 1,500 by Sunday night) they also called in more constables (bringing the total to 1,000), divided the town into military districts, closed all the public houses at 4:00 p.m., and prohibited all public gatherings of more than six people. In the deadliest show of force yet, a group of constables charged into several crowds with bayonets fixed and even fired upon a few rioters on Sunday night.[32] Such muscular policing altered, but did not end, the riots. The green and khaki multitudes managed to prevent most of the large battles and flying attacks on churches and shops that had characterized the first few days of the riots, but they were often unable to stop the wrecking of individual houses or the many quieter warnings—a note slid under a door, a whispered conversation between neighbors—that led people to flee their homes. For the rest of the week, as overt acts of violence became less frequent, hundreds of families crowded the narrow streets of north and west Belfast, trundling their belongings onto horse carts, setting off to find new homes among more welcoming hosts. In some cases Protestant and Catholic families simply swapped homes as they crisscrossed the city.[33] In Sandy Row, the destination of many fleeing Protestants, neighbors searched around for keys that would fit the doors of empty tenements, and some refugees moved in without even asking their new landlords.[34] Altogether, according to government figures, 247 houses were wrecked or damaged and 837 families fled their homes during and immediately after the riots.[35] The number of temporary refugees therefore likely numbered in the thousands, an enormous transfer of people for a city during peacetime.[36]

The manifest inability of the authorities to stop the violence, particularly the home wreckings, led some people to take the law into their own hands. Four days into the riots, on Monday, August 19, two competing placards appeared on the dead walls of the town, both announcing different initiatives to put down the riots. The first was a proclamation by the mayor, Sir John Savage, announcing that all public houses were to be closed until the following Friday, that the military were authorized to disperse all outdoor gatherings and to enter any house from which shots were fired, and that both the military and the police "have positive orders to fire upon riotous mobs."[37] The second placard was an altogether more vernacular production, inviting Catholics from "the unprotected districts of Belfast" to a meeting at the Foresters' Hall in Hercules Place, the same spot at which the Hannahstown procession had been planned. "If the authorities will not protect us we must protect ourselves," said the placard. "We want peace, but to obtain it we now find that we must be prepared to exact it from the armed mobs that threaten us with murder."[38] It is unclear what the outcome of this meeting was, but it was in line with a long-standing tendency among Catholics to adopt vigilante methods when they felt the police had failed them. Similar initiatives had occurred during the riots of 1857, when a number of Catholics had formed a "gun club" to raise money for firearms, and in 1864, when middle- and working-class Catholics had formed an ad hoc committee to combat Protestant rioters (and the largely Protestant local police) during the O'Connell riots of that year.[39] The Catholic press, which consistently portrayed the 1872 riots solely as acts of Protestant aggression, endorsed this Catholic vigilantism. At the height of the riots the *Daily Examiner* published an appeal to the Catholics and the authorities:

> We know our words have some weight with the Catholics of Belfast.... And, therefore, the counsel which we give will be respected, and it is this—As soon as they perceive that the authorities have determined to put down disturbance; to save them from the cowardly onslaughts which have been made upon them, that moment they must give up the contest, and quietly return to their homes.... When we have confidence in the power of the law, we shall cease to resist; but be it known to the authorities, and to our enemies, rather than live under the ascendancy of an Orange mob, we, Catholics of every rank, are prepared, and willingly, to shed the last drop of our blood.[40]

In the days and months to come, many Catholics would call for the creation of a permanent Catholic vigilance committee to protect innocent Catholics from future outbreaks, but nothing seems to have come of the idea at this time.[41]

During previous riots Catholics had explained their distrust of the state by pointing to the apparent bias of the local police, who were nearly Protestant to a man and reported directly to the ultra-Protestant Belfast Town Council. Now that the local police had been replaced by the RIC, Catholics shifted their criticisms to the magistrates who coordinated the police response, most of whom were local Protestant grandees. According to the Catholic papers, the magistrates were not allowing the constables to use their guns against the Protestant rioters, and this was encouraging the mayhem.[42] Arguing that constraints upon the constables' behavior had made the forces of law and order "purely ornamental," the *Northern Star and Ulster Observer* asked, "What avails it to burden them with loaded rifles merely for show?"[43] Protestants also expressed their disgust with the state, although most of their vitriol was aimed at the constables (most of whom had been called in from the Catholic southern county of Tipperary), not the magistrates. A person identified only as "Pax" told the *Daily Express* in Dublin that "the Protestants of Belfast are of opinion that except when controlled by a magistrate or sub-inspector Roman Catholic constables in charge of men have not acted with impartiality."[44] This Protestant hostility toward the constabulary would be a recurrent theme in future Belfast riots as well, culminating in a virtual insurrection against the greenjackets during the massive riots of 1886, but there was a countervailing tendency as well. After the 1872 riots several constables reported being treated very kindly by the Protestants among whom they were posted, many of whom brought food, drinks, and even chairs and vehicles to the exhausted men.[45]

Of course, most riots, if they last long enough, will lead people to question the efficacy of the state. There was nothing uniquely Catholic or Protestant (or Irish) about that. In fact, at the tail end of the riots several groups of middle-class inhabitants, Protestant and Catholic, formed unofficial peace committees to try to suppress the violence by remonstrating with the violent partisans on their own side.[46] As with the Catholic defense committees, there was a precedent for such non-state pacification efforts during earlier riots, but such groups had little permanent impact on communal relations. It is unclear whether the peace committees of 1872 did much good, either: by Wednesday, August 22, a day or two before the peace committees formed and six days after the riots began, the combined influences of exhaustion and heavy rains had largely quelled the violence.[47] By then there were nearly 4,000 constables and soldiers in Belfast, and the city had been "proclaimed" under the Peace Preservation Act, a measure that empowered the police to impose a curfew, search for arms, and arrest anyone they suspected of malicious intent.[48] There were also, according to the government, 170 wounded civilians (thirty-seven of whom required hospital treatment), seventy-three injured constables, and one dead constable (a man named Morton, shot while searching for arms on Tuesday night).[49] The government does not seem to have registered the death of James McSorley, whom the *Whig* reported dead by a constable's bayonet on the first full night of rioting, but McSorley's Catholic friends and relatives surely did.[50]

The aftermath

Every riot begins in a different way, but they nearly all end with finger-pointing. From the minute the first stone had been thrown, newspapers, magistrates, Dublin officials, and ordinary people had all rushed to assign blame, and the recriminations continued long after the last shots had been fired. Some people blamed the press for stirring things up, and some segments of the press blamed other segments. Some blamed the Orangemen for refusing to show the same tolerance toward Catholics on Lady Day as Catholics had shown them on the Twelfth, while some blamed the Catholics for deliberately provoking the Orangemen with their novel procession. Some blamed the magistrates, some the police, some the mayor, and some the army. Some people blamed the iniquities of British rule, others blamed the volatilities of the Irish character. Much of this was unilluminating and predictable—Catholic newspapers said Protestants were the aggressors, Protestant papers said the Catholics had acted disloyally and irresponsibly, and everyone said the police should have done more—but, if one listened carefully, one could hear a few interesting discussions going on in the corners.

One discussion centered on whether the constables should have shot more people. They had certainly shot some: on Sunday, the fourth night of the riots, a party of constables on the Shankill Road coming under attack while rescuing a man had opened fire, wounding at least one person; on Tuesday, during the attack in Norfolk Street in which Constable Morton was shot and killed, the police had returned fire, injuring several; in Cupar Street on the same day another constabulary party opened fire in similar circumstances; and on Wednesday, in the week's largest shooting incident, constables fired over sixty rounds at a Falls Road house from which they were themselves coming under fire (Lord Lieutenant Spencer heard a rumor that four rioters had been killed on this occasion, their bodies concealed by relatives in the gathering dusk, but no deaths were officially recorded).[51] Still, many of the government's critics felt that more shooting should have been done earlier, before the riots had had a chance to spread. Someone, identified only as "Strong Measure," wrote to the *Northern Whig* that the mobs did not fear the police or soldiers but that "they should be taught to fear them, and taught by a lesson so severe that the memory of it will not die out of the recollection of our dangerous classes for a generation to come."[52] Several days into the riots the Catholic *Northern Star and Ulster Observer* declared, "Nothing is left but to shoot down the rioters like mad dogs, whenever, being called on to disperse, they refuse to obey the command."[53] The Mayor's proclamation of Monday, August 19—that the constables and solders "have positive orders to fire upon riotous mobs"—was a belated attempt, five days into the riots, to do just that.[54]

The decision to shoot or not to shoot was something that constables and magistrates continually struggled with throughout the riots. Usually they decided not to shoot. Town Inspector Bailey, the head of the constabulary force stationed in Belfast, told the police court that he would have ordered his men to fire on a Catholic crowd in the Pound on the first night of the disturbance—he would have had the rioters "shot down like dogs," he said—but it was too dark to see the stone throwers, and he might have shot innocent people by mistake.[55] As it happened, Bailey was ill for the rest of the riots and unable to participate beyond that first night, and his illness probably saved several lives, since most of the remaining magistrates were much more hesitant to shoot people.

In early September the Belfast Town Council addressed this issue at its monthly meeting. Several members of the Council had acted as magistrates during the riots, and several now explained why they had refrained from shooting rioters. For Samuel Browne, who had been at the Battle of the Brickfield on August 17, it was a question of practicality as well as humanity:

> an opportunity never arose but any magistrate, possessing common sense or common feeling, could have directed the troops to fire upon them, for the simple reason that it was the duty of the authorities and the magistrates to keep the parties asunder who were thirsting to get at one another. No man in his senses would have fired at one mob and then fired at another.

Mayor John Savage said that he was proud that, despite his placard announcing that the police and military had "positive orders" to shoot, "no life has been lost by my act or deed." He would rather pay the extra taxes to clean up the town, he said, than take human life. Another Town Council member, one Dr. Whittaker, considered the issue within a wider context. "It is not easy," he said,

> in a country like this, famed for its incapability of devising administrative measures for the management of large crowds, and where no warrant of any power can shield a magistrate from the effects of an illegal action, to act with the determination and success which could be obtained under a more arbitrary form of Government.[56]

Whittaker was alluding to the famous reluctance by British courts and legislators to define the conditions under which a magistrate could order his men to fire on disorderly crowds. In both Ireland and Britain the leading man on the spot had the power to use lethal force whenever it was necessary to preserve lives or property, but he was also required to use the minimum amount of force that would get the job done. Should he fire unnecessarily he would be liable to prosecution, but should he fail to fire when necessary he could be held responsible for any damage that subsequently took place; neither the judiciary nor any government had ever seen fit to define the man on the spot's duty more clearly than that, a circumstance that we will explore more fully in Chapter 6.

One of the few dissenting voices during the Town Council debate belonged to William Dobbin, who announced that "if life becomes insecure, and property becomes insecure, [I] would be willing, as an individual, to submit to any amount of despotism necessary to give security for life, and security for property, without which life is not worth possessing."[57] Dobbin's use of the term "despotism" was significant, for it indicated that what lay behind this question of shooting rioters was a much larger question about the kind of government Ireland should have. London's *Daily Telegraph* went right to the heart of the matter in its commentary on the riots:

> A despotic Government, of course, would rapidly settle the matter; but constitutional rulers cannot prescribe the "whiff of grapeshot" or dose of Snider bullets, except in the last resort. Public feeling recoils from "volleys" or file-firing, and the gentleman who last recommended the "trail of a six-pounder" justly met with little countenance. If then we are precluded from dealing sharply with brainless ruffianism, the other alternative of letting the factions fight it out—a course many would like to see adopted—would be really nothing less than the abdication of authority.

After briefly (and presciently) considering whether fire hoses might be useful against Belfast rioters, the *Telegraph* concluded that the real problem in Ireland was that local officials were too tangled up in local affairs to act impartially. "The best plan for Ireland would be a despotic Viceroy and an Irish Civil Service trained into impartiality between all the factions," the *Telegraph* concluded—but if, in the meantime, rioters provoked the police into shooting them, then they had no one to blame but themselves.[58]

Another postriot discussion, which was indirectly related to this question of shooting rioters, concerned the predisposition of the Irish people to engage in this sort of violence. When British papers advocated a shoot-first policy—as several, including the *Pall Mall Gazette* and the *Hampshire Telegraph and Sussex Chronicle*, did—it was often because they believed that only strong measures could keep the peace among people as naturally turbulent as the Irish. Just as "you cannot expect the Ethiopian to change his skin nor the leopard its spots," the *Preston Guardian* declared, so with the Irish: "his combativeness defies annihilation."[59] The *Telegraph* claimed, significantly, that the closest cousins to the rioters of Belfast were not leopards or Ethiopians but the "Hindoo and the Moslem" of India, although Belfast rioters distinguished themselves even from these notorious brawlers by having absolutely no reason to fight other than simple love of fighting. Bread riots, anti-machine riots, political disturbances—all these the *Telegraph* could understand, but Belfast riots "have no aim, no cause, no practical object; they represent human passion and religious intolerance in their naked fury. They begin in violence and end in violence."[60]

Invocations of the turbulent Irish character were necessary to explain an apparent paradox at the heart of these riots. Belfast, after all, was by many measures the most "civilized" city in Ireland, the one that came closest to resembling the great industrial cities of Britain, and the one where the religious and secular impact of Protestantism was the greatest. If these primitive squabbles continued there, it was not because Belfast lacked the outer trappings of civilization, but because, as the *Telegraph* put it, "prosperity does not diminish the passions of intolerant factions."[61] The lesson of these riots, for those in Britain already disposed to think so, was that the Irish were not capable of exercising self-rule: if the Irish continued to tear each other apart even in a prosperous city like Belfast, what would happen if they were granted their own parliament? "Set Ireland to govern herself," wrote the *Pall Mall Gazette*, "and Ireland would immediately relapse into her chronic strife and social war."[62] The *Times* agreed, noting sarcastically, "These are the people whom we are invited to soothe by 'legislation according to Irish ideas,' by surrendering their destinies into their own hands." In fact, the only thing Britain could hope to do was to sit back and wait for the Irish to grow up.

> Having made up our minds what is really just and expedient for Ireland, we must be content to stand by it, and be satisfied to uphold order and law while the people are growing out of their evil traditions. It needs the lapse of generations to eradicate such animosities as those of Belfast. Time is our only safe ally; and all we can do is to see that time is not lost by such mischievous revivals of the old malady as the present outbreak. They or any other riots should be put down at once, at all costs; but they will have done some service if they remind our Statesmen that the one thing Ireland now needs is a strong hand steadily and patiently applied.[63]

Few people who argued in this vein seem to have recognized that the continuation of British rule in Ireland was not exactly making these conflicts disappear. One Belfast paper did make this connection, however: the nationalist *Daily Examiner*, responding to the *Times*, wryly noted that the recent riots in Exeter against new early closing rules for the pubs had not led anybody to suggest that the English were unsuited to self-rule.[64]

As we will see in the next chapter, attributing communal violence to the inherent flaws of non-British people was a rhetorical device by no means reserved for the Irish. Yet not all British observers used these riots as an excuse to abuse the Irish character and argue against Home Rule. The liberal London journal the *Spectator*, for instance, blamed the riots not on the deficiencies of the Irish people but on the deficiencies of the British state in Ireland. The people of Belfast, it said, like the people of Ireland generally, did not trust the men who administered the law. To preserve the peace in Ireland, and to impress its virtues upon the "Irish imagination," the law had to be administered in a way that was "firm, courageous, and above all, impartial." So far this sounded like the platitudinous speech Earl Spencer had given during his preriot visit to Belfast harbor, but, whereas Spencer believed that Ireland was already being ruled impartially and firmly, the *Spectator* declared that it was not. Either because they actively sympathized with one side or the other, or because they were believed to do so, the agents of the state were, said the *Spectator*, bringing the law itself into contempt. The solution the *Spectator* offered was to introduce a new class of civil servant to Ireland, one that "would rival the Indian Civil Service in efficiency of administration and in severe impartiality," but which would be drawn from the Irish population itself. Under such a system,

> Irishmen would quickly understand that the magistrate under the new system was a man of no party, whose first duty it was to preserve order, if possible without shedding blood, but, if necessary, by sweeping the streets with cavalry and cannon. Such firmness, especially when recognised as the characteristic, not of an individual here and there, but of a class, would win respect, even though now and then the duty of the magistrates will come into contact with the will of the people. The country would feel that if governed somewhat sternly, it was self-governed, and a respect for law and dislike of disorder would naturally grow up.[65]

This prescription was deeply flawed—for one thing, there was already a system of centralized, "impartial" magistrates and policemen in Ireland—but the *Spectator's* analysis of the problem was astute. Just like riots in other parts of the empire, the Belfast riots of 1872 exposed the weakness of the state's position in Belfast, showing just how easily a great city could slide into anarchy and just how feeble the state's authority among the people really was.

And what of the state itself? How did the men who administered Ireland interpret the violence and evaluate their own response? On the question of shooting rioters, most important officials in Dublin believed that the police should have shot more people sooner. H. G. Thompson, Earl Spencer's private secretary, wrote to Lord Dufferin in Canada, "If ten or a dozen had been shot on Friday the whole affair would have collapsed."[66] The Red Earl agreed, telling Lord Halifax, "I confess that much as I dislike the idea of killing men in a crowd, I think it often would save great loss of property & life if at the outset after due warning an effective volley were fired."[67] Immediately after the riots Spencer sent General Sandhurst, the head of military forces in Ireland, to interview the magistrates in Belfast and devise a standard policy for policing future riots.[68] Interestingly, Sandhurst's recommendation was slightly at odds with the popular shoot-first principle. He recommended that the first forces on the scene should be constables armed only with·truncheons, and if these men failed to disperse the crowd then an armed reserve, heretofore hidden from sight, should come forward with guns blazing. Sandhurst believed that rioters were trainable: if all they ever saw were constables armed with guns, they would not fear the guns, because they would know that the constables would only fire upon them in extraordinary circumstances. But if they knew that the guns would be used—if the only guns they ever saw were spitting bullets at them—then both the truncheons and the guns would be more effective.[69] After much discussion, the two resident magistrates of Belfast agreed with Sandhurst's plan, as did the chief secretary and the lord justices in Dublin.[70] On the surface it was a plan consistent with police practices in Britain itself, for it enjoined the police first to try dispersing riots with minimum force and only to bring out the guns as a last resort. Unlike in Britain, however, where there were no armed policemen at all, firearms were always within easy reach of the semi-military RIC. In fact, once Belfast got the permanent military force that Sandhurst recommended (the 78th Highlanders, who had been so unpopular with both Protestants and Catholics, were to be stationed there), and once its constabulary force was augmented by the recommended 200 foot soldiers and twenty-five mounted men, the availability of deadly weapons would be all the greater.[71] Sandhurst's recommendations about leading with unarmed men, however, were not immediately adopted, and subsequent riots (especially the antipolice riots of 1886) were all the deadlier for it.[72]

Meanwhile, local officials in Belfast were not at all sure that what their city needed was more guns. Just as they had been reluctant to order constables and soldiers to fire on crowds during the riots, now they wanted the government to reevaluate the heavy-handed policing tactics that they felt had exacerbated the riots. Twice, the Town Council asked Earl Spencer to institute a parliamentary inquiry into the riots (as had been done after the riots of 1857 and 1864), and twice Spencer refused. In their second letter to Spencer the Town Councilors wrote, "the present riots show that it is not an increase in the Police force of the Borough that is required so much as a complete change in the semi-military character, arms, discipline, organization, and management of the present force."[73] This was a common complaint against the RIC—they were too military, too comfortable with rifles and parade-ground drills, not suited to ordinary policing duties—and it was an especially cogent one in Belfast, where the nature of urban policing required very different skills than most constables, recruited from rural areas and trained to combat insurgents and agrarian crime, possessed.[74]

But such concerns failed to move the central government, which trusted its own men much more than it trusted local forces. Over the next few years the main question for the central government was how to handle Protestant and Catholic marches now that the Party Processions Act had been repealed. During the Belfast riots many officials had noted that the ordinary law gave magistrates enough power to disperse illegal assemblies regardless of whether they included the "party" tunes, flags, emblems, and banners that had been banned by the Party Processions legislation. For his part, Spencer felt that the repeal of the Party Processions Acts was a good thing, since it enabled magistrates to put down dangerous processions simply on the grounds that they endangered the peace, avoiding the question of "party" displays altogether.[75] To make this clear, the following year Dublin Castle sent a circular to all resident magistrates in Ulster informing them that they had the power to disperse any assembly that, from its general tenor, was likely to cause a breach of the peace.[76] Over the next few years, however, as nationalist demonstrations became more common and the threat of insurrection continued to percolate, Thomas Burke, the undersecretary at Dublin Castle, tried to get the government to define more precisely the conditions under which an assembly could be said to be "disloyal," so that they could be prohibited on those grounds alone. Two different chief secretaries rebuffed Burke's request, claiming that it was impossible to define precisely what sorts of symbols or emblems might be disloyal.[77] One of these chief secretaries, James Lowther, made it clear that he regretted the repeal of the Party Processions Act and felt that Ireland required the strictest measures. "There can be no doubt," he said, "that it is highly undesirable that more than 3 or 4 persons should be allowed to walk about together at any time in Ireland, especially upon Saints days." The law was the law, however, and "We ought not to embark in any absurd crusade against either party so long as they create no disturbance."[78] The possibility of disturbance was the important thing; emblems, even disloyal emblems, could not be suppressed.

It was of course much easier to have these discussions in the comfort of Dublin Castle or the viceregal lodge than in the midst of a full-blown riot. The law was one thing, its application quite another, and in the heat of the moment magistrates and policemen could sometimes overstep the bounds of legality. This does not seem to have happened too often during the Belfast riots of 1872—indeed, the local authorities turned out to be much more reluctant to use deadly force than their superiors were—but the state's adherence to the principles of minimum force and strict impartiality could be severely tested when things got too hot. Indeed, as Chapter 6 will show, the way British officials applied the rule of minimum force (and other rules) depended very much upon what they thought about the people they were policing. Before we explore this dynamic, however, we first need to say more about how British officials, and other British observers, interpreted these outbreaks.

4

Interpretations: How Communal Riots Confirmed and Strengthened Britain's Civilizing Mission

One of the problems with communal riots, from the British perspective, was that they seemed to gainsay the entire imperial project. If the fundamental aim of that project was to civilize the savages while providing a secure environment for British settlement and commerce, then this required, at a bare minimum, the creation and maintenance of internal peace—the *Pax Britannica* of legend. How, then, to explain the persistence (indeed, the worsening) of communal violence in a place like Belfast, which was widely regarded as the most "British" city in Ireland, thanks to its industrial might and Protestant culture? Nor was it only Belfast that presented this conundrum: many of the most "British" parts of Asia were also prone to such violence. As this chapter will demonstrate, British officials, journalists, and other molders of public opinion addressed this problem in several ways. One solution was to flip the equation around, or anyway to stand it on its head: if communal violence was a problem in some parts of the empire, observers argued, then perhaps those areas needed more, not less, British influence. Others suggested that if the people of the empire were refusing, despite the blessings of civilization, to put away these childish quarrels, then there must be something fundamentally (perhaps even biologically) wrong with them. Some took this notion further, arguing that the recurrence of these riots showed that these people were not ready to control their own affairs: if things were bad now, just imagine what would happen if Britain were to depart! Such interpretations—and they appeared at all levels of power, in nearly all parts of the empire where communal violence occurred—managed, by a curious sleight of hand, to transform communal riots from evidence of empire's failure into evidence of empire's indispensability. We have already seen how British imperialism helped foster communal violence. In this chapter we will see how British observers used such violence to confirm and strengthen their empire's civilizing mission, largely ignoring their own part in helping to bring these conflicts into being.

Primordial hatreds

One of the most common ways of interpreting communal riots was to see them as extensions of ancient conflicts that had been passed down through generations. Such supposed antiquity gave these quarrels an "integrity" (the word is Churchill's, referring to Protestants and Catholics in Ulster) that rendered them impervious to intervention. After all, what were a small group of policemen, magistrates, or legislators, however wise and disinterested, against centuries of hereditary hatred? This idea—call it the primordial hatreds thesis—may have been sincerely held, but it was also a way both to absolve the British state of responsibility for these outbreaks and to affirm the essential superiority of British civilization, which had long ago (it was said) progressed beyond this atavistic state. Among its many shortcomings, however, what the primordial hatreds thesis failed to comprehend was that there was a difference between communal tension and communal violence. Even if we accept that Hindus and Muslims, say, will always distrust one another (a problematic assumption in itself), we need not accept that actual violence between the two groups is inevitable. Because it removed each outbreak from its immediate context, the primordial hatreds thesis could not explain why violence happened when and where it did, and it therefore could not offer any practical remedies.

Gyanendra Pandey has explored this dynamic in India in his classic text, *The Construction of Communalism in Colonial North India*. The primordial hatreds thesis found in colonial riot narratives, Pandey shows, acted as "an emptying out of all history—in terms of the specific variations of time, place, class, issue—from the political experience of the people, and the identification of religion, or the religious community, as the moving force of all Indian politics."[1] This strategy of relegating communal violence to the realm of the ineffable and the spiritual was essential for a colonial state that saw itself as the antithesis of "the primitive, pre-political, one might even say proto-historic character of the local society."[2] Pandey argues that these misreadings of Indian society served a valuable purpose: not only did they justify the intervention of (rational and civilized) outsiders in (irrational and primitive) local conflicts, but they also provided a ready-made excuse when those outsiders failed to stop the violence. What was missing, of course, was any hint that the outsiders themselves might be part of the problem.

Pandey's argument relates primarily to colonial knowledge about northern India, but the primordial hatreds thesis could be endlessly repurposed, shaping riot narratives in the press (locally and in Britain), government dispatches, political speeches, popular fiction, and informal discussions about violence right across the empire. After the Muslim–Parsi riots of Bombay in 1874, which we will explore in the next chapter, the *Northern Echo* in northeast England averred that "there glows the same unquenchable animosity between the Moslem and the Parsee [today] as when Saad Ebn Wakass crushed the forces of Rustam at the battle of Cadesia; and the Scimetar of the Moslem chased the disciples of Zoroaster from the precincts of Persia."[3] Little had changed, in other words, in over a thousand years. Operating within a slightly more realistic time frame was the London newspaper *The Era*, which explained an 1859 attack on native Christians in southern India as the product of a caste system that "has been embedded in the minds of the population by centuries of usage," helpfully pointing out (in a manner that echoed the ahistorical riot narratives examined by Pandey) that a similar riot had occurred "in the same place, and from the same cause, thirty years ago."[4]

Of course India was not the only place where, in Pandey's words, British riot narratives "range[d] freely through time and space, unfettered by either," or where Britons imagined all such riots to be "simply the reflexive actions of an irrational people."[5] If anything, British observers were even quicker to apply the primordial hatreds thesis to Ireland. Nearly every Protestant Catholic riot in Ireland—and even many that involved Irish communities outside of Ireland—elicited complaints that the Irish were trapped in the past, acting out ancestral feuds, or unable to forget or ignore an insult.[6] In the previous chapter we saw several examples of this during the Belfast riots of 1872, but such ideas found expression throughout our period.[7] Following the Belfast riots of 1864, for instance, the London *Times* observed, "These people are still in the 17th century; they grovel in the petty partisan disputes of that evil time; they cannot rise to a conception of the dignity implied in the position of citizenship in an empire like that of Great Britain."[8] Nearly thirty years later Lord Morley, chief secretary of Ireland, asked his officials what was behind a (nonsectarian) faction fight in Cork and was told that "it was the old quarrel between the two Earls in the time of Queen Elizabeth." "Here," Morley drily remarked in his memoirs, "was the fatality of history indeed."[9] The fault, then, was not in Britain's manner of ruling

Ireland, but in the Irish people themselves, who failed to act as proper historical, independent, and rational people should.

There was more than a hint of social Darwinism in some of these analyses. Just as Indians, blacks, and (less commonly) the Irish were held to be less fully advanced down the path of civilization than the English, so, too, did their religious conditions seem to bespeak an earlier phase of evolution. Alfred C. Lyall, in his influential book *Asiatic Studies*, described the study of Indian religion as akin to stepping "suddenly out of the modern world of formal definite creeds, back into the disorderly supernaturalism of pre-Christian ages.... There we seem to have the nearest surviving representative of a half-civilised society's religious state, as it existed before Christianity and Mahomedanism organised and centralized the beliefs of all nations, from Ireland to the Indus."[10] Indeed, in Lyall's telling, trying to make sense of Indian religion was like studying an especially disorderly collection of geographical strata:

> Here is India still full of the mythologies, mysteries, and metaphysical theosophies of the ancient world, not lying one below the other, as in the religious stratification in which all these fossils may still be discovered even in Europe, but mixed and crowded together without order or coherence. The Christianity which we profess at this day in England is the outcome of an immensely long upward growth; the fruit of a tree whose roots are in primitive ages; yet the distance which separates Protestant England from the scenes and manners of the Pentateuch is no unfair measure of the breadth which lies between Englishmen and Hindus along the line of religious evolution.[11]

Naturally, British ideas about the primitiveness or otherwise of native religions varied considerably from person to person and place to place, but attitudes such as Lyall's were fairly widespread in India and elsewhere, and they helped to reinforce the idea that religion-based violence was essentially primitive and atavistic.

If such violence was, as Lord Carlisle said of Belfast in 1858, not only the result of "childishness and folly" but also an "entire anachronism," then perhaps it followed that Britain's civilizing mission had failed, or was incomplete, or was—perhaps—unrealizable.[12] This latter idea seems to have been the conclusion of the *Times* correspondent reporting on the Belfast riots of 1864, who wrote, "oil and water are not more unsympathetic than are the Northern Protestant and the Celt; and no influence of clergy or of employers, or of interest, seems capable of amalgamating them, and the effort at reconciliation is eminently hopeless."[13] On the other hand, perhaps these societies simply needed more time to grow up. This was what Irish undersecretary Thomas Larcom told Carlisle after those same Belfast riots: "Ireland will outgrow all this in time, but it may be a very long time: meanwhile it is something to see in spite of all that is said to the contrary ... the country is rapidly improving."[14] The problem with this sort of optimism was that many places—even, or especially, those places that had come most fully under the influence of British modernity—were manifestly not "outgrowing" these disputes anytime soon.

Sticking with Belfast, inarguably the most "British" part of Ireland, here is Lord Carlisle, just returned from a stint as lord lieutenant of Ireland, speaking in the House of Lords in 1858: "The town of Belfast ought, in many respects, to be the most civilized and well-ordered place of residence in Ireland; whereas it certainly now might be considered the least so."[15] Six years later, in the midst of the procession disputes that we examined in the previous chapter, British observers frequently noted the seeming paradox that Ireland's most industrial, prosperous, and Protestant city should be also its most violent. A *Daily Telegraph* report from August 19 was typical: "Here, in the most thriving town in Ireland, where the progress of enlightenment and general prosperity has unquestionably been greater within the past few years than in any other spot you can point out on the map, scenes have prevailed for ten successive days which surpass the tales of Maori savagery."[16] In 1917, more than half a century after British observers first began puzzling over Belfast's imperviousness to the improving forces of civilization, former Irish chief secretary Lord Morley prefaced his memories of the Belfast riots of 1886 (by far the worst of the nineteenth century) in the following terms:

> Belfast is one of the triumphs of modern trade. The shipyards turn out mighty vessels that rival the noblest constructions of the Mersey or the Clyde. The linen factories employ great hosts of skilful workers. Its inhabitants boast of the number of new houses that are built every year; of the enormous sums that are annually collected by the officers of the revenue; of the fact that the duties of customs paid at Belfast exceed those of any port in the United Kingdom, excepting Liverpool and London. Yet, strange to say, this great and flourishing community, where energy, intelligence, and enterprise have achieved results so striking, has proved to harbour a spirit of bigotry and violence for which a parallel can hardly be found in any town in western Europe. The outbreaks of disorder in 1857, in 1864, in 1872 were as formidable as any that have taken place in these kingdoms even in the most agitated times of the nineteenth century. There is no such anachronism in our day as the circumstances that make the anniversary of the battle of the

> Boyne and the feast of the Assumption days always of anxiety, and often of terror, in one of the most industrious and thriving societies in the realm.[17]

As in most British accounts of the city's violence, there is little hint here that the British presence in Ireland might be part (even a small part) of the problem.

It was easier for British observers to explain the anachronism of violence in other parts of the empire besides Ireland, for not only were Asians and West Indians less touched by British modernity, they also belonged to what Britons saw as manifestly inferior races. Nevertheless, one often catches a note of perplexity here as well, especially since rioting often happened in precisely those pockets of the empire that were the most Westernized. Take Bombay, for instance, one of the most prosperous commercial and industrial centers of India, and one that, with its bustling harbor and grandiose Victorian architecture, physically resembled many British cities. After the Bombay riots of 1874, when Muslim gangs attacked the wealthy and Anglophile Parsi community, the London *Times* wrote, "Bombay is so much and so happily under the influence of European ideas that the Governor may sometimes forget that he is in Asia, but it is evident that even in Bombay the moderation, industry, and intelligence of the Parsees are no security against deadly feuds of Race and Religion."[18] The *Glasgow Herald* made a similar point during the Bombay riots of 1893, although it also recognized how colonial modernity might be making violence worse:

> From the standpoint of Western civilisation Bombay is, of course, the last place in India we should look to for one of these mad outbursts of fanaticism. That city has long been subjected to all the civilising and other influences of the European industrial system. Its numerous factories enable it to rival in smokiness the great English city which feels most keenly the competition of its cheap labour. But grinding toil has manifestly neither deadened the faith nor mitigated the intolerance of the people. On the contrary, the large concourse drawn together by the attraction of steady work, if it has not made the city specially liable to religious riots, renders them more terrible when they do occur.[19]

While some British observers felt that Britain's civilizing influence *ought* to be encouraging non-Western peoples to abandon their primordial hatreds, there was usually much less talk of Indians or blacks "outgrowing" these conflicts than there was about the Irish, who, apart from everything else, had at least benefitted from a substantial infusion of British blood that was absent in farther-flung locales. In the more "primitive" lands, most observers agreed, the state must content itself, in the words of Alfred Lyall, to "keep the peace and clear the way."[20] We will examine these race- and character-based explanations of violence in the next section.

Before leaving this topic, it is important to recognize that not everybody subscribed to the primordial hatreds thesis. Some sympathetic Britons saw that their own government might be partly to blame, and of course the colonized people themselves often made this point. In an interview with the *Pall Mall Gazette* after the Bombay riots of 1893, the Indian nationalist and MP Dadabhai Naoroji said, "There is no such thing as [Hindus and Muslims] always hating each other." The fundamental causes of the violence, he said, were the political and economic conditions brought about by the English themselves, for the English administration "is impoverishing in its effects" and English officials were "out of touch with the natives." What India needed was more officials of Indian "race," who could foresee trouble and ease tensions before they became violent. "You speak of the peace and quiet you bring, and yet look at these riots," he told the British reporter. "[Y]ou have only been with us a hundred years, and India existed and managed to get on for ages before you came."[21] As we will see in Chapter 7, other Indian observers made similar points that year, blaming government policies of "divide and rule," rather than ancient hatreds, for the riots. In Ireland people challenged this idea as well. After the Belfast riots of 1872 the *Daily Examiner*, the organ of the Catholic Church, blamed not ancient hatreds but the British government for the tumult: "the distressing scenes recently enacted in Belfast, taken in conjunction with the feebleness of the Government, is a clear and concise proof that Irishmen should be allowed to take care of themselves. If we had a local government, no lawless rowdies would be permitted to hold unmolested the streets of Belfast."[22] Some Creoles in British Guiana made similar observations in 1856, such as the correspondent who wrote to *The Creole* that "since the accession of Governor Wodehouse to the Government of this magnificent province, every law enacted by him has tended to create the greatest discontent and ill-feeling among those with whom, I am proud to say, all prejudice was fast subsiding."[23] In Ceylon, following the Buddhist–Catholic riot in Colombo in 1883, Sinhalese Buddhists blamed government favoritism toward Catholics for the violence, while the *Ceylon Examiner*, the organ of Colombo's Burgher community, criticized the police for their "criminal thoughtlessness and incompetency," insisting that they, not the riotous mobs, were "the real criminals" with "blood on their hands."[24] The real cause of this violence, in accounts such as these, was not primordial enmity but British mismanagement, and possibly favoritism.

The explanatory power of fanaticism

Another common way for Britons to explain communal riots was to blame them on the rioters' innate defects of character. If British modernity was incapable of extinguishing ancient feuds, perhaps there was something fundamentally wrong with the people themselves: perhaps they were simply impervious to the improving forces of British civilization. Probably the word that appeared most frequently in British riot narratives was "fanatic" (along with its cognates). "Beyond tolerance and impervious to communication," says Alberto Toscano in his recent study of the idea of fanaticism, "the fanatic stands outside the frame of political rationality, possessed by a violent conviction that brooks no argument and will only rest, if ever, once every rival view or way of life is eradicated.... He or she is also a subject who will not change, an intransigent, incorrigible subject."[25] Fanatics have "a kind of monolithic invariance" across time and space, Toscano observes, and as such they align quite closely with the timeless colonial subjects analyzed by Pandey and others.[26] In a colonial context, to call someone a fanatic is to address what Toscano calls "the seemingly intractable problem ... of governing subject peoples who could draw on a reservoir of religious virtue and oppositionalism against the forces of a secular modernity that they could only enjoy, at best, in a derivative or subordinate manner."[27] In other words, those accused of fanaticism were those who seemed to be turning to tradition to resist colonial modernity, but in doing so they only made themselves seem more irrational and uncivilized in the eyes of the colonizer.

If the newspapers are to be believed, the Victorian Empire was positively crawling with fanatics. In 1859 London's Liberal *Era* newspaper espied "childish, absurd, ridiculous fanatics" among the Hindus of Travancore in southern India.[28] In 1862 the Liberal *Bristol Mercury* found Irishmen enacting a feud "which, for folly, ferocity, and downright impiety, is not to be surpassed by any proceedings of fanatical Arabs or Chinese rebels,"[29] and two years later the Radical *Birmingham Daily Post* was unsure who was more ludicrous, the "Hindoo fanatics" who threw themselves under wheeled idols during India's Juggernaut festival, or the "'religious' rioters at Belfast" who "imperil the lives and destroy the property of their neighbours." Perhaps it was simply the case that, "[s]o long as there is a good deal of rioting and a satisfactory amount of bloodshed, both sets of fanatics are content."[30] In 1872 the Liberal *Daily News* decried Belfast fanatics who lacked any "avowed object" and were "simply out to enjoy and prolong the anarchy which they have produced."[31] And in 1874 the *Pall Mall Gazette*, *Daily*

News, *Northern Echo*, *Glasgow Herald*, and London *Times* were among those British papers who blamed "fanatical" Muslims for the Muslim–Parsi riots in Bombay.[32]

These examples all come from the third quarter of the nineteenth century, but most any period of the Victorian era would reveal similar expressions—and, as these examples suggest, such language would also span the ideological spectrum.[33] Nor was it only the press that used this language. In 1858 a resident magistrate reported "fanatical mobs" with "evil passions" rampaging through Belfast during a minor disturbance.[34] In 1874 the home secretary of India Alfred Lyall criticized the Bombay police for deferring to the prejudices of "[i]ntemperate and fanatic men" when they suppressed an allegedly anti-Muslim book at the start of the Bombay riots of that year.[35] On the same occasion the advocate general of India argued that magistrates should be able to call on military force "in the first instance" to suppress riots, because "an excited mob of persons ruled by strong fanatical feelings or prejudices" could not be contained otherwise.[36] The former Bombay police commissioner S. M. Edwardes (1909–16) was also quite free with the epithet in his 1923 history of the Bombay City Police, singling out the Julhais (Muslim handweavers living near Ripon Road) as an especially "ignorant and fanatical" group easily inspired to violence.[37] British officials tended to see the Indian cow-protection riots of the 1890s through a similar lens, describing them as the work of lower-class fanatics shocked into a violent frenzy by high-caste agitators. As historian Richard Cashman has observed of the cow-protection riots in the Deccan, "Most officials failed to recognise the complex causes of the riots, or to see them as a reaction to rapid modernization and British-introduced change, they found it more convenient to attribute the continuance of riots to the truculence of Poona Brahmans."[38] In Bengal, Acting Lieutenant Governor Antony MacDonnell advised one of his magistrates to be "conciliatory" toward Hindu agitators because, "[a]fter all they are not reasonable beings in this matter but blind fanatics."[39] At the same time, Lord Harris, the governor of Bombay, felt confident that one could appeal to the "respectable people of both communities ... to discourage the violent expressions of religious fanaticism amongst their people," although no such direct appeal was likely to work, he felt, among Bombay's most violent underclass.[40]

As these examples suggest, British observers often used the language of fanaticism to dismiss the religion of the masses as not really *religion* at all, but rather a collection of irrational prejudices, superstitions, and vulgarities. When it was Christians doing the rioting, British commentators enjoyed pointing out the chasm between "proper" Christianity—that is, the Christianity of peace, charity, and middle-class morality—and the rioters' form of Christianity. Thus the *Liverpool Mercury*, after a riot involving Irish immigrants in that city, was dismayed that these Irishmen should show "their love of the religion of peace by fiendish hatred, by skull-splitting, by shooting, and even by organised attempts to maim and murder" and demanded that the forces of law and order "teach them that such Christianity as this cannot be tolerated."[41] When it was non-Christians (or non-Europeans) doing the rioting, it was even easier to dismiss their so-called faith as fanatical superstition. After all, a people whose form of religious worship consisted of little more than "ecstatic howlings" (as Anthony Trollope observed of Guianese Creoles in 1859) could hardly be expected to bear insult or contradiction with equanimity.[42]

Another way to express the same idea was to deny that certain religious rites and festivals were truly religious. British descriptions of the Muharram festival, in which Shia Muslims mourn the martyrdom of the third imam, and which in parts of India and the West Indies sometimes entailed considerable violence, were a case in point. In 1885 Sir Henry Norman, investigating a police shooting at a Muharram festival in Trinidad, denied that the event was truly religious since many Hindus and blacks took part in it, while many "respectable" Muslims did not (and also because it was the occasion for much rum drinking and ganja smoking).[43] Likewise, S. M. Edwardes said that when he took the job of Bombay police commissioner in 1909 the Muharram festival had long since lost its religious character and had instead "degenerated into an annual scandal and become a menace to the peace of the city."[44] As for Ireland, the *Aberdeen Journal* doubted whether Protestant Orangemen, who marched every July in part to affirm their Protestant faith, could have any faith "in a religion that does not parade itself with fife and drum, and flags and symbols, and throw defiance in the teeth of its adversary, and proclaim its fervour and its readiness to fight after the Irish fashion of Donnybrook fair."[45]

In addition to these generalized stereotypes about fanatics and their so-called religions, there were also stereotypes specific to individual groups of subject people that helped to explain their propensity for violence. To begin with Muslims, Francis Robinson has noted that in many British texts "the term 'Muslim' was usually accompanied by the term 'fanatic,'" a rhetorical habit that "often concealed an unwillingness, and perhaps an inability, to analyse what was really taking place in Muslim societies."[46] The stereotype of the fanatical Muslim stemmed partly from British concerns about pan-Islamism and, in particular, about the Wahhabi fundamentalists who violently challenged British power in northwest India in the second half of the nineteenth century. It also, somewhat contradictorily, stemmed from a belief that lower-class Indian Muslims were ignorant of the teachings of their own faith—indeed, they were little more than idiosyncratic Hindus[47]—and therefore easily led into acts of violence by their leaders. Sir John Strachey believed that even though rural Muslims "know little or nothing of the tenets of the religion they profess," they were nonetheless "fanatical in their hatred of the Hindus." As far as "true Muhammadans" were concerned, moreover, Strachey felt their aversion to Hinduism was much stronger than their hostility to Christianity or their "fanaticism against our government," a fact that he thought should be some consolation to the ruling race.[48]

A particular highlight of this genre, which also makes virtuosic use of the primordial hatreds thesis, is Winston Churchill's account of his experiences with a field force trying to suppress the Pathans of Afghanistan in 1897:

> It is, thank heaven, difficult if not impossible for the modern European to fully appreciate the force which fanaticism exercises among an ignorant, warlike and Oriental population. Several generations have elapsed since the nations of the West have drawn the sword in religious controversy, and the evil memories of the gloomy past have soon faded in the strong, clear light of Rationalism and human sympathy.... But the Mohammedan religion increases, instead of lessening, the fury of intolerance. It was originally propagated by the sword, and ever since, its votaries have been subject, above the people of all other creeds, to this form of madness. In a moment the fruits of patient toil, the prospects of material prosperity, the fear of death itself, are flung aside.

Churchill continues to say that everywhere the West rubs up against Islam one sees "the forces of progress" at war with "those of reaction," the "religion of blood and war" clashing with "that of peace." He is astounded by the "extraordinary credulity" of Muslims who follow their "Mad Mullah" into battle, describing numerous instances of people being "swept away" in tides of "fanaticism" as they rise up against Britain's armies.[49] Although Churchill was not describing communal violence as such, his account nicely illustrates the ideological framework into which he and his colleagues tried to fit episodes of Muslim violence.[50] Muslims were bloodthirsty, unreasoning, intolerant, and fierce. The Muslim knows "no law but the sword" (according to the *Times* in 1874), "can never forget that his race and creed were once dominant in India" (according to the *Times* in 1893), and is of an "excitable race" (as Lord Harris put it in 1893).[51] No wonder Muslims reacted violently to even the smallest insult to their faith, for they "will always, until the end of the chapter, be an inflammable race" (in the words of the *Glasgow Herald* in 1874).[52] As Subho Basu has argued, the stereotype of the fanatical, turbulent Muslim not only influenced how police dealt with Muslim violence, but it also helped to reconfigure violence *by Muslims* (in Basu's study, labor protests among Calcutta millworkers) into *Muslim violence*—that is, violence borne of the inherent flaws of Muslims' character and faith. Such a rhetorical framing heavily influenced police behavior toward Muslims, which in turn informed Muslim attitudes toward the police (and even, Basu suggests, toward themselves), a dynamic that we will explore in a more general way in Chapter 6.[53]

Yet, whatever their flaws, Muslims were familiar withal. However alien and childlike their faith might appear to British eyes, they were also monotheists guided by a core scripture that originated at a definite historical moment and was rooted in the Judeo–Christian tradition. Islam was at least accessible to Western minds, and for this reason many British officials preferred Muslims to Hindus. "I have always liked the Mahomedans," wrote Sir George Campbell after three years in the Indian Civil Service, "and in religion I think they are only a kind of more advanced Protestants."[54] Hinduism was another matter.[55] Complex, amorphous, and polytheistic, Hinduism's origins were murky, its core texts (if such it really had) sprawling and tangled, its devotional practices mysterious, and its morality highly mutable. "If a religion be a creed with certain distinctive tenets," wrote Sir John Strachey, "the Hinduism of the mass of the people is not a religion at all."[56] For Bampfylde Fuller, Hinduism was "not so much a faith as a system of society."[57] To most Western minds the Hindus' holy images were grotesque and obscene, their holy men freeloading mendicants, and their caste system appalling. "Never has human society been more complicated or artificial," declared Fuller on the latter topic.[58] Edmund C. Cox, the Bombay policeman, repeated in his history of that city the canard that a "Hindu's every act of daily life is a religious observance" and declared that this absolute faith and credulity could easily "degenerate into superstition." For Hindus, "Nothing in the way of supernatural agency is too gross to be believed."[59]

All this meant that the motives of Hindu rioters were even more opaque than those of their Muslim opponents, and so, as with Muslims, it was easiest to describe the masses as blind, credulous fanatics easily goaded into action by scheming leaders. This was a common response to the cow-protection riots of 1893. While most officials recognized Hindu veneration of the cow as a motivating (if childish) factor in the riots, they also believed that the Hindu masses would not have been so vociferous in their objections to Muslim cow-slaughter had they not been stimulated from on high. Typical was the assessment of Charles Crosthwaite, lieutenant governor of the North-West Provinces, who told the viceroy that the "Babus" of the Indian National Congress were responsible for whipping the people into a frenzy over the cow-killing question but that, "in letting loose fanaticism and goading it on, the Congress is playing with a power it cannot control."[60] The press also used stereotypes about the gullible and benighted Hindu masses to explain the violence, as when the *Birmingham Daily Post* observed that there was "little doubt but that the money gained from the fanatic and credulous masses has gone into the pockets of the political agitator."[61]

For many westerners it was easier to comprehend Hinduism by analogy with something familiar, and Catholicism, with its priests, saints, and mysterious rites, offered a sort of ready-made "vocabulary" (the word is Thomas Metcalfe's) for that purpose.[62] When Lord John Russell, in his famous "Durham letter" of 1850, ridiculed Catholicism's "mummeries of superstition" and its tendency to "confine the intellect and enslave the soul," he might just as well have been articulating prevailing British notions of Hinduism.[63] There were several points of similarity between the two faiths—and, as we will see below, this made it tempting to compare Irish and Indian rioters—but one of the main similarities, especially for those seeking to explain the two groups' supposed propensity for religious quarreling, was the alleged power of priests over their ignorant and submissive followers. Priests held the mysteries of both faiths, acting as intermediaries between believers and the deity, and, in the Protestant imagination, often used their position to extort wealth and obedience from their followers. The masses' "boundless veneration" of the priesthood (as Cox said of the Hindus) could take several forms, among them a willingness to fight anybody who opposed their faith.[64] The same was often said of Irish Catholics. Here is the *Belfast Morning News*, a staunchly Protestant paper, describing the Irish cities of Kilkenny, Cork, and Limerick, whose ranks it feared Belfast might join if it did not control its Catholics.

> In these Romish cities, where priests are regnant, and their mobs omnipotent, and the authorities bow to their behests, no Protestant minister dare lift his voice in the streets or highways, to proclaim the peaceful message of the Cross—he would be stoned or murdered.[65]

The power of Catholic priests was not simply a preoccupation of the press. Like their counterparts in India, British officials sometimes laid the blame for Catholic violence at the feet of priestly agitators. In 1853, for instance, Lord Palmerston suspected that Irish Catholics attacking Protestant street preachers had been goaded into these attacks by their priests, "for the people if left to themselves would probably seldom commit them."[66]

Of course, when it came to explaining communal violence in Ireland, there was already a convenient stereotype that did not rely solely upon one side's Catholicism. This was the image of the "fighting Irish," linked in the popular imagination to the supposed "hot-bloodedness" of the "Celtic race," a condition of such passionate intensity that it apparently afflicted Protestants as well as Catholics. "The Celt is a finely-mettled creature," wrote a leader writer in the *Preston Guardian*, stuffing the Irish of all creeds and ancestries (and genders) into the same box, "but he lacks equillibrium [sic], and when his exuberance is associated with any particular idea in the domain of either religion or politics, he cannot exist without a row—he must 'go off,' and that means much fighting, window-breaking, head-damaging, and policeman-bruising."[67] According to the *Saturday Review* it was simply part of "Irish human nature" to respond violently when insulted, a habit into which they had been "carefully indoctrinated" by Catholic priests and "Orange divines."[68] Lord Carlisle similarly put the Belfast riots of 1857 down to "a propensity for mischief, and a taste for fighting," while the *Liverpool Mercury* blamed the violence of the Liverpool Irish on their "hereditary passion for a row."[69] "Ireland is Ireland," wrote a resigned *Aberdeen Journal* in 1860, "and Irishmen Irishmen, and whether they go off to fight for the Pope, or stay at home in the full employment of fighting their neighbours, it seems unreasonable to expect either Protestant or Roman Catholic to act, if anything, like any other people."[70]

All of these stereotypes implicitly distanced imperial subjects from the British norm. If a passionate and turbulent "Irish human nature" helped to explain an Irish riot, then by implication the nonrioting Briton must be placid and restrained. If Hindus and Muslims were fanatical in their faith, then Britons must be cool and rational. If Bengalis were (as one *Times* editorial put it), effeminate, imitative, loquacious, and possessing a "conspicuous lack of original faculty and virile strength," then the opposite was true of their British rulers.[71] Often these stereotyped explanations of communal violence blurred into one another. John David Rees, a former ICS man, might have been talking about the Irish when he observed that it was the "emotional and excitable temperament" of the Bengalis that allowed them to be "induced to imitate, and take part in, attacks upon Mahomedans" (the men doing the inducing, on this occasion, were of course high-caste "Babus").[72] When the *Daily News* described the Bombay Parsis as "a most intelligent, enterprising, and progressive element" and quoted approvingly Sir Henry Anderson's judgment that they were "an agency by which the civilization of the West will be able to influence the destiny of that magnificent country," the newspaper might equally have been describing the Portuguese of Guiana, who were likewise admired as "[i]ndustrious, thrifty, patient, and persevering" subjects—or, indeed, any other commercial elite around the globe (for instance the Malays of Cape Town).[73] Sinhalese Catholics, meanwhile, came in for much the same criticism as Indian Muslims who allegedly failed to understand the teachings of their own religion, as when the *Ceylon Examiner* wrote, following the 1883 Colombo riots:

> An excitable imaginative people, with a deep veneration for the forms and ceremonies of their religion, but without sufficient education and self-control to allow the truths of that religion habitually to influence their conduct, especially in times of excitement, they were carried away by their feelings.[74]

There was also the all-purpose stereotype of the lazy and barbaric savage, which could be used to explain communal violence pretty much anywhere, but especially when the rioters were of African descent. This, as we have seen, was among the explanations offered by Philip Wodehouse of the anti-Portuguese riots in Guiana in 1856 when he said that rural blacks were living "a life little less savage than that of the beasts of the field."[75] The violence of such people could never have any rational purpose.

Cross-colonial analogies

The facility with which British observers drew upon a common stock of stereotypes to describe such disparate people as the Irish, Pathans, Africans, and Bengalis naturally leads us to investigate more fully those moments when they drew more explicit comparisons between imperial subjects, a practice that usually occurred in order to show one or the other group in an unflattering light. These comparisons are interesting because they help us gauge the extent to which British observers saw specific outbreaks as part of a larger pattern and the facility with which distinct episodes could be drained of their individuality and subsumed into a larger picture of undifferentiated "unrest" overseas. Such cross-colonial analogies had a way of flattening out the map of empire, positing a great mass of atavistic fanatics "out there" who needed more (not less) British rule to help bring them into the modern world. In this way they helped to buttress their civilizing mission.

The first thing to note is that, obvious though such comparisons might seem to us, explicit comparisons of one colony with another were a minor part of the British interpretive repertoire; it was much more common to subsume rioters (of whatever community) into a generalized stereotype of fanaticism than to explicitly link them with other communities around the globe. Furthermore, such analogies were more common in the press than in official documents—and when they did appear in official documents, they tended to be used to explain political rather than communal problems. When Irish nationalism began to dominate British politics from about the 1870s, for example, references to Charles S. Parnell, the Fenian Brotherhood, and other Irish nationalists started appearing in official correspondence about India. In the midst of the cow-protection riots of 1893 Home Department Secretary Charles J. Lyall suggested that the Hindu cow-protection movement "is much more dangerous to the peace of India than Fenianism ever was to that of Ireland."[76] At a more general level, W. W. Hunter, a member of the Bengal Civil Service, pointed out that Indian Muslims held "sentimental grievances" against the British for the usurpation of their historic power, "which not less in India than in Ireland keep the popular heart in a state of soreness to their Rulers."[77] On occasion, however, officials did make comparisons between Irish and Indian communal violence, as when Lord Elgin, the viceroy of India, observed that "Hindus and Mahomedans attack Europeans, just as Irishmen would join in a row [against the authorities], whether Orangmen [sic] or Home Rulers."[78]

Even if they did not write down many direct comparisons between one colony and another, however, imperial officials undoubtedly made such comparisons informally. Indeed, the imperial system was designed to encourage such comparisons, since it moved administrators around the globe like pawns on a chessboard. Lord Mayo, for instance, who served as Viceroy of India from 1869 to 1872, came from a prominent Anglo-Irish family and had served (as Lord Naas) as chief secretary of Ireland on three separate occasions; one of his admirers felt that his Irishness gave him special insight into India, "on account of the analogies between some Irish and Eastern institutions."[79] Another official of Irish origin, the Catholic Antony MacDonnell, served in various capacities in India before returning to Ireland as the country's leading civil servant. Both Mayo and MacDonnell had to deal with communal violence in Ireland and India, and it would be surprising if their experience of one place did not inform their understanding of the other.[80] Even more striking in this respect is Sir Philip Wodehouse, who had the distinction of being governor of British Guiana during the 1856 Angel Gabriel riots and governor of Bombay in 1874 during the Muslim–Parsi riots. During the former, as we have seen, he relied heavily on special constables to put down the violence, and this experience was probably what lay behind his ill-considered advice to Parsis to form themselves into self-defense organizations in 1874, the implications of which we will explore in the next chapter. Moreover, as the discussion of policing in Chapter 6 will demonstrate, the similarity in riot-control techniques across the empire suggests that many officials were drawing on a common fund of imperial knowledge and experience when it came to the practicalities of communal disputes.

It was in the press, though, that cross-colonial analogies were the most common. Often the analogies suggested themselves when violence in one part of the empire happened to coincide with violence in another. In October 1886, after a heavily reported summer of rioting in Belfast, the Radical *Birmingham Daily Post* found a felicitous parallel in the news of Hindu–Muslim riots in Delhi and Etawah:

> The essential similarity of human nature all the world over is forcibly brought home to us by the intelligence of religious rioting in India, where the Mohammadens and Hindoos apparently find the same satisfaction in proving their doctrine orthodox by apostolic blows and knocks, as do their Catholic and Protestant fellow-subjects in Belfast. What the anniversary of the battle of the Boyne is to the Irish Orangeman, the Dusserah and Mohurrum Festivals appear to be to the fanatics of Northern India, and the recent concurrence of the religious festivals of the rival creeds is said to be mainly responsible for the alarming outbreaks at Etawah in the Bengal Presidency, and at Delhi.[81]

The Irish–Indian comparison was a particular favorite, especially since it afforded journalists the opportunity to argue that the Irish, despite their apparent closeness to Britain, were actually no different than other colonial fanatics. Thus in 1872 the Conservative *Daily Telegraph* found that "[a]nything more thoroughly 'heathen'" than a Belfast riot "could not be found in the whole Eastern world; indeed, if we want a parallel, we must go back to search the records of the great Indian cities in the Ganges Valley."[82]

As with other aspects of British riot interpretation, cross-colonial analogies were never the monopoly of one political creed. Although Conservative organs such as the *Telegraph* and *Times* were more likely than others to compare the Irish to colonial "savages," we also find the Liberal *Leeds Mercury* accusing Irish rioters of "fighting with a ferocity of which New Zealand savages would be ashamed," and the *Bristol Mercury* (which was usually sympathetic to Irish causes) arguing that Irish violence was "only to be paralleled amongst the fanatical Mohammedans of Arabia or the most degraded American Indians."[83] We must be careful not to read too much into this, however: often comparisons of the Irish to non-Europeans were simply ironic flourishes meant to call attention, through calculated exaggeration, to a domestic evil.[84] Often, too, these analogies arose when other pieces of imperial news were preoccupying journalists' minds. This was undoubtedly the case in 1872, for instance, when news of the Belfast riot coincided with news of Henry Morton Stanley's successful "rescue" of David Livingstone on the shores of Lake Tanganyika, a convergence that prompted a *Telegraph* writer to observe, "If Mr. Stanley had described such scenes [as the Belfast riots] in Ujiji-land, we should not have been astonished."[85] With these caveats in mind, what we can say about these analogies is that they helped to situate communal violence within the realm of the primitive and the atavistic, and, further, that they positioned such disturbances as essentially un-British. In this way they helped to demonstrate the necessity of continuing Britain's civilizing mission across the globe.

The necessity of continued British rule

As we have seen, outbreaks of communal violence among imperial subjects led some British observers to wonder whether liberal principles were really an appropriate basis for ruling an empire. If the people of India, Ceylon, the West Indies, or even Ireland were not truly free individuals—free from ancient prejudices, free from the domination of priests and feudal princes, free from their own primitive passions—then were they really fit subjects for a liberal regime that required its members to be not only free but also rational?[86] If they could not handle even the modest liberties guaranteed to them as British subjects—freedom of worship, freedom of expression, due process before the law—then how could they be entrusted with even greater political liberties? Qualms about the intelligence or sophistication of imperial subjects did not prevent Britain, in most instances, from guaranteeing them minimal protections before the law, but the supposed shortcomings of imperial subjects did provide a philosophical basis for denying them representative institutions. John Stuart Mill famously articulated this idea in *On Liberty*, when he described despotism as a legitimate method of governing "barbarians":

> Liberty, as a principle, has no application to any state of things anterior to the time when mankind have become capable of being improved by free and equal discussion. Until then, there is nothing for them but implicit obedience to an Akbar or a Charlemagne, if they are so fortunate as to find one.[87]

Episodes of communal violence seemed to justify such a view. "What can we do more?" asked a petulant *Times* after the Belfast riots of 1864.

> We forbid the violence which each party burns to exercise towards the other, and we do not confine ourselves to negatives, but offer them, instead of these endless brawls, the enjoyment of a common liberty and the means of a boundless development of wealth and prosperity. But because we offer these things in vain, because the Irish prefer to the prosperity which is within their grasp the prosecution of childish and obsolete feuds, is England to be considered responsible for these evils, or to lose her well-earned character for justice and liberality in the eyes of foreign nations?

The problem, the *Times* concluded, lay "in the Irish people themselves, not in the political institutions by which they were governed."[88] As we have seen, after the 1882 Salem riots the *Madras Times* made a similar point about Indians, whom it declared "not sufficiently civilized or philosophical to be benefitted by" liberal laws allowing free religious expression.[89]

If these imperial subjects were not "capable of being improved by free and equal discussion," then it stood to reason that they were not ready to take charge of their own affairs. "What sort of a country," asked the *Saturday Review* after the Belfast riots of 1864,

> would Ireland be to live in if she were left wholly to her own devices, without the restraining and controlling influence of English law, English authority, and English opinion? A country rent with civil and ecclesiastical discords which apparently defy all the healing virtue of time and experience, and even of education, is the very last country in the world to sustain the perilous responsibilities of separate political existence.... It is only as citizens of the British empire and subjects of the British Crown, that Celt and Saxon, Papist and Protestant, have a chance of learning to dwell peaceably together in the same land.[90]

If the Irish were to run their own country, the same paper insisted a few months later, "the only kind of tranquility they are likely to maintain is that which was enjoyed by the surviving portion of the historical Kilkenny cat."[91] The more Irish Home Rule appeared on the legislative agenda after about 1870, the more antinationalist partisans made this argument, to the point that it was becoming something of a cliché by the end of the century. In an article on the Belfast riots of 1872 headlined "An Experiment in Home Rule," the *Pall Mall Gazette* argued that under Home Rule "Ireland would immediately relapse into her chronic strife and social war;" the same riots proved to the *Preston Guardian* that the Irish were "not prepared for absolute freedom."[92] Twelve years later the *Ipswich Journal* likewise declared that internecine Irish violence would inevitably follow "should self-government be given to a people incapable of self-restraint," and the *Graphic* similarly worried about what would happen if "the 'English garrison' were withdrawn" from Ireland.[93] "The absolute truth of the matter," wrote one Henry Jephson to the *Times* in 1886,

> proved year after year beyond all contradiction except assertion—is, that peace is only preserved in Ireland by the sheer weight of the Imperial authority. Withdraw that authority, and the two factions in Ireland, or, as they have recently been called, "the two Irelands," will, on the first serious provocation, be at each other's throats.[94]

A similar sort of rhetoric could be seen regarding other parts of the empire. Philip Wodehouse believed that the 1856 riots in British Guiana demonstrated, "beyond the possibility of doubt, that the mass of the population are in no degree better able to govern themselves than they were at the time of the emancipation; some will say even less so." This was especially evident, he thought, in the large Creole villages: "With everything around them that they can wish for, they make no progress, moral or material; while there seems every possibility of the rising generation proving even worse than their fathers."[95] With India, meanwhile, this sort of argument was almost as common as with Ireland. Commenting on India's 1893 riots, the *Glasgow Herald* spoke for many British observers when it said,

> At present the British authority enforces peace between the rival races and the rival creeds; if that authority were withdrawn or paralysed, the immediate consequence would be a series of internecine conflicts between the followers of the Prophet and of Brahma, the duration and results of which it is impossible to foretell, but which would certainly substitute for the present situation of order and security a reign of bloodshed and utter confusion. In one sense this state of things augurs well for the permanence of our rule.[96]

Charles Crosthwaite, lieutenant governor of the North-West Provinces, made the same point that year when he told the viceroy that "the people of India can only be kept in order and peace by a strong firm authority which they know cannot be interfered with, or set aside, and which therefore they respect."[97] Indeed, in the coming century the notion that Britain's restraining hand was the only thing preventing Muslims and Hindus from tearing each other to bits would become one of the strongest arguments for continuing to withhold Indian self-rule. It was also one of the guiding assumptions of those Indians who advocated for, and achieved, a separate state for Indian Muslims.

These arguments all rested on the assumption that only the British state—wise, impartial, and firm—was capable of mediating, policing, and resolving communal disputes. This was an assumption shared by both British journalists and British officials, and it was deployed wherever and whenever communal riots occurred. In 1865 Lord Wodehouse (later Lord Kimberley), the lord lieutenant of Ireland, lamented to Sir George Grey the occurrence of riots in Belfast in the following terms: "It is a frightful and disgraceful state of things no doubt that a country which professes to be civilized should be divided into hostile factions (orange and green) who are only prevented from killing each other by the presence of a strong impartial force of armed men."[98] The *Times* expressed the same idea following the 1874 riots in Bombay: "When we are bound to interfere, and we are always so bound when the law is broken—our first aim ought to be the strictest avoidance of partisanship, and our second to allow for much that we cannot approve, while at the same time we put down the disorder unsparingly."[99] The historian A. F. Pollard made a similar point in 1912, observing, "the abandonment of her task by Great Britain would leave India a prey to anarchy."[100] Like a stern father with his unruly children, the state had to be both powerful and just in handling these brawls; that it was not, and could not be, in any way responsible for the violence was taken for granted.

Was there anything to be done about these riots, then, other than to "keep the peace and clear the way"? In Chapter 6 we will examine specific policing strategies across the empire, but here it is worth observing that Britain's overall strategy, when there was one, was simply to wait for the people to outgrow these puerile quarrels. This idea found expression in different ways at different times, but the fundamental assumption remained the same: given enough time under a progressive, liberal, British regime, even the most intractable conflicts would begin to erode. The *Daily News* put it this way in a comment on the 1893 Indian riots: "It is evident that the best way of making these mobs forget that they are Hindoo or Mussulman is to teach them to remember their common brotherhood of citizenship and loyalty to the throne. The best cure for these fantastic hatreds is the hope of material prosperity and the chances of a career."[101] In 1864 the *Leeds Mercury* offered a somewhat simpler prescription of "time and the growth of common sense" for the warring factions of Ireland, expressing the quintessential liberal belief that progress, especially under British tutelage, was inevitable.[102]

What all these analyses ignored, however, was that violence was not disappearing over time but was, in many places, getting worse. The Belfast riots of 1886 were far, far worse than the outbreaks of 1857, 1864, 1872, and the innumerable smaller episodes of the mid-Victorian period, and the catastrophic "Troubles" of 1919–21 would be worse still. In India, too, the scope and complexity of communal conflicts were expanding year by year, and as the cow-protection quarrels of the 1890s gave way to larger, more overtly political conflicts in the first half of the twentieth century, some regions began to experience something not far short of anarchy. From the standpoint of the early- to mid-twentieth century, to speak of British rule as the only thing keeping rival communities from killing one another would have seemed like nonsense, for here was British rule, and here were communities killing one another. These were not mutually exclusive conditions, and to claim otherwise required some acrobatic feats of logic (recall Strachey's Caveat, discussed in the Introduction, which praised the "absolute peace" of British India apart from the "not unfrequent" outbursts of violence between Hindus and Muslims). Plenty of people, especially those on the receiving end of the civilizing mission, noticed the fallacy of this argument. As we have seen, following the Belfast riots of 1872 the nationalist *Daily Examiner* argued that the riots showed Ireland needed less British rule, not more. "If we had a local government," it argued, "no lawless rowdies would be permitted to hold unmolested the streets of Belfast."[103] We have also seen Dadabhai Naoroji making the similar suggestion that the employment of more Indian officials in responsible positions might help to prevent clashes between Hindus and Muslims.[104] Even some British observers thought that self-government might ease, rather than exacerbate, communal tensions, as when the *Bristol Daily Mercury* suggested that Irish Home Rule would be a "panacea for Irish troubles" on the grounds that, "if the two [sides] were left to themselves, a very different temper would soon come over each. The majority would learn the wisdom of tolerance, while the minority would come to see that it is much better to live amicably with their Catholic neighbours than to be in perpetual hot water."[105] Such views, however, were decidedly in the minority during this period.

Conclusion

Overall, what is most striking about British responses to communal violence is their essential sameness from place to place and era to era. The same tropes, assumptions, and even words recur again and again, suggesting that there was an underlying unity not only to how Britons perceived communal violence, but also to how they perceived their larger imperial purpose. From Georgetown to Belfast to Bombay, the purported causes of conflict—fanaticism, childishness, an inability to escape the past, the tumultuousness and gullibility of the lower orders, (but emphatically *not* British rule)—were essentially the same. Similar causes called for similar remedies—firm and impartial rulers, ample time to absorb the healing balm of British modernity—and this, in turn, justified the (indefinite) continuation of British rule. The *Times*, commenting in 1886 on riots in India that had occurred just after the conclusion of riots in Belfast, drew together most of the interpretive strands we have been following in this chapter:

> It will perhaps occur to some to reflect how very much more easy it is to deal with the mutual antipathies of Mussulman and Hindoo than with the religious animosities of different Christian sects. Human nature seems very much the same in Belfast and in Delhi, but when Orangemen and Roman Catholics unfurl their banners on the same day, the resulting riot is a much more serious affair than anything that has happened in India. The fact may be a testimony to superior strength of character on the part of Christian professors, but it does not shed much lustre either upon Western religion or Western civilization. If the flame of religious fanaticism burned in India with anything like the intensity it sometimes attains in the north of Ireland we should never have heard of the *pax Britannica*. Still, although the enforcement of mutual tolerance in India is within our power, every one of our Indian subjects who is capable of reflection on such questions at all must be fully aware that there is no other authority actual or possible in Hindostan capable of securing the same blessing.[106]

This closing thought, that there was no other power capable of keeping the peace in India, applied equally to every part of the empire where rival communities fought. To compare India to Ireland, or Ireland to New Zealand, or any portion of the empire to any other portion, was to affirm that Britain had a unique, global role to play in keeping the peace within less fully evolved societies. Only the global British state—competent, rational, and disinterested—was capable of mustering the firmness and integrity that these people needed to overcome their ancient hatreds. Such, anyway, was the broad consensus of British commentators regarding communal violence in the Victorian Empire. How these ideas informed the behavior of imperial officials on the spot is the subject of Chapter 6, but first we will take a detailed look at just how hard it was for some officials to live up to the role of disinterested referee by dropping in on the city of Bombay in February 1874.

5

The Ruling Race Stumbles: Bombay, 1874

If Frank Souter was a reflective man, and it is by no means certain that he was, he might have chalked up the whole bloody row to his own good intentions. In his past life Souter had been a soldier, a hero of a minor episode of the 1857 Indian rebellion and a bandit hunter in Hyderabad and the Deccan, but his present job as Bombay police commissioner required very different skills.[1] He had been on the job for ten years by the time of the great Bombay riots of 1874. He knew the city, knew a few of its languages, a bit of its history. He knew that there had been riots in the city well before his time, in 1851, when a gang of Muslim ruffians had attacked the peaceable and prosperous Parsis over some alleged insult to their prophet.[2] In his own time he had seen Sunni and Shia Muslims come to blows during Muharram, a religious festival that, even at its best, looked to British eyes like little more than an excuse for the superstitious masses to relive some obscure and ancient quarrel. Maintaining order in such a city was a tricky business: one had to be sensitive, careful not to offend the local bigwigs but ready to pounce on any rumblings coming up from the lower depths. One had to be politic, a listener, sympathetic—but forceful too, when the time came, able to show the inhabitants that the British state was supreme here, that there mustn't be any nonsense. Souter was quite comfortable in the latter mode, but he was less adept at being sensitive and politic, and this, in essence, was his failing in 1874.

The trouble seemed minor at first. In 1873 a Parsi vaccinator named Rustomjee Hormusjee Jalbhoy had quietly published a book in Gujarati with the jaunty title, *The Renowned Prophets and Nations, Comprising the Lives of Zoroaster, Moses, Christ, and Mahomet, and Abridged History of the Ancient Aryans, the old Parsees, and Complete History of the Jews, the Christians, and the Mahomedans, together with an Account of the Creation of the World from the earliest period to the present time.* After circulating among the Parsis for several months the book came to the attention of the city's Muslim leaders when someone (Jalbhoy suspected his neighbor Sooliman, with whom he had a quarrel[3]) complained about a passage that seemed to imply that Muhammad had fathered a son by a prostitute. The offending passage (translated, in fact, from Washington Irving's biography of Muhammad) concerned the mother of Muhammad's son Ebrahim, whom the text described with a Gujarati phrase meaning "kept woman." The Muslims who objected to the phrase (most of whom almost certainly did not read Gujarati) believed it to be a deliberate insult, but the Parsis insisted that the phrase simply meant concubine, and that it was never meant to insult Muhammad or Islam.[4]

Well-intentioned or not, Souter's handling of this controversy turned a teakettle tempest into a mighty storm that, at its height, destroyed people's homes and killed several men. His decisions in this matter, along with his subsequent actions and inactions, would also seriously undermine the state's prestige among some of its most loyal subjects. The Bombay riots of 1874 were by no means the biggest riots the city had ever seen, nor were they the most consequential. They did not fundamentally alter the course of Indian history or inaugurate a new era in the communal or political life of Bombay. What they did, rather, was to rip a tiny hole in the carefully woven fabric of Britain's Indian Empire, a hole through which the people of Bombay glimpsed the masters of the empire scrambling about in most unbecoming and embarrassing confusion. Eventually the forces of order regained their composure, but that moment of confusion and embarrassment would be difficult to forget.

Parsis and Muslims

The 1874 riot was not the first time Souter had become entangled in a communal dispute involving the Parsis. The previous year he had intervened in a dispute between rival bands of Parsis at the Towers of Silence (funerary structures for the Parsi dead) on Gibbs Road. The dispute concerned ownership of a parcel of land on which the towers sat, and when things became violent, Souter and his men charged onto the site and arrested several dozen people. This would have been enough to earn him some enemies among the Parsis, but he earned many more when he defiled this sacred space by riding onto the tower grounds on horseback, violating the strict laws of purity that governed Parsi religious life.[5] The Parsis' antipathy for the police commissioner, which would only deepen in 1874, was unusual for a community that was in many ways the most Anglophilic in Bombay. The Parsis were a small community in a vast, multiethnic metropolis, monotheists descended from Zoroastrian refugees from the Muslim conquest of Persia in the seventh century. Memories of this expulsion, and of subsequent periods of persecution by Muslims in India, were an important part of the Parsi identity, giving them a particular distaste for Muslims (Bombay's second-largest religious community) even if, by the Victorian period, the Parsis had little to fear from them either economically or politically.[6] In this city of oligarchs—a city that owed its existence to the commercial ambitions of European empires past and present—Parsi merchants, bankers, shipbuilders, and factory owners were oligarchs *par excellence*, a tight-knit club of likeminded men whose wealth rivaled that of the Europeans. They were magistrates, judges, municipal councilors, philanthropists, and newspaper editors; they ran the city's hotels, dominated its liquor trade, owned much of its real estate, and imported most of its fine European goods. They had both enabled and profited from Britain's military expansion in Asia, building ships for the Royal Navy and exploiting new markets once those ships had cracked them open, doing especially well in the opium trade with China.[7] They were, in other words, perfectly aware that they owed their considerable wealth and influence to British might and British commerce, and they did not lightly make enemies of the representatives of the ruling race.

Not all of the Parsis were wealthy, of course, nor were they all admirers of the British, but of all the communities in Bombay, they were the ones to whom the British were best able to relate, although not always perfectly, and not always without condescension. After the 1874 riots the Bombay-based *Times of India* would observe that the Parsis, "a mere half lakh of people" who "speak English provokingly well" and "affect to display public spirit," were disliked by many Europeans "with that special kind of repugnance reserved for the behoof of poor relations or intrusive kinsfolk from a distance."[8] Although they admired their enterprise (one British writer claimed, apparently in all seriousness, that the Parsis were "the most energetic people living, except the French"[9]), many Britons were not quite prepared to admit the Parsis into the ranks of the civilized. Still, they were people with whom one could do business, and they were people one could talk to (in English), and that helped to set them apart from the other communities of Bombay. Like the Jews of Europe, however—and the comparison was a common one—their very success made them objects of envy and suspicion among more than a few Europeans, to say nothing of their fellow Indians.

The Parsis' antagonists in 1874 differed from them in almost every conceivable way. If the Parsi community was small and close-knit, the Muslims, numbering over 130,000 to the Parsis' 44,000, were numerous and fragmented.[10] At roughly a fifth of the city's population, Muslims differed from one another by sect, origin, language, and occupation.[11] Some groups resembled the Parsis in their wealth and cohesiveness. The Bohras, for instance, were a small community descended from Hindu converts who had given Bombay its first Muslim solicitor, barrister, doctor, and engineer, but even they were further divided into Sunni, Aliya, Daudi, and Sulemani sects. There were other elite groups, such as the Memons and the Khojas, who were smaller still. There was also a transitory population of Arabs and Sidis (from the Middle East and sub-Saharan Africa, respectively) who worked for the shipping companies as seamen and laborers. Bombay was the principal port of embarkation for Indian Muslims undertaking the Hajj, so many of these latter groups were connected to the pilgrimage trade in some way. Most Bombay Muslims, however, were poor Sunnis who spoke Marathi and Konkani and worked as laborers and factory workers.[12] They lived in crowded quarters in the "native town," near similar neighborhoods of poor Hindus; their lives were hard, their work unpleasant and irregular, and many retained strong ties to their homes in rural India or overseas.[13] When they did find employment they were overworked and poorly remunerated. (The *Bombay Gazetteer* of 1909 noted that Bombay's mill workers—not all of whom, of course, were Muslims—worked on average 80 hours a week, as compared with 55.5 hours for Lancashire mill workers, and earned just 13 rupees a month, much less than the equivalent of 81 rupees earned in Lancashire.[14]) Their *chawls*, or tenements, generally consisted of one 12' x 8' room shared by two to three families—that is, ten to fifteen adults, plus numerous children—and no furniture to speak of, apart from rough wood boxes and iron trunks, a few kitchen implements, and blankets instead of beds.[15] The distance between such people and the affluent Parsis was immense.

It is impossible to know what went through Souter's mind when a delegation of leading Muslims approached him in February 1874 to complain about the controversial Parsi book. He would certainly have been aware of the Raj's general policy of allowing free religious expression, its distaste for censorship, and its stance of religious neutrality. On the other hand, as police commissioner he would have been concerned above all with preserving the public peace. Would the Muslims run riot if he failed to do something about the Parsi book? Two years earlier rival groups of Muslims had rioted during Muharram, and it was not impossible that some of them might cause trouble again, especially with another Muharram just around the corner. Souter may also have considered the bigger picture: ever since the revolt of 1857 there had been grave concern in official circles about the loyalty of the empire's Muslims. There were two reasons for this. First, during the rebellion many north-India Muslims had rallied to the cause of restoring the Mughal Empire at Delhi, and, although Bombay's Muslims had remained quiet, it was unclear just how much they might have sympathized with that cause. Second, since the late 1860s there was another Muslim threat emanating from India's northern frontier, a radical political and religious ideology known as Wahabbism that seemed to have some purchase among the city's more politically engaged Muslims.

Working to purify Islam of external contamination by means of a strict interpretation of the Quran, and aspiring to unify all Muslims under a single global caliphate, the Wahhabis' goals were simultaneously spiritual and temporal. In British eyes what was troubling about Wahhabism was not so much its fundamentalism as its anti-imperialism: Muslims might do what they liked among themselves, for all that most British officials cared, but the unified caliphate to which Wahhabis aspired would require no less than the dismembering of British India, and this was another matter entirely. A series of wars along India's northwest frontier in the middle of the nineteenth century had galvanized the Wahhabi movement both outside and inside of India, and in the 1860s the state had launched a severe internal crackdown on Wahhabi militants.[16] The excitement peaked just a few years before the Bombay riots, when, in 1871, a Punjabi Muslim murdered the officiating chief justice of the Calcutta high court, and the following year a deranged Muslim killed the viceroy, Lord Mayo.[17] These episodes helped to fix Muslims in British minds as an unpredictable and potentially disloyal people, an attitude captured in the title of an 1871 book by the Bengal civil servant W. W. Hunter: *The Indian Musalmans: Are They Bound in Conscience to Rebel against the Queen?* Although most officials recognized, like Hunter, that "the Indian Wahábis are only a small fragment of a great sect,"[18] they also tended to think of Islam as fundamentally intolerant, of Indian Muslims as longing to restore the power they had enjoyed under the Mughals, and of the Muslim masses as easy prey for fanatical rabble-rousers.[19] Was Wahhabism a threat in Bombay in 1874? Certainly some Bombay Muslims were Wahhabis. Charles Forjett, Souter's predecessor as police commissioner, claimed that some of the city's most influential Muslims were Wahhabis, but that, far from being disaffected, they had actually helped him root out sedition in 1857. In 1869 Souter had reported that there were 100 Wahhabis in the city but that there was no evidence that they were connected to the conspirators in Bengal. And in 1889 James Maclean—editor, journalist, and author of the authoritative *Guide to Bombay*—would assert that there were surely some Wahhabis in Bombay at this time, even though none had appeared as such on the 1872 census.[20]

To return to February 1874: even if Souter was not worried about Wahhabism specifically, it is likely that he was acting under some notion that it was wise to placate the city's volatile Muslims. This would help to explain why, after meeting with the delegation of Muslim leaders who came to complain about the book, he sent for Rustomjee Hormusjee Jalbhoy, the book's author/translator, and asked him to hand over all unsold copies to the police. Jalbhoy expressed surprise that his book had caused offense, but he complied with Souter's request. Souter then contacted the book's Parsi subscribers to ask them to allow their copies to be stored temporarily in the police office, and soon every known copy was in police custody.[21] Muslim leaders, satisfied with Souter's handling of the affair, held a large meeting on February 12 at which they attempted to put the matter to rest, assuring their people that the police had taken prompt and decisive action.[22] The spies Souter sent to the meeting reported that the Muslims seemed to be in a placid mood, but just to be safe Souter soon sent out more spies to mingle with the Muslims and report any signs of discontent. Souter's main concern, he later said, was not that violence would break out immediately, but that someone might make trouble during Muharram, due to start the following week. The spies heard nothing, however, and the leaders of the Muslims likewise felt that the storm had blown over.[23] If there had been a plan to riot, Souter said later, "the plot must have been confined to a very few of the Mahomedan roughs of Bombay."[24]

Even as Souter's men were reporting that everything was quiet, however, terrifying rumors were spreading through Parsi neighborhoods that the Muslims were planning a pogrom. Dorabjee Pestonjee, a fruit vendor in the Crawford Markets, was one of those who spread the rumors: having been informed by a Muslim friend that trouble was afoot, he warned a few fellow Parsis and then fled with his family to a relative's house in Cumballa.[25] Jalbhoy, the publisher of the book, heard a similar rumor, only it was more personally threatening: Muslim men, he heard, were addressing crowds from the steps of mosques and urging them to kill Jalbhoy and attack the Parsis. Jalbhoy reported the rumors to Alfred Edginton, the deputy commissioner of police, who had received a similar warning from a Parsi delegation the previous day. Then Jalbhoy, too, fled Bombay.[26]

Day 1: Friday, February 13

The storm broke on Friday, February 13. On that morning Hindus and Parsis noticed a larger crowd than usual heading toward the Jama Masjid—the large central mosque, which happened to be near many Parsi and Hindu homes—for Friday prayers.[27] Stories differed about what went on inside the mosque: some said the speakers were violently calling for vengeance against the Parsis, but others disputed this, and Souter's own spies inside the mosque reported nothing especially alarming.[28] The *Times of India* reported "ruffianly-looking Mahomedans" gathered around the mosque with sticks, and a few Parsis later reported coming under a barrage of stones and insults from people gathered on the mosque's terrace, but such reports are difficult to verify.[29] At some point in the early afternoon, however, a large group of men (the Parsis said five thousand, others said several hundred) left the Jama Masjid and ran toward the Parsi homes and fire temples in nearby Sheikh Abdool Rahmon Street and the Bhendy Bazaar. As they ran, they shouted "Din, din," which, according to the *Bombay Gazette*, was "a cry which always has an electric effect upon Mussulman fanatics, and which often has been the forerunner of barbarities perpetrated in the name of the religion of the Prophet."[30] British observers would have many more occasions to deploy this rhetoric of fanaticism in the days to come.

The first Parsi home the Muslim crowd attacked was that of Framjee Bicajee, a police inspector living on Sir Jamestjee Jejeebhoy Street. The reason they targeted Framjee is unclear. After the riots a Muslim memorial would claim that Framjee had come out of his house and struck some Muslim boys who were running past yelling "din, din," and also that bottles "and other injurious things" had been thrown from Framjee's house.[31] Another version, provided by a Muslim correspondent to the newspaper *A'rya Mitrá*, had it that while the congregation was leaving the mosque a Parsi constable (presumably Framjee) picked a fight with a peaceful Arab who was walking by with a stick in his hand. According to this version, the constable called the Arab a *suar*, or hog, and tried to grab his stick, whereupon Arab bystanders rushed him and commenced the destruction.[32] Whatever the cause, the attackers showed Framjee little mercy, smashing his windows, breaking down his door, and rushing upstairs to menace his family. They beat up Framjee (though not, apparently, his family) and then destroyed everything in the house—mattresses, clothes, furniture—before rushing across the street to the Alibag, a sort of Parsi poor house. There they raided the kitchen, hurling pickles and destroying pots and pans. They also invaded the adjoining fire temple, easily overpowering the elderly priest there and extinguishing the temple's sacred fire. All Parsi temples (and many Parsi homes) had such a fire, a symbol of divinity and a channel to God, which they carefully tended and were careful never to contaminate or extinguish—it was forbidden even to approach the fire except in a state of utmost purity. When the rioters doused the temple's sacred fire, and when they proceeded to tear up sacred texts and spit into the sacred well, they were committing acts of deliberate defilement meant, in all likelihood, to avenge what they saw as the defilement of their own faith in the pages of Jalbhoy's book.[33]

Meanwhile other bands of Muslims ran through the Bhendy Bazaar and Sheikh Abdool Rahmon Street, where there were several Parsi fire temples and a great many Parsi homes. In Sheikh Abdool Rahmon Street they invaded a doctor's office and smashed his bottles of medicine and chemicals. Then they battered down the door of an elderly man named Jejeebhoy Dhunjeebhoy, and once inside they destroyed Japanese cabinets, chairs, tables, clocks, couches, silver lamps, rare glasses, family photos, and a Chinese box full of women's saris. They also broke into a small cabinet and stole several gold ornaments, hacked with clubs and iron hooks at pictures of Persian kings and heroes hanging high on the walls, and tore apart sacred writings and family heirlooms. What they couldn't carry they threw out the windows to waiting crowds who snatched eagerly at the silk and satin dresses fluttering down.[34]

In other streets, other depredations: the usual pattern was for armed gangs to invade a Parsi home, chase the women and children onto the roof, beat the men, destroy the furniture, rob gold and other valuables, and then run off to do it all again. One crowd invaded the fire temple in the Bhendy Bazaar. Another attacked buildings and homes belonging to Hindus, possibly by mistake. Most of these marauders, according to the police and the English press, were Arabs and Sidis, with perhaps a few Pathans among them—outsiders, in other words, migrants and seamen from the Middle East, Africa, and Central Asia.[35] It is difficult to know how accurate this picture is—people trying to defend the reputation of their city often blame such violence on strangers—but what happened over the next few days would seem to confirm that Sidis, at any rate, were prominent among these early rioters.

The worst was over by the time the police finally showed up. They quickly dispersed the rioters with truncheons, shot no one (for they had no guns to shoot), and made sixty-four arrests. The official list of wounded included eight Muslims and five Parsis (one of whom subsequently died), and the total cost of property damage and theft ran to roughly 30,000 rupees.[36] Although Souter would later dispute this point, the *Bombay Gazette* claimed that the riot had continued for two hours, from one to three in the afternoon, before the police arrived on the scene, presumably (it suggested) because of some lag in getting word of the riot from the "native" policemen who first witnessed it to their European officers, who then informed the central authorities.[37] The question of what had taken the police so long to quell the disturbance would linger, especially among the Parsis, for days and weeks to come.

Day 2: Saturday, February 14

The suddenness with which the attacks had broken out and the tardiness with which the police had responded threw many Parsis into a panic. One Parsi, looking over the destruction of the fire temple in the Bhendy Bazaar, reportedly said, "It was to avoid such treatment as this that we left Persia, and now are we to suffer like things as British subjects?"[38] On Saturday, beset by rumors of renewed Muslim violence, some Parsis began taking steps to defend themselves. As Donald Horowitz has observed, rumors of impending violence during a riot of this sort can "mobilize ordinary people to do what they would not ordinarily do," empowering "those proposing the most extreme action."[39] This, it seems, is precisely what happened among the normally peaceable Parsis. A witness writing to the *Times of India* from Calcutta nearly two weeks later described the atmosphere in the Parsi neighborhoods:

> Go where you would in Parsee quarters, you would but hear—"The police declared their inefficiency to protect us. We will protect ourselves, and henceforth we will see who dares to defile and plunder our hearths and homes." And true to these spirit-stirring, valour breathing words, the Parsees, as it were, by enchantment turned themselves into a military community in a few hours, and organized plans of defence that would do credit to any nation in the world. Defence funds were raised, and thousands of rupees were in a few hours collected. The wherewithal to fight, if necessity arose, were provided and furnished all round. Having thus arranged for accoutreing and equipping themselves, they stood on the defence at various places, and surely it would be no exaggeration to say that it was a refreshing sight to see their faces beaming with valour which welled up to defend their just cause.[40]

One might expect the state to have balked at this spirit of Parsi vigilantism, but that does not seem to have been the case. Indeed, if the Parsi sources are to be believed, the Bombay government positively encouraged them to take matters into their own hands. On Saturday afternoon a deputation of Parsi leaders called on the governor, Sir Philip Wodehouse, to ask him to call out the military and declare martial law, but he refused, urging the Parsis instead to organize their own defenses.[41] We have met Wodehouse before: he was the governor of British Guiana during the Angel Gabriel riots of 1856, and his experience there seems to have informed his response to what was happening in Bombay. The two events were, in fact, strikingly similar: in both cases a large community, regarded by many Britons as fanatical and half-savage, had risen up against an economically privileged minority whom the British saw as at least semicivilized. In Guiana the government had relied heavily on special constables, drawn from the European and East Asian populations on the plantations, to suppress the riots, and that is what Wodehouse now recommended to the Parsi delegation. "I cannot call the military into the town until I hear that the police are quite unable to cope with the rioters and suppress the riot," he told them. "The members of your community ought to learn the lesson of defending themselves from the rioters, and not to depend wholly on Government, but form themselves into what they call in England special constables." He also reportedly asked, more than once, "Are you Parsees quite unable to defend yourselves?"[42] This was not what the Parsis wanted to hear, and they only grew more outraged when Souter refused their subsequent request for military guards in their neighborhoods.[43]

In the short term, the governor's complacency appeared to be justified, for there was very little violence on Saturday, apart from a melee on the Falkland Road when police killed a Muslim weaver who was attacking Parsi homes.[44] The violence would resume the next day, however, and from a most unexpected quarter: "The Parsees," Souter later remarked, "had been regarded as a peaceable people, and it was never contemplated that they would act as they did."[45]

Day 3: Sunday, February 15

To make sense of what happened next, we need to leap forward a few days to look at what the Parsis would say in the immediate aftermath of the riots, once the inevitable swirl of recriminations had begun. Two themes would stand out in the Parsi riot accounts. First, they were severely disappointed in the government's response to the initial attacks. The Parsi newspaper *Bombay Samachar* expressed the general mood when it explained that Parsis "have now begun to think what should be done to make themselves independent of Government on occasions like these. They see their grand mistake in relying too much on Government."[46] Second, many Parsis, like many British observers, would come to blame the violence on inherent flaws in the Muslim character. One anonymous Parsi, borrowing a bit of British imperial vocabulary, wrote to the *Times of India* after the riots, "I make bold to state that one can never have a high opinion of Mahomedan veracity, and in my opinion, if the cant proverb 'the proverbial untruthfulness of an oriental' is applicable to any of the Asiatic races, it is to the Mahomedans chiefly."[47] Other Parsis, while insisting that not all Muslims were bad, nevertheless contemptuously described those who had rioted as "Mahomedan fanatics," or, as the *Bombay Samachar* put it, "plundering Mussulman loafers and their companions, the coward beggars and opium eaters."[48] Still other Parsis alleged that this was part of a broader pattern of Muslim disaffection. A Parsi styling himself "Coriolanus" wrote to the *Bombay Gazette* to warn the British of the folly of giving in to Muslim intolerance, for Muslims "still have a very poor opinion about the strength of British rule in India," and, if their violence were allowed to pass unpunished, "it requires no great foresight to predict a second mutiny, if only on a small scale."[49]

Given such attitudes about both the Muslims who had attacked them and the state that had abandoned them, it is hardly surprising that some Parsis (though probably not the majority) should seek revenge. They had their opportunity on Sunday when three large Muslim funeral parties paraded to the cemetery at Sonapore. The police accompanied the processions, which were larger than usual but mostly peaceful, but when the processions reached the graveyard a band of Parsis armed with bludgeons and stones charged the mourners. A detachment of Sidis rounded on the Parsis, and a great fight broke out. The police eventually managed to restore order and continue the ceremonies, but after the funerals another fight broke out when a group of Sidis, returning home under police escort, encountered a band of armed Parsis in the district of Breach Candy. More stones and bludgeons, more Parsi homes wrecked, and another dispersal by the police: at the end of the affray thirteen Muslims and seven Parsis lay injured, five of whom (four Muslims and one Parsi) would subsequently die. Now, at long last, Souter decided to call out the military.[50]

There were other fights around Bombay that Sunday, many of them initiated by Parsis. One Englishman told the *Bombay Gazette* that he had been taking his bath when he heard a noise from the street, and, looking out the window, he saw a Muslim post office worker accosted by a number of Parsis. The man had almost managed to escape when a well-dressed Parsi rushed out of his house and smote him with a big club.[51] Near the Fort a group of Parsis attacked and seriously wounded three Muslims, and another group attacked a police inspector named O'Connor outside a Parsi fire temple and nearly killed him.[52] James Maclean, editor of the *Bombay Gazette*, reported that he and a Muslim companion were nearly attacked by a band of bludgeon-wielding Parsis disguised as Muslims outside a fire temple. The Parsis "were quite in the mood to beat my Mussulman companion to death," Maclean recalled, before he and his friend made their escape under a hail of stones. When Maclean confronted Souter a little later about the apparent inactivity of the police, Souter replied, "Well, what am I to do? I am working night and day to keep the peace, but we have no police force. The Bench of Justices chose to cut down the strength of the European mounted police; half a dozen of whom would be of more use to me now than a hundred natives." Having affirmed the superiority of six Europeans on horses to a hundred Indians on foot, Souter went on to blame the Parsis for the day's violence.[53] Maclean, however, believed that Souter had it backward. From his conversations with Parsis, he believed that they were working under two distinct impressions. First, they believed the native policemen were mostly Muslims and therefore biased against them. Second, they believed that Souter himself had strong anti-Parsi prejudices and that this was affecting his handling of the riots.

To support the second allegation the Parsis to whom Maclean spoke told him a story that they would later relate to the India Office in a memorial signed by Byramjee Dadabhoy, registrar of Bombay, and several other prominent Parsis. As Souter was riding past Byramjee's house, so the story went, he saw all the Parsis in the neighborhood out on their verandas openly vowing revenge. Souter yelled at them, "Damn you Parsees, you have provoked this row. The Mussulmans were quite orderly, but you provoked the row." "But, sir," Byramjee responded, "one of our Parsees is killed." "I am very glad of it," Souter is supposed to have said, "and I should like to see all the Parsees killed, and I will tell the Governor not to help the Parsees, and I will remove all the police force." For his part Maclean believed this story, and, while allowing that Souter might have been speaking out of irritation rather than deep conviction, he still felt that the outburst had been "injudicious."[54]

Day 4: Monday, February 16

By Monday the editors of the English-language papers were beginning to worry that prolonged unrest might be sapping the state's authority. Criticizing the Bombay government for not calling out the military at once, the *Bombay Gazette* warned that "a very slight disturbance, if it be not at once put down with a strong hand, may quickly gain dimensions making it a serious danger to the State."[55] This was a typical attitude for nonofficial Europeans to take: frightened by any eruption of indigenous violence, the methods and motives of which they only vaguely understood, European communities in India (and elsewhere) often advocated swift and harsh repression lest the rioters turn their sights on them. Worried about the damage these riots were doing to the state's prestige, the *Indian Statesman* said, "The majesty of the law has already been set at too much defiance in the very head-quarters of Government, and unless Sir Philip

Wodehouse is prepared to abdicate in favour of King Mob, he must stretch out a strong hand upon the turbulent masses."[56] Far more was at stake here than the fates of a few Parsis and Muslims, according to this line of thinking: if the violence continued much longer, the state's very credibility might collapse.

As it happened, there was not much violence on Monday. In the morning a group of Muslim leaders met to discuss ways to calm their people, and they sent a delegation to the influential Parsi Jamsetjee Jejeebhoy to ask him to do the same among the Parsis.[57] As a result of this initiative a series of reconciliation meetings would take place over the next few days, but they mostly involved the leaders of the two groups and had little influence on the people doing the rioting.[58] Meanwhile, in the Crawford Market, a rumor went around that the Muslim butchers were poisoning the mutton, prompting Parsis to throw away large quantities of perfectly good meat; they even sent some meat samples to graduates of the Grant Medical College for chemical analysis. Fearing a renewed assault, and placing little faith in the authorities, many Parsis rushed to hide their valuables in the bank, others arranged to sleep in ships in the harbor rather than in their homes, and still others hired Europeans from the Sailors' Home to defend their property.[59] By this time well over a hundred Parsi families who lived near Muslim districts had relocated to the relative safety of the predominately Parsi Fort district, where they intended to stay with relatives and friends until the trouble subsided.[60]

Their fears were not without foundation. The biggest excitement of the day surrounded yet another Muslim funeral procession that almost descended, like the others, into violence. Hajee Ahmed, a native of Bombay—and not, like many of the wounded or killed rioters, a Sidi or Arab from overseas—had died in the Jamsetjee Jejeebhoy Hospital the previous day. He had been wounded during the Muslim funerals on Sunday, where, old and feeble as he was, he had probably gone not to riot but simply to mourn. His death caused great anger among Muslims who vowed to hold an even grander funeral procession for this new martyr, openly threatening to attack Parsis along the way. Rather than suppressing the funeral, however, Souter called on the newly arrived soldiers to accompany the procession, a task they performed with two artillery pieces in tow. It was, according to the *Gazette*, the grandest funeral ever seen in Bombay. Thousands of people gazed down from their windows and roofs as mourners and soldiers threaded their way through the narrow streets, bayonets gleaming, cannons rumbling, and officers (including Souter) jogging back and forth on horseback. Some of the skullcapped men carrying the bier bowed their heads in mourning, others shouted in anger, and many of the processionists danced and sang as chickens squawked and scrambled at their feet. A flicker of excitement shot through the crowd when some Parsis were spotted watching the procession from a rooftop, but the Parsis kept their peace, and soon the mourners were squeezing through the narrow cemetery gate to bury Ahmed in silence. When it was over the Muslims slowly dispersed, the Parsis came out of hiding, and the day, against all odds, resumed its peaceful course. On this occasion the *Gazette* credited Souter and the military with skillfully managing a potentially explosive situation.[61]

Aftermath

By Tuesday the excitement had begun to dissipate. After days of hesitation, Wodehouse finally telegraphed to Poona for more military assistance, and several hundred horsemen and infantry arrived to guard the trouble spots. The government also ordered the seafaring Sidis to stay on their ships, beating a drum to warn them against disembarking. One or two additional assaults took place on Tuesday, but nothing serious.[62] The big question now was whether to allow the Muharram processions, due to start on Wednesday, to proceed. This was a delicate question. On the one hand, to prohibit the processions would anger the many Muslim neighborhoods that planned to carry *tabuts*[63] in this, their biggest communal festival of the year. The Bombay government was aware of the danger, and may in fact have exaggerated the danger in its subsequent report to London when (in a rhetorical strategy common to other British riot narratives, as we saw in the previous chapter) it downplayed the religious meaning of Muharram and focused instead on its communal significance; Muharram in Bombay, the report claimed, was "more an exhibition of triumph than a ceremonial connected with religious worship" and as such was especially important to "the more ignorant Mahometans."[64] On the other hand, permitting the processions would further infuriate the Parsis and might set the stage for yet more violence. Souter, possibly stung by the Parsis' allegations against him, strongly recommended prohibiting the processions. The Bombay government agreed, issuing a prohibition on Tuesday night, the day before the processions were to begin.[65] Muslims were predictably outraged by what they saw as a violation of their religious liberty, and using language that might have come from the Protestant Orangemen of Ulster, a group of Muslim leaders sent a petition to Wodehouse complaining that "it would be extremely unfair to deprive the Mahomedan community of the exercise of one of their most valued religious rights, on account of the improper conduct of a very small portion of their community." Wodehouse, however, was unbending.[66]

If Wodehouse hoped to silence his critics with this stern new attitude, however, he promptly reversed course that evening. During a convocation address at the University of Bombay, after announcing (to great cheers) the government's firm line against Muharram processions, Wodehouse offered the following reflections on the extent of his powers during times of popular unrest. There was, he said,

> no simple and efficient and practical punishment which can be instantly applied to those creating riots in this city. I say further, that there is no power in the Legislature of this Government to provide, off-hand, full legal powers to do what is necessary on the spot for keeping down such disturbances. I believe prompt punishments to be of the essence of dealing with disturbances of this nature, but yet the means of bringing them about here is not in existence.[67]

What Wodehouse appears to have had in mind was the Code of Criminal Procedure, whose provisions allowing civilians to call out the military did not formally encompass Presidency Towns such as Bombay. But such legal hairsplitting was very much out of tune with the mood in the city, and immediately the English and Parsi press bombarded Wodehouse with ridicule and incredulity.[68] The *North-West Herald* called Wodehouse "a man of such slender character and attenuated mental calibre as to render it inexplicable how it came to pass that he was entrusted with the administration of an important province."[69] Most newspapers were more restrained, but they nevertheless insisted that the state did in fact have significant powers to suppress unrest, and that it had done so again and again in different parts of the country. The *Indian Statesman* summarized this line of argument in an editorial a few months later: "Executive power in India is fettered by none of the formalities prescribed by English law; and the fullest latitude is left to a Governor in making provision for public safety during an emergency."[70] Wodehouse, according to these critics, was tying his own hands by insisting on a fictive legality that nobody else in India bothered much about during an emergency. This, as we will see below, was an argument with which Wodehouse's superiors in Calcutta and London were in full agreement. In the short term, Wodehouse's critics needn't have worried. Muharram began on Wednesday, February 18, and, thanks largely to the military presence and the ban on processions, but also thanks to the peacekeeping efforts of Muslim and Parsi leaders, the city remained mostly quiet throughout the festival.[71] There was one brief clash near the Fort on Saturday when a group of Parsis attacked some Sidis on their way home from work, but on the whole it was a peaceful, if corseted, Muharram.[72]

All that were left now were the recriminations. No sooner had the first Parsi home been invaded than Parsis had begun asking (in the words of one) "Where—where—where are the police?"[73] Months later, many Parsis would still be singing this tune. Keenly aware of their rights as British subjects, the city's leading Parsis maintained (in a memorial sent to the authorities in London) that Souter's initial decision to confiscate Jalbhoy's book had violated "the principle of religious toleration and the right of free discussion" that British rule supposedly guaranteed.[74] Just like John Sayers Orr in Georgetown or the Protestants of Belfast—and, indeed, in terms very similar to those used by the outraged Muslims who opposed the suppressing of Muharram—the Parsis of Bombay took seriously Britain's promise of freedom of belief and expression. They were determined to force the state to live up to its own liberal ideals, for, from their perspective, not only had Souter acted unjustly in banning the book, but he had then failed to protect Parsi homes when the emboldened Muslims decided to press their advantage. In both respects, the Parsis maintained, their liberties as British subjects had been infringed.

Parsis were not the only ones critical of the government's handling of the riots; the newspapers, too, found plenty to criticize. One person, identified only as "Hermit," wrote to the *Englishman* on February 21 about the damage the riots would do to Britain's imperial reputation.

> The record of the disturbances, which has just disgraced our administration at Bombay, will ever remain as a dark blot on the history of British India, proclaiming to the world that the British have been unable to afford to a peaceful, industrious and well-behaved section of their Indian subjects, the same protection as they had, for so many centuries received from the native rulers who [preceded] us in the government of the country.[75]

The *Times of India* was also concerned about the Raj's image, reminding the authorities that "if Government were to exhibit the slightest weakness, it would be taken advantage of," not only in India but right across the empire. Indeed, too much public introspection on the part of the state—such as the formal inquiry that many Parsis were demanding—would also weaken the government's prestige. "It is not that we fear indulging in boldness of speech, but we endorse the doctrine that there is 'a time to be silent,' and in dealing with Asiatic politics, we ought never to forget that the imperial interests of England may at times be best served by a prudent reticence."[76] The less said about the state's failings, in other words, the better.

This did not keep others from piling on the abuse. While Wodehouse's infamous speech at Bombay University had made him the target of considerable ridicule, Souter attracted most of the venom from Parsis, Muslims, and the English press. His critics accused him of two principal failings: first, he had erred in suppressing Jalbhoy's book, and, second, he had been too slow to end the disturbances once they began. The first charge was in some ways the more serious, for it suggested that Souter was capitulating to Muslim intolerance and unable to protect free expression in the city. One person, styling himself as LEX, wrote to the *Bombay Gazette* to say that Souter's suppression of the book might have seemed like a wise measure at the time, "but a little reflection would have convinced Mr. Souter that he was doing the very thing he is bound above all others to abstain from, that is bringing the law into contempt." The book was either lawful or unlawful, LEX maintained: if lawful, Souter should never have suppressed it; if unlawful, the courts were there to hear the Muslims' complaints. Circumventing the law like Souter had done was a dangerous game, for it only made "these insolent and turbulent people more insolent and more turbulent."[77]

Underlying the second charge against Souter was a widespread belief that the Muslims had planned their attack against the Parsis and that Souter ought, therefore, to have anticipated it. "Can any sane man," asked FMB in the *Times of India*,

> believe that Mr. Souter—with all his experience, knowing well the riotous nature of these fanatics, also knowing, as a matter of fact, that in the very heart of the native town the storm had been brewing, that the residents in the neighbourhood were afraid of the outbreak … could be such a simpleton as to be misguided by outer appearances, and not to take the ordinary precaution of keeping a few mounted police in the very places where the disturbances were most dreaded?[78]

The Oriental made similar complaints, stating that the duty of a police commissioner "in an alien country like India" was to discover "the secret action of deep-lying forces which convulse society" and to respond accordingly.[79] Clearly there was some standard here to which Souter was not living up.

That standard had been set in large part by Souter's predecessor at the police office, Charles Forjett, whose daring exploits against the insurgents of 1857 were legendary.[80] Forjett had been born in India and knew some of its languages, and he was famous for periodically disguising himself as an Indian and mingling incognito among the people like a king slumming among peasants. During the Muharram of 1857, while Indian troops were mutinying in the north and rumors were circulating that the sepoys in Bombay were plotting the same thing, Forjett had disguised himself as a Muslim in order to listen for signs of disaffection. In the company of an Arab ally (who happened to be a Wahhabi) he snooped around the city's mosques and coffee houses, ears cocked, listening for treason. On hearing any seditious talk, he recalled in his memoir, "I immediately threw off my disguise and seized [the offender] on the spot; and such was the fear inspired by the police, and such the opinion in regard to its ubiquity, that though the number assembled was a hundred, or two hundred, or more, they immediately hastened away, leaving the man who was taken into custody to his fate."[81] In perhaps his most famous exploit, Forjett tortured and bribed one Gunga Pursad into allowing him and some other policemen to spy on some rebellious sepoys while they met at Pursad's house. Listening night after night through holes in the wall, Forjett gathered enough evidence to arrest and convict the ringleaders, six of whom were subsequently transported for life and two of whom were executed by being blown apart from the mouths of cannons on the Bombay Esplanade.[82]

Frank Souter was simply unable to live up to this man. Where Forjett had kept his ear to the ground (or wall) to catch the first tremors of disaffection, Souter had relied on spies to take the pulse of the Muslim neighborhoods, and they had failed. Where Forjett had ruthlessly punished Bombay's rowdies and did not flinch from overwhelming displays of violence, Souter had refused to call out the military until the worst of the fighting was over. The *Bombay Gazette*, which roundly abused Souter throughout the riots, attacked the beleaguered commissioner precisely on the grounds that he was not Forjett. What Bombay needed, the *Gazette* argued, was a police commissioner who could "foresee and prevent disturbances, and this is just what Mr. Souter cannot do. He has at least as numerous and well-drilled a force as Mr. Forjett had; but he cannot produce the same good results with it." Once a row was already under way, Souter could certainly be effective, delighted to "ride vigorously into the middle of a riotous mob and scatter them in all directions," but Bombay needed a man who could penetrate the secret world of the natives and stop trouble before it started, and this was beyond Souter's abilities.[83]

Meanwhile, Muslims had their own particular objections to how the riots had been policed. For them the riots were not a series of one-sided and unprovoked attacks by wicked Muslims upon innocent Parsis, but rather a series of battles in which both sides had committed excesses, the Parsis no less than the Muslims. And yet, as Muslim leaders wrote Wodehouse in "great surprise and astonishment," "good many of our caste people are in custody and none of the Parsees are arrested." They also, as we have seen, objected strongly to the ban on Muharram processions, which they regarded as a severe infringement of their religious liberty on a scale unseen for at least two hundred years.[84] Both sides, in other words, had grounds for accusing the police of failing to live up to the ideals of British liberalism, and both sides knew precisely the language in which to couch their complaints.

Souter responded to this near-universal abuse by deflecting the blame. His spies, he told the Bombay government in his official report, had strict instructions to listen for any mutterings of discontent among the Muslims, and they had reported none. The leaders of the Muslims had also assured him, after he rounded up every copy of Jalbhoy's book, that their people were mollified. Not only had the Muslim leaders not warned of any impending riot, he said, but no Parsi had come to him to express concern either—apart from a few of Jalbhoy's neighbors, who were worried that there might be some disturbance during Muharram. Even without such warnings, he continued, on the morning of the outbreak he sent spies to watch the Muslims at the Jama Masjid, but these spies also reported nothing; it was not until the riot was already under way that he knew something was wrong.[85] Yet Souter's exercise in self-exculpation was unlikely to appease his critics, for it still showed him as an essentially passive presence, sitting in the police office and receiving news from underlings and delegations, when the thrust of his critics' complaints was that he should have been more like Forjett, dying his moustache and donning a turban in order to go out and see things for himself. To this charge Souter offered no response.

While he refused to blame himself for what had happened, Souter also tried not to place too much of the blame on his own men. His detectives, he said, had done their work admirably, and his European policemen had been energetic and courageous. He had fewer good things to say about his Indian policemen, but he did manage to give them some faint praise. "To say that Native constables are not as intelligent, energetic, and self-reliant as would be desirable is merely to say that they are Natives," he told his superiors; yet despite that shortcoming, "they have behaved extremely well and followed their European leaders with considerable courage, and have been most steady and obedient."[86] The trouble, Souter felt, was not that he had poor policemen but that he didn't have enough of them. The blame for this—and, by extension, the blame for any inadequacy in the state's handling of the riots—lay with the presidency and municipal governments of Bombay, who had repeatedly refused his requests for more men and better barracks.[87]

The Indian government in Calcutta was not persuaded by Souter's arguments. Home Secretary Alfred C. Lyall, while allowing that Souter's actions were "well meant," judged his suppression of the book injudicious and said he should have reported the matter to his superiors. "Intemperate and fanatic men," Lyall said, invoking the well-worn stereotype of the fanatical Muslim, "are not always appeased by deference. We cannot undertake to lock up every book which the Mahomedans disapprove; nor would the Mahomedans for a moment consent to comply to a similar demand made on behalf of another sect against any of their polemical works."[88] Other Calcutta officials agreed, adding that Souter should also have done more in the riots' early stages to nip the problem in the bud, a notion that was well in line with the prevailing idea that the best way to forestall a riot was to make a deadly example of its early leaders.[89] We will explore this idea in some detail in the next chapter.

In a rearguard action probably designed to silence his critics, Souter eventually tried a bit of his own imaginative detective work to determine the extent to which the riots had been prearranged. About a month after the riots, he sent a letter to the influential Parsi Sir Jamsetjee Jejeebhoy telling him that he was forming a committee of influential Muslims, Parsis, "and perhaps a Hindoo or two" to visit all the Muslim riot prisoners and, in the presence of a police officer, question them about the origins of the riots. Did Sir Jamsetjee have any Parsis he could recommend for the committee? After consulting with other Parsi leaders Sir Jamsetjee decided not to take part in this plan, and in his response to Souter he lectured the police commissioner on the duties of his own office, telling him that such a committee would have no legal standing, would be ineffective, and would be performing a task that the police themselves ought to be doing. The *Bombay Gazette* was pitiless in its ridicule when it obtained the correspondence between Souter and Jejeebhoy on March 19: "Has Mr. Souter no friends able to restrain him from writing letters? We all know that in the saddle he is the doughtiest of cavaliers, but at the desk, whenever he sits down to put pen to paper, he seems fated to commit innumerable follies." Souter's plan, the *Gazette* said, was sheer idiocy. "If Mr. Souter is really such a simpleton as to imagine that the truth about conspiracies can be found out in this easy way, we need no longer be surprised at anything that may happen in Bombay." Once again raising the bar well above Souter's head, the *Gazette* argued that Sir Charles Forjett would have ferretted out the Muslim agitators before the riots even happened, "and he would also have ascertained if money as well as fanaticism was not brought into use by the conspirators; but it never seems to have entered Mr. Souter's head that he should pursue his own independent inquiries instead of resting satisfied with the comforting assurances of respectable Mahommedans that all would be well."[90] In the end, both Souter and Wodehouse told their superiors that there had almost certainly been no conspiracy to riot, since they had found no evidence to that effect.[91] Many Parsis believed otherwise, and after the riots they formed a committee that forwarded to London several statements from Parsis who said they had been warned the night before that an attack was coming.[92]

The final word, of course, belonged to the government in London, and from those heights the whole thing looked much less complex than it did on the ground. Apart from the official reports from India (which were published at the command of the House of Commons), the authorities in London learned much of what they knew about the Bombay riots from the press, which carried telegraphic reports direct from the subcontinent, sometimes polished with a little editorial gloss. Most British newspapers explained the violence as a simple matter of clashing "races," blaming not government mismanagement or the extremism of individuals but rather the character defects of the rioters themselves. Most papers preferred to blame the Muslims, who, according to the *Pall Mall Gazette*, were "always an arrogant and aggressive sect, lately heated by revivalist ideas" and "unable to endure the notion of being scoffed at by the worshippers of fire." The *Glasgow Herald* said Muslims were an "inflammable race" but that, nevertheless, they had some legitimate grievances, like Irish Catholics, to which the British government should attend.[93] The Parsis, meanwhile, were (according to the *Times*) culturally much like the Bengalis, or "some say the Jews," while the *Daily News* praised them as "a most intelligent, enterprising, and progressive element in the population."[94] To the British press it was quite clear, given these racial characteristics, who were the predators and who were the prey in this affair.

This simplified narrative led to the logical conclusion that the necessary stance of the government was to project an image of firmness and impartiality. Expanding upon its Irish analogy, the *Glasgow Herald* worried that Wodehouse's reluctance to call out the troops would be taken as a sign of weakness.

> What would be said of the magistrate of an Irish town who, in answer to a request for protection by Orangemen or Roman Catholics, should tell them to fight for their creeds? No doubt, the advice would be very Irish, but as certainly it would be contrary to our ideas of what should be done under the circumstances by an impartial administrator of justice, to whom races and creeds should be nothing, and order everything.[95]

The *Northern Echo* was slightly more tentative. Drawing a comparison with the Murphy Riots in England, a series of anti-Catholic pogroms stoked by an evangelical preacher, which had ended just a few years earlier, the Darlington newspaper wrote,

> It will be a great temptation to the sorely-pressed governors of our dependencies to imitate the example set them at home, and as our magistrates gagged Murphy because the Catholics would have broken the law if he spoke, so they may wish to suppress all books which can be taken as a pretext for a Moslem riot or a Hindoo tumult. The temptation, however great, must be resisted; the evil precedent must not be followed.

However, the paper continued, Britain's imperial rulers must remember that their first duty was, "first of all, to maintain order; and then to preserve unimpaired the freedom of the press."[96] Order, most British papers agreed, was the most important thing, and if the state had to be a little heavy-handed in preserving it, then so be it.

This certainly was the attitude of the man whose opinion mattered most in Britain. Lord Salisbury was the secretary of state for India and the man to whom Souter, Wodehouse, and the central government at Calcutta were ultimately responsible. In the words of Andrew Roberts, Salisbury at the India Office "saw fear, awe and respect for the law as the key to British rule."[97] In this, Salisbury differed little from most Conservatives in Britain and most Europeans in India. As an example of this attitude, Roberts cites an 1874 letter from Salisbury to Lord Northbrook, the Liberal viceroy with whom he often butted heads: "We are often told to secure ourselves by their affections, not by force. Our great-grandchildren may be privileged to do it, but not we." The following year Salisbury would tell Wodehouse (in an unrelated discussion), "India is held by the sword, and its rulers must in all essentials be guided by the maxims which befit the government of the sword."[98] Such sentiments echoed much of what the British press was saying about the riots in Bombay: abstract principles like freedom of religion were all well and good, but in the final analysis it was the sword, not the constitution, that would guarantee Britain's supremacy in India.

It was only to be expected, then, that Salisbury should have found fault with the Bombay government's shambolic response to the riots. Wodehouse, in his report to the Indian government in Calcutta, had repeated the argument he made at Bombay University that he could not bring out the military until it had been shown that the police were unable to cope with the disturbances, and "in no single instance in these riots was it found that the police could not master the rioters as soon as they acted in a body against them."[99] Calcutta had disagreed, arguing that the military should be used as soon as a serious riot seemed imminent, especially given "the character of the population which composes many of our Indian cities" and "the political danger of any appearance of inability on the part of the executive Government to put down a disturbance."[100] Salisbury was of the same mind, and his pronouncement on the matter is a classic expression of the Conservative attitude toward India, particularly in its assumptions about the differences between India and England:

> I must express the distinct dissent of Her Majesty's Government from the view thus taken of their duty by the Government of Bombay [i.e., Wodehouse]. In England, military force is only used for the repression of civil disturbances in the last resort. This usage has its origin and its justification in political circumstances peculiar to England. It is wholly inapplicable to India. There is nothing distasteful to Indian feelings in the employment of troops for the maintenance of order. The nature of Indian institutions, the excitable character of the people, and the many causes of conflict which are supplied to them by diversities of race and creed, impose upon every Indian Government a special obligation to repress with an unfaltering hand the first beginnings of disorder.[101]

To Salisbury the excitability of the Indian people and the fragility of British rule meant that riots must be put down immediately, with jackboots and bayonets, cannons and cavalry, not knock-kneed natives clutching sticks. To show weakness in such circumstances was to court disaster. This was a judgment with which the Indian government agreed, informing Wodehouse that, while there was no "substantial distinction" between the laws of England and India, there was a

> real and substantial distinction between the social and political circumstances of the two countries, which should induce those in authority to apply the law differently, and which render it expedient to resort to Military force in India more readily than in England.[102]

Uniform rules, in other words, need not entail uniform execution. One could hardly ask for a better demonstration of the paradox at the heart of Britain's liberal imperium.

In the matter of Frank Souter, meanwhile, Salisbury turned out to be surprisingly forgiving. He did not fault Souter for suppressing Jalbhoy's book (the publication of which he deemed "indefensible"), but he did criticize his failure to take early preventive measures against disturbances. Still, once the rioting began, Souter had shown himself a "vigorous and resolute officer" who displayed "the conspicuous gallantry which he has always evinced throughout his official career."[103] Gallantry and vigor were the sorts of things Salisbury could admire in an officer, and these, everyone agreed, were qualities Souter had in abundance. It was the caution and discretion of Wodehouse that Salisbury (and Wodehouse's many Anglo-Indian critics) found so troubling; such scrupulous legalism could only backfire in a place like India. Bolstered by Salisbury's endorsement, Souter would remain in his post until 1884 (outlasting the aging Wodehouse by seven years), and after his death the city honored him with a marble bust in the hall of the Bombay municipal council.[104]

Rather than leave the last word with Salisbury, however, I would like to close with a response to Salisbury (and, by implication, to the government of India) that appeared in the *Times of India* in August 1874. The *Times* had frequently criticized Wodehouse for his timidity and Souter for his complacency, but now it offered a subtle and penetrating rebuttal of Salisbury's jackboot doctrine, and, in the process, it put its finger on one of the chief difficulties of governing an empire like Britain's. In England, the newspaper said, magistrates could call out the military from time to time without undermining respect for the civil authorities, because the English people recognized the law as the law, "whether its agents dressed in blue or red." In India, however, the state's foundations were much shakier.

> If we accustom the people to the action of the military as the one resource of the Government for dealing with rioters, it will be found impossible to restrain them when a war, or a camp of exercise, or any accident, deprives the authorities of the actual presence of troops. There will be peace while it is known that soldiers are at hand to enforce peace; when it is known that the soldiers are not at hand there will be disturbance.

In terms reminiscent of General Sandhurst's recommendations for Belfast in 1872, this writer maintained that Britain needed to train Indians to accept civil, not just military, authority; otherwise they would come "to regard law and Government as non-existent" in the absence of actual soldiers. If that happened, India would become like certain continental European nations, where soldiers were routinely used to maintain order and the police were regarded "as little other than spies." This system of military repression might work for a while, "until some day the troops are sent to the frontier, when a revolution breaks out as a matter of course."[105] What the author was arguing, in essence, was that the civil state needed to do a better job of cultivating its legitimacy in India; a "government of the sword" could only hold the country for so long. However embarrassing the riots had been for the local authorities, however much the violence had damaged the state's prestige, the thing to do was to strengthen the civil power, not to sound the bugles and charge the cannons at the first tremor of unrest. This prescient warning, however, seems to have fallen on deaf ears.

6

Policing: How Cultural Assumptions Guided the Policing of Communal Riots

As the postriot discussion in Bombay in 1874 demonstrated, how the British state policed communal riots depended, to a large extent, on what British officials thought about the people they were policing. Whenever a riot broke out, their top priority was to restore order, but how they did that was determined by their ideas about the communities involved and their theories about the basis of the imperial state's power. Riots require police officials to make innumerable minute decisions—about using firearms, liaising with local leaders, requesting military support, protecting bystanders, protecting property, distributing manpower, assigning procession routes, and so forth—all of which guide a riot in its unique direction. Those decisions are often made on the basis of clearheaded tactical assessments, but they are never free from cultural assumptions or political predispositions. A riot among a familiar people, speaking a familiar language and acting in a predictable way in pursuit of identifiable aims, is very different from a riot in an alien environment where few or none of these conditions exist. The latter situation was where British colonial policemen normally found themselves when communal violence was brewing.

One would therefore expect British policing practices to vary from place to place and to deviate especially far from policing practices at home—the more alien the rioters, the less likely they were to be policed like Britons—and so indeed they did. But they were not policed as differently as we might expect, for across the British Empire (and this was true well beyond public-order policing) there existed something like a uniform set of standards by which all British policemen were to abide. As the state's most visible representatives, policemen had to embody the dignity, justice, and impartiality of the ruling race (even, or perhaps especially, when policemen were "natives"), and this meant following rules laid down by men who already knew what a rule-bound police force was supposed to look like, since that was what they had at home. At a minimum, the police were to be bound by the rule of law—which was, after all, one of the great rhetorical pillars of Britain's liberal imperium.[1] This is not to say that colonial policemen never broke the rules, but simply to say that there were rules for them to break, and that these rules were derived from Britain's own historical experiences and principles. In form, if not in function, the colonial police were to be as British as they could manage to be, even in the most un-British environments.

The striking thing about the policing of communal violence in the empire, as this chapter will demonstrate, is how this uniformity of principle nevertheless produced a great divergence of practice. To examine this phenomenon I will investigate the chief public-order policing tactics that British forces had in their repertoire, which I have grouped into three categories (prevention, quelling, and punishment) that cover the life span of most riots. The uniformity of British policing principles will be most evident in the sections on quelling riots, but the other sections will reveal a similarly uniform set of norms and expectations. They will also reveal how, as in most aspects of empire, local realities—including the cultural attitudes police officials brought to their duties—could derail the universalist aspirations of Britain's civilizing mission.

Preventive action

The fundamental principle guiding all British riot policing was that state agents must act as impartial guardians of law and order, showing neither special favor nor special antipathy toward any faction or community. For this reason officials often became mediators in communal disputes, working to ease tensions before they caused open conflicts. The closer officials were to the people, the better they were able to prevent violence by meeting with communal leaders, negotiating disputed procession routes, and generally adopting the same balance-of-powers techniques that governed British diplomacy in Europe. This enterprise met with varying degrees of success, but the idea of the state as neutral arbiter remained a vital component of Britain's imperial self-image.[2]

Preventive mediation was only possible, of course, when violence was anticipated in advance. This was most often the case with processions, festivals, and other prearranged communal displays, and so it was in these areas that the state was most active. In places with frequent processions, such as the north of Ireland, parts of India, and Caribbean islands such as Trinidad, policemen and magistrates spent countless hours charting acceptable routes, regulating schedules, and defining appropriate visual and aural components of processions. Music (especially when played by Hindu processions near mosques) was a source of particular tension; the usual compromise, whereby musicians would cease making music when passing near houses of worship, was effective enough during times of general peace, but when some larger controversy was simmering, the police could not always trust in the forbearance of musicians or bystanders. On these occasions officials might prohibit processions outright, but the usual practice, even during contentious periods, was to defer to established custom, or what was known in India as "customary usage." If things had "always been done this way," then, invoking the principle of religious noninterference, the state would generally defer to that tradition and hold those who sought to interfere with the tradition responsible for any breach of the peace.

The difficulties attaching to the regulation of communal displays were numerous and inescapable. For one thing, as Katherine Prior has said about India's North-West Provinces, what exactly constituted "customary usage" was open to multiple interpretations, and British understandings of local history and customs were usually flawed or incomplete. This meant that, far from settling communal disputes, the British insistence on upholding customary practices simply provided a vocabulary through which each side could articulate, and sometimes fight out, their conflicting claims.[3] Second, blanket bans on communal displays, such as the one imposed on Ireland from 1850 to 1872, were often unenforceable (leading people to question the power of the state), susceptible to the perception of unfair dealing (thereby damaging the state's reputation for impartiality), and, even when successful, likely to channel communal energies into other, equally damaging paths (as when Irish Catholics managed to hold processions that fit within the letter, but not the spirit, of the law). Third, policemen intervening in local disputes often found it very hard to avoid the appearance of favoring one side over the other; some disputes were simply not amenable to compromise, whatever the intentions of the state, and often one party came away feeling injured when it did not get its way. In a study of British interference with musical processions in Ceylon, Michael Roberts has shown how antinoise regulations, enacted to prevent religious processions from disturbing nonparticipants, fell harder on Sinhalese Buddhists than on Muslims or Catholics, despite the neutrality of the laws' language. This was because the variety of religious expression that the regulations declared objectionable—that is, noisy processions—was an activity that only one part of the community (i.e., the Buddhists) engaged in. Buddhists therefore felt ill-used by the state, restricted in their own religious devotions while other communities seemingly faced no corresponding constraints, even as the state continued to adhere formally to its doctrine of religious neutrality.[4]

It was a similar story elsewhere. We have already seen how Irish Protestants regarded the enforcement of the Party Processions Act to be one-sided, since it prohibited their Orange processions without stopping Catholics from conducting religious or municipal processions that were every bit as partisan; even though Parliament eventually repealed the ban, it could not so easily suppress the Protestant anger and suspicion that the ban had aroused. We have also seen how the state's handling (or mishandling) of processions in southern India contributed to the Salem riots of 1882, which greatly shook local confidence in officials' impartiality. Another example, this one from northern India, makes the point even more clearly. In the mid-1860s a classic "music-before-mosques" dispute broke out in Hooghly, Bengal, following the completion of a new mosque and imambara along a traditional Hindu procession route. Clashes in 1863 and 1864 led the local government to ban music in front of the mosque, with the lieutenant governor, Sir Cecil Beadon, publicly expressing his objection to "the votaries of one religion noisily and obstrusively parading their ceremonies" and criticizing Hindu marriage processions (the principal occasions for the clashes) as "unseemly demonstrations."[5] Local Hindus complained to the viceroy that the ban, and Beadon's attitude, violated the 1858 proclamation of religious neutrality and, by extension, their own religious freedom. The Hindus were quite specific on these points: their memorial to the viceroy not only invoked the 1858 proclamation but also the "right of way over all public roads and thoroughfares" as well as the principle of customary usage. They also argued that their own religious freedom was bound up with that of others: interference in the activities of one community may affect "the Hindoos in one place, the Mahomedans in another, the Christians or the Jews in a third place."[6] For his part, Beadon insisted that the ban "was issued simply with a view to preserve the peace, an object equally to the interest of all classes and creeds," thereby failing to recognize that an antimusic ordinance must inevitably fall harder on Hindus, for whom music is a central component of religious observance, than on Muslims, for whom it normally is not.[7] Beadon seems eventually to have upheld the ban, but not before the state's reputation for fairness had been tarnished among many Hindus, and of course the question of what to do when new buildings challenged customary usages remained largely unanswered.[8]

Processions and other public displays were also a source of contention in the West Indies, and here, as elsewhere, police efforts to regulate the use of public space often exposed them to charges of bias. In 1860, for instance, a letter to the

British Guiana newspaper *The Creole* complained that the Georgetown police were stopping Creoles from playing music in the streets while Portuguese musicians were left alone—a petty, if telling, instance of the zero-sum-game of communal politics.[9] Much more serious was the 1884 Hosay Massacre in Trinidad, by far the deadliest preemptive strike against communal displays anywhere in the Victorian Empire. It occurred during Muharram—known locally as "Hosay," after the shouts of "Hussain!" that accompanied it—when several processions of East Indians and Afro-Trinidadians tried to enter the town of San Fernando despite being forbidden to do so. The ban on entering San Fernando (and other towns) had been enacted because of the rowdiness that often attended Hosay, although what worried the authorities in this case was not the prospect of violence between communities but rather the possibility that Hindu and Muslim Indians might join up with Afro-Trinidadians in an intoxicated frenzy that could turn anti-British. When the processionists outside San Fernando refused to turn back, the police opened fire, killing ten people on the spot, mortally wounding another twelve, and injuring many dozens more.[10] Despite the fact that, as historian Prabhu P. Mohapatra wryly observes, "the maximum penalty for [violating the ban] was six months imprisonment, not summary execution," a state inquiry found the killings to have been justified.[11] State violence on this scale was utterly unknown in the policing of British, Irish, or even South Asian processions.[12]

Another sort of preventive action undertaken by policemen throughout the empire was to work with community leaders—priests, imams, teachers, employers, and so on—to defuse tensions before violence broke out.[13] This was a popular tactic not only because it helped extend the reach of outnumbered officials but also because it fit British notions about the hierarchical nature of "native" societies.[14] Whenever possible, British officials preferred to work with clearly identifiable agents, men with names and status and "natural" authority, who could speak to, and sometimes for, the faceless mob. During moments of communal crisis street preachers in Belfast, imams in Bombay, and priests in Colombo were all liable to be summoned to police offices or governors' quarters and asked to carry messages from the rulers to their people. On some extraordinary occasions, as in India's North-West Provinces in the turbulent 1890s, the state even appointed local headmen to report on incipient disturbances.[15] When they managed to quiet tensions, as the Catholic priests of Belfast did for most of the summer of 1886, such intermediaries might win laurels for their moderating influence.[16] When they failed, however—and they often failed because they had less influence than the British supposed—then local leaders might take the blame. Thus Lord Palmerston blamed Catholic priests for inciting violence against street preachers in Ireland in 1853, the *Times of India* argued that Muslim leaders should have done more to quell the Bombay riots of 1874, and Ceylon's Governor Longden suspected "native priests" of stoking Catholic intolerance in Colombo in 1883.[17] At other times, however, British officials saw popular violence as the result of the "wrong" leaders having more influence over the people than their "natural" leaders did.[18] This hierarchical conception of the causes of mass violence—in which the actions of the "fanatical" masses were supposedly traceable to the influence of communal leaders—helps to explain the British obsession with identifying, punishing, and sometimes even shooting "ringleaders" and "agitators" during a riot, while rank-and-file rioters might—as in Guiana in 1856—get a free pass. Blind, gullible fanatics could only be partly responsible for their actions, after all, whereas the leaders who goaded them to violence, or who failed to restrain their fanaticism, were much easier to identify and hold accountable.

Quelling riots: minimum force, theory and practice

As with preventive action, decisions about how to stop riots once they started were also inflected by the cultural, racial, and even class assumptions of the officials in charge. One area in which this was apparent was in discussions about the level of physical force that should be used to put down a riot. Should overwhelming displays of firepower—armed policemen, horses, soldiers, perhaps even artillery—be employed to disperse rioters, or were subtler measures more appropriate? As a general rule, the weaker the state's "soft power," or legitimacy, the more it relied on massive displays of force to restore order. Different groups had differing ideas about the wisdom of displaying overwhelming force, of course. Often it was the mouthpieces of middle-class, settler, or loyalist opinion that were the loudest in calling for massive displays of force, partly because they feared for their own persons and property, and partly because of the contempt they felt for the turbulent masses. Newspapers, in particular, put considerable pressure on officials who might otherwise have acted with restraint to use lethal violence against rioters. During the 1857 Belfast riots, for instance, newspapers repeatedly accused the authorities of not doing enough to quell the violence, none more vividly than the Whiggish *Belfast Daily Mercury*, which insisted, "The law is strong enough to put down rabble violence—and it must be put down—shot down—exterminated, if necessary, for the peace of society is not to be disturbed and endangered by giving an impunity to the scum of Belfast ruffianism."[19] When another riot threatened Belfast the following year, the new chief secretary, Lord Naas (later to become viceroy of India as Lord Mayo), decided to take no chances. At the first sign of trouble he ordered a regiment of cavalry and a regiment of infantry to Belfast and ordered that "[c]avalry should alone be used in clearing the streets," an impractical and heavy-handed measure that was usually avoided during other Irish (and British) riots.[20] Heavy-handed they may have been, but these military displays pleased the press: the *Belfast Morning News* remarked approvingly, "Wherever one moved, he saw a body of police; and in High Street the presence of the infantry with grounded arms, and the dragoons moving up and down to keep the horses in exercise, conveyed a salutary lesson to one class of the inhabitants, and gave assurance to another that the town was not, for another night, to be overrun by gangs of any class."[21] Similarly impractical, but no less impressive, were the two artillery pieces that accompanied 1,300 soldiers through the Belfast streets in 1864, to say nothing of the naval vessels and cannons deployed to Bombay to 1893, about which I will say more in the next chapter.[22] In contrast, during the turbulent year of 1848, when many British authorities feared a revolution at home, policemen in Ayrshire, Scotland, deemed a mere fifty-nine cavalrymen sufficient to disperse a dangerous Orange parade, a number that a subsequent report suggested was unusually high.[23]

Demonstrations of overwhelming force had little practical value in dispersing rioters—indeed, they could even be counterproductive, insofar as they alerted people that a serious row was brewing—but their psychological impact was considerable, or so many officials and journalists believed. These displays sent the message that the state was taking an outbreak seriously and that it had the means to impose its will, even if this required massive death and destruction. The purpose, in other words, was deterrence, and the readiness with which officials resorted to such measures depended on their own evaluation of the fragility of the state's power—the more fragile the state, the more necessary such displays were felt to be—and on their attitudes toward the people doing the rioting. In most colonies the conventional wisdom about imperial subjects was that they only respected governments that ruled with strength and determination, that it was in the nature of Indians or Irish or blacks to act turbulently unless restrained by a state powerful enough to earn their respect. Lord Minto, viceroy of India in 1908, expressed the prevailing sentiment there when he told the India secretary, "government by the strong hand is what appeals to the majority of the different populations of this country."[24] Minto would presumably have agreed with Sir Charles Crosthwaite, lieutenant governor of the North-West Provinces, who in 1893 yearned for the days when "the Governor General was looked upon as a supreme authority second only to the Almighty."[25] This was the rule-by-bluster school of imperial power, and not all officials subscribed to it. During riots in Calcutta in 1891, for instance, Police Commissioner J. Lambert made a deliberate decision not to call attention to the troops he had requested to quell the unrest, choosing instead to post soldiers by a canal and cavalrymen in side streets during a contentious religious procession so that they "might attract as little attention as possible."[26] Such circumspection seems to have been relatively rare, however.

Of far more practical utility than overwhelming displays of force was the simple expedient of shooting at rioters. This tactic was the most controversial, and the most commented upon, arrow in the state's quiver, and it highlighted like no other the tension between the liberal impulse to earn the trust of the people and the authoritarian impulse to preserve order at all costs. To understand this tension we must understand the rules and expectations—formulated, in large part, in Britain itself—under which imperial police forces were operating.[27] Throughout Britain and the empire there were three basic rules, set out in policing manuals, judicial decisions, and parliamentary committee reports, governing the use of lethal force during riots.[28] First, lethal force could only be used as a last resort, after all other means of dispersing a violent crowd had been tried. As an 1837 Irish police manual put it, constables were expected to "observe the utmost forbearance that humanity combined with prudence can dictate, before incurring the awful as well as legal responsibility of firing upon the people, a measure which should never be resorted to until the very last extremity."[29] Second, the decision to use lethal force had to be made by a responsible magistrate or police head; individual policemen and soldiers could not fire without orders. Third, the force had to be the minimum necessary to disperse a violent crowd. Excessive or wanton violence was strictly forbidden. Other rules—that rioters must be warned before opening fire; that live rounds, not blanks, should be used to disperse rioters; and that state forces were always permitted to fire in self-defense—were also fairly consistent across the empire.

The most important principle was the rule of "minimum force," that is, the requirement that the force used to disperse a violent crowd had to be no more than was strictly necessary to stop the violence. This principle was rooted in the British tradition of resistance to state tyranny, but its legislative origins are somewhat complex. The foundation stone of British public-order policing, the Riot Act of 1715, was designed not to restrain the police but to empower them to use whatever force they thought necessary in dispersing riots.[30] According to this law any gathering of twelve or more people that refused to disperse after the Riot Act had been read (by a magistrate, mayor, sheriff, or sub-sheriff) became a felonious gathering after one hour, and its members became eligible for the harshest punishment, which, in the eighteenth century and much of the nineteenth, was death. Under the Riot Act, soldiers and policemen had the power to suppress riots with considerable brutality, as they did, for instance, during the Gordon Riots of 1780, when the military killed 285 London rioters and sent 173 to hospital, after which the hangman dispatched another 25.[31] In a famous statement following the Bristol riots of 1831, Lord Chief Justice Tindal explained that, under common law, a magistrate did not even have to wait an hour before dispersing an unlawful assembly if persons or property were in immediate danger. In order to stop a riot in its first stages the military could, and in many cases should, open fire at once. "The beginning of tumult," Tindal explained, "is like the letting out of water; if not stopped at first, it becomes difficult to do so afterwards; it rises and increases, until it overwhelms the fairest and most valuable works of man."[32] Under statutory as well as common law, then, killing rioters need not be a last resort, but might instead be a wise first step in stopping a rising tide of violence.

Over the course of the nineteenth century, however, the British public became less tolerant of lethal state violence. Partly because of the infamous Peterloo Massacre of 1819 (when state forces killed eleven unarmed people at a reform rally in Manchester), and partly because of growing democratization and press scrutiny, the authoritarian violence embedded in the Riot Act and common law gave way to a growing insistence on restraint, at least domestically. Peterloo and subsequent episodes of state violence were highly problematic for the government and the elite classes generally, for they galvanized reform movements, inspired labor unrest, and generally led to the sort of popular outcry that Britain's rulers thought it wise to avoid. "It was not philanthropy," writes David Philips of this period, "but fear of another Peterloo, which led the authorities to keep the armed forces under fairly tight control in cases of internal disorder."[33] Scrutinized by the public as never before, magistrates, police captains, and military commanders in the Victorian era often erred on the side of permissiveness when policing large crowds in Britain, lest any heavy-handedness bring cause for rebuke. This was the case in spite of continued official pronouncements that (as an 1867 Home Office memorandum put it) state forces were justified in "using any degree of Force" to disperse rioters or prevent acts of felony.[34] The balance was often a difficult one to maintain—sometimes permissiveness could look like weakness when things went wrong in one direction, and firmness could look like tyranny when things went wrong in the other—but it was a balance that officials in Britain worked earnestly to maintain, often with considerable success.[35]

This balancing act between repression and restraint was part of what Charles Townshend has called the "British way" of policing popular disturbances.[36] Another component of the "British way" was the state's steadfast refusal to create universal guidelines governing the use of lethal force, beyond the basic requirement that state forces must use no more, and no less, lethal force than was absolutely necessary to end a disturbance. Discretion about the use of force lay entirely with the leading official on the spot, and, while prior to a disturbance he might search in vain for clear official guidance about when to use lethal force, he could be prosecuted if it was subsequently felt that during the disturbance he had violated the principle of minimum force. It was an unenviable position in which to find oneself, made all the more difficult by the fact that official directives in these matters were not only vague but sometimes actually working at cross-purposes. Thus the imperative underlying Tindal's 1831 Bristol ruling—that riotous crowds ought to be dispersed with deadly force at once—sat uneasily with an 1887 Home Office memo that doubted whether an early display of force was always the most appropriate way to disperse a crowd, noting that "'Dispersing' an unlawful assembly is, in practice, a very difficult thing to accomplish, for persons once assembled cannot be dispersed (like a flock of birds) by a shout or clap of the hands."[37] Which of these legally sanctioned procedures was the right one to follow?

Two parliamentary inquiries, one into shootings at a colliery in Featherstone in 1893 and the other into a military shooting during a Belfast police strike in 1907, pointedly refused to clarify matters. The former simply affirmed that firing upon crowds was sometimes necessary to prevent or stop serious crimes and insisted that such firing must "be conducted without recklessness or negligence." The latter, asserting that full responsibility rested with the leading official on the scene, bluntly declared, "it is not possible nor even desirable to attempt to regulate that responsibility more clearly."[38] As Townshend says, "The result of these investigations was not to tighten up the rules governing the use of military force to preserve public order. Rather it was to stress that the very imprecision of the rules, so disturbing to soldiers, was part of the British way. Vagueness was a barrier against despotism."[39] Townshend is speaking here about the rules governing the military in Britain, but his observation is equally valid with respect to colonial policemen.

All of the elements of this British way of policing unrest—the minimum force rule, the legal responsibility that attached to the leading man on the spot, the carefully maintained vagueness about when and where lethal force could be used—found their way into the theory, if not always the practice, of imperial policing. A 1909 circular distributed to police forces in Bengal nicely summarizes the riot-control regulations that were in place across most of India by this time:

> It is of course well understood that the order to fire should only be given in the last resort, when it is impossible to disperse the mob by any other means; but when the order is given, the firing should be at once effective, and must be such as, with the minimum of injury, to convince the crowd of the necessity of immediately dispersing.[40]

The congruence with domestic British regulations was probably strongest in Ireland, where the semi-military Royal Irish Constabulary was subject to many of the same rules governing the military in Britain. The regulations handbook used by the RIC for much of the 1880s and 1890s, for instance, drew its riot-control regulations entirely from British common and statutory law (including the Riot Act), making it quite clear that Irish riots were to be policed like British riots.[41] Conversely, sometimes Irish violence became the occasion for articulating riot-control regulations for the entire UK. This happened after the 1907 Belfast police strike, when a parliamentary committee affirmed that the military must only ever be used as a last resort when suppressing unrest—not only in Ireland, but anywhere in the United Kingdom.[42]

Another sign that the expectations governing the policing of the colonies were essentially the same as in Britain was the frequency with which state bodies investigated major episodes of police violence to assess whether the police had acted with restraint. Since most of these investigations relied heavily on the testimony of the leading man on the spot, officials usually got the assurances they were seeking. An official report following a riot at Bareilly, North-West Provinces, in 1871, was typical:

> After great forbearance, and attempting by every means in his power to disperse the mob … the Magistrate brought up a reserve of eight Police, and ordered four to fire. Six of the rioters were wounded, and the mob dispersed. The coolness and determination of the two English Officers prevailed, and no second volley was required.[43]

The archives are full of such reports, praising the "steadiness" and "reserve" of state forces in the face of intense "provocation" from hostile crowds. In these reports the decision to fire is always given only after all other methods have been exhausted, and the force used is always the minimum necessary to disperse the crowds. We may doubt whether these official explanations of state violence, often drawn solely from the testimony of policemen on the scene, accurately reflect what happened, but there is little doubt that there was at least a formal commitment on the part of colonial officials to police riots with restraint.[44] Unsurprisingly, many policemen bucked at this insistence on "minimum force;" one former policeman bitterly recalled "the inevitable post-mortem" that occurred after shots had been fired, when "authority in its wisdom when considering the affair in comfort and peace, might think that excessive force was used."[45] Indeed, despite the tendency to whitewash these episodes, on rare occasions state inquiries might actually result in punishment for individual policemen. This happened in 1886 when eight members of the RIC were convicted of murder after repeatedly firing into crowds during a summer of rioting in Belfast.[46]

The uniformity of these norms did not mean that policing (even ordinary, everyday policing) was conducted in the same way in the empire as it was in Britain, of course, or that the imperial police were always subject to the same constraints as their metropolitan cousins. In Britain policing was a local affair, with each county and borough maintaining its own unarmed force and receiving very little in the way of guidance or assistance from London.[47] Nearly all of Ireland, by contrast, was policed by a single force, the RIC, which was heavily armed, lived in barracks, conducted military-style drills, and was generally more suited to combating insurgents than catching criminals.[48] In contrast to both Ireland and Britain, the dependent colonies had a hodgepodge of local and provincial forces, most of them manned (though not commanded) by "native" subalterns and relying on armed reserves to put down disturbances. As many scholars have observed, the Irish model of the semi-military policeman, trained in the methods of counterinsurgency, was a major influence on colonial police forces, although other models, such as the Metropolitan Police of London, were influential as well.[49] The different policing arrangements across the empire say a lot about the priorities of the state in each place. Mostly what they say is that outside of Britain the state feared sedition more than it feared criminality, while in Britain the opposite was the case. This meant, in turn, that colonial policing tended to rely on coercion rather than consent, a situation that reflected the larger power dynamics underpinning the imperial relationship.[50]

It is difficult to say exactly how many rioters were killed by state forces in Victorian Britain, but the numbers certainly declined steadily over time: eleven Kentish laborers at Bossenden Wood in 1838; up to twenty-four workers in the Newport rising of 1839; four or five during the Plug Plot riots of 1842; four during a riot at Mold, Wales, in 1869; two during the Trafalgar Square riot of 1887; and another two at Featherstone, Yorkshire, during a labor dispute in 1893. The total is therefore probably between forty and fifty police killings during Victoria's reign, with the vast majority of deaths occurring in the period 1838–42. In many of these episodes, especially those occurring after 1842, public outcry (channeled through an increasingly representative press and Parliament) prompted government inquiries of one kind or another. Such inquiries usually found the killings regrettable but necessary, but they also made a point of criticizing any excessive police violence and rearticulated the need for policemen to act with caution and restraint.[51]

In the empire, however, despite similar normative constraints on police power, the trajectory was in precisely the opposite direction, with policemen and soldiers opening fire much more frequently as the period progressed. As with Britain, precise numbers are difficult to calculate, but the scattered evidence available from police and magistrate reports, parliamentary debates, official inquiries, and newspapers clearly indicates a more lethal environment for rioters than in Britain. In Ireland the constabulary opened fire in at least seven different places between 1853 and 1887, and on sixteen separate occasions during the long summer of sectarian rioting in Belfast in 1886.[52] Thomas Fennell, a member of the constabulary for several decades beginning in the 1880s, believed "that all instances of firing"—several of which he detailed in his memoir—"might have been avoided; in fact were not justified," since they violated the principle of minimum force.[53] In India such incidents were simply too numerous to count, but in 1893 alone the police killed some eighteen rioters in Bombay and another twelve to eighteen in Rangoon, with innumerable smaller incidents throughout northern India.[54] This was probably the largest number of police killings in a single year during the nineteenth century, but police forces' reliance on lethal force was a common feature of many Indian riots before and after this time.[55] Police killings in the West Indies are even more difficult to calculate, but the incidents we have already examined (twenty-two dead in Trinidad in 1884 and anywhere from one to sixteen in Guiana in 1856), along with other scattered episodes, clearly indicate that state killings were likewise more common here than in Britain.[56] Moreover, in many places around the empire the number of police shootings increased sharply in the early decades of the twentieth century, as nationalist movements gathered steam and communal riots became more frequent. During three days of communal disturbances in Calcutta in 1918, for example, the police killed at least forty-three people and injured four hundred (although actual casualties may have been much higher), and in Ceylon in 1915 state forces killed at least sixty-three and injured many more during a series of anti-Muslim pogroms.[57]

One obvious reason that rioters were killed more often outside Britain than inside is that the colonial police (including the RIC) carried firearms, while their British counterparts did not. Occasionally armed soldiers would be called in to police riots in Britain, but in the great majority of cases it was unarmed local police who handled such outbreaks, whereas even local constabularies in most colonies had armed reserves at the ready. The reason for this was that colonial police forces were normally expected to operate as counterinsurgency forces as well as ordinary "bobbies on the beat."[58] Apart from the threat of anti-state violence, in most places British officials operated under the assumption that, as the *Times* said after a riot in Lurgan, Ireland, in 1879, public disorder of any kind might arise at any minute, "like a squall in a tropical sea, without giving any signs of its approach." If, the *Times* continued, the Irish "were less ready to break each other's heads on the smallest provocation, it would, perhaps, be possible, as it has long been in England, to arm the police with staves, and to reserve more deadly weapons for purely military use," but this, sadly, was not the case.[59] This image of a hot-blooded populace always on the brink of violence had little basis in reality—in Ireland, as elsewhere in the British world (including Britain), most riots were in fact eminently predictable, since they tended to accompany processions, festivals, and other communal gatherings—but it remained a powerful justification for the greater force with which areas outside of Britain were policed.

Another reason for the greater number of state killings outside of Britain is that there were simply more riots in the colonies, and this created more opportunities for the police to use deadly force. During the 1893 cow-protection riots in India, just one province—the North-West Provinces and Oudh—reported some 1,048 disturbances, far more, in all likelihood, than Britain experienced during the entire nineteenth century.[60] In the north of Ireland, meanwhile, many places saw yearly disturbances that coincided with the Catholic and Protestant marching seasons, such that some spots, such as Belfast, developed their own entrenched cultures of urban violence. Riots were much less frequent in Ceylon and the West Indies, but episodes of state violence were less frequent there as well, suggesting that there was some correlation between frequency of riots and frequency of state killings. On the other hand, there is a distinct possibility that the presence of numerous, heavily armed state forces in Ireland and India might have exacerbated, rather than reduced, the severity of riots by attracting curious bystanders, providing a target for partisans, and generally signaling that a violent confrontation was expected.[61] Riots certainly were more common outside of Britain, in other words, but this does not absolve British forces of some responsibility for what happened once a riot began.

A third explanation for the greater number of state killings outside of Britain is linked to the other two. If imperial police forces had deadlier weapons and more opportunities to use them than their British counterparts, they also had a stronger predisposition to see lethal force as an acceptable riot-control tactic. This predisposition arose in large part out of a persistent fear of mass violence—whatever its origins, and whatever its objects—that haunted imperial officials. As we will see in the next chapter, official fears about the unpredictable nature of mass violence certainly shaped the state's handling of the 1893 cow-protection riots in India. Lord Harris, the governor of Bombay, warned the viceroy that several of his senior officials were worried that the Hindu revival, of which cow protection was one manifestation, "has an object ulterior to that of cow protection, and sinister to our Raj," and during the riots he and others frequently acted as if the state was, in fact, facing a seditious threat.[62] Another, closely related, official assumption was one we have already noted: many British officials, failing to understand the true causes or purposes of mass violence, often believed that the only thing the turbulent inhabitants of places like Belfast, Bombay, or Georgetown respected was a column of armed soldiers marching through the streets. After the 1856 British Guiana riots, Governor Wodehouse defended the floggings and forced labor, to which he was subjecting riot prisoners, in the following terms: "I think that the people of England are no longer under the delusion that these people can be controlled by precisely the same forms of law as prove sufficient in highly civilised communities."[63] Non-British populations, in short, sometimes required non-British methods of control.

This imperial double standard was something that Irish nationalists were especially sensitive to, since it seemed to contradict the terms of Ireland's political union with Great Britain. Following a police shooting in Youghal, Ireland, in 1887, Irish MP T. P. O'Connor told the House of Commons (somewhat hyperbolically), "In England you have a superabundant hesitation before shooting down any rioters. In Ireland the police have orders to shoot the people down without hesitation."[64] Former Irish constable Thomas Fennell put his finger squarely on the fundamental paradox, that uniform rules were producing different practices, when he wrote in his memoir,

> English laws are supposed to be the fairest in the world. Much, however, depends on how the law is administered. For Englishmen in England, the law in recent times has been justly administered; but for Irishmen, even in England, the same could not always be said, especially when the cause was of a political character. In Ireland, it can be safely stated that the law has not been fairly administered.[65]

This gap between principle and practice was at the heart of Britain's liberal dilemma, not only in Ireland, but in the empire as a whole. The rule of minimum force was theoretically in effect well beyond Britain's shores, but how that rule was implemented depended upon how secure the state felt itself to be, what the police thought about the people they were policing, and how willing officials were to stretch the definition of "minimum" for the sake of maintaining order. Unsurprisingly, perhaps, the "last resort" for which policemen were supposed to wait before opening fire arrived much sooner in Ireland than in Britain, and sooner still in parts of the nonwhite empire. Likewise, the further one got from Britain, the more capacious terms like "restraint" and "forbearance" became, and the greater was the "minimum force" necessary to restore the peace. The words remained the same, but their meanings varied widely.

Quelling riots: blanks, bullets, or buckshot

Uniform rules, differentially applied: such was the British way of policing communal violence in the empire. One place to observe this phenomenon up close is in the discussions that took place late in the nineteenth century about the kinds of ammunition to be used in quelling riots. The subject first arose in Ireland in 1879 following a sectarian riot at a Home Rule demonstration in Lurgan. During the tumult, the RIC opened fire, and two siblings, a brother and sister, were hit, the brother fatally. The Tory government decided that hereafter the constabulary should be issued with buckshot, rather than balls, when sent into a riot, on the grounds that buckshot was less deadly and traveled shorter distances than live rounds.[66] This change became public following an eviction riot in Dungannon the following year, when the constabulary shot and killed a man with buckshot. In the House of Commons, outraged Irish MPs used the killing as an opportunity to question the entire basis of policing in Ireland. Thomas Sexton, arguing "that Ireland was the only civilized country in which the distinction between the civilian and military force was not well recognised," called for the constabulary to be reconstituted on a civilian basis.[67] Edmund Leamy wondered whether the switch to buckshot was (as the government maintained) really done for humane reasons, sarcastically remarking,

> It seemed that bullets had a trick of killing innocent people; but it was expected that this benevolent buckshot... would be more nicely discriminating, and search out and punish the guilty only. A bullet, they were told,

> would pass through and kill three men; a discharge of buckshot would kill one man dead, fatally wound three, and probably seriously wound 20 or 30 others; and so law and order would, in this way, be vindicated in accordance with justice and humanity.[68]

Asked by T. P. O'Connor how many police firings there had been in the last year, the new Liberal chief secretary, William Forster, said that there had been "only four," two of them during sectarian processions, one during an eviction, and one when a party of police came under fire from a private house.[69] Forster also insisted that the constabulary were bound to observe the principle of minimum force and promised to review the buckshot order. In the meantime, he said, he looked forward to the day when Ireland could be policed more like England, "[b]ut in the present state of things he felt it was impossible."[70]

Buckshot, it turned out, was deadly enough. In May 1881 Thomas Sexton asked Forster whether he still regarded "the use of buckshot as humane, seeing that in every case in which it has been used the consequence has been loss of life."[71] Forster insisted that it was humane, and his intransigence on this issue soon earned him the nickname "Buckshot Forster."[72] Still the objections continued. In 1887 Irish MP Patrick Chance told the Commons that the real reason the constabulary switched to buckshot was that they were having trouble hitting people with single rifle bullets; buckshot enabled the police "to fire with a better chance of hitting someone," even at a range of 100 or 150 yards. "I have no doubt," he said, "whoever invented this method of assassination prides himself upon the increased returns the Government are likely to get for the ammunition expended."[73] In 1904 the government reversed the buckshot policy when it issued the RIC with new Lee-Metford Enfield carbines, which could not be loaded with buckshot. Asked about this in Parliament, the chief secretary, George Wyndham, replied that the change was made "on the grounds of economy" and because the new bullet "is a more humane missile at close ranges, and less liable to inflict accidental damage at long ranges."[74] Of course, these considerations had been the purported rationale for implementing the buckshot-only policy in the first place; perhaps, as Irish MPs suspected, single bullets had been the more humane choice all along.

Ireland was unique in that its debate over police ammunition took place in Parliament. Elsewhere in the empire the state's policing decisions were subject to little public scrutiny, and they therefore followed an even more lethal trajectory. This was the case in 1893 when the Government of India began looking into the matter of police ammunition. The widespread nature of the cow-protection riots that year had raised questions about the efficacy of the state's response, and, by coincidence, very similar questions were being asked in Britain at the same time in the wake of the riot in Featherstone, Yorkshire, where soldiers had shot and killed two men. While Parliament merely requested copies of official correspondence relating to the Indian riots, it set up a full-scale inquiry into the killings in Yorkshire, and among that inquiry's recommendations was that blank cartridges ought not to be issued to soldiers on riot duty, since blanks seemed only to inflame a violent crowd. Instead, the commissioners argued, only buckshot or ball should be used, so as to impress crowds with the seriousness of the state's repressive intentions.[75] Inspired partly by this report, and concerned about the apparent futility of firing blank cartridges at rioters (which had been tried, with little effect, during a riot at Rangoon), the Indian Government solicited the advice of provincial governors, who, in turn, either referred the matter to their district magistrates or offered their own views without seeking further input.[76]

The responses were mostly in line with what the Featherstone Commission had recommended for Britain. In Madras the inspector general of police and the majority of the district magistrates recommended the "absolute prohibition of the use of blank cartridges" on the grounds that this was "likely to excite the mob." At the same time, Madras recommended that "some warning should be given before firing commences, and this warning must be of such a kind as to be immediately intelligible not only to the rioters directly opposed to the police, but to the whole mob."[77] In Bombay the officials recommended that buckshot, not ball, should be used in the first instance (as in Ireland), but they agreed that blanks should never be used.[78] In the Punjab the lieutenant governor described the use of blanks as "a stupid proceeding, calculated to defeat its own object and to lead to greater bloodshed in the end."[79] Officials in the Central Provinces noted that in no case over the last twenty-five years had they found it necessary to shoot at rioters, but they felt that the inhabitants of this district were "so closely allied in their characteristics to their neighbours" in the North-West Provinces and Bombay that whatever rules were adopted in those provinces should also be adopted in the Central Provinces as well.[80]

The most interesting response came from Sir Charles Crosthwaite, lieutenant governor of the North-West Provinces, where much of the recent rioting had taken place. It would, he said, "be most dangerous to publish an order that blank cartridge shall be used always or generally in the first instance." Crosthwaite believed that there had not been "any undue haste to open fire" in most cases of which he was aware, nor had any commanding officer been guilty of "any indiscretion." It was important to remember, he said,

> that the first duty of the Government of India is to preserve order. The population usually is peaceful, but when once disturbed it is excitable and easily led to commit excesses. The number of police in proportion to the population and area of each district is so small that if a riotous mob once got the upper hand, it would be very difficult to restore order before much loss of property and life had resulted.

Though conscious of the fragility of British power in India, Crosthwaite was also concerned about any potential interference that might come from the government in London if the Indian government publicized its determination to use only live rounds against Indian rioters. "If the Government issues the only order which is right," he said, "namely that ball or buck-shot cartridge shall be used, there will be an outcry in the native papers and a risk of interference from England, where opinion on matters of this kind appears to be in a very uncertain state. Anything is preferable to having the orders of the Executive Government in this country overruled. Every fresh act of such interference saps the foundations of authority." Better, Crosthwaite felt, for the Government of India to keep quiet about its decision to use only lethal ammunition than to risk provoking a humanitarian storm back home.[81]

Lord Elgin, the new viceroy as of 1894, endorsed the consensus against blank cartridges. He also agreed with Crosthwaite that the government should avoid publicizing its decision lest it cause an outcry in Britain, but he nevertheless acceded to the desires of his council that the new regulations forbidding the use of blank cartridges should be published. The difficulty that officials faced in India, Elgin observed in a letter to the secretary of state for India, was one that was not faced by their counterparts in England. In England soldiers were under the command of a single officer,

> but in this country small bodies of police, under the command of a Head Constable, may be compelled to use their weapons. It is a plausible argument that they ought to be ordered, or allowed, to fire blank cartridge first, but I think it is sounder to try to make them feel that they must not fire at all, if they can avoid it, and that the fact of their guns being always to be regarded as deadly weapons will increase the sense of responsibility.

Elgin did not have to explain that many of the policemen so entrusted were Indians; one could infer as much from the somewhat patronizing tone he adopted in discussing them. "At the same time," he continued, "the races of India are so different that it is impracticable to lay down a general rule for conveying the preliminary warning to rioters."[82] The upshot, then, was that police were no longer to use blanks, but only bullets or buckshot, and they could do so with or without warning—and the only portion of this new regulation that would be advertised to the Indian people was that blanks would no longer be used during riots.

The only significant dissenter from this anti-blanks consensus was C. A. Elliott, lieutenant-governor of Bengal, a province that also saw significant rioting in 1893 and 1894. In September 1893, in the Saran district, police had fired buckshot at a crowd of Hindus after a round of blanks had failed to disperse them, killing two people and injuring several more. Then in July 1894, during a conflict between rival bands of Muslims in Rajshahai, three policemen had fired buckshot, without orders, into the air and injured three or four bystanders.[83] In reporting the latter incident to Lord Elgin, Elliott lamented the "want of discipline" displayed by the policemen and promised that they would be punished. He also said that he had taken it upon himself not to enforce the circular that the government had issued discouraging the use of blank cartridges. "I remonstrated officially directly the Circular came out," he said, "and Lord Lansdowne [the previous viceroy] told me he disapproved of the order which was issued while he was in Burma." Elliott did not explain why he refused to go along with the ban on blank cartridges, but it was not, apparently, because of any personal squeamishness. In an earlier letter to Elgin he had explained his "maxim" for dealing with rioters: "Never fail to let it be seen that there are large elements and classes among the people whom you absolutely distrust, and whom you are ready and able to put down with a strong hand."[84] H. Thirkell White, an Indian Civil Service official who had ordered the firing of blanks during the riot in Rangoon, also continued to believe that blanks, though sometimes ineffective, were still more humane than live rounds. As he recalled in his 1913 memoir, the firing of blanks in Rangoon did not infuriate the crowd: it simply had no effect at all. In a similar circumstance, he said, he would again try firing blanks first.[85]

The prohibition against blank cartridges remained in place despite these objections, and eventually the government did publicize the new live-fire order. A memorandum sent to all commissioners and divisions in Bengal in 1909, a portion of which I quoted above, explained the reasons for this order:

> Experience has shown that the use of blank cartridge does not succeed in checking a determined mob, and in fact often produces the opposite effect,

> and may ultimately result in more loss of life than would have been the case had the firing been effective in the first instance. The issue of blank cartridge on such occasions has, therefore, been absolutely forbidden.... It is of course well understood that the order to fire should only be given in the last resort, when it is impossible to disperse the mob by any other means; but when the order is given, the firing should be at once effective, and must be such as, with the minimum of injury, to convince the crowd of the necessity of immediately dispersing.[86]

Here we have the apotheosis of the paradox underlying British public-order policing. Deadly force had to be used "in the first instance" to prevent greater bloodshed, but policemen could only use deadly force in "the last resort," after all other methods had failed. The paragraph almost collapses under the weight of its own contradictions.

Quelling riots: special constables and volunteers

Another tactic that officials sometimes used in suppressing riots was to enlist special constables, or civilian deputies, sometimes via preexisting forces of civilian volunteers or militias. This was a practice that also had its origins in Britain, where common law held that private citizens may—indeed, in some instances, must—use any necessary measures, including lethal force, to stop a violent or felonious riot.[87] In Britain special constables were frequently recruited from among the "peaceable" middle classes, most famously during the Chartist demonstration in London on April 10, 1848, and also during the anti-Catholic Murphy Riots of the 1860s, when anywhere from 100 to 500 specials were enrolled in towns where violence was anticipated.[88] These unpaid men were usually sworn in by a police chief or magistrate, issued a baton and an arm-band, empowered to arrest miscreants, and assigned a district to patrol. The practice was in some ways an urban outgrowth of the volunteering tradition of the eighteenth century, when farmers and laborers had come together in militias or yeomen corps to defend against foreign invasion and internal revolt, often under the direction of the local gentry. The practice was also a holdover from the days when policing was the responsibility of unpaid volunteers rather than professional policemen. The drawbacks of this practice were considerable—an amateur constable, vested with a modicum of legal power and impunity, might easily become a petty tyrant[89]—but it was strongly appealing when the police felt outnumbered, and it could be quite effective as long as (in the words of historian Roger Swift) the specials could be trusted to act with "good sense."[90]

Outside of Britain, where police numbers often were smaller and their authority weaker than at home, the idea of enlisting help from trustworthy civilians was even more appealing; the difficulty was finding civilians who could act with the requisite impartiality. During the Belfast riots of 1864, when the authorities enrolled 2,000 special constables to assist the beleaguered local police, one magistrate spotted several specials carrying their police batons in a massive, illegal funeral procession for a Protestant who had been killed by the police. This magistrate (who had opposed the decision to enroll special constables) also claimed that among the specials were a "notorious brothel-house keeper and a robber."[91] Stung by this experience, during the Fenian scare of 1866–7 and the Belfast riots of 1872 and 1886 the authorities decided not to enlist special constables, partly because few impartial volunteers would be available, partly because the specials would be outgunned by the rioters, and partly because even the most upright specials would inevitably be seen by some communities as a partisan force.[92] During the 1874 riots in Bombay, when Governor Philip Wodehouse suggested that the Parsis ought to form themselves into "what they call in England special constables," he was criticized not only by indignant Parsis but also by the Anglo-Indian *Times of India*, which pointed out that "Bombay Parsees are not Englishmen, inheriting from a hundred generations the habits of self-government," and by the *Glasgow Herald*, which likened Wodehouse's suggestion to an Irish magistrate telling rival bands of Orangemen and Catholics that they should "fight for their creeds."[93] In 1893 Antony MacDonnell contemplated making Bengal's Hindu ruling councils (*sabhas*) into special constables charged with keeping their own people quiet, but he felt it would be necessary to threaten them with prison in order to motivate them.[94] That same year the police in Bareilly, did make a number of Hindu grandees (*chaudhuris*) into special constables, but this seems to have been taken as an insult rather than an honor: one vernacular paper complained that these "highly respectable people" were being forced to guard the streets "like common constables."[95]

If enrolling special constables was an imperfect expedient during a riot, so, too, was enlisting the amateur volunteer corps that existed in many parts of the empire. Often comprised of white settlers who trained and drilled with weapons and horses throughout the year, most volunteer groups had the approval, and sometimes the active support, of the authorities to whom they loyally pledged their assistance in the event of a crisis. Most of the time the authorities were grateful for their help. During the 1893 riots in Bengal the Behar Mounted

Volunteers (manned by planters) received the thanks of Antony MacDonnell, the lieutenant governor of Bengal, for escorting a convoy of cattle destined for slaughter safely past hostile Hindu villagers.[96] That same year the Bombay Volunteer Rifles guarded strategic spots in their city, earning the thanks of the government at a formal banquet in the Bombay Town Hall.[97]

Nevertheless, mobilizing volunteers and special constables was a bit like grabbing a tiger by the tail. White settlers (nonofficial Europeans, in the imperial parlance) were normally much more aggressive toward nonwhites than were agents of the state; whenever a riot broke, they (and their spokesmen in the press) could usually be counted on to demand the strongest measures—floggings, shootings, martial law—to restore order. The *Bombay Gazette's* expression of evenhanded contempt for both the Muslims and the Parsis during the 1874 riots was typical of nonofficial European responses to these outbreaks: "There is not a pin to choose between the Parsee rough and the Mussulman rough, and both ought to be shot down without mercy if there is any more rioting, unless the Government is prepared to let the reign of anarchy be established permanently in Bombay."[98] In Belfast the nonaligned middle-class press also tended to advocate the harshest measures to suppress disorder. "There is a vast deal too much tenderness displayed by the authorities towards such brutal ruffians," declared the *Belfast Daily Mercury* in a typical outburst in 1857, "They ought to be, when detected in their murderous onslaughts, shot down like dogs."[99]

Such violent enthusiasm among the "respectable" inhabitants of a locale could be quite valuable to outmanned and poorly trained colonial police forces, provided it could be harnessed and effectively supervised. This appears to have been the scenario in Guiana in 1856, when the state relied heavily upon white and East Indian volunteers to patrol rural areas.[100] Even so, many of these volunteer forces—especially in rural plantation societies—behaved more like vigilante squads than aids to the civil power. In Chapter 1 we encountered the Guianese special who boasted to the *Liverpool Daily Post*, "We have only killed some sixteen this time, the next we shall see what will be done," and went on to confess, "I am most thoroughly disgusted with niggers."[101] During riots in Bengal in 1897 the officiating lieutenant governor complained that local volunteers were going on unauthorized river expeditions in search of miscreants and showing up armed at Calcutta's genteel Saturday Club. "One of the greatest difficulties in the situation," he told the viceroy, "is to be found in the unreasoning panic with which the non-official Europeans have been generally stricken."[102] At another level of mayhem altogether, in Ceylon in 1915 planter militias became virtual death squads, flogging and executing rioters without trial in an outburst of semiofficial violence that helped turn many moderate Sinhalese into committed nationalists.[103] In the short term, such "assistance" from white volunteers and specials could certainly help quell a disturbance, but in the long term their behavior could undermine British efforts to present the ruling race as just and dispassionate guardians of the peace.

After the riots

Most of the state's energies went into preventing and quelling riots, but official involvement with communal disturbances did not end after the last stone had been thrown. First, the rioters had to be punished, usually (but not always) through the judicial system, and sometimes *en masse*. Second, policemen and magistrates normally wrote up reports of the event, usually chronological narratives of the major events and the state's response that described the minutiae of the riots without much attempt at interpretation or analysis. Third, officials might decide that local or regional policing arrangements needed adjusting: they might add more policemen, relocate a military barracks, add more weapons, or tinker with rules and procedures. Fourth, in some extraordinary (or extraordinarily well-publicized) cases, Parliament might set up an inquiry, or MPs might request copies of reports and correspondence from officials on the spot. Sometimes these investigations would result in more far-reaching reforms, such as the decision to abolish the Belfast police force in 1865. Finally, in a handful of cases policemen or soldiers might be disciplined for misconduct during a riot; usually these were "native" policemen or troops, not Europeans, and the nature of their penalties varied widely. As with preventive and policing measures, each of the state's postriot actions derived from a set of empire-wide norms, but the behavior of individual officials varied greatly according to their own cultural assumptions and the local contexts in which they found themselves.

The only significant generalization that we can make about the judicial punishment of rioters is that non-Europeans tended to receive heavier punishments than Europeans. In Britain and Ireland convicted rioters usually received fines ("forty shillings and costs" was the usual fine in Belfast) or, in more serious cases, prison sentences ranging from several weeks to several years.[104] At the more lenient extreme were the Irish Catholics arrested in 1866 for attacking an Orange march at Donaghmore, who received sentences of one month each.[105] At the other extreme were the Catholics who attacked an Orange march in Coatbridge, Scotland, in 1857, who received four years for their parts in a riot in which no party sustained serious injury.[106] In India punishments were typically much harsher. Following Muharram disturbances in Bareilly (North-West Provinces) in 1871 and 1872 several people were sentenced to death, and some to transportation, along with many others who received shorter jail terms and fines.[107] Slightly less severe, but still substantial, were the punishments handed down to rioters after the 1882 Salem riots in Madras: one person was transported for life, two were transported for five years, and nine were sentenced to prison terms ranging from five years to one day (others were fined between 1,000 and 10,000 rupees).[108] And in British Guiana, as we have seen, the old slave punishment of flogging was still very much in use in 1856, as indeed it was in Ceylon as late as 1915.[109] This sort of judicial punishment for rioting was all but unknown in Victorian Britain and Ireland, although it is perhaps significant that flogging remained an acceptable disciplinary technique in the British army until 1881.

Impartiality in the administration of postriot justice was just as difficult to achieve as impartiality in riot policing. For one thing, rival communities often used the courts to settle personal scores, prompting responses such as that of an Irish Crown Solicitor who asked permission to stop prosecuting rioters in Belfast in 1872 on the grounds that so many of the cases were being brought "to gratify a feeling of bigotry" and were likely to "intensify the feeling hatred" between the two sides.[110] Another problem was that the state's prosecution of rioters frequently appeared one-sided or halfhearted to at least some portions of the community. Riot offenses were notoriously difficult to prove, relying as they did on the testimony of injured parties who, in many cases, belonged to the opposing camp. When such cases broke down, or when they failed to produce the desired results, either side might cry foul, and the state's reputation for impartiality would suffer. Thus did the zero-sum game of communal violence extend to the postriot period: any judicial defeat for one's own side might automatically be seen as a victory for the other, and partisans carefully scrutinized the pattern of arrests, indictments, and sentences for any sign of bias.

The same was true of riot inquiries. Most inquiries, whether commissioned by Parliament or another body, were instructed to identify the causes of an outbreak as well as the steps that might be taken to prevent its recurrence, and in identifying causes they often ended up assigning blame. The usual practice was to spread the blame around a bit—to apportion some to the party who provoked the attack, some to the attackers, and perhaps a little to the police—but this formula rarely satisfied communal partisans, who preferred to assign all the blame to their enemies. Thus the Orange Order derided the parliamentary inquiry into the 1857 Belfast riots—which severely censured Orangeism but reserved some criticism for Catholics and the authorities—as a "perversion of justice" and accused the commissioners of violating their "sacred duty" to dispense justice "impartially, without fear, favour, or affection."[111] Even the decision to hold an inquiry could be contentious, partly because of the cost (to the municipal reputation as well as the municipal finances), partly because of fears that it would stir up renewed violence, and partly because one or the other side might doubt that they would be treated fairly.[112]

In reality, the cliché about inquiries—that they are a good way to give the impression of taking action without actually taking action—held true for most of the riots in which Parliament took a direct interest. The most consequential inquiry was that into the 1864 Belfast riots, which recommended the replacement of the ineffective, unarmed, and (among Catholics) unpopular local police with the semi-military, centrally controlled RIC.[113] But apart from Ireland, whose MPs carried at least some weight at Westminster, the most Parliament was prepared to do in the wake of colonial violence was to request reports and correspondence relating to specific episodes (e.g., the 1856 Guiana riots, the 1874 Bombay riots, and the 1893 India riots). Not only did Parliament stop short of setting up full-blown commissions of inquiry, it also took little action as a result of the reports that it requested. Inquiries on a smaller scale, usually organized by provincial or colonial governments, could sometimes bring about minor changes, however. Following the Catholic–Buddhist riot in Colombo in 1883 the Ceylon government formed a permanent reserve of fifty "armed and drilled" men to put down future disturbances, installed telephones in each Colombo police station, and introduced new rules for granting procession permits.[114] Rarely did a local government decide upon any disciplinary action against policemen for using excessive force. Sometimes an individual might be disciplined or sacked for misconduct—as happened to a Sinhalese police inspector following the Colombo riot, who was demoted after being accused of killing a Catholic and demanding bribes from the Buddhists[115]—but most local inquiries, as noted earlier, simply praised the steadfastness and restraint of state forces and asked no further questions.

Another common postriot measure was the imposition of what were known as punitive police. These were special, sometimes armed police forces that would be stationed in a locale for several months or years after an outbreak, usually at local expense. Their purpose was partly to deter renewed rioting, partly to inflict a financial punishment upon unruly locales, and partly to impel local leaders, via their pocketbooks, to discourage such violence in the future.[116] Something approaching this practice could be seen in Ireland—when constables were called in to quell a riot, the expense was sometimes borne by local ratepayers[117]—but for the most part this "wholesome burden" (as the *Times of India* put it) was a South Asian phenomenon.[118] Not everybody agreed that the best way to forestall future riots was to punish an entire community, of course. In Bombay the vernacular *Karnátak Patră* argued in 1893 that punitive police would "prove worse than a deliberate fomentation of quarrel" between Hindus and Muslims:

> For the poor people will thereby be further irritated for their inability to meet the heavy demands of Government on their scanty means, and it is quite possible that the Hindu and Musalman sepoys forming the punitive police may sympathize with their respective parties and thus give a more serious aspect to the animosity now existing between the unarmed and half-fed rayats.[119]

Such views carried little weight with the British administration, however, where the overriding concern was to impress the people with the deadly force at its command.

Conclusion

This chapter has argued that, while there was a considerable range of tactical responses available to British officials faced with communal violence, the essential choices they had to make boiled down to two competing imperatives. On the one hand, this was a liberal empire subject to the rule of law, and its people were entitled to many of the same considerations as Britons: police restraint, due process, an impartial judiciary, and the rest. On the other hand, colonized people were *not* Britons, and colonial governments did not enjoy the same level of legitimacy among their subjects as the state did in Britain. There were therefore strong reasons, as far as many imperial officials were concerned, to treat the people of the empire differently than Britons, especially when it came to preserving order. They might rely on exemplary violence—the clatter of hooves, the crack of rifles—to demonstrate the power of the state and deter further defiance. They might impose exemplary punishments—floggings, transportation, long prison sentences—for the same purpose, or collective punishments like punitive police and blanket prohibitions of certain forms of communal expression. How individual officials struck the balance between conciliation and coercion depended largely upon local circumstances and personal predilections, but it is clear that, on the whole, public-order policing in the British Empire was determined by several core cultural assumptions. The first was that the people of the empire, especially Asians but also Irish and blacks, only respected a government that they feared. People accustomed to despotism, it was believed, had an innate respect for authoritarian rulers, so strong displays of force might serve a "moral" purpose by demonstrating the power of the British state. The second core assumption was that the non-British peoples of the empire were fundamentally irrational. Their motives were inscrutable, their temperaments were volatile, and their hatreds were primordial, perhaps even hereditary. They therefore could not be trusted to act in a reasonable manner once their passions were inflamed. The third core assumption was that any local flare-up, even if it only involved one "native" community attacking another, could easily grow into a conflagration that might endanger Europeans and the rule of law itself. This was the primary reason officials worked so hard to prevent or quell such disputes. The fourth core assumption was that non-British lives were worth less than British lives: otherwise there would have been fewer state killings in the empire and more serious investigations into those that occurred. The fifth core assumption was that British forces were capable of maintaining a stance of strict impartiality, tempered by a sense of justice and fair play, which would keep them above the communal fray.

Every one of these beliefs was some distance removed from reality, but the distance varied from place to place and episode to episode. Most of the time, the way British forces policed communal violence exposed something of a gulf between imperial rhetoric and imperial reality. The basic rules governing riot policing may have been essentially the same across the empire, but their application was not. By exposing this (apparent) hollowness at the heart of British liberal imperialism—by creating circumstances in which the state's impartiality and competence could be called into question—communal riots lay bare Britain's fundamental failure to construct a legitimate state to which all colonized communities could pledge their allegiance. These riots were, in short, seriously embarrassing for the state, and that embarrassment had significant consequences, the most important of which was the creation of a sort of vacuum into which communal vigilantes might step in order to assert their own rival claims to competence and legitimacy. We will explore this process more fully in the last chapter, but we will also catch glimpses of it in the next chapter, on the great Indian cow-protection riots of 1893.

7

The Cow Row: India, 1893–1894

By most accounts Lord Harris, the governor of the Bombay presidency at the time of the province's worst riots of the nineteenth century, preferred the thwack and whiff of the cricket pitch to the chaotic din of Bombay city life. Like many top officials in the late Victorian Empire Harris had come to India on the strength of his political and family connections rather than any demonstrated administrative skill. His great-grandfather had led an army against Tipu Sultan at the end of the last century (a service for which he was granted a peerage), his grandfather had been wounded at Waterloo, and his father had been governor of Trinidad and Madras. The younger Lord Harris (then George Canning) had grown up in the latter locale until he went off to boarding school in England.[1] At Eton and then Cambridge he showed promise as a batsman, and he subsequently captained both the English national cricket team and the county team of Kent. It was for cricket, not statesmanship, that Harris was known and admired in England, and it is for cricket that he is remembered (if remembered he is) to this day. He had dabbled in politics, serving for a decade as an undersecretary in the India and War Offices, but it is nevertheless surprising that Lord Salisbury should have entrusted him, from 1890 to 1895, with the governorship of so large and complex a province as Bombay, an area more than twice the size of Britain and infinitely more heterogeneous. Or it would be surprising if we were to imagine that Harris's job was more about promoting the welfare of the province than about upholding the grandeur and dignity of the ruling race.

Upon arriving in Bombay in 1890 Harris quickly found the clamor and torpor of Bombay city uncongenial and proceeded to spend most of the next five years either at the governor's estate at Poona or at the hill station of Mahableshwar, organizing cricket matches (but for no more than "ten days a year," he would later insist), consuming vast quantities of alcohol, and generally letting his subordinates handle the day-to-day affairs of the province.[2] To critics who accused him of spending more time cricketing than governing, he retorted, with typical insouciance, that at least he was pursuing a healthy pastime and not "lying on a sofa, smoking cigarettes, and reading French novels."[3] Of course, even cricket had its uses in the great civilizing project of empire. One of his Parsi friends (Harris, like many governors, was partial to Parsis) aptly described Harris as the "guru" of Indian cricket: the man who, though he did not introduce the game to India, ensured that it thrived among the different communities of Bombay.[4] Like most public school sportsmen of his day Harris believed that cricket's virtues were not only physical but moral. The mental acuity and physical fitness demanded by cricket could, he believed, be handmaidens to the ethos of honesty and fair play that was at the core of British imperialism. He also nurtured a hope (as he put it many years later) that cricket in India might "bring the several races together more and more" in a "spirit of harmony," enabling them to pursue their rivalries on the sporting ground rather than the streets and bazaars.[5] It was a noble but deeply flawed project, for, not only were Bombay's cricket clubs organized along communal lines—as governor, Harris approved the setting aside of different seaside plots for Parsi, Hindu, and Muslim clubs—but European cricketers also maintained their own club, which enjoyed special privileges denied to Indians.[6] Instead of confining communal rivalries to the cricket grounds, this arrangement simply provided one more arena in which those rivalries could be pursued, much as sectarian sporting rivalries have done in other parts of the world (not least Britain itself).

There was something inescapably symbolic, then, about the fact that Harris was playing cricket in Poona when riots broke out in Bombay in August 1893. Rather than hastening to the scene of what were to become the city's worst riots to date, Harris remained in Poona, overseeing the dispatch of troops and, on the second day of the riots, meeting with the Bombay Governing Council and urging communal leaders to restrain their people.[7] It wasn't until the ninth day of the disturbances, when things had mostly calmed down, that Harris visited the city, and then (again the symbolism is inescapable) primarily to attend a cricket match. He toured the disturbed districts for an hour and was back in Poona the next day, much to the disgust of the vernacular press, which accused him of indifference to the people's suffering.[8] The criticisms were not without merit. Even his admirers offered Harris only faint praise. When the Parsi newspaper *Rást Goftár* noted that Harris "directed operations from Poona and personally saw that as many troops were despatched as were wanted and that they were despatched with the least avoidable delay,"[9] this was the most any locals were prepared to say in his defense. Much more common was the judgment of the radical Hindu paper *Mahrátta*, which accused the governor of "singular weakness in dealing with the question of the recent disturbances."[10]

Harris was not the only British official to attract criticism during the violence of 1893, nor was Bombay the only place where Hindus and Muslims came to blows that year—far from it. But his behavior was emblematic of the careless detachment that was coming to characterize British officialdom in the closing years of the nineteenth century. Although there were still some men (for instance Antony MacDonnell, Harris's opposite number in Bengal whom we will encounter shortly) who favored active state mediation to head off disputes, the future of British India lay with men like Harris, withdrawn behind the high walls of their compounds and ruling the country at arm's length. The riots of 1893 marked something of a shift away from the intimate, community-based policing that had characterized much of the Victorian period, toward a more remote but also more repressive system that relied less on mediation and more on regulation, surveillance, and force. It was the beginning of a period when, as Sandria Freitag has observed, "religiously focused unrest began to be treated as a security issue," when any outbreak of violence, no matter how solipsistic, was seen as a potential threat to British rule.[11] It was also the beginning of a period when British officials began to demonstrate less detailed knowledge (and curiosity) about Indian life and, correspondingly, much greater fear of the country's subterranean currents. It was, in short, the beginning of the end of the illusion that the British state would ever enjoy any sort of legitimacy in India, and the violence of the period made this abundantly clear.

The spark

The riots of 1893 and 1894 were the largest popular disturbances in India since the Sepoy Revolt of 1857, but to Sir Charles Lyall, home secretary of the Indian government, the most obvious parallel was not 1857 but 1848. In that year, as anyone with knowledge of recent European history knew, sparks struck in Paris had quickly caught fire elsewhere (narrowly missing Britain), and within a short time the spirit of revolt had engulfed an entire continent. And what had transmitted this spirit, in Lyall's judgment? For one thing, the world was getting smaller. News, true and false, spread rapidly from place to place, exciting passions everywhere. "The news of the overthrow of the monarchy of Louis Philippe," Lyall wrote, "had its effect in turning men's thoughts to revolutionary outbreaks in Prussia, Austria, Italy, and Russia." Something similar had happened in India: when Hindus and Muslims fought each other in Rangoon, he observed, their counterparts in Delhi would hear about it a few days later and immediately "begin to look at one another with suspicion." Lyall also identified "the increasing heat of political, religious, and race discussion" in the Hindu newspapers as a cause of the riots (newspapers had been central to the outbreaks in Europe as well) and he complained specifically about the extent to which the nationalists of the Indian National Congress had seduced the Hindu papers into taking positions that worried many Muslims. Like most British officials at the time Lyall also blamed the violence on the cow-protection societies, Hindu revival groups devoted to saving and sheltering the Hindus' sacred beast.[12] These societies, or *sabhas*, Lyall faulted for recklessly provoking clashes with Muslims—and of course the newspapers and other communications technologies were only abetting their incautious behavior.

Although Lyall did not use the word, the causes of violence that he identified all fit under the heading of modernity, specifically the style of colonial modernity brought about by British rule. The railroads, newspapers, and telegraphs were obviously byproducts of Britain's modernizing influence, but so, too, were the secondary causes Lyall identified. Indians educated by (and sometimes in) Britain were becoming the most outspoken opponents of British rule, and the Congress movement reflected their aspirations, even if its role in the cow-protection movement was not nearly as important as Lyall imagined. The religious revivalism of the cow-protection *sabhas* was also an outgrowth of British modernity, insofar as it was a movement that simultaneously rejected much of what modernity entailed (secularism, above all) while using modern tools (the newspaper, the railroad, the telegraph) to spread and grow.[13] Not for the first time—and here 1857 probably is the more appropriate parallel—the spark that ignited a continent had been lit, in part, by the British themselves.[14]

The "cow row," as British policemen called it, began in earnest in the North-West Provinces in late June 1893, during the Muslim festival of Bakr-Id.[15] This was a time when Muslims traditionally sacrificed cows, a practice that was newly controversial since the advent of the Hindu cow-protection movement about a decade earlier. Hindu cow-protection groups, or *Gaurakshini Sabhas*, had been active in India since the early 1880s, originating in the Central Provinces and finding particularly strong followings in northern areas with large Muslim populations such as Bihar, Punjab, and north-central India.[16] The character of the *sabhas* varied: some sought to establish pounds in which to care for cows, others wanted to keep cows out of the hands of non-Hindu butchers, and still others pressured the government to ban the slaughter of cows (and even goats and sheep) altogether. Their means also varied. Some *sabhas* simply held meetings and raised subscriptions, while others distributed pamphlets, employed itinerant preachers, paraded cattle through the streets, placed collection boxes stamped with a cow's image in different spots around cities and towns, extorted contributions from nonmembers, and even conspired to interfere directly with the killing of cattle.[17]

When clashes occurred it was usually because the *sabhas* and their followers had tried forcibly to rescue cattle or stop a sacrifice. It would be impossible to detail all of the violence associated with the movement, but it is instructive to examine some of the larger (and better documented) episodes.[18] The first major riots were in and around the city of Azamgarh in the North-West Provinces. In the spring of 1893 the local *sabhas*, heretofore quite moderate, became markedly more aggressive. The previous year Britain had begun allowing Indians to serve on legislative councils for the first time, and this had led many *sabhas* to press for some sort of legal restriction on cow slaughter.[19] Feeling the wind in their sails, the Azamgarh *sabhas* introduced compulsory contributions from all Hindus (often in the form of *chutki*, or a pinch of food set aside by each family member during mealtimes) and declared that failure to contribute to the movement was equivalent to eating beef, which was grounds for "exclusion from caste."[20] They also orchestrated several dramatic cattle rescue operations, inflaming relations with the region's Muslim minority, who numbered 225,000 to the Hindus' 1.5 million.

Things worsened as the Bakr-Id festival approached at the end of June, when rumors began circulating that Muslims intended to sacrifice more cattle than usual. Police officials worked to defuse potential crises, securing promises from Muslim leaders that they would sacrifice no more than was customary and from Hindus that they would not interfere with Muslims' customary practices. After much toing and froing H. Dupernex, the relatively inexperienced magistrate of Azamgarh, secured a promise from Muslim leaders that they would sacrifice cows only between the hours of 9:00 a.m. and 12:00 p.m. on June 24, the day before the festival proper. This they did, largely without trouble, but the following day large bands of Hindus—some from as far away as Bengal—roamed the district attempting to prevent additional sacrifices, whether they conformed with established custom or not. The result was some thirty or forty clashes in and around Azamgarh.

There were also serious disturbances in the Ghazipur district southeast of Azamgarh city. On June 24, the day before Bakr-Id, Inspector Pollock took twenty-seven armed policemen to Mauza Patiya, just north of Ghazipur, to protect Muslims from attack. The following day some 7,000 to 8,000 Hindus, many of them armed, descended on the mosque to stop the sacrifices, encouraging one another by shouting that the police were unarmed, an illusion that Pollock dispelled when he ordered his men to fire a few shots into the air. This show of force, along with the arrival of more police, convinced the Hindus not to go any further. A riot was avoided, and the terrified Muslims decided not to sacrifice a cow after all. There was a similar confrontation at nearby Zahurabad, where police ended up arresting twelve Hindus. Two days later a crowd of seven thousand lathi-wielding Hindus showed up at the Shadiabad police station with twelve Muslims whom they'd kidnapped from the village of Khatipur. With the cooperation of the police chief, a Hindu named Manohar Das, they forced the Muslims to swear never to sacrifice cattle again. Das was subsequently suspended, tried, and imprisoned for his part in the affair (which included refusing to hold an inquiry and failing to enter the event into the station logbook), and in all police arrested 129 people, of whom 87 were convicted by a magistrate or sent for trial. The government then imposed a heavy force of punitive police upon the district for two years.[21] In the Azamgarh region as a whole, the police arrested over 800 people (of an estimated 35,000 rioters), mostly those alleged to have committed grave crimes such as robbery and murder.[22]

Meanwhile, in a sign of just how quickly and widely these disturbances would spread, another row broke out a few thousand kilometers away in Rangoon (Burma was then administratively part of India). The contestants were Hindu and Muslim Indian migrants, minorities in an overwhelmingly Buddhist city who apparently shared some of the rivalries of their confreres back home. On the day of Bakr-Id a group of Muslims tried to sacrifice a cow in a walled compound belonging to Yacoobji Duda, who lived on Twenty-Ninth Street near a mosque and just across the street from a Hindu temple. They had done this on previous years without trouble (and Duda had gone to considerable effort, including arranging appropriate drainage for the blood, to ensure that the sacrifice would not offend Hindus), but this year the Hindus demanded that no sacrifices be performed within two hundred feet of their temple. Worried about the potential for violence among the "large numbers of Hindus who are not amenable to reason," the deputy commissioner, A. S. Vincent, forbade the Muslims to carry out the sacrifice. What Vincent saw as a simple expedient to preserve order, however, Muslims saw as capitulation to Hindu thuggery and an abandonment of the state's duty to preserve their religious liberty. Adding to their outrage was the magistrates' decision to post military policemen at the entrances to Twenty-Ninth Street on the morning of Bakr-Id to prevent Muslims bringing a cow to Duda's compound. As Muslims gathered at their mosque that morning some began trying to breach the police barricade (which was only a block away), throwing bricks, stones, bottles, and other missiles. Something hit Vincent in the head, and after issuing a warning Vincent ordered the police to fire—first with blanks, which had no effect, and then with buckshot and ball, which managed to subdue the crowd long enough for the military to arrive and secure the area. Some fifteen civilians and one police horse died in the affray, and many dozens of civilians and policemen suffered injuries of one kind or another.[23]

Bombay

In the coming weeks similar clashes, many triggered by reports of what had happened in Azamgarh and Rangoon, broke out in the North-West Provinces, Punjab, Bihar, Gujarat, Maharashtra, and Bombay. Bombay's riots were among the worst.[24] The immediate trigger was a riot in distant Prabhas Patan, western Gujarat, where Muslims destroyed Hindu temples and killed several Hindus during Muharram. This provoked mass demonstrations in Bombay among Hindus, particularly those associated with a militant new *sabha* known as the Gaupalan Upadeshak Mandali, founded in 1893 by a Bhatia mill owner named Lakhmidas Khimjee.[25] For months campaigners had been troubling the police commissioner, R. H. Vincent, to restrict cow slaughter in Bombay's streets; that April Vincent had only just managed to persuade the *sabha* not to hold a massive procession of thousands of cows through the city.[26] In late July, as news of the riots in Prabhas Patan arrived in Bombay, the cow-protection societies held mass demonstrations in which they denounced the Muslim rioters, accused the authorities of favoring Muslims, and demanded that the government prohibit the killing of cows across all of India.[27] Muslims began holding their own meetings in response, and among their complaints was that local Hindu authorities were treating Muslims unfairly.[28] Both sides, in other words, were openly expressing their distrust of the state's impartiality at the same time as they were accusing one another of unprovoked aggression.

The dam burst on Friday, August 11, just after midday prayers at the Jama Masjid, which was, unusually, full to overflowing. I will allow R. H. Vincent's official report to tell this part of the story, since, although it provides just one man's perspective on a very complicated affair, it is a nice illustration of how British officials explained these outbreaks to one another. According to Vincent, at about one o'clock a crowd emerged from the mosque shouting "din din," hurling stones, and racing for the Maruti Temple in Hanuman Lane, where, rumor had it, a drum or bell had been beaten during the Muslims' prayers. The police, along with some "respectable" Muslims, managed to disperse this initial group of rioters under a hail of stones and road metal, but no sooner had they done so than reports of violence in other parts of town began to arrive. Feeling overwhelmed, Vincent called for infantry, marines, and artillery to help deal with the mounting crisis.[29]

At this point Vincent's official report, heretofore cool and precise, begins to rival even the most sensational news reports in its breathless account of events.

> Meanwhile the tide of the riot had spread with astonishing rapidity through almost the whole of the native town. Infuriated mobs of Musalmáns surged from street to street, carrying havoc and destruction in all directions. To trace the course of the tumult is beyond my powers, for the rioters seemed to be in every place at once; and when they were driven back and dispersed by the Police and Military from one locality it was only to unite again in another and wreak their wanton rage on the hated Hindus and any who sought to hinder them.... Little care was taken by the Musalmáns to limit their aim to the enemies of the Faith, for passing tram-cars and public conveyances were freely pelted irrespective of the race of the passengers.... Raging from street to street the infuriated crowds desecrated Hindu temples, broke idols and hurled them on to the roads, to be trodden under foot, while they inflicted savage assaults on the Hindus who came in their path. These unfortunate people were in an abject state of terror.

In Vincent's telling, the city was in the grip of a sort of mad fury, without object or rationale, almost an act of nature rather than the product of human volition. Among the most destructive rioters, Vincent said, were the "Chili Chors," or horse cart drivers ("Chili Chor" was a nickname meaning "fodder thieves"). Their targets that day were the Hindus in the Kumbharvada neighborhood, where they almost succeeded in sprinkling a temple with the blood of four slaughtered cows; then they tried to destroy the stables of the Tramway Company at Byculla, presumably in order to harm a professional competitor. Vincent also noted the ferocity of the "Julais," Muslim weavers "not a few of whom are Wahabis," who targeted Pardeshi milk sellers in their neighborhoods and were only dispersed after a "prolonged struggle" with mounted police who confronted them with swords drawn.[30]

In a rhetorical move typical of British riot narratives, Vincent then explained that, although the outbreak had its origins in religion ("fanatical" was the adjective he used), it now descended into baser realms. The criminal castes, "commonly known as budmashis," used the chaos as an occasion to rob passersby and shops. In the Bhendi Bazaar the "mob" tried to unharness police horses and barricade themselves inside the bazaar. In other places gangs threw stones at policemen and soldiers and then tried to steal their weapons. Some Muslims assaulted a body of Hindus returning from work along the docks. Others extinguished lamps and frightened away those lamplighters who had not already fled in search of shelter. Meanwhile, groups of Hindus gathered in Arthur Road "with the object of taking the law into their own hands;" although the police arrested some of these men, others slipped away to embark on a series of retaliations. Within the first hour of the riots a band of Hindus had assaulted a Muslim driver passing through a Hindu quarter, robbing the two European women who were traveling in the coach with a small child. Another Muslim driver, along with two other European passengers, met a similar fate at the hands of another band of Hindus (Vincent was careful to point out that he knew of no similar attacks by Muslims upon nonofficial Europeans).[31]

Having examined the police commissioner's particular impressions of the start of the riots, we might now set aside his report and look at what other official bodies were doing. Immediately after the initial outbursts Vincent had called in a body of marines from naval vessels, infantrymen from Poona, and forces of armed police from Thana and elsewhere. Within a few hours, and into the following day, several hundred "native" and European soldiers flooded into the city, bringing with them artillery pieces which they placed in commanding positions over the disturbed areas, including one aimed at the jail to protect it from rescue parties.[32] The Bombay Volunteer Rifles, a body comprised of European civilians, also came out to guard strategic spots such as the jail, tramway stables, and gasworks.[33] According to Edmund C. Cox, a midlevel policeman on hand just after the riots, the soldiers "had a very good time" during the riots.

> The troops in the city had to be provided with house accommodation, and rich natives were only too anxious to secure protection from the rioters for themselves and their families by entertaining a party of soldiers in their houses. They vied with each other in extending hospitality to the military; and they did their best with good food and the best of champagne to welcome their temporary guests.[34]

Baptist missionary H. E. Barrell was less charmed by the military buildup. "Picture the slaughter," he wrote in a dispatch to the Baptist *Missionary Herald*, "of a single seventy-pounder loaded with canister, sweeping a street with 10,000 people or more traversing it!" Barrell also reported that a cannon was aimed at one of the big mosques and that, "as in the Mutiny," soldiers had orders to destroy the mosque in the event of an organized uprising by Muslims.[35]

Whether these were in fact the artillerymen's orders is unclear, but it is certainly true that these forces had little qualms about using deadly force: from the very beginning soldiers and policemen had been firing upon rioters and charging them with swords and bayonets. From behind the curtains of his bungalow Barrell could hear the cries of an officer—"Attention!" "Get ready!" "Charge"—followed by "shouts and a general stampede." Later, "a gentle hum would begin, increasing in the course of half an hour to a shouting mob, then a riot, and then, when the clash of sticks began, there would be a rifle report, and then a stillness like the grave."[36] For all of their firepower, however, the soldiers seem to have acted with some restraint, choosing for instance to fire at rioters' legs instead of their vital regions.[37] The Parsi paper *Bombay Samáchár* credited the chief magistrate, Mr. Cooper, with "hesitat[ing] to give the order for firing upon the rioters, taking pity on them and treating them as so many misguided children," and it also praised the restraint of the special magistrates who had been recruited from among the respectable classes.[38] Of course, as we saw in the previous chapter, restraint in these scenarios was in the eye of the beholder. Certainly the broader purpose of the state's massive display of force was clear enough: to terrorize the lawless into submission and to demonstrate to the law-abiding that the state was capable of protecting life and property, even if it had to sacrifice some lives and property along the way.

These repressive measures had little immediate impact. On Saturday, the second day of the riots, Hindu and Muslim gangs roamed the streets with apparent impunity, attacking individuals, businesses, homes, and houses of worship with whatever weapons they could find—firewood, road metal, stones, sticks studded with nails. Others looted and plundered, often from those belonging to their "own" side. Muslim funeral processions for people killed the previous day came under attack from bands of Hindus, and during one of these affrays a group of Muslims tried to seize the rifles of the soldiers sent to disperse the rioters.[39] So bad were things that terrified sweepers and scavengers employed by the Health Department were refusing to go on their rounds, causing a dangerous accumulation of night soil and other refuse that festered until the authorities began providing these sanitation workers with military escorts.[40] Meanwhile, in the northern textile mills, Marathi-speaking workers began showing a worrying capacity for collective action by staging several work stoppages.[41] H. E. Barrell, the Baptist missionary, claimed that the "worst feature" of the riots was the desecration of scores of temples and mosques, a somewhat odd position for a Protestant minister to take. Outside one temple he saw an "idol" smashed to bits in the center of the road, "and standing over the broken fragments was the poor priest, with his hands clasped, and looking round in abject misery." Mosques, generally more solidly built than temples, fared a little better, but the people hiding inside them were every bit as vulnerable: Barrell told of several Muslim clerics and worshippers murdered in their mosques—atrocities that, he felt, "will not be forgotten as long as this generation lives."[42]

The worst of the violence was over by the end of the third day, Sunday, although isolated incidents persisted for weeks, as did the occasional scare. Well before the dust had cleared, Vincent decided to take his wife riding through the disturbed districts to help soothe rattled nerves—"a very plucky thing," in the judgment of policeman Edmund Cox—but even in late September, six weeks after the riots, the sound of an exploding soda bottle was enough to send shop shutters banging shut.[43] People's apprehension was understandable. These were, by a large margin, the worst riots Bombay had ever seen—at least eighty dead, over 800 wounded, more than 1,500 arrests, and 50,000 refugees who fled the city during the height of the unrest[44]—and it would be a long time before things returned to normal.

Bengal and Bihar

Throughout the Bombay riots, as indeed in the unquiet weeks preceding them, Lord Harris had remained at his compound in Poona, dispatching troops, receiving reports, and letting subordinates like Vincent (and his wife) handle the difficult job of restoring calm. Very different was the approach of Harris's counterpart in the Bengal Presidency, Antony MacDonnell. MacDonnell, nicknamed the "Bengal Tiger" by his subordinates,[45] was an Irish Catholic who had worked his way up through the Indian Civil Service for the better part of thirty years, acquiring the kinds of local knowledge and relationships that the inexperienced (though better-connected) Harris lacked. If we were to be Victorian about it, we might attribute the two men's different styles to their "races"—Harris the phlegmatic Englishman, MacDonnell the fiery Celt—but the truth was that the officiating lieutenant governor of Bengal (for such was MacDonnell's title) was simply more experienced, more capable, and more comfortable with the thorny realities of Indian life than his aristocratic colleague.

While Harris was holed up in Poona, reading reports and waiting for the bloodletting to run its course, MacDonnell was actively working on ways to prevent or contain the unrest. In Bengal and the neighboring region of Bihar the danger lay mostly in rural districts, among peasants living on the estates of powerful *zemindars* and, in the princely states, ruled by maharajas who had a fair degree of internal autonomy. In such places, where British control was mediated or indirect, MacDonnell believed (as he told the viceroy) that the state should be kept "as much as possible in the background," since the police had a tendency to get mixed up in the controversy and "cannot be trusted to act impartially."[46] Instead MacDonnell reached out to local leaders, secular and religious, to implore them to control their own people. In this way he would reserve the state's forces for those occasions when it became necessary to get "all shades of opinion to agree on the desirability of maintaining order."[47] He also encouraged his officials to create conciliation committees, or *panchayats*, to work out ways that cows might be slaughtered without offending Hindus. Toward this end he appointed H. LeMesurier, the collector of Hooghly, as a special "conciliator" to travel around and meet with local leaders.[48] Summing up his creed in a letter to a subordinate, MacDonnell insisted that his officials try conciliation before using force:

> Of course I know that force is our main reliance: and you will not find me squeamish in using it. But as I told you once before a conciliatory attitude does not [cost] your powder. On the contrary if you show yourself desirous of conciliating then the swift & strong show of force when occasion arises is all the more effectual. While you should certainly suppress all overt acts & act equally strongly when danger is apprehended you ought to do all that is possible to bring the two creeds together. They may keep aloof & retain their sullen readiness for outrage, but your attitude will be unmistakable. Swift to strike & to punish if you cannot prevent, but withal conciliatory. After all they are not reasonable beings in this matter but blind fanatics.[49]

MacDonnell also encouraged careful surveillance of the *sabhas*. Across Bihar, local police forces compiled the names and tracked the movements of the principal organizers—they were especially interested in the allegations of embezzlement of *sabha* funds by itinerant *sadhus*, as well as rumors that funds were being used to pay rioters' court costs—and passed on the information to MacDonnell.[50]

If Harris was the Raj at its most remote and frivolous, MacDonnell was the Raj at its most competent and energetic, holding back here, thrusting forth there, and adopting creative solutions to forestall unrest. Nevertheless, by November 1893 he was forced to admit that his conciliation efforts "have been attended with scant success."[51] The most troubled area was Bihar, where *sabhas* had been active since the mid-1880s. In the Gaya district, where fearful Muslims had taken to disguising themselves as Hindus to buy cattle at fairs, there were seven or eight serious riots (plus thirteen or fourteen instances of "cattle-snatching") in the summer of 1893.[52] Meanwhile, so uniform were the various outbreaks in Bihar's Patna district—with *sadhus* fasting until cattle were saved, attacks taking place on market days, and other common features—that the district commissioner suspected that the cow-protection agitators were "controlled by some as yet unknown agency."[53]

The biggest outbreak in Bihar involved a convoy of some 120 cattle heading to slaughter at the military barracks at Dinapur. In and around the town of Basantpur, which sat along the route, Hindus had been anticipating the arrival of the cattle for some time: several *sadhus* were fasting in the hope of saving the cattle, and the local *sabha* planned a mass public rescue, which it put into effect when the cattle passed through the district on September 6. After a violent collision, a local indigo planter named Bean managed to disperse the crowd and enabled the drovers to take the cattle to the police station at Basantpur, where, after refusing to sell the cattle to a local landowner for 1,000 rupees, the police inspector secured the animals in a walled compound. Around nine o'clock that evening a crowd of about one thousand people surrounded the compound with sticks and spears to demand the cattle's release, crying out (as MacDonnell later reported) that the *sadhus* had "foretold the doom of the English Raj because of the cow-killing business." The police inspector (whom MacDonnell thought had "done fairly well," for a Bengali) ordered his men to fire blanks at the crowd. When this failed he ordered his men to fire buckshot, wounding several and killing two. Soon the local mounted volunteers (planters from a nearby estate) arrived to escort the cattle to their destination, and no further violence took place.[54]

Responses

In the immediate aftermath of the riots journalists and officials went through the usual round of hand-wringing and finger-pointing. Across India some 107 people had died in about forty-five separate incidents in 1893, an unusually high level of violence in a country where public disturbances were common but deadly riots comparatively rare.[55] Vernacular newspapers, especially those with a nationalist bent, predictably accused the government of partiality and incompetence. The Anglo-Indian press, along with loyalist communities like the Parsis, were much more forgiving of official missteps and sought instead to pin the blame on either the cow-protection societies, the Muslims who opposed them, or both. Most interesting, however, were the official responses. These ranged from the blasé to the alarmed, and they were nicely encapsulated in the attitudes of the men heading the three provinces that had seen the worst rioting: in Bombay, Lord Harris was sanguine to the point of callousness; in Bengal, Antony MacDonnell was realistic in his assessment and creative in his remedies; and in the North-West Provinces, where the riots had begun, Sir Charles Crosthwaite nearly allowed fear to chase him down the path of despotism.

We can begin with the press response, which was, on the whole, livid. Although the Anglophone papers were (uncharacteristically) reluctant to criticize the government's handling of the riots, the same was not true of the vernacular Hindu and Muslim papers, many of whom blamed the state for the outbreaks.[56] D. F. McCracken, head of India's Thagi and Dacoity Department, summarized the press response in a report in August 1893:

> Muhammadan organs in the Native Press throw the blame upon the new education and sometimes on the Government which they declare does not maintain strict neutrality and leans towards the Hindus. Hindu organs on the other hand charge Government officials with deliberately sowing dissension between the two communities or of favouring the Muhammadans at the expense of the Hindus in order to divide and rule.[57]

The Hindu press was especially outspoken. The usual charge was (in the words of the government translation of Bengal's *Dainik-o-Samachar Chandrika*) that the government had "for some time past shown undue favour to the Mussulmans, and in matters affecting Hindus and Mussulmans has occasionally adopted a policy of repression towards the former."[58] Such favoritism was allegedly evident in the police escorts provided to Muslim funeral parties and in the state's willingness to tolerate large crowds at mosques when no such toleration was afforded Hindus gathered at temples.[59]

A great many papers alleged that the state's behavior was part of a deliberate policy of divide and rule—of using the cow issue "to weaken the people by creating quarrels among them and by setting class against class."[60] Several papers hinted darkly that it was just this sort of religious agitation that had provoked the rebellion of 1857.[61] In language reminiscent of 1857 the Hindu *Gujaráti*, which had been a vocal proponent of the cow-protection movement before the riots, argued that the violence

> once more proved, if any proof were at all needed, how those who are responsible for the maintenance of order are not in close touch with the unseen social under-currents, and how a most deplorable and irretrievable catastrophe might happen one day from a state of unpreparedness and the absence of timely vigilance and promptitude.[62]

Another Hindu paper, the *Din Bandhu*, saw in the riots a fundamental threat to British power, observing that "the Mahomedans behaved as if they had assumed the reins of government of the British Empire."[63] Other papers blamed not the government's cupidity but its incompetence, as when Bengal's *Sulabh Dainik* suggested that the magistrate of Azamgarh was "sleeping all the time" when he should have been taking precautions; the same paper also accused the magistrates, most of whom were "beef-eaters," of "insolence, shortsightedness, and ignorance of the religion of the people."[64]

All of this was acutely embarrassing to the ruling power, however much they disavowed any actual responsibility for the outbreaks, and much of the discussion among high-level officials concerned the extent to which these riots presented a real threat to British authority and British prestige. Soon after receiving reports of the first riots the viceroy, Lord Lansdowne, had written to Sir Charles Crosthwaite, head of the North-West Provinces, expressing his concerns about the fragility of British power. "These incidents," he wrote, "bring home to one our numerical weakness in this country, and how easy it is for a large area to get out of hand."[65] Crosthwaite needed little convincing on this score, for his essential policy during and after the riots was to treat the *sabhas* not as communal organizations but as "distinctly seditious societies."[66] The "Congress party," he told Lansdowne, was secretly running the *sabhas*, using the " 'Cow' cry" to "get all of Hindoodom at their back" and organizing a "political agitation under the guise of religious and humane sentiments."[67] "The truth is," he said, "the Hindus are at present full of insolence, and think they can drive the Government."[68] D. F. McCracken, head of the Dacoity and Thagi Department, was also alarmed, observing, "The primary danger is that the Cow-protection question furnishes a common platform on which all Hindus of whatever sect, however much at variance on other questions, can and do unite." Noting the "inflammable and seditious character" of the language these societies used, McCracken felt the movement was

> part of the Hindu revival of which the National Congress is another manifestation, the aspiration at the root of both being directed to the formation

> of an Indian nation and the displacement from power, place and emolument the ruling race, who may however be permitted to guard India for its new Governors.[69]

What began with an attack on the Muslims, in other words, might end with an attack on the British themselves.

Fearful that the state was losing control over a vast portion of the subcontinent, Crosthwaite proposed measures to suppress the *sabhas* and rein in the vernacular press. He advocated laws and amendments to the Penal Code that would make it illegal for societies to compel contributions from people and that would punish people who belonged to societies of this sort. He also wanted to make it illegal, under pain of imprisonment, to belong to a society whose aim was to prevent the use of government cattle pounds or to stop the sale of cattle to Muslims. Landlords and headmen, too, ought (he felt) to be made legally responsible for reporting illegal activities by *sabhas.* As regards the press, Crosthwaite suggested making it illegal for newspapers to publish damaging information if the editor had reason to suspect the information was false, even if the editor did not have definite knowledge to this effect. These reforms were urgently needed, Crosthwaite's secretary reported, "for it is certain that we are face to face with a very dangerous organization which threatens in some districts to become the government *de facto* of the country, and if not suppressed will certainly cause very great trouble in the not distant future."[70]

Crosthwaite's superiors were not quite so frantic. In London Lord Kimberley, the India secretary, thought Crosthwaite showed some signs of "losing his head." Referring to his proposals for press regulation, Kimberly acknowledged that the Indian press was irritating, but he believed it also served a vital function as a "safety valve for explosive opinions." The experience of Russia was instructive in this regard, he felt: there the effect of press censorship was "to drive the disease inwards, and the product is Nihilism with a Tsar whose life is in perpetual danger."[71] Indeed, Kimberley professed to see some good in the violence, insofar as it made "all combination of the Hindoos and Mahometans impossible, and so cuts at the root of the Congress agitation for the formation of a united Indian people, who are to force us to surrender power into their hands."[72] The Indian government in Calcutta was also unmoved by Crosthwaite's alarm. Acknowledging that Crosthwaite was "as bold as a lion," Lansdowne nevertheless noted a "pessimist twist in his mind" and questioned his more forceful proposals.[73] Lansdowne did, however, share a related worry that the cow agitation, while not expressly revolutionary, might be exploited by those who wished to expose Britain's weaknesses. "It is clear," he told Kimberley, "that the agitation is widespread, and organized by men who are thoroughly disloyal to us, and who join this movement, not on account of their religious convictions, but because they see in it a means of shaking our authority and increasing our difficulties."[74] Lansdowne's fears (to say nothing of Crosthwaite's) were understandable but overblown: there certainly were enemies of British rule among the *sabhas*, but it is extremely doubtful that they pursued violence purely for the sake of embarrassing the ruling power.[75] Even the radical nationalist Bal Gangadhar Tilak, who alleged that the government's failure to stop the rioting betrayed a pro-Muslim bias, saw no intrinsic political value in widespread violence; on the contrary, during the uproar, he held several communal meetings devoted to restoring the peace (during which participants made a point of expressing their loyalty to the government).[76]

In Bombay Lord Harris initially shared Crosthwaite's fears. In a dispatch to London at the end of August he worried that the *sabhas* were becoming more political, perhaps at the instigation of "young Congress wallahs" who would use the movement "not merely as a lever against Mahomedans but also against the British Raj." No doubt thinking of the 1857 revolt, Harris particularly worried that the movement might try to "unsettle the minds of our sepoys," a development that could make things "extremely nasty."[77] A month later, however, he had come to share Kimberley's complacency, writing, "It sounds brutal, but I really believe the blood letting has cleared the system advantageously.... We have these difficulties between Hindus and Mahomedans annually, & get accustomed to them." No doubt seeking to justify his own decision not to visit Bombay during the riots, Harris said that it was best not to get too excited if, say, "we get a solemn warning from the Hindus of this or that place that all their throats are going to be cut on such & such a day." Hindus were naturally excitable, he said, and "999 out of 1000 times" their fears came to nothing. "Perhaps," he told Kimberley, "you will think I am acting too confidently & too hopefully; but it is the correct reflection of what I notice round about me; & therefore I don't believe the great danger lies in Bombay."[78] Of course, Kimberley, viewing the situation from the tranquil corridors of the India Office, thought no such thing. "The feud between Hindoo and Mahometan is no new phenomenon," he told Harris reassuringly, and the present trouble "may after all be only one of those recrudescences which always occur in such matters, and the agitation may again subside."[79]

In Bengal and Bihar there was little sign of panic. Most local officials doubted that the *sabhas* were seditious; in fact, many worried that the large number of Indian officials—deputy collectors, munsifs, employees of the postal and education departments—who joined (and sometimes led) the *sabhas* were making it seem as if the groups had the imprimatur of the government.[80] Nor was Bengal's lieutenant governor, Antony MacDonnell, especially worried. "The foundations of the Empire are surely not to be shaken by a handful of scoundrelly preachers in a few districts," he told Lansdowne.[81] MacDonnell was not as quite as sanguine as Harris, however, for he felt that the *sabhas* did present a serious law-and-order dilemma. Having failed to establish effective conciliation committees at the outset of the trouble, MacDonnell now presented several typically creative proposals for dealing with the societies. Perhaps, he suggested, the *sabhas* could be forced to register with the government, their members tracked by the police, and perhaps even required to serve as special constables during times of disturbance.[82] The government might even turn the *sabhas* "to good account" by making them into bodies devoted to "protecting and improving" cattle, complete with official badges.[83]

Although MacDonnell understood the potential threat of the cow-protection movement to British authority, he maintained that Crosthwaite's draconian proposals were likely to backfire.[84] Anything that looked like a government attack on the Hindu religion, or any interference with customary practices generally, might actually give a boost to the movement and lead it to "assume that seditious character which Sir Charles Crosthwaite is disposed to attribute" to it. "The attention of the entire Hindu population in all Provinces would be arrested, and a tremor of excitement would pass through the land, of which all that could with certainty now be said is that its effects would be evil, far-reaching, and possibly ineradicable." The worst thing that could happen to the British Raj, in MacDonnell's estimation, was "a conflict between the Government and the people over a religious question." Nor was interfering with the "liberty of the press" either practical or politic. A certain strengthening of existing laws might be desirable—for instance fining an entire village for property damage, or making landlords legally responsible for violence and coercion on their estates—and better enforcement of those laws was certainly necessary, but legislation targeting the *sabhas* or the press, he felt, was likely to do more harm than good.[85]

There were some officials under MacDonnell (principally in Bihar) who saw things differently, however. T. M. Gibbons, manager of the princely state of Bettiah Raj, was convinced that the "ultimate object" of the cow-protection movement was "to excite the people to sedition to the subversion of the British power." Although he confessed that he had no proof of this, he pointed to a string of unusual and suspicious visitors to Bettiah in the past few years, as well as to a general spirit of disaffection:

> In Bihar and in the North-Western Provinces there is a general belief abroad that all our Government do is governed by purely selfish motives. Our

> irresponsible writing, our habit of threatening when we do not immediately get our own way with them, added to our general levelling propensities are destroying the loyalty of Bihar, the most loyal people in India; we are losing all touch with them.

Among other suggestions, Gibbons argued that the police should use "ball and not blank cartridge" when firing on crowds, that they must "fire low," and that the government should "hang the first policeman who fires in the air."[86] H. C. Williams, magistrate and collector at Darbhanga, proposed similarly forceful measures: "special detectives" to "shadow" preachers, troops to march regularly through disturbed districts, and "some kind of censorship" of the *sabhas'* publications.[87]

Proposals of this sort carried a distinct echo of the counterinsurgency measures that had been used against Irish revolutionaries over the past three decades, so it is unsurprising that officials who saw the *sabhas* as potentially revolutionary often invoked the Irish example, either to explain the *sabhas'* insurrectionary potential by analogy, or to suggest that Britain's Irish policy might be directly emboldening Indian nationalists. In his dispatch from Darbhanga, for instance, H. C. Williams observed that Muslims believed the Hindus were "following the example of Ireland" in "trying to get everything their own way."[88] When Sir Charles Lyall, the home secretary of India, argued against publishing everything the government knew about the *sabhas*, he pointed out that the government had never published all it knew about the Irish Republican (Fenian) Brotherhood, and "this great Hindu movement is much more dangerous to the peace of India than Fenianism ever was to that of Ireland."[89] Lord Lansdowne, himself an Anglo-Irish landlord, worried that with cow-protection the nationalists had found an issue that would link them with the "great mass of the Hindu population" much as "[t]he Home Rule movement did not become really formidable until Parnell had taken up the agrarian question."[90] A few Indian papers were also alive to the Irish analogy. Repeating the standard Hindu nationalist line that the government was partial to Muslims, the *Mahrátta* (the newspaper of Bal Gangadhar Tilak) suggested that this was much like Lord Salisbury's policy of "supporting the Protestant population of Ulster against Irishmen generally."[91] Curiously (but significantly) the one high-ranking Irish Catholic who took part in this discussion, Antony MacDonnell, offered few such parallels, apart from a fleeting reference to the tendency of the *sabhas* to engage in the sort of "exclusive dealing" (that is, patronizing only their own coreligionists) that was common amongst Irish boycotters.[92] Perhaps MacDonnell's greater familiarity with the

Irish case helped him recognize that the cow-protection movement was not, in fact, truly analogous.[93]

Epilogue

In the end, MacDonnell's moderation carried the day.[94] In January 1894 the Indian government circulated secret instructions to the provincial governments, along with one of MacDonnell's letters from the previous November, outlining the steps that could be taken under existing law to curb the activities of the *sabhas*. No new repressive legislation of the sort Crosthwaite advocated was deemed necessary, although the government did decide to amend the Police Act, the Criminal Procedure Code, and Indian Penal Codes to require local headmen and landholders to inform the government about illegal activities under their purview. The government also instructed local commissioners to submit regular reports on the *sabhas'* activities. And it directed that, in urban areas, the slaughter of cows for purposes other than religious sacrifice was to be confined to designated slaughterhouses, and the sale and transportation of cattle and beef was to be carefully regulated.[95] ("[A]nd a nice lot of trouble we police had to enforce the regulations," grumbled Edmund Cox in his memoir.[96]) Thus, despite the fears expressed by Crosthwaite and others that the cow-killing agitation might be seditious, the Indian government decided that it was more dangerous to outrage Hindu opinion by openly suppressing the *sabhas* than to allow them to continue their campaign. In this instance, at least, surgical judiciousness won out over the blunter instruments of panic.

At the local level, the riots of 1893 prompted several changes to policing practices that would fundamentally alter the people's relationship with the state. In Bombay the police acquired greater coercive powers and, in the words of historian Prashant Kidambi, became "an increasingly obtrusive element in the social relations of the street and the neighbourhood."[97] In 1902 the Bombay police acquired the power to direct the timing, routes, and behavior of processions and assemblies; to regulate music and public addresses; and generally to exercise a degree of control over commercial and public life that put them in ever more frequent conflict with the people.[98] Indeed, across India the enhanced surveillance of cow-protection *sabhas* led to greater state surveillance of associational life, culminating in a full-blown surveillance-and-security state in the next century, a development that signaled the end of any hope that Britain could hold India primarily through "soft power."[99]

These measures did not immediately end the violence, however. The following year there were renewed outbreaks in several places, especially in the Maharashtra towns of Yeola and Poona, both in the Bombay presidency. The Yeola clashes began with a Hindu boycott of Muslim businesses, evolved into a dispute over musical processions, and culminated in a pig carcass being hurled into a mosque.[100] Lord Harris, aloof as ever, told the viceroy, "The odd thing is that it has nothing to do with cow-killing. It is arrogance as regards processions and music-playing; and what has started it, and what is working it now, I can't make out."[101] The Poona riot also stemmed from a music-before-mosques dispute, in the course of which Muslims attacked a Hindu procession and Hindus responded by rampaging through a mosque.[102] What set the Poona riot apart was the unusual interest that it attracted in Britain, particularly among no less a personage than Queen Victoria, who, in a series of frank communications with the Indian government, insisted that her officials must protect Muslims from Hindu extremism. After being assured by a somewhat anxious viceroy (now Lord Elgin, after the retirement of Lansdowne) that the government's policy was to observe strict impartiality between the sects, Victoria made her sympathies clear:

> The Queen-Empress *entirely* concurs in the necessity and wisdom of a policy of religious impartiality; but she cannot help feeling that the Brahmins are those who incite the people *against us*, and that the Mahomedans are the real supporters of the *British* rule; and she does think that they should be protected from insults and disturbance in their very peaceful and quiet worship, which is so opposed to idolatry.[103]

This sort of talk was extremely dangerous coming from the crowned head of all India, and both Harris and Elgin were at pains to keep Her Majesty's views quiet, lest they give the impression that the government shared Victoria's special affection for Muslims.[104]

Cow-protection, and the associated question of music-before-mosques, continued to produce riots into the twentieth century, although outbreaks of plague and famine in 1896–7 changed the dynamic in many ways. As we will see in the next chapter, the fears entertained by the likes of Crosthwaite and Lansdowne that the cow-protection movement might become seditious proved prescient, for the *sabhas* did indeed feed into the nascent mass campaign for Indian independence. The fact that the nationalist movement grafted itself onto what was essentially a sectarian Hindu movement was to be profoundly important for the future of Indian nationalism, which failed, in the long run, to develop a genuinely popular nonsectarian ethos. Any Muslims who remembered the cow-protection disputes of the 1890s would (understandably) be reluctant to join a nationalist movement that included notorious cow-protection agitators in its ranks, as the Congress movement soon would do. Perhaps, such Muslims might conclude, what they needed was their own organization to advocate for their own special interests. And in this way, although nobody could have foreseen it at the time, the communal riots of the 1890s turned out to have serious consequences not only for the British Raj but also for the very shape and size of independent India.[105]

8

Consequences: How Communal Riots Weakened the British Empire

None of the riots examined in this volume fatally wounded the British Empire, but a case could be made that they corroded it. As we have seen in each of the four extended riot narratives in this book, communal riots were both a symptom and a cause of a deficit of state legitimacy. Distrust of the imperial state's motives, alienation from the forces of law and order (especially when they drew their personnel from outside of the community), and a feeling of having been abandoned by important sectors of the state were all features of these disturbances. Not only did such attitudes lead many people to commit or condone acts of violence, but the violence itself also exposed the state's weaknesses and deepened antistate attitudes among imperial subjects. Each of these riots, in short, was profoundly embarrassing for the British state. The precise weight of this embarrassment varied from episode to episode and from person to person, but one can see its effects in the stones thrown at Philip Wodehouse as he departed Georgetown harbor in 1857, in the insults heaped upon Frank Souter and Wodehouse (again) in Bombay in 1874, and in the chorus of complaints about state partiality and incompetence that rang across India in 1893. These outbursts were fairly trivial in themselves, but they bespoke a larger crisis of state authority that could not easily be shrugged off. The more embarrassed a state became during a riot, for instance, the more imperial subjects—frightened, infuriated, or both—tended to gravitate toward their own communal vigilantes, many of whom could claim to act with more efficacy, and often more legitimacy, than the constituted authorities. State failure could therefore have a galvanizing effect within rival communities, promoting ties of group solidarity as well as giving rise to communal organizations that might be turned not only against communal rivals but also against the state itself. To guard against such dangers, and to overcome other embarrassing consequences of these riots, British officials sometimes responded with forceful, even draconian measures that, while perhaps curtailing the violence in the short term, nevertheless served to further alienate the populace and strengthen communal activists in the long term.

This chapter explores these corrosive consequences of communal rioting, arguing that in many cases it was the British response to violence, rather than the violence itself, that was most damaging to the long-term stability of British imperial power. It will also explain how the communal politics of the Victorian era fed into the nationalist politics of the twentieth century, an evolution that had profound consequences not only for the British Empire but also for the post-British societies that emerged in its wake. I do not wish to overstate the role of these Victorian-era riots in weakening the British Empire—there were many other forces, both internal and external, that would play a greater role in destabilizing the empire both in the Victorian era and in the decades to come—but I do hope to demonstrate how communal violence both exposed and exacerbated some of the empire's structural defects at the very moment when British wealth, power, and self-assurance seemed to be at their peak. In the twentieth century these defects would become impossible to rectify or ignore, particularly in Ireland and India, arguably the most important pillars of the empire. The communal wars that eventually broke out in these countries were much more destructive than anything the Victorians experienced, and their patterns of violence were novel and complex, but their origins clearly lay in the dynamic of communal fragmentation and antistate alienation that began during the Victorian period.

The embarrassment of riots

Nothing is quite as embarrassing for a modern state as the collapse of social order in one of its territories. Rebellions, natural disasters, foreign invasions, epidemics, outbursts of unsanctioned violence by state agents—all of these events can be calamitous, and some can be quite embarrassing, but none of them cut to the heart of a state's avowed purpose like internal violence and disorder. If this is true of states in general, it was especially true of the British Empire during its heyday: social peace was a key component of the *Pax Britannica* upon which the empire staked its legitimacy, a vital precondition of all the other benefits that were meant to flow from British rule—modernity, prosperity, moral improvement, and the rule of law, to name a few. Social peace was also necessary to secure the British state's support among alien populations. Any state that cannot guarantee the smooth functioning of society—any state that cannot protect its people's lives and property—will have a difficult time securing the loyalty and obedience of the people over whom it rules. How much more must this be the case for an imperial state, imposed from without, with few organic claims to legitimacy? The British state needed to maintain at least an aura of competence (if not omnipotence) in the territories it ruled; violence and disorder, if it occurred often enough and lasted long enough, could seriously darken that aura.

This is why the embarrassment of communal violence mattered so much. As R. L. Stirrat has said of the 1883 Colombo riot, such outbreaks "threatened that sense of superiority and unfailing competence essential to the identity of any colonial regime."[1] As we have seen in all four of our extended case studies, many of the people who witnessed, suffered from, or took part in a riot came to see the British state as partisan or inept, whether they had good reasons for doing so or not. Unfettered by strict censorship or other regulations, discontented journalists, activists, revivalists, and other local observers were free to broadcast their abuse far and wide, often in language that was shockingly bold. During the Bombay riots of 1874, to take one example, we saw more than one Anglophone writer call the police commissioner a "simpleton" and one paper, the *North-West Herald*, call the governor "a man of such slender character and attenuated mental calibre as to render it inexplicable how it came to pass that he was entrusted with the administration of an important province."[2] Often it was self-proclaimed loyalists who were the most abusive of the authorities. Thus the Presbyterian preacher Hugh Hanna inveighed against the "imbecility of the Belfast magistrates" who tried to prevent his public preaching in 1857, calling them "positively a greater evil than the mob."[3] Hanna's anger, like that of other loyalists around the empire, derived from a sense that the state had abdicated its responsibility to protect its supporters, but their attacks were no less stinging for having come from friendly quarters.

Newspapers—local and metropolitan, Anglophone and vernacular—were the most reliable critics of government behavior during these riots. Because they tended to speak for the propertied classes, the chief complaint of the Anglophone press was that the state had been too timid in checking the unrest—that, for instance, the police should have shot more people at the outset of a disturbance, as we saw both the *Bombay Gazette* and the *Belfast Daily Mercury* recommend in Chapter 6.[4] Categorical derision of the authorities was also a common feature of British publications. The *Economist*, to take one influential metropolitan example, argued that the Belfast riots of 1864 were the consequence "of imbecility, of inadequate precautions and more inadequate remedies, of dismay, party rancor, paralysing sympathies and antipathies on the part of the magistrates and police."[5] Following the 1882 Salem riots the Calcutta weekly *The Friend of India and Statesman* rendered a similar judgment about officials in Madras, concluding its review of press reports about the violence thus: "[i]ncompetence and mismanagement seem to sum up the general verdict on the condition of the authorities before and during the *émeute*."[6] The *Ceylon Observer* likewise criticized the behavior of British officials in Colombo for their "monstrous" folly in sanctioning the Buddhist procession that sparked the Colombo riot of 1883, while the *Ceylon Examiner* (a Burgher, rather than English, publication) attacked the police (the "real criminals" with "blood on their hands") for their "criminal thoughtlessness and incompetency" which brought the law itself into "disrepute."[7] Indeed, quite a few Anglophone observers worried that unchecked violence might encourage popular contempt for the law, or for the law's guardians. Thus a correspondent to the *Times of India* worried that the 1874 Bombay riots were creating "an indelible blot on the character of the British Raj." The solution, this writer felt, was for the authorities to impose martial law, and thereby "do a little wrong in order to do a great deal of good."[8] This was precisely the sort of logic that would underpin some of the greatest state atrocities of the nineteenth and twentieth centuries (one thinks of the Morant Bay rebellion in Jamaica, the shelling of Dublin during the Easter Rising, the Amritsar Massacre, and much more), and, as we will see below, the temptation to "do a little wrong in order to do a great deal of good" in the matter of communal violence was increasingly one to which British officials succumbed as the Victorian period drew to a close.

The loudest critics of the government, of course, were the "native" or vernacular papers, who usually pounced on any sign of incompetence or partiality to tell their readers (many of whom were already parties to the dispute) that the state was their enemy. One of the most colorful expressions of this demotic distrust of the state came from the Fenian newspaper *The Irish People* after the Belfast riots of 1864, when it accused both sets of rioters of

> playing the most subtle and successful game of those who, so long as they can get our countrymen to contend about "opinions," can safely deal with the property and prosperity of the nation as the monkey did with the beef, which it quietly devoured, while the quarrelsome cats tore each other to pieces over the bones.[9]

We cannot know for certain how Irish readers responded to observations like this, or what Indian readers thought about accusations that (as the Azamgarh

Sanjivani said in 1893) "the North-Western Provinces authorities brought about the riots with the view of harassing the Hindus" or that (as Rawalpindi's *Taj-ul-Akhbar* said) "Government officials deliberately provoked ill-feeling between the two communities in order to win a name for themselves by suppressing the disturbances which they had originated," but the frequency with which these accusations were made suggests that these ideas had some popular currency.[10] Moreover, as my discussion of vigilantism will shortly demonstrate, the palpable distrust with which Belfast Catholics regarded the local police, the self-defense initiatives Bombay Parsis adopted in 1874, and other concrete manifestations of anti-state alienation clearly indicate that these ideas were prevalent among important segments of the imperial populace.

Certainly many British officials were aware of the damage that communal violence could do to the empire's prestige. Following the 1864 Belfast riots the chief secretary of Ireland wrote confidentially to his undersecretary, "The Belfast business has done much harm in this country—The general feeling is that the arm of govt. is weak. This is the greatest misfortune we can endure."[11] This sentiment, as we have seen, likewise animated Lord Lansdowne during the 1893 Indian riots, as it did many other India officials. Shortly after the 1893 riots began, Dennis Fitzpatrick, lieutenant governor of Punjab, told Lansdowne that the government had so far acted impartially—by which he meant they had "hit" the Hindus hard in the North-West Provinces and "hit" the Muslims hard in Rangoon and Bombay—but that this could change if the rioting lasted much longer. There was a "very serious danger," Fitzpatrick said, that "things might in some parts of the country take such a turn that, in spite of all we could do, we could not keep ourselves clear of the quarrel; that we should be forced from our position of neutrality, and be compelled to some extent to take a side, and after that, of course, whatever we did, would be put down to prejudice and partiality."[12] (Fitzpatrick did not seem to be aware that the Hindu press was already accusing Britain of favoring the Muslims in these disputes or that just ten days earlier Antony MacDonnell, officiating lieutenant governor of Bengal, had admitted to Lansdowne, "There is a bias in favour of Mahomedans on the part of my officers which must not be allowed to appear."[13]) Around this time Sir Alfred Lyall also noted the dangers that communal riots presented to the Raj's position of neutrality, observing that when Indian communities came into conflict

> the parties actually engaged are apt to be impatient of and to disregard the neutral flag of toleration; nor does our Government at present obtain unanimous applause for its appearance in the character (so novel on the

> Asiatic stage) of an impartial bystander, prejudiced only in favour of order and material prosperity. And thus it has come to pass that our neutrality has been challenged simultaneously, yet from different and indeed opposite points of view, by Hindus, Mahomedans, and various energetic partisan leaders of Christians in England.[14]

For Lyall—as, indeed, for many other proponents of Britain's civilizing mission—it was a frustrating experience trying to convince imperial subjects that the state's intentions were noble. As Kipling would memorably lament, no matter how earnestly one took up the white man's burden, "the silent, sullen peoples / shall weigh their gods and you."

This helps to explain why, when British officials spoke of restoring order after a riot, they frequently spoke of restoring people's "confidence" in the forces of law and order, for at bottom every breakdown of order called into question the state's competence (or even willingness) to protect the life and property of its subjects.[15] Many officials, especially in India but also elsewhere, were acutely aware of the fragility of their position. Looking back on his long career in the Indian Civil Service, Sir Bampfylde Fuller reflected, "Our influence in India rests not so much upon our strength as upon prevailing ideas of our strength; and if anything occurs to weaken these ideas, the people of the country prepare themselves for a change of rulers."[16] In 1906 Lord Minto, Indian viceroy, made a similar remark to Lord Morley, who as secretary of state for India had more conciliatory instincts than the viceroy: "We are here a small British garrison, surrounded by millions composed of factors of an inflammability unknown to the Western world, unsuited to Western forms of government, and we must be physically strong or go to the wall."[17]

If communal riots called into question the state's repressive capacity, they also called into question its intentions, especially its intention to be (or to be seen to be) an impartial referee standing above communal rivalries.[18] In fact, the state's frequent insistence on its own impartiality (recall Lyall's insistence, noted above, that the state in India was "prejudiced only in favour of order and material prosperity") created unrealistic expectations among imperial subjects that policemen, magistrates, and other officials would always act disinterestedly, and when they failed to do so—or when, in the zero-sum game of communal politics, state officials simply gave one side something that their opponents did not want them to have—the state's prestige could be fatally compromised. We have seen numerous examples throughout this book of individual officials failing to act with strict impartiality, so we need not belabor the point here, except to point out that this was a problem right across the empire. In Ireland there were the Protestants of the Belfast local police who, prior to the force's dissolution in 1865, marched in sectarian processions one day and policed communal riots the next.[19] In India there was the Hindu policeman Manohar Das, in charge of the station at Shadiabad during the cow-protection riots, who sided with armed Hindu agitators, made local Muslims promise never to sacrifice cows again, neglected to make a note of the unrest in the station diary, refused to conduct an inquiry, and ended up in prison for a month.[20] A few years later, in Calcutta, Muslim millworkers viciously attacked policemen (whom they already suspected, for good reason, of being anti-Muslim) after the police tore down an unauthorized mosque, and even some Hindus took part in this antipolice activity, among the worst disturbances Calcutta had ever seen, in a striking display of the depths to which the police force's reputation had sunk in that city.[21] In Ceylon, meanwhile, a certain Police Inspector Goneratna had an apparent proclivity for accepting bribes from both Catholics and Buddhists before and during the Colombo riot of 1883, which earned him a demotion despite his insistence that the ecumenical character of his enemies actually proved his impartiality.[22] Indeed, wherever the British relied upon local people to help them keep the peace—which is to say, nearly everywhere the Union Jack flew—they found it impossible to keep the state fully disengaged from communal disputes, and their reputation for impartiality suffered accordingly.

Individual failings aside, however, what mattered more than actual state partiality was the perception of unfair dealing among imperial subjects. Every serious communal riot that I have examined—in Ireland, South Asia, and the West Indies—provoked complaints of state bias from at least one, and frequently all, parties to a dispute.[23] Even when state agents contorted themselves to maintain their impartiality, often by seeking compromises that would appease all sides, somebody was sure to accuse them of siding with their enemies. This is what happened to Frank Souter in Bombay when he tried to placate Muslims by suppressing the allegedly anti-Mohamed book published by a Parsi. The Parsis duly complained that Souter was kowtowing to Muslim intolerance, and when more Muslims than Parsis were arrested during the riots, and when the authorities decided to suppress the Muslims' Muharram processions to prevent more violence, Muslim leaders made the same allegation. In Ireland, where the government deliberately sought to improve the efficiency and impartiality of the police by taking power away from Protestant elites and giving it to a centralized constabulary and magistracy, it succeeded only in angering Protestants while failing to appease Catholics.[24] In Ceylon both Catholics and Buddhists accused the police of favoritism so frequently that the government agent investigating the 1883 Colombo riot told London that both sides "so generally abuse the police and declare they favoured the opposite side that I am led to the belief they acted impartially and performed a very trying duty to the best of their ability."[25] This argument may have satisfied London, but it would do little to restore the state's credibility among the Sinhalese.

There was another way that state bias (or apparent bias) could foster violence. This happened when one side to a communal dispute believed that they had the state on their side—that is, when one side felt it could act with impunity because they were carrying out the wishes of the state.[26] The 1883 riots in Colombo were partly a result of such a misapprehension by Buddhist revivalists who believed that the governor, Sir James Robert Longden, was secretly a Buddhist who would protect them in their procession dispute with Catholics. The rumor probably originated with Migettuwatte Gunananda, a leading Buddhist revivalist who made no secret of his friendship with the governor, going so far as to emblazon the royal coat of arms above the Buddha statue in his temple and telling his followers that the British favored Buddhism over the island's other religions. There were other rumors as well: that the government had granted the Buddhists permission to hold processions at any time of the day or night, that Queen Victoria herself had given Migettuwatte special permission to hold processions regardless of what local officials said, and so forth. All of these rumors were equally baseless, but they emboldened Migettuwatte's Buddhist followers and encouraged them in their determination to hold a controversial procession past a Catholic church, which resulted in Colombo's worst riot of the nineteenth century.[27] As we saw in Chapter 1, another mistaken feeling of impunity animated the Guianese Creoles who attacked Portuguese homes and shops in 1856. After the initial unrest in Georgetown, Creole emissaries went from town to town pretending to read from official directives calling for the Portuguese to be driven from the country, performances that were apparently so convincing that some people were actually surprised when soldiers came out to stop the destruction.[28] Such episodes give us a sense of just how difficult it was for the state to keep clear of communal conflicts: even if state agents managed to control their own behavior, they could not control people's imaginations.[29]

Vigilantism

Most riots, no matter their cause, provide opportunities for vigilantism. When a state is incapable of preserving order there will usually be people ready fill the void, either to defend their communities, to settle old scores, or simply to loot and plunder, often under the guise of communal self-defense organizations. When a state appears not just to be losing control but actually to be taking sides (and there was always, as I have been arguing, someone who believed that the British state was taking sides), then the vigilante can also claim a certain moral legitimacy in order to gain the support of the community. If disorder is prolonged or frequent enough, the state can face a severe legitimacy problem: its monopoly on the legitimate use of force can dissolve as ordinary people turn to their own violent extremists for protection or vengeance.[30]

This problem was most acute in Ireland, especially in its northeast corner, where rival groups of Protestants and Catholics sometimes enjoyed such power among their respective communities that they could afford to ignore or even bully the constituted authorities—that is, when they were not actively colluding with them. In July 1865 the lord lieutenant of Ireland received a panicked letter from a retired Irish MP complaining about the violence at the general election that month. Local magistrates, the MP said, were leading armed parties of Protestants to the polls, and, owing to the cheapness of firearms, he feared that soon "*both* sides will be armed & civil war will rage." The north of Ireland was "not fit to live in during July," he said (even when there was not an election on, July was the traditional Protestant marching season) and although the Catholics had so far borne the provocation with great patience, their forbearance was now "*coming to an end* and they are determined to protect themselves if the Govt. does not."[31] The lord lieutenant, John Wodehouse (later Lord Kimberley), professed himself unconcerned by these developments, assuring his correspondent that the newspaper reports were exaggerated and that even England experienced the occasional bout of election violence. Panic, he said, would get one nowhere.[32]

In fact, a little bit of panic was probably in order. By the end of the nineteenth century the northeastern corner of Ireland had developed one of the empire's most vigorous vigilante traditions, one that would ultimately help undermine British rule and lead to the partitioning of the island. In fact, just the year before Wodehouse heard from the panicked magistrate, in 1864, large groups of Irishmen had shown profound distrust of the authorities, local and national, during more than a week of rioting in Belfast. Catholic laborers, angry at repeated Protestant attacks on female Catholic millworkers, had rampaged through the center of town and attacked a Protestant school, proclaiming themselves the defenders of Catholics who were unprotected by the police. In retaliation, Protestant shipyard workers had stormed into several shops in town, appropriating weapons (but promising to return them once the Catholics were routed), and then chasing the Catholic laborers into the sea in a fierce and deadly battle. Both groups, but especially the Protestants, were consciously performing deeds that they felt should have been done by the police: the Catholics distrusted the largely Protestant local force (which would, largely for this reason, be abolished the following year), and the Protestants felt the police had shown themselves incapable of restoring law and order. Drawing on a long tradition of Protestant self-reliance in Ireland, the shipyard workers claimed that they were assisting, not subverting, the civil power—helping to "to crush the fearful riot" as a celebratory ballad put it—when they were really trying to preserve a measure of Protestant supremacy in a rapidly shifting communal landscape.[33]

The post-1850 history of Belfast (and, to a lesser extent, other parts of north-east Ireland) is in many ways the history of a steadily building antistate alienation among both Catholics and Protestants, a crisis so severe that by 1912 large numbers of the latter had decided to form a paramilitary force to fight the British state in order to remain within the United Kingdom. It was a crisis propelled and sustained by a steady drumbeat of rioting throughout the period, rioting that both exposed the limits of state power and created opportunities for vigilante activity. The problem for Catholics, not only in Belfast but throughout the north of Ireland, was that the local levers of power were almost wholly controlled by Protestants, either in the form of municipal governments or rural landowners-cum-magistrates, many of whom felt they had a duty to preserve Protestant supremacy. As an instance of Catholic vigilantism we might point to the Catholic Gun Club formed during the Belfast riots of 1857 to help Catholics purchase guns and (ostensibly) defend their neighborhoods from Protestant attack.[34] Although the connection is difficult to trace, it seems likely that this tradition of Catholic "self-defense" eventually fed into the insurgency campaigns of the early Irish Republican Army, which, while primarily fighting for Irish independence, also presented itself as an organization devoted to protecting Catholics from violence at the hands of Protestant vigilantes and their state allies.

The Irish Protestant tradition of vigilantism sprang from a different source and was even more powerful. What worried Protestants in the north was not the partisanship of local officials—who, after all, were usually on their side—but the steady undercutting of those officials by a central government determined to give Ireland a more efficient, disinterested, and professional law-enforcement apparatus. The Protestant tradition of defending themselves from their enemies found its strongest expression in the Orange Order, a fraternal organization founded in 1795 that enjoyed massive popular support in the last decades of the Victorian era. Through processions, petitions, and other acts of defiance the

Orangemen pledged themselves to uphold the so-called Protestant Ascendancy and to resist any government that left them stranded in a hostile Catholic sea; sometimes (as with the Belfast shipyard workers) they claimed to be acting as adjuncts to the state in preserving order, and sometimes they showed a striking readiness to fight the state in order to preserve what they saw as their "civil and religious liberties." This spirit of Protestant vigilantism was abundantly demonstrated during the Belfast riots of 1886, when working-class Protestants assailed the Royal Irish Constabulary, rumored to be carrying out orders to force Protestants into a Catholic-dominated Irish state, and made large parts of Belfast no-go areas for several days. Such alienation reached its apotheosis in 1912 with the formation of the Ulster Volunteer Force, a paramilitary organization devoted to violently resisting Irish Home Rule. To a very large extent, the modern history of Belfast (and Northern Ireland generally) has been shaped by communal entrepreneurs who have managed, for varying lengths of time, and with varying degrees of success, to claim for themselves the legitimate functions of a state.

Distrust of the state, and the corresponding impulse to organize independently for communal self-defense or self-assertion, was also evident in other parts of the Victorian Empire, albeit on a lesser scale. The Bombay riots of 1874 are a good example, since they prompted Parsis, usually the most tranquil and loyal community in the city, to form neighborhood defense organizations outside of the state's purview. As we saw in Chapter 5, Bombay's governor, Sir Philip Wodehouse, seems to have encouraged the Parsis to defend themselves along the lines of English special constables, but this does not alter the fact that their vigilantism demonstrated a profound, indeed astonishing, level of distrust of the ruling power. According to the *Bombay Samachar*, a Parsi paper, Wodehouse's "frightening" abdication of responsibility led Parsis of all varieties to lose "all confidence in the Government." Some were contemplating emigration to America, and others were beginning to question the entire "future of India" under British rule:

> The Parsees have now begun to think what should be done to make themselves independent of Government on occasions like these. They see their grand mistake in relying too much on Government. On the strength of Government protection the Parsees had abandoned their habits of manly exercise and taken entirely to mental labours. They now feel that physical exercise is of first importance, and that henceforth every Parsee street should have a gymnasium. The employment of sailors, Purdasees, and others to guard streets is a sure sign of want of confidence.[35]

Thus did Bombay's most loyal community become, at least for a time, one of its most alienated. By the time of the 1893 Bombay riots it seems as if the Parsis, to judge from their spokesmen in the press, had regained their trust in the state, so we must be careful not to see this momentary efflorescence of vigilantism as evidence of a total withdrawal from participation in the British system. For that to happen, communal entrepreneurs must have numerous occasions, over considerable periods of time, to demonstrate that they can protect their people better than the state can. Without prolonged or recurring evidence of state failure, vigilante groups cannot sustain the kind of institutional presence necessary to become a true rival to the state. In the Victorian era most colonial governments managed to reassert themselves fairly quickly after a disturbance, but their successors in the twentieth century would not always be so fortunate.

Communalists into nationalists

For most of this study I have been examining communal violence in isolation from larger political forces, especially colonial nationalist movements advocating self-rule, but to fully grasp how communalism, and the state's responses to it, changed over time it is necessary to understand these evolving political contexts. Put simply, as the nineteenth century faded into the twentieth, communal violence, and the communal mobilization out of which it sprang, began to acquire a more nationalist flavor. The moment of transformation that British officials had long feared—the moment when rival communities stopped fighting one another and began fighting the state—never quite arrived, for violence is not (despite what the British sometimes assumed) a disease that spreads indiscriminately, shared first among acquaintances and then unleashed upon strangers. What actually happened was far more destructive than that. Rather than putting aside their rivalries, many communities clung to their Victorian-era quarrels even as they became more aggressive in their attacks upon the British. This meant that the competing communities forged in the riots of the Victorian period survived into the twentieth century largely intact, and the political liberty that each individual group of nationalists demanded tended (despite their protestations to the contrary) to be an essentially communal sort of liberty. That is, successful nationalist groups tended to justify their demands for freedom by pointing to the solidarity and homogeneity of their own particular religious or ethnic communities, rather than demanding equality for all subject communities equally. Communalism, in short, became an essential building block of anticolonial nationalism.

Scholars of nationalism in South Asia and Ireland would undoubtedly object that the leading nationalist organizations in both places (the Indian National Congress, the Irish Republican Brotherhood, and the various Irish nationalist parties) were in fact avowedly nonsectarian in both ideology and practice. If they came to be dominated by one communal group (Hindus in the former, Catholics in the latter), this was not because they excluded minorities, but because other communities—deluded perhaps by their own communal leaders, or bought off by a cynical, divide-and-rule government—deliberately held themselves aloof. The failure to form a genuinely inclusive nationalism was not the fault of secular nationalists, so this argument might run, but of those who sabotaged the secular nationalists' inclusive vision. This argument is true up to a point, but it fails to account for two (closely related) factors. First, in the late nineteenth century nationalist leaders throughout the empire began to realize that one of the best ways to mobilize the masses was to appeal to their communal identities. The Catholic Church in Ireland, Buddhist revivalists in Ceylon, Hindu (and, in places, Muslim) revivalists in India, and a host of other communal movements and institutions often provided the surest way for a secular, cosmopolitan nationalist elite to connect with a far more traditional and conservative public. Second, the communal riots of the Victorian era, which kept old grievances alive and gave birth to new ones, created (or revived) communal fault lines that ordinary people found it difficult to cross. The nationalist elite might be able to envision a free nation in which all communities got along together, but many ordinary people—at least the ones who had lived through the fires of communal warfare—thought otherwise. The appeal of these communal (rather than national) bonds became dramatically clear in the violent partitioning, largely along communal lines, of both India and Ireland at the moment of each country's independence. Although many factors had to converge before partition became a viable, much less desirable, option for British and nationalist statesmen in these countries, the decision to create a largely Muslim Pakistan and a largely Protestant Northern Ireland out of previously unitary polities owed much to the communal violence of the Victorian period.

We can date the merging of communalism and nationalism in Ireland to the 1870s, when the combined powers of militant nationalism (in the form of the Irish Republican Brotherhood and its offshoots) and legislative reformism (in the form of the parliamentary Home Rule movement) made some form of Irish political autonomy a feasible, if still somewhat distant, objective. Until that time, sectarian violence in places like Belfast and Derry had had only a tenuous connection with the question of Ireland's political future; much more important were the parochial questions of parading, public preaching, and control of public space. These questions never went away, but, as the Irish national question came to dominate British politics, individuals and organizations that had previously served a largely communal purpose began to take on political roles. Thus, Hugh Hanna, the Belfast Presbyterian minister who had begun his career by proselytizing among Catholics and had risen to prominence by upholding the right to open-air preaching in the 1850s (and who, as we have seen, helped foment the 1872 Belfast riots), ended his career as one of the city's most outspoken and popular opponents of Irish Home Rule. Likewise, the Orange Order, devoted primarily to the task of defending ordinary Protestants from "papist" aggression for most of the century, had by the 1880s become the most important expression of demotic Protestant opposition to Home Rule. On the nationalist side the Catholic Church began to support legislative Home Rule in the 1870s, while underground sectarian organizations gave way to the revolutionary (and ostensibly nonsectarian) nationalism of the Irish Republican Brotherhood, also known as the Fenians. The scaffolding of Irish nationalism and unionism, in other words, was built upon a foundation of communalism.

The reasons Irish nationalism never became truly nonsectarian are complex and lie well beyond the scope of this book. They range from the internal collapse of Ulster liberalism to the cultural and economic appeal of a British (as distinct from Irish) identity for Irish Protestants, and they have been ably analyzed by many other historians.[36] But one crucial factor was surely the fact that secular cosmopolitan nationalists were trying to build a cross-communal movement on ground that was already cracked. The communal riots of the nineteenth century had created suspicions and grievances that no manufactured identity, no putative common Irishness articulated by an educated elite, could overcome. Moreover, the involvement of the British state in these riots, and Britain's larger failure to construct a version of a state upon which both Catholics and Protestants could agree, meant that there was very little basis upon which to build an inclusive, legitimate Irish state. During the Irish crises of 1916–22, which saw tremendous sectarian violence on both sides and resulted in the poisonous partitioning of the island, many of the protagonists knew what they were fighting for because they had the example of the Victorian era fresh in their minds. Catholic attacks on Protestant schoolchildren, Protestant policemen openly encouraging anti-Catholic violence, Orange parades quashed while nationalist parades flaunted the ban, preachers disturbed, parades attacked, houses sacked, shipyards that became battlefields, policemen murdered, policemen murdering—all of these memories jostled with, and frequently overwhelmed, more abstract ideas about liberty, national identity, and religious faith within both communities, adding the sharpness of personal experience to the high-toned political principles of the elite. In places such as Belfast, Lurgan, Lisburn, and Derry—all northern cities that saw considerable violence in the Victorian era—collective memories of violence, emotional rather than intellectual in nature, probably did just as much to divide the country as any purely rational considerations.

For a compelling instance of how the patterns of Victorian communalism blended with the ideology of nationalism to create a severe crisis of state legitimacy, we might turn once again to Belfast. As during the nineteenth century, the epicenter of violence in the early twentieth century (concentrated in the period 1920–22) was the Belfast shipyards, where Protestant workers (many of them returning servicemen) expelled Catholics who had moved into skilled positions from which they were traditionally excluded. The ensuing forced evictions in residential neighborhoods also conformed to Victorian patterns, as did allegations of police partiality (this time mostly made by Catholics). Perhaps the most poisonous legacy of the Victorian era for the new state of Northern Ireland, founded in 1921, were the "B" Specials, a volunteer paramilitary force whose caps and armbands, as well as their name, harkened back to the civilian special constables of an earlier era, although their openly sectarian nature—their members were nearly all Protestants, their remit to protect the "loyal" population from "rebel" violence—also drew from the centuries-old tradition of Irish Protestant self-defense.[37] In a sense, the spirit of vigilantism that the Victorian riots had engendered—with Protestant volunteers stepping forward to defend their people when the state's police forces proved inadequate—became a central pillar of the sectarian Northern Ireland state, which would continue to rely on the assistance of Protestant volunteers for decades to come. And this reliance, in turn, helped to ensure that the Northern Irish state failed to enjoy much legitimacy among Catholics, many of whom would eventually turn to their own communal vigilantes (the Irish Republican Army, or IRA) to protect them from the state and its civilian Protestant allies.

In India the pattern was similar. Political nationalism, emerging in an institutionalized way in the 1880s but only developing a popular base after the First World War, built upon a foundation of communal distrust and memories of violence that, even with the best wills in the world, secular nationalists could not overcome. A word of caution is in order here, for India is a vast country in which many religious communities managed to live in perfect harmony until 1947 (and beyond), partly because they had no poisoned well of collective memories on which to draw. Nevertheless, those areas that did see substantial rioting in the nineteenth century—a northern band stretching from Punjab to Bengal, along with large portions of the Deccan and Gujarat—were also those areas where communal disputes made pan-communal nationalism, not to mention a unified independent India, all but impossible. As in Ireland, much of the infrastructure on which Indian nationalists built was communal in nature, most notably the Hindu revival organizations that had emerged late in the century and helped to precipitate the cow-protection riots of the 1890s.[38] Despite the suspicions of British officials, the early Hindu revivalists were not front organizations for the nationalist Indian National Congress (INC), but they did provide a fund of experience and popular mobilization upon which the INC could draw. By the late-Victorian period, Indians were learning, in John McLane's words, to couch their claims "in terms of legal rights and legislative enactments" and began looking to "the courts, Parliament, and the legislative councils, and even the Indian National Congress as arenas for dispute and solutions."[39] Moreover, the activities of Hindu revivalists allowed Muslim organizers to capitalize on the feelings of insecurity and grievance that the cow-protection riots instilled among Muslims, leading them to create their own sectional organizations (most importantly the Muslim League, founded in 1906) to promote putatively "Muslim" interests. "Perhaps no issue," says McLane, speaking of the cow-protection movement, "dramatized so well the problem of minority rights under a future Hindu majority rule."[40] Barbara and Thomas Metcalf summarize the polarization dynamic thus:

> The fact that many individual members of Congress supported cow protection contributed further to the view of most Muslim leaders that their interests were best served by organizations that focused exclusively on Muslim interests. For some Hindu nationalists, the behaviour of the cow activists evoked a sense of pride, for it challenged the enduring image of Hindu passivity and inaction.[41]

In short, the cow-protection movement, and the violence that it spawned, were important preconditions for the emergence of distinctive Hindu and Muslim forms of Indian nationalism.

The career of Bal Gangadhar Tilak, the most important originator of the *swadeshi* (self-sufficiency) movement in the Bombay presidency (and the Deccan generally), is perhaps the best illustration of how nineteenth-century cow-protection fed into twentieth-century Hindu nationalism. Prior to the riots of 1893 Tilak had been part of a fringe minority of Hindu nationalists, outspoken in the cause of Hindu liberation but otherwise without much influence among the masses. However, the apparent ineffectiveness of the Bombay government in quelling the violence allowed Tilak and his followers to credibly charge the British government with pursuing a policy of divide and rule—that is, of seeking to weaken Hinduism by allowing Muslim extremists to act with impunity in their dispute with the cow-protectors. At first the moderate Hindus of Bombay and Poona were reluctant to adopt this line, but after repeated riots in the area from 1893 to 1895—and after repeated demonstrations of official incapacity and, as they saw it, partiality—many came around to Tilak's way of thinking. These allegations were not quite fair—as we have seen, and as Richard Cashman observes, British officials did make a "genuine effort" to stop these riots—but the state's failure nevertheless gave Tilak and his growing number of Brahman supporters a "a convenient explanation for all the ills which plagued the Deccan."[42]

S. M. Edwardes, police commissioner of Bombay from 1909 to 1916, explained how Tilak used the cow-protection riots to promote his radical nationalist agenda:

> The riots left behind them a bitter legacy of sectarian rancor, which Bal Gangadhar Tilak utilized for broadening his new anti-British movement, by enlisting in its support the ancient Hindu antagonism to Islam.... As his propaganda grew, assuming steadily a more anti-British character, Tilak decided to invest it with a definitely religious sanction, by placing it under the special patronage of the elephant-headed god Ganesh or Ganpati. In order to widen the breach between Hindus and Muhammadans, he and his co-agitators determined to organize annual festivals in honour of the god on the lines which had become familiar in the annual Muhammadan celebration of the Muharram.[43]

The strategy worked, at least partly: within a few years Ganapati festivals were drawing large Hindu crowds across the Deccan, becoming a popular communal display to rival Muslims' Muharram processions (in which many Hindus had formerly participated) and leading to occasional clashes with Muslims.[44] Tilak's ultimate aim, however, was much more ambitious: to turn these Hindu religious festivals into a political movement for self-rule, and thereby to link the nationalism of the Brahman elite with the traditionalism of the masses.[45] The Ganapati movement never fully realized this hope, partly because the government considered the movement sufficiently subversive to stifle it under legal restrictions.[46] It would take several years and a new set of causes (notably the 1905 partition of Bengal[47]) for communal mobilization to become fully intertwined with anticolonial nationalism in India, but Tilak's strategy of capitalizing upon anti-British as well as anti-Muslim sentiment in the wake of the cow-protection riots showed how Indian nationalism could—and eventually would—make its fateful merger with communal politics.[48]

In Ceylon, political nationalism likewise gained strength from communal violence, although here it was government patronage of Buddhism that facilitated the merger. A Buddhist revival had been under way for two decades by the time of the great Buddhist–Catholic riot in Colombo in 1883. The revivalists' initial aim was to counteract the work of European Protestant missionaries by using the missionaries' own techniques of pamphleteering and controversialist lectures, but in the early 1880s the movement received a boost from the Russian and American Theosophists Madame Blavatsky and Col. Henry S. Olcott, mystics with a soft spot for Asian religions who visited Ceylon several times in the early 1880s.[49] In 1883 the Colombo revivalist Migettuwatte Gunananda, famous as a skilled controversialist, caught the rising wave of Buddhist self-assertion with a grand procession to celebrate renovations to his Buddhist temple, which happened to be situated in a Catholic neighborhood. The ensuing riot, while not serious by South Asian standards, was a rare enough occurrence in tranquil Ceylon, and it convinced the government to reach out in a more concerted manner to the island's Buddhist leaders, who were perceived to be crucial to Ceylon's stability. In the wake of the riot, following some energetic politicking by Buddhist leaders—and by Henry Olcott, who traveled to London to lobby on their behalf—the state formally recognized Buddhists' rights to religious processions, declared Buddha's birthday (Wesak) a holiday, appointed Buddhist registrars of marriages, and enacted other reforms meant to placate the Buddhist elite.[50] In fact the governor, Sir Arthur Gordon, pointedly resisted subsequent requests to declare a policy of religious neutrality in Ceylon so as to preserve the notion that Buddhists had a special position in the colony.[51] This pro-Buddhist policy worked, insofar as it ensured that Ceylon's Buddhist leaders remained moderate and conservative, but they also became increasingly assertive in their nationalist ambitions. A key moment in the politicization of Buddhist revivalism was the bloody repression of the anti-Muslim riots of 1915 (discussed below), during which the police imprisoned many Buddhist leaders who, upon their release, went on to lead the island toward independence. As in Ireland and India, Ceylon's path from revivalism to nationalism was long and winding, but it undoubtedly began with the communal violence of the late nineteenth and early twentieth centuries.

State violence

This entwining of communalism with nationalism was just what British officials had always feared. As long as rival communities were attacking one another the problem was largely one of law and order. The riots could be serious, and (as I have been arguing) they could also damage British prestige, but such damage was usually limited in time and space. Once those communal energies began to find expression through nationalism, however, communal tensions acquired a new political importance: they became a threat not only to the public peace but also to the state itself. In a sense, the politicization of communalism was an inevitable product of Britain's neutrality policies, since those who opposed the communal practices of a rival community must also oppose the state as guarantor of that community's liberty. But what worried British officials was not so much the abstract threat to religious liberty that communal conflict represented but the prospect of a frontal assault upon British power as such, partly because of the unique power (as they saw it) of religious fanaticism to motivate the unthinking mob, and partly because a successful defiance of authority in one arena (e.g., a communal riot) might encourage defiance in others (e.g., anticolonial terrorism). They knew, as Rod Thornton has said, that because they were outnumbered they needed to rule with "some measure of consent.... Ruling had to involve a balance that set the lightness of the yoke against the need to garner the prestige and respect that came from occasional punitive action."[52] Yet that was not always an easy balance to strike, and the instinct of many officials was to tighten the yoke, not loosen it, when British prestige was at stake, especially as the Victorian period drew to a close.

How British officials responded to the growing problem of communal self-assertion took different forms at different times, but the general trend across the empire was to relinquish their preventive and mediating roles and to concentrate instead on repression. In northern India the shift began in the 1890s. As we have seen, it was around this time that some elements of the Indian state began treating communal unrest as a threat to the security of the Raj. As part of this process British officials were starting to withdraw from their customary roles as communal arbiters and to rely instead on each community's "natural leaders" to settle disputes. As the revivalist and nationalist movements gained pace, however, Britain's preferred "natural leaders" appeared to be losing their grip on the people and ceding ground to illegitimate "agitators" who preyed upon the people's natural fanaticism, or so British officials believed.[53] This caused the gradual weakening of ties between British officials and their favored local leaders, and the result was a state that was more detached from Indian society, less intimately involved in local conflicts, and more inclined to rely on heavy displays of force to keep the peace. In Arun Mukherjee's words, "It was a shift away from crime prevention and control to containment of public disorder. This, in turn, necessitated greater reliance on military and paramilitary forces as against the civil police."[54]

The dual policy of reaching out to "natural leaders" while relying on increasingly coercive policing was especially evident in the city of Bombay. Prashant Kidambi has shown how the riots of the 1890s (some of them fueled not by cow-protection but by resistance to government antiplague measures) led the police to intervene more aggressively in the "native town" by cultivating relationships with informal community leaders such as "jobbers, rent collectors, petty landlords, Pathan moneylenders, the proprietors of taverns and tea shops, brothels, gymnasiums and street-bosses of various kinds commonly known as *dadas*."[55] The difficulty, however, was that it was not always clear who the right leaders were, how local power dynamics might shift over time, or how cooperation with the police might undermine a leader's position among his own people. From 1902 these enhanced surveillance techniques were joined by a new batch of "unprecedented" police powers that allowed the authorities to control communal processions, regulate the use of public spaces such as eating houses and thoroughfares, arrest or deport paupers and beggars, and ban public displays that might "inflame religious animosity or hostility between different classes" or otherwise cause disorder.[56] The upshot of this more aggressive policing style, introduced as a direct response to urban mass violence, was, in Kidambi's words, to "amplif[y] the scale and dimension of the potential conflict between the police and local society."[57] Among other things, these measures made the state a more visible enemy (and an easier target) for communal organizers than it had been before.[58]

The changing relationship between the people and the state was evident in other parts of India as well. After a riot at Yeola, Maharashtra, in 1894 a correspondent wrote to the *Times of India* of the long-term dangers of relying too heavily upon the military to quell disturbances:

> A frequent display of the military not only shows the people that the civil arm is powerless, but it also familiarises them with fights with the army, and familiarity is sure to beget contempt; and, moreover, if Government cannot enforce peace except by relying on the military, it must admit itself to be a weak Government and will not inspire its subjects with the necessary

> respect. You must depend for the purposes of Government upon moral force and not upon battalions. That schoolmaster will rule his class best who brings out his rod on the fewest occasions, while he who always flourishes it over the head of his pupils does not inspire them with any regard for him. Sir, if occurrences like these are repeated the prestige of the government will be in jeopardy.[59]

This was precisely what would happen over the next few decades across much of India. The gradual ascendance of a doctrine of overwhelming force was not, as it was intended to be, a sign of British strength, but rather an admission of weakness, and the result was to even further "alienate the police from the people," as Mukherjee has said of the situation in Bengal.[60] Such alienation, which was by no means confined to episodes of communal violence, would be resoundingly confirmed in 1905 when a government inquiry identified widespread, and well-founded, hatred of the police across much of Indian society.[61]

The West Indies also saw a shift toward more draconian policing at the end of the Victorian era. Carnival processions by Creoles were one area in which closer state regulation of public behavior began, from the 1870s, to provoke clashes between crowds and the police, but some of the worst violence occurred during celebrations associated not with black revelers but with East Indian immigrants.[62] As their numbers grew in the second half of the century, Indian plantation workers began holding elaborate Muharram processions, in which, despite the festival's sectarian origins, both Hindus and Muslims commonly participated. Muharram (or Hosay) festivals therefore became something of an Indian national festival, although the participation of blacks—both as spectators and processionists—also made them something more. Troubled by the licentious behavior of the revelers and the violence that sometimes accompanied the processions, West Indian governments began trying to curtail, if not completely smother, the festival: British Guiana banned Muharram processions in large towns in 1871, and Trinidad followed suit in 1882. This set the stage for clashes between celebrants and the police that rivaled the procession disputes of Ireland and South Asia.[63]

The most notable episode of state violence during a procession, as we saw in Chapter 6, was the Hosay Massacre in Trinidad in 1884, when soldiers and armed policemen killed some twenty-two Muharram processionists and wounded more than a hundred others when marchers tried to enter the town of San Fernando against government orders. Unusually for a police shooting in the West Indies, the Colonial Office decided to investigate the episode, dispatching

Sir Henry Norman, governor of Jamaica, to look into the affair. Norman's report, which asserted that the firing was justified if regrettable, was a masterpiece of colonial self-exculpation. What made the show of force necessary, Norman concluded, was not so much the rowdy behavior of the revelers (although this was deplorable enough), but the way the festival seemed to embolden the Indians, giving them a sense of strength and solidarity that could be quite dangerous to the ruling power. An Indian "coolie" in the West Indies, Norman observed, "not only becomes a man of more independent spirit than he was when in India, but according to some reliable evidence, he often becomes somewhat overbearing. There is little doubt that the Indian immigrants looked upon the processions as a sort of means of demonstrating their power."[64] Such an agglomeration of "overbearing" Indians, Norman implied, would inevitably seek an object against which to test its strength, and, lacking any enemies of a communal sort, they might lash out directly at the British. If the Hosay Massacre signaled a new, firmer line against communal processions in the West Indies, then, Norman's report affirmed that deadly force was a perfectly justifiable way to control recalcitrant populations. For Trinidad, this meant the almost complete disappearance of Muharram celebrations in the years after 1884; for the West Indies generally, it marked a new era of repressive policing that lasted well beyond the end of British rule.[65]

Ireland also experienced a drift toward more repressive and centralized policing, which both fed upon and fed into popular distrust of the state, although here the process began much earlier than in India or the West Indies. The Belfast riots of 1864 had convinced the central government that that city's local police force, controlled by the Town Council and almost entirely Protestant, was inadequate and probably sectarian, so the force was disbanded and replaced with a permanent detachment of the semi-military constabulary. Whereas the old force had been poorly equipped to handle riots, however, the new force was not especially good at ordinary, everyday policing, and even during riots their approach could be overbearing and counterproductive. During the riots of 1886 Belfast Protestants fought fierce battles with the RIC—most of whom were southerners and therefore suspected of Catholic sympathies—which resulted in a number of deaths and even a murder trial for some of the constables.[66] Elsewhere in the country the RIC were aggressively enforcing evictions and committing the occasional act of lethal violence at nationalist demonstrations, ensuring that they remained unpopular with large segments of the Catholic population even while their reputation among northern Protestants reached its nadir. Repeated government suspensions of *habeas corpus* and other civil liberties during the 1870s and 1880s, enacted to combat nationalist and anti-landlord agitation, also alienated broad swathes of the Irish public from the police and their political masters in Dublin. It surely was no coincidence, then, that when the Irish struggle for independence began in earnest in 1919 the RIC, targeted by guerrillas and ostracized by civilians, was among the first buttresses of British power to collapse.[67]

In both Ireland and South Asia (and, to a lesser extent, the West Indies) the strains of the First World War pushed this uneasy relationship between the state and the people almost to the breaking point. The economic and social dislocations brought on by the war created conditions favorable to radical nationalism, and as anti-British radicals became ever more assertive they coaxed British forces into ever more draconian modes of repression—and this, in turn, encouraged yet more anti-British activity among nationalists. In Ireland the endgame arrived with the Anglo–Irish War of 1919–21, and India saw the rise of a full-blown popular nationalist movement during the same period. Communal violence was a part, but only a part, of these postwar imperial crises, and it would take us well beyond the scope of the current study to provide a satisfactory account of the ways communalism shaped the post-1914 period. The essential point is that the legacies of Victorian-era communal violence could be found during and after the First World War both in the communal infrastructures that the nationalist movements used to build their support base, and in the distrust with which imperial subjects continued to regard the police, the army, and their political masters.

There is one part of the empire where the twisting strands of communal violence, repressive policing, and postwar nationalism are somewhat easier to tease apart, and this is Ceylon. Like so many of the riots we have examined in this book, the massive Ceylon riots of 1915 began with a procession dispute—this one in the town of Gampola, where Muslim immigrants had built a new mosque and subsequently objected to Buddhist processions going past it. The dispute wound its way through the courts for a few years until a settlement was reached that allowed Buddhists to process past the mosque on condition that they not play music within 50 yards of it (this was the standard solution to such disputes in India). The controversy attracted considerable attention across the island, fraying nerves in neighboring Kandy and in western coastal districts where Sinhalese Buddhists resented Muslim merchants (known as Coast Moors) for their hold on the retail trade, resentments that grew sharper once wartime shortages began causing prices to rise. Fueled by economic resentments, procession-related grudges, and xenophobia, Buddhists began attacking Muslim shops and mosques in Kandy on May 29, the day after Wesak (the holiday marking Buddha's birthday that had been institutionalized in the wake of the 1883 Colombo riots). The violence quickly spread to other towns and villages across the island in a rolling anti-Muslim pogrom that resembled the anti-Portuguese riots in British Guiana more than half a century before.

Although the violence was clearly communal in nature and posed no real threat to the state, British officials—who, like their counterparts in Ireland and India, had begun to lose touch with the grass roots of local society—saw in these disturbances a proper revolt against British authority during a time of war (some influential officials suspected German instigation).[68] After hesitating for a few days the governor declared martial law and left it in place for nearly three months, during which time roving bands of policemen and soldiers, assisted by civilian planter patrols, combed the island for miscreants, flogging many and shooting others on sight. In all 140 people died during the unrest, more than 100 of them at the hands of official and nonofficial British patrols, and over 4,000 were imprisoned. Many of those arrested were moderate, heretofore loyal Buddhist temperance activists whom the authorities (following the same paranoid logic that had led their Indian counterparts to blame the cow-protection riots on Congress "wire pullers") believed to be secretly orchestrating the riots in order to overthrow British rule.[69] It was a colossal overreaction, transforming (in Charles Blackton's words) "fundamental attitudes [toward British rule] almost as radically as did the Easter Rising in Dublin in 1916 or the Amritsar massacre in 1919."[70] If Sinhalese temperance activists had not been radical nationalists before the mass arrests and deadly reprisals, in other words, they certainly were afterward, and if Ceylon had been a peaceful, even sleepy corner of the empire before 1915, it was not so anymore. An outbreak of fierce communal violence, carried out in the wake of a period of increasing communal self-assertion among Sinhalese Buddhists (a development that was itself traceable to an earlier period of communal violence), had coaxed the British state into committing brutalities that violated nearly every principle of Victorian liberal imperialism and transformed what began as a communal dispute into a movement for national independence. It was a remarkably unambiguous instance of a colony traveling the path from communal violence to national liberation by way of violent state repression.

Conclusion

In this chapter I have been arguing that communal riots—or, more specifically, the state's fear of the embarrassment these riots could cause—contributed to a vicious cycle of state violence and collapsing state legitimacy around the empire. All riots have a way of exposing the limits of state power, however briefly, and of empowering those who would defy the state's monopoly on legitimate violence. Riots in themselves are rarely fatal for a state, but they can erode its authority, especially in an imperial context where the state's authority is already uncertain. The longer the riot, the bigger the threat, and the more scope is given to communal vigilantes who would impose their own visions of law, order, and communal interest upon the wider society. By embarrassing the imperial state—by chipping away at its façade of omnipotence, by calling its impartiality into question, by turning its policemen into targets and belligerents (rather than mere referees)—communal riots in the British Empire lent courage to those who wished to establish rival centers of power. In the Victorian period this was not yet a serious problem for the British Empire, but it would become so in the twentieth century.

Across the empire two related trends, driven by the dynamic interaction of embarrassment and vigilantism, were discernable. First, nationalism and communalism began to entwine. From the nationalists' perspective, not only did communal movements offer a ready-made forum for mobilizing the masses on behalf of a broader political (i.e., anti-British) cause, but communal riots themselves also helped to expose (and to accelerate) the very weakening of British legitimacy that the nationalists were aiming for. Second, at the very moment when the state's authority was beginning to suffer, thanks to the defiance of nationalists and the embarrassment of communal riots, state forces were starting (often under the pressure of world war) to behave more aggressively toward imperial subjects who defied their authority. These two trends fed on each other: as the state lost ever more legitimacy, British officials relied ever more on violence to maintain their power, and in so doing they lost ever more legitimacy among subject populations. The ultimate beneficiaries, of course, were those nationalists who could turn the communal aspirations of subject peoples toward anti-imperial goals.

this vicious cycle of state violence and collapsing state legitimacy that accompanied the empire. All riots have a way of exposing the limits of state power, however briefly, and of empowering those who would defy the state's monopoly on legitimate violence. Riots in themselves are rarely fatal to a state, but they can erode its authority, especially in an imperial context where the state's authority is already uncertain. The longer the riot, the bigger the threat, and the more scope is given to communal vigilantes who would impose their own visions of the order and communal interest upon the wider society [illegible]

Notes

Introduction

1 Sir John Strachey, *India* (London: K. Paul, Trench, Trübner, 1888), 364.

2 Ibid., 367.

3 Strachey, *India*, 2nd ed. (London: K. Paul, Trench, Trübner, 1894), 395.

4 Not all European empires took this approach, of course—one thinks of the ancient, land-based empires of the Russians, Ottomans, or Austrians—but even these regimes had to reckon with the nationalist aspirations of subject peoples, either by accommodating (or appropriating) their aspirations or by suppressing them. In either case, they were addressing a growing popular sense that states derived their legitimacy from the benefits they conferred upon the people. Among the major European powers, perhaps the clearest expression of this idea occurred during the Berlin Conference of 1884–5, when even the most rapacious powers felt it necessary, when carving up the continent of Africa, to cloak their avarice in the language of humanitarianism.

5 Niall Ferguson, *Empire: The Rise and Demise of the British World Order and the Lessons for Global Power* (New York: Basic Books, 2003).

6 The classic popular account is Jan Morris, *Pax Britannica: The Climax of an Empire* (New York: Harcourt, Brace, 1968). For a recent exploration of the same theme, see Barry Gough, *Pax Britannica: Ruling the Waves and Keeping the Peace Before Armageddon* (New York: Palgrave, 2014). The most thorough examination of the *Pax Britannica* idea is in Ali Parchami, *Hegemonic Peace and Empire: The* Pax Romana, Britannica, *and* Americana (London: Routledge, 2009), 59–164.

7 For a recent assessment of this debate, see Stephen Howe, "Minding the Gaps: New Directions in the Study of Ireland and Empire," *Journal of Imperial and Commonwealth History* 37, 1 (2009), 134–49.

8 Kate O'Malley, *Ireland, India and Empire: Indo-Irish Radical Connections, 1919–64* (Manchester: Manchester University Press, 2008); Michael Silvestri, *Ireland and India: Nationalism, Empire and Memory* (Houndmills, Basingstoke: Palgrave Macmillan, 2009); Julia M. Wright, *Ireland, India and Nationalism in Nineteenth-Century Literature* (Cambridge: Cambridge University Press, 2007); Tadhg Foley and Maureen O'Connor, eds., *Ireland and India: Colonies, Culture, and Empire* (Dublin: Irish Academic Press, 2006); C. A. Bayly, "Ireland, India and the Empire: 1780–1914," *Transactions of the Royal Historical Society (Sixth Series)* 10

(2000), 377–97; Peter Gray, "Famine and Land in Ireland and India, 1845–1880: James Caird and the Political Economy of Hunger," *The Historical Journal* 49 (2006), 193–215; Jill Bender, "The Imperial Politics of Famine: The 1873–74 Bengal Famine and Irish Parliamentary Nationalism," *Eire-Ireland* 42 (Spring/Summer 2007), 132–56.

9 Donald Horowitz uses the term ethnic riot to describe many of the same kinds of violence that I describe here, but this term seems unsuitable to the Irish case, where, despite differences of religion and political outlook, the contending parties spoke the same language, were physically indistinguishable, and engaged in most of the same cultural practices. The term sectarian, which is normally used to describe Protestant–Catholic violence in Ireland, is probably more accurate, but it does not work for violence in other parts of the empire. Donald Horowitz, *The Deadly Ethnic Riot* (Berkeley: University of California Press, 2001).

10 My understanding of the relationship between cleavages at the national or central level (i.e., the major fault lines that outsiders usually apply to these outbreaks) and local cleavages (i.e., the complex bundle of motives that drive individuals to engage in such violence) aligns quite closely with that of Stathis Kalyvas, whose *The Logic of Violence in Civil War* (Cambridge: Cambridge University Press, 2006) offers a systematic way to disentangle local dynamics from abstract, theoretical enmities.

11 Charles Tilly, *The Politics of Collective Violence* (Cambridge: Cambridge University Press, 2003). Horowitz also discusses several kinds of violence that are similar to, but not quite the same as, his conception of an ethnic riot: violent protests, pogroms, feuds, lynchings, genocides, terrorist attacks, gang assaults, and ethnic fights. My use of communal riot encompasses ethnic fights and pogroms, but the other categories differ significantly from the kinds of violence we will consider in this book (although communal riots may be a part of, or contain, instances of these other kinds of violence). Horowitz, *Deadly*, 19–26.

12 "Disturbance" is another term one encounters in the contemporary sources, but this has a way of minimizing the violent nature of these episodes as well as downplaying the role of human agency in bringing these "disturbances" about.

13 Sir Andrew Reed, *The Irish Constable's Guide*, 3rd ed. (Dublin: Alex Thom, 1895), 287.

14 Peter Robb, "The Challenge of Gau Mata: British Policy and Religious Change in India, 1880–1916," *Modern Asian Studies* 20, 2 (1986), 285–319 (285).

15 Theodore Koditschek, *Liberalism, Imperialism, and the Historical Imagination: Nineteenth-Century Visions of a Greater Britain* (Cambridge: Cambridge University Press, 2011), 1.

16 R. W. Kostal, "A Jurisprudence of Power: Martial Law and the Ceylon Controversy of 1848–51," *The Journal of Imperial and Commonwealth History* 28, 1 (2000), 1–34 (2 and 27); R. W. Kostal, *A Jurisprudence of Power: Victorian Empire and the Rule of Law* (Oxford: Oxford University Press, 2005), 461–5.

17 Nasser Hussain, *The Jurisprudence of Emergency: Colonialism and the Rule of Law* (Ann Arbor: The University of Michigan Press, 2003), 4. See also Martin J. Wiener, *An Empire on Trial: Race, Murder, and Justice under British Rule, 1870–1935* (Cambridge: Cambridge University Press, 2009); and Elizabeth Kolsky, "Codification and the Rule of Colonial Difference: Criminal Procedure in British India," *Law and History Review* 23, 3 (Fall 2005), 631–84.

18 Charles Townshend, *Making the Peace: Public Order and Security in Modern Britain* (Oxford: Oxford University Press, 1993), 5.

19 For explorations of this tension in other realms of Victorian imperialism, see Uday Singh Mehta, *Liberalism and Empire: A Study in Nineteenth-Century British Liberal Thought* (Chicago: University of Chicago Press, 1999); Kolsky, "Codification"; Koditschek, *Liberalism*; and Jennifer Pitts, *A Turn to Empire: The Rise of Imperial Liberalism in Britain and France* (Princeton: Princeton University Press, 2006).

20 While my language skills have not allowed me to make use of vernacular newspapers published in South Asia (few of which survive anyway), I have utilized (with due caution) the voluminous Reports on Native Newspapers (RNN) produced by the Indian government (copies of which are available in the National Archives of India and elsewhere), which translated and summarized the responses of vernacular papers to communal violence. For a useful discussion of the limitations of these reports as a historical source, see Sukeshi Kamra, *The Indian Periodical Press and the Production of Nationalist Rhetoric* (New York: Palgrave Macmillan, 2011), 8–16. Throughout this book, direct quotes from vernacular newspapers are drawn either from these government productions or from translated excerpts published in English-language newspapers.

21 Gyanendra Pandey, *The Construction of Communalism in Colonial North India* (Delhi: Oxford University Press, 1990); Bernard Cohn, *Colonialism and its Forms of Knowledge: The British in India* (Princeton: Princeton University Press, 1996); Nicholas Dirks, *Castes of Mind: Colonialism and the Making of Modern India* (Princeton: Princeton University Press, 2001).

22 Patricia A. Gossman, *Riots and Victims: Violence and the Construction of Communal Identity among Bengali Muslims, 1905–1947* (Boulder, CO: Westview Press, 1999); Sandria B. Freitag, *Collective Action and Community: Public Arenas and the Emergence of Communalism in North India* (Berkeley: University of California Press, 1989). See also Michael Roberts, "Noise as Cultural Struggle: Tom-Tom Beating, the British, and Communal Disturbances in Sri Lanka, 1880s–1930s," in *Mirrors of Violence: Communities, Violence, and Survivors in South Asia*, ed. Veena Das (Delhi: Oxford University Press, 1990), 240–85; and Katherine Prior, "Making History: The State's Intervention in Urban Religious Disputes in the North-Western Provinces in the Early Nineteenth Century," *Modern Asian Studies* 27, 1 (1993), 179–203.

23 For an argument on behalf of applying South-Asian historiography to Ireland, see Sean Farrell, "Ulster Sectarianism and the Lessons of South Asian Historiography," *History Compass* 8, 9 (September 2010), 1023–35. See also the special issue of *History Ireland* devoted to Ireland and India: *History Ireland* 18, 4 (July/August 2010).

24 There is a vast literature associated with the "new imperial history." Two useful starting points are Kathleen Wilson, ed., *A New Imperial History: Culture, Identity and Modernity in Britain and the Empire, 1660–1840* (Cambridge: Cambridge University Press, 2004); and Stephen Howe, ed. *New Imperial Histories Reader* (New York: Routledge, 2009).

25 Richard Price, "One Big Thing: Britain, Its Empire, and Their Imperial Culture," *Journal of British Studies* 45, 3 (July 2006), 602–27.

26 According to Barry Gough (*Pax Britannica*, 12), the term first appeared in print in an article on India in the *Contemporary Review* in 1878. The phrase became current in the 1880s, appearing in a handful of periodicals and books on different aspects of the empire, and had become an accepted truth by the first part of the twentieth century.

Chapter 1

1 Someone claiming to have been a school friend of Orr's wrote to the *Montreal Weekly Pilot* (July 15, 1854) that the name "very much annoys him." His mother would make a similar claim after his death in a letter to *The Creole* published on December 6, 1856. On the other hand, one of the pamphlets Orr distributed in Georgetown describing his travails in New England included a song—a parody of a popular spiritual tune—that began, "We went to Bunker Hill for to hear Gabriel . . ." Supreme Court of Criminal Justice, Monday, April 28, *British Guiana. Copies or extracts of correspondence between the Governor of British Guiana and the Secretary of State for the Colonies, on the subject of the recent disturbances in that colony*, HC 1856 (432) XLIV (hereafter, *1856 British Guiana Riots Correspondence*), encl. 3 in no. 5, 65.

2 *Berkshire Chronicle*, November 17, 1832. The precise nature of Orr's Leicester Square performance is unclear, but it seems he was preaching a millennial sermon, for, as he was ordered to find bail, he threw his hands above his head and yelled, "Beware! It is preaching the word of the Lord which will save the land only. Look at the signs of the times—look at the awful crisis!"

3 *Morning Post*, July 25, 1848. When they arrested him the police found that he had been distributing pamphlets, presumably written by himself, entitled "The Signs of the Times, as expressed in the House of Commons, on the 10th of April, and the

12th of June, 1848." These were dates of significant Chartist activity in that unsettled summer.

4 Navvies were migratory laborers ("navigators") who constructed railways, docks, and canals across the British Empire and North America. Many of them were Irish Catholics.

5 Deposition of William Blair, in "Report of the Procurator Fiscal, Greenock, respecting the Riot at Greenock on the night of Monday 28 July 1851," TNA, HO 45/3472P, no. 15–30.

6 Ibid.; *Glasgow Courier*, July 17 and 22, 1851.

7 Edward Savage quoted in Jack Tager, *Boston Riots: Three Centuries of Social Violence* (Boston: Northeastern University Press, 2001), 130. In Boston, Orr spoke at Chelsea, East Boston, Dorchester, and Charlestown, and in the latter spot he went to jail for disturbing the peace and illegally selling pamphlets. See John Bach McMaster, *A History of the People of the United States*, vol. 8 (1850–61) (New York and London: D. Appelton, 1913), 87. In Chelsea, surrounded by a guard of ship carpenters, he preached in front of the Irish "fifty-houses" neighborhood, where he was attacked by Irishmen who were, in turn, attacked by Yankees who destroyed several homes and then destroyed a crucifix at a Catholic church in East Boston. Shortly thereafter he was arrested in Worcester and then again in Boston after further disturbances. See Tager, *Boston Riots*, 131.

8 McMaster, *History*, 86–7.

9 Mark Foynes, "Manchester's 'Disgraceful Riot,' July 3 and 4, 1854," *Horizons*, 22 (Winter 2002), https://www.nhhistory.org/edu/support/nhimmigration/disgracefulriot.pdf (accessed December 26, 2014); McMaster, *History*, 87.

10 "American Jottings: The Know-Nothing Movement," *Chambers's Journal* (February 3, 1855), 70–3; Tager, *Boston Riots*, 131. There is some uncertainty about whether it was Orr who incited the riot in Bath. According to a correspondent to the *Montreal Weekly Pilot* (extracted in *Dumfries and Galloway Standard,* August 30, 1854), the preacher's name was Brown, not Orr.

11 Quoted in Richard Gott, *Britain's Empire: Resistance, Repression and Revolt* (London: Verso, 2011), 441.

12 John Sayers Orr to Philip Wodehouse, January 1, 1856, *1856 British Guiana Riots Correspondence*, encl. 1 in no. 1, 6; Supreme Court of Criminal Justice, Monday, April 28, ibid., encl. 3 in no. 5, 60; *The Creole*, December 6, 1856, letter from Mary Ann Orr.

13 Wodehouse himself was fairly new to Guiana. A well-connected son of a Norfolk squire, he had spent most of his career in Ceylon, rising to the substantial post of government agent of the Western Province, the most populous and important part of the island. He had played a controversial role in handling a rebellion by Sinhalese chiefs in 1848, first supporting and then disavowing Governor

Torrington's decision to impose martial law on the island, a measure that caused considerable suffering and provoked a parliamentary inquiry. Torrington never forgave Wodehouse for turning against him—in private letters to London he called Wodehouse a scoundrel and a liar—but Wodehouse remained on the island until 1851, some years after Torrington's own ignominious departure. He then became superintendent of Honduras where he remained until 1854, when he moved into the governor's mansion in Georgetown. Wodehouse therefore had some experience with turbulent imperial subjects, and he knew the byzantine world of colonial officialdom quite well, but he had not yet directed the government response to a serious crisis. On Wodehouse's career in Ceylon, see R. W. Kostal, "A Jurisprudence of Power: Martial Law and the Ceylon Controversy of 1848–51," *The Journal of Imperial and Commonwealth History* 28, 1 (2000), 1–34; and Lord Torrington to Lord Grey, October 9, 1849, in K. M. de Silva, ed. *Letters on Ceylon 1846–50. The Administration of Viscount Torrington and the "Rebellion" of 1848: The Private Correspondence of the Third Earl Grey (Secretary of State for the Colonies 1846–52) and Viscount Torrington* (Kandy & Colombo: KVG de Silva & Sons, 1965), 167–75.

14 John Sayers Orr to Philip Wodehouse, January 1, 1856, *1856 British Guiana Riots Correspondence*, encl. 1 in no. 1, 6–7.

15 W. Walker, Government Secretary, to John Sayers Orr, January 2, 1856, *1856 British Guiana Riots Correspondence*, encl. 2 in no. 1, 7.

16 The literature on nineteenth-century anti-Catholicism in the Atlantic world is vast. A useful recent overview, comparing manifestations of anti-Catholicism in North America and the British Isles, is John Wolffe, "North Atlantic Anti-Catholicism in the Nineteenth Century: A Comparative Overview," *European Studies* 31 (2013), 25–31.

17 On the post-emancipation crisis in British Guiana, see Alan H. Adamson, "Monoculture and Village Decay in British Guiana: 1854–1872," *Journal of Social History* 3, 4 (Summer 1970), 386–405.

18 Steve Garner, "Atlantic Crossing: Whiteness as a Transatlantic Experience," *Atlantic Studies* 4, 1 (2007), 117–32 (122); Brian L. Moore, "The Social Impact of Portuguese Immigration into British Guiana after Emancipation," *Boletín de Estudios Latinoamericanos y del Caribe* 19 (December 1975), 3–15; Mary Noel Menezes, *Scenes from the History of the Portuguese in Guyana* (London: Sister M. N. Menezes, 1986), 5.

19 Moore, "Social Impact," 5.

20 Garner, "Atlantic Crossing," 122–3.

21 Moore, "Social Impact," 6–7.

22 Maurice St. Pierre, "The Nature and Development of Social Conflict in Guyana," in *Governance, Conflict Analysis, and Conflict Resolution*, ed. Cedric H. Grant and R. Mark Kirton (Kingston, Jamaica: Ian Randle Publishers, 2007), 177–93 (183).

23 Anthony Trollope, *The West Indies and the Spanish Main* (London: Chapman and Hall, 1860), 182. W. H. Holmes, writing in 1862, used almost exactly the same words in describing the "industrious, thrifty, patient, and persevering" Portuguese, while characterizing the Creoles as unreliable, averse to plantation labor, and suitable for replacement by Indian and Chinese "coolies" on the sugar (or, better, cotton) plantations. W. H. Holmes, *Free Cotton: How and Where to Grow It* (London: Chapman and Hall, 1862), extracted in George W. Bennett, *An Illustrated History of British Guiana* (Georgetown, Demerara: Richardson and Co., 1866), 102–4.

24 Henry Kirke, *Twenty-Five Years in British Guiana* (London: Sampson Low, Marston, 1898), 272.

25 Moore, "Social Impact," 4.

26 Ibid., 9–12; Menezes, *Scenes*, 13.

27 Guiana's were not the only anti-Portuguese riots in the West Indies, nor indeed were they the only riots of a communal nature, but, owing to the unusually cosmopolitan character of the colony at this time, they were probably the worst. Their only serious rival was the outbreak at Basseterre, St. Kitts, in February 1896, which originated in a wage dispute between black workers and a Portuguese plantation owner. As in Guiana, the rioters burned and looted many Portuguese shops, and it took a force of marines from Antigua to put them down. Four or five rioters died on this occasion, and about 150 rioters were charged. See Frank Cundall, *Political and Social Disturbances in the West Indies: A Brief Account and Bibliography* (Kingston: The Institute of Jamaica, 1906), 21–2.

28 P. E. Wodehouse to H. Labouchere, February 24, 1856, *1856 British Guiana Riots Correspondence*, no. 1, 3.

29 A. R. F. Webber, *Centenary History and Handbook of British Guiana* (British Guiana: "The Argosy," 1931), 245; Moore, "Social Impact," 13.

30 P. E. Wodehouse to H. Labouchere, February 24, 1856, *1856 British Guiana Riots Correspondence*, no. 1, 4; Supreme Court of Criminal Justice, Monday, April 28, ibid., encl. 3 in no. 5, 59; John W. Braithwaite's evidence, Supreme Court of Criminal Justice, Monday, April 28, ibid., encl. 3 in no. 5, 66; Moore, "Social Impact," 13.

31 Supreme Court of Criminal Justice, Monday, April 28, ibid., encl. 3 in no. 5, 60.

32 Evidence of R. G. Butts, ibid., 70.

33 Ibid., 60–3.

34 Ibid., 64–5.

35 Webber, *Centenary History*, 244.

36 P. E. Wodehouse to H. Labouchere, February 24, 1856, *1856 British Guiana Riots Correspondence*, no. 1, 4.

37 J. T. Hynes to P. E. Wodehouse, February 15, 1856, *1856 British Guiana Riots Correspondence*, encl. 3 in no. 1, 7.

38 P. E. Wodehouse to H. Labouchere, February 24, 1856, *1856 British Guiana Riots Correspondence*, no. 1, 4.

39 No Portuguese were seen in the crowd, apart from one who was chased and beaten for allegedly having stabbed a Creole. *Demerara Royal Gazette*, no date, extracted in *Hereford Times*, March 29, 1856.

40 P. E. Wodehouse to H. Labouchere, February 24, 1856, *1856 British Guiana Riots Correspondence*, no. 1, 5.

41 Ordinance no. 4, of 1856, *1856 British Guiana Riots Correspondence*, encl. 5 in no. 1, 8–9.

42 P. E. Wodehouse to H. Labouchere, February 24, 1856, *1856 British Guiana Riots Correspondence*, no. 1, 5.

43 Webber, *Centenary History*, 246; Moore, "Social History," 13.

44 P. E. Wodehouse to H. Labouchere, February 24, 1856, *1856 British Guiana Riots Correspondence*, no. 1, 4. Wodehouse seems to have been mildly obsessed with the role of Creole women in these disturbances, frequently noting their outrageous behavior and entertaining, but eventually refusing, several suggestions "that one or two should be flogged, as examples."

45 Webber, *Centenary History*, 246.

46 "Alarming Negro Riot in Georgetown," *Liverpool Daily Post*, March 21, 1856.

47 P. E. Wodehouse to H. Labouchere, February 24, 1856, *1856 British Guiana Riots Correspondence*, no. 1, 4.

48 J. W. Boddam-Whetham, *Roraima and British Guiana, with a Glance at Bermuda, the West Indies, and the Spanish Main* (London: Hurst and Blackett, 1879), 121.

49 Monica Schuler, "Liberated Africans in Nineteenth-Century Guyana," in *Slavery, Freedom and Gender: The Dynamics of Caribbean Society*, ed. Brian L. Moore, B. W. Higman, Carl Campbell, and Patrick Bryan (Kingston, Jamaica: University of the West Indies Press, 2001), 133–57 (143).

50 P. E. Wodehouse to H. Labouchere, February 24, 1856, *1856 British Guiana Riots Correspondence*, no. 1, 4.

51 Rev. Charles Rattray quoted in Schuler, "Liberated Africans," 144.

52 L. G. Tucker to R. G. Butts, Inspector-General of Police, February 24, 1856, *1856 British Guiana Riots Correspondence*, encl. 6 in no. 1, 21.

53 *Demerara Royal Gazette*, no date, extracted in *Hereford Times*, March 29, 1856. Other rioters reportedly said, "If the Governor thought we were doing wrong in destroying the Portuguese shops he would have sent up soldiers." James E. Roney to Wodehouse, February 22, 1856, *1856 British Guiana Riots Correspondence*, encl. 6 in no. 1, 13.

54 P. E. Wodehouse to H. Labouchere, March 10, 1856, *1856 British Guiana Riots Correspondence*, no. 3, 37.

55 *The Daily Chronicle*, February 18, 1887, quoted in Menezes, *Scenes*, 46.

56 Extracts from the Official Gazette of British Guiana, February 23, 1856, *1856 British Guiana Riots Correspondence*, encl. 12 in no. 1, 29–31.
57 J. Brommell to William Walker, February 19, 1856, *1856 British Guiana Riots Correspondence*, encl. 6 in no. 1, 15.
58 Hugh M. Greene to William Walker, February 19 and 20, 1856, *1856 British Guiana Riots Correspondence*, encl. 6 in no. 1, 15.
59 Webber, *Centenary History*, 246.
60 L. G. Tucker to R. G. Butts, Inspector-General of Police, February 21 and 24, 1856, *1856 British Guiana Riots Correspondence*, encl. 6 in no. 1, 21–2.
61 P. E. Wodehouse to H. Labouchere, February 24, 1856, *1856 British Guiana Riots Correspondence*, no. 1, 5–6; P. E. Wodehouse to H. Labouchere, March 10, 1856, ibid., no. 3, 34; Webber, *Centenary History*, 246.
62 P. E. Wodehouse to H. Labouchere, February 24, 1856, *1856 British Guiana Riots Correspondence*, no. 1, 4.
63 Schuler, "Liberated Africans," 143.
64 C. G. H. Davis to William Walker, February 20, 1856, *1856 British Guiana Riots Correspondence*, encl. 6 in no. 1, 16; Webber, *Centenary History*, 246.
65 L. G. Tucker to R. G. Butts, Inspector-General of Police, February 24, 1856, ibid., encl. 6 in no. 1, 21.
66 Sam Bean to William Walker, February 20, 1856, ibid., encl. 6 in no. 1, 11–12.
67 R. Henderson to William Walker, February 21, 1856, ibid., encl. 6 in no. 1, 17.
68 John Ross to William Walker, March 7, 1856, ibid., encl. 1 in no. 3, 49.
69 Robert Short to William Walker, February 19, 1856, ibid., encl. 6, in no. 1, 11. The manager in question was a Mr. Waith of La Bonne Intention estate on the east coast. He also reported to the local magistrate that the "Congos" (that is, Africans born in Congo or Angola) were "far worse than the Creoles."
70 L. G. Tucker to R. G. Butts, Inspector-General of Police, February 24, 1856, ibid., encl. 6 in no. 1, 22.
71 P. E. Wodehouse to H. Labouchere, March 10, 1856, ibid., no. 3, 34.
72 C. Bishop to William Walker, February 22, 1856, ibid., encl. 6 in no. 1, 23.
73 Despite the objections of humanitarians (and some officials), flogging was still being routinely used as a punishment for serious offenses by the end of the century. See Kirke, *Twenty-Five Years*, 314–18.
74 James E. Roney to Wodehouse, February 23, 1856, *1856 British Guiana Riots Correspondence*, encl. 6 in no. 1, 14.
75 Augustus Frederick Gore to William Walker, February 25, 1856, ibid., encl. 1 in no. 3, 42.
76 P. E. Wodehouse to H. Labouchere, March 10, 1856, ibid., no. 3, 34.
77 P. E. Wodehouse to H. Labouchere, February 24, 1856, ibid., no. 1, p. 5; P. E. Wodehouse to H. Labouchere, March 10, 1856; ibid., no. 3, 34.

78 Supreme Court of Criminal Justice, Monday, April 28, ibid., encl. 3 in no. 5, 57–87; Webber, *Centenary History*, 248; Kirke, *Twenty-Five Years*, 184.
79 P. E. Wodehouse to H. Labouchere, March 10, 1856, *1856 British Guiana Riots Correspondence*, no. 3, 35; T. Lucie Smith to P. E. Wodehouse, May 9, 1856, ibid., encl. 2 in no. 5, 57.
80 In a nice piece of transcolonial jurisprudence, the Attorney General quoted from a judgment of the House of Lords in an 1844 case against Irish nationalist Daniel O'Connell, to the effect that any attempt to stir up "ill-will between different classes of Her Majesty's subjects" was an illegal proceeding. Report of the Trial of John Sayers Orr, Supreme Court of Criminal Justice, Monday, April 28, ibid., encl. 3 in no. 5, 59.
81 Webber, *Centenary History*, 248.
82 T. Lucie Smith to P. E. Wodehouse, May 9, 1856, *1856 British Guiana Riots Correspondence*, encl. 2 in no. 5, 57.
83 Webber, *Centenary History*, 247.
84 P. E. Wodehouse to H. Labouchere, March 10, 1856, *1856 British Guiana Riots Correspondence*, no. 3, 35. Wodehouse said that he gave every prisoner the option of serving out his or her sentence instead of accepting labor duties and restrictions on their place of residence, and only two chose the former. Using this system, no fewer than 510 people were sentenced to labor duties ranging from six to eighteen months.
85 P. E. Wodehouse to H. Labouchere, March 10, 1856, ibid., no. 3, 35.
86 Ibid., 36.
87 Webber, *Centenary History*, 248–51.
88 The initial provision of police arms was 300 muskets and 30,000 ammunition cartridges. Joan Mars, *Deadly Force, Colonialism, and the Rule of Law: Police Violence in Guyana* (Westport, CT: Greenwood Press, 2002), 75; Memorandum from Philip Wodehouse, March 5, 1856, *1856 British Guiana Riots Correspondence*, encl. 5 in no. 3, 55.
89 H. Labouchere to P. E. Wodehouse, April 1, 1856, *1856 British Guiana Riots Correspondence*, Dispatches from the Secretary of State, no. 1, 87.
90 Ibid., 88.
91 H. Labouchere to P. E. Wodehouse, April 16, 1856, *1856 British Guiana Riots Correspondence*, Dispatches from the Secretary of State, no. 3, 88–9.
92 P. E. Wodehouse to H. Labouchere, March 10, 1856, ibid., no. 3, 36.
93 Adamson, "Monoculture," 396.
94 P. E. Wodehouse to H. Labouchere, March 10, 1856, *1856 British Guiana Riots Correspondence*, no. 3, 37.
95 William Hudson to William Walker, March 7, 1856, ibid., encl. 1 in no. 3, 50–2. When this letter was published a few months later, leading Creoles were outraged

at the racist sentiments it contained. See the letter from "Observer" in *The Creole*, December 5, 1856, as well as the editorial leader in *The Creole*, December 13, 1856.

96 "Alarming Negro Riot in Georgetown," *Liverpool Daily Post*, March 21, 1856.

97 *The Creole*, December 6, 1856.

98 See, for example, the editorial leader in *The Creole*, December 27, 1856.

99 *The Creole*, December 13, 1856.

100 *Devizes and Wiltshire Gazette*, September 17, 1857.

101 Report of Demerara papers in *Morning Post*, September 15, 1857; Webber, *Centenary History*, 250; *The New Local Guide of British Guiana* (Demerara: "Royal Gazette" Office, 1862), 36–7.

102 Webber, *Centenary History*, 254.

103 *The New Local Guide of British Guiana* (Demerara: "Royal Gazette" Office, 1862), 42.

104 Kirke, *Twenty-Five Years*, 186–7.

105 The letter, dated November 9, 1856 and originally sent to the office of the *Examiner*, was reprinted in the *Paisley Herald and Renfrewshire Advertiser* on December 13, 1856.

106 *The Colonist*, November 26, 1856.

107 The 1889 riot started after a Portuguese man named Manoel Gonsalves murdered his mulatto lover. He was found guilty and sentenced to death, but when the acting governor commuted the sentence to hard labor for life, many Creoles were outraged. One of their own had recently been executed for the same offense, and many alleged that there was one law for the Portuguese and another for the Creoles. Shortly thereafter, at the Stabroek Market, a Creole boy stole a piece of bread from a Portuguese shop, and the owner chased him down and beat him. The rumor went around that the boy had been killed, and angry black crowds attacked Portuguese stalls in the market. Within a few days another general rising against Portuguese shops had broken out across Georgetown and beyond. Once again the police proved insufficient to stop the rioting, and the authorities enlisted special constables. The Sheriff of Demerara, worried that the black soldiers under his command would join the crowds and turn on the black policemen (with whom they had a long-standing rivalry), refused to call the soldiers out. He also made it known that he would not hesitate to order his policemen—now considerably more militarized than in 1856—to fire at riotous crowds, a threat that he eventually carried out. As during the Angel Gabriel riots, Guiana's jails filled to overflowing with riot prisoners, so the authorities decided to release numerous petty criminals to make room for the rioters, a decision that some East Indian inmates resisted because they preferred the food and shelter of jail to life on the plantations. See Kirke, *Twenty-Five Years*, 273–81.

Chapter 2

1 On the varieties of precipitating events, and the chain of events that normally precedes a triggering event, see Donald Horowitz, *The Deadly Ethnic Riot* (Berkeley: University of California Press, 2001), 269–325.

2 Heather Streets, *Martial Races: The Military, Race and Masculinity in British Imperial Culture, 1857–1914* (Manchester: Manchester University Press, 2004), 33; Nicholas Dirks, *Castes of Mind: Colonialism and the Making of Modern India* (Princeton: Princeton University Press, 2001), 177–80; Tan Tai Yong, *The Garrison State: The Military, Government and Society in Colonial Punjab, 1849–1947* (New Delhi: Sage Publications, 2005), 52–9.

3 Steve Garner, "Atlantic Crossing: Whiteness as a Transatlantic Experience," *Atlantic Studies* 4, 1 (2007), 117–32 (122).

4 *Sanjivani*, July 29, 1893, Report on Native Newspapers (hereafter, RNN) (Bengal) for the week ending August 5, 1893, 623.

5 See, for example, James Connolly, "Labour and the Proposed Partition of Ireland," *Irish Worker*, March 14, 1914: "That the Irish people might be kept asunder and robbed whilst so sundered and divided, the Orange aristocracy went down to the lowest depths and out of the lowest pits of hell brought up the abominations of sectarian feuds to stir the passions of the ignorant mob."

6 Gyanendra Pandey, *The Construction of Communalism in Colonial North India* (Delhi: Oxford University Press, 1990); Dirks, *Castes*; Bernard Cohn, *Colonialism and its Forms of Knowledge: The British in India* (Princeton: Princeton University Press, 1996); Bernard Cohn, "The Census, Social Structure and Objectification in South Asia," in *An Anthropologist Among the Historians and Other Essays* (Delhi: Oxford University Press, 1987), 224–54; Suranjan Das, *Communal Riots in Bengal, 1905–1947* (Oxford: Oxford University Press, 1991), 14; Sandria B. Freitag, *Collective Action and Community: Public Arenas and the Emergence of Communalism in North India* (Berkeley: University of California Press, 1989).

7 Lord George Hamilton to Lord Elgin, October 3, 1895, The Earl of Elgin and Kincardine papers, BL, IOR F84/13, no.37 (to viceroy). A similar ambivalence about communal violence can be seen in the opinion of Sir John Strachey that "Nothing could be more opposed to the policy and universal practice of our Government in India than the old maxim of divide and rule; the maintenance of peace among all classes has always been recognised as one of the most essential duties of our 'belligerent civilisation'; but this need not blind us to the fact that the existence side by side of these hostile creeds is one of the strong points in our political position in India." Sir John Strachey, *India: Its Administration and Progress*, 4th ed. (London: Macmillan, 1911), 338–9.

8 Two years later Hamilton wrote, "I am sorry to hear of the increasing friction between Hindus and Mahomedans in the North-West and Punjab. One hardly knows what to wish for. Unity of ideas and action would be very dangerous politically; divergence of ideas and collision are administratively troublesome. Of the two, the latter is the least risky, though it throws anxiety and responsibility upon those on the spot where the friction exists." Lord George Hamilton to Lord Elgin, May 7, 1897, The Earl of Elgin and Kincardine Papers, BL, IOR F84/15, no. x (to viceroy).

9 David Arnold, *Police Power and Colonial Rule: Madras 1859–1947* (Delhi: Oxford University Press, 1986), 121.

10 "A Note on Hindu–Muslim Antagonism, Bengal, 1923," Police Files on Pre-1947 Communal Disturbances (author unspecified), BL, IOR, MSS Eur F161/142.

11 G. R. Thursby, *Hindu-Muslim Relations in British India: A Study of Controversy, Conflict, and Communal Movements in Northern India, 1923–1928* (Leiden: E. J. Brill, 1975), 174.

12 *Saturday Review*, April 1, 1865.

13 *Glasgow Herald*, August 14, 1893.

14 *Daily News*, September 5, 1893, on the Hindu–Muslim riots in northern India: "The best cure for these fantastic hatreds is the hope of material prosperity and the chances of a career."

15 On the origins of Orangeism see Hereward Senior, *Orangeism in Ireland and Britain, 1795–1836* (London: Routledge and Kegan Paul, 1966).

16 Mark Doyle, *Fighting like the Devil for the Sake of God: Protestants, Catholics, and the Origins of Violence in Victorian Belfast* (Manchester: Manchester University Press, 2009); Sean Farrell, *Rituals and Riots: Sectarian Violence and Political Culture in Ulster, 1784–1886* (Lexington, KY: University Press of Kentucky, 2000); Sybil Baker, "Orange and Green: Belfast, 1832–1912," in *The Victorian City: Images and Realities*, vol. 2, ed. H. J. Dyos and M. Wolff (London: Routledge & Kegan Paul, 1973), 787–815; Catherine Hirst, *Religion, Politics, and Violence in Nineteenth-Century Belfast: The Pound and Sandy Row* (Dublin: Four Courts Press, 2002).

17 One of the most troubled spots in Britain was Liverpool. See Frank Neal, *Sectarian Violence: The Liverpool Experience, 1819–1914: An Aspect of Anglo-Irish History* (Manchester: Manchester University Press, 1988).

18 Dipesh Chakrabarty, "Communal Riots and Labour: Bengal's Jute Mill-Hands in the 1890s," *Past and Present* 91 (May 1981), 140–69; Arun Mukherjee, *Crime and Public Disorder in Colonial Bengal, 1861–1912* (Calcutta: K P Bagchi, 1995).

19 On the violence associated with Irish "navvies" in the British Isles and North America, see David Brooke, "The 'Lawless' Navvy: A Study of the Crime Associated with Railway Building," *The Journal of Transport History* 10 (September 1989),

145–65; David Brooke, *The Railway Navvy: "That Despicable Race of Men"* (Newton Abbot: David & Charles, 1983), 108–22; and James E. Handley, *The Navvy in Scotland* (Cork: Cork University Press, 1970), 267–320.

20 There is a considerable literature on sectarian conflict in North America. For Canada, see William J. Smyth, *Toronto, the Belfast of Canada: The Orange Order and the Shaping of Municipal Culture* (Toronto: University of Toronto Press, 2015); and Hereward Senior, *Orangeism: The Canadian Phase* (Toronto: McGraw-Hill Ryerson, 1972). For the United States, a good starting place is Michael A. Gordon, *The Orange Riots: Irish Political Violence in New York City, 1870 and 1871* (Ithaca: Cornell University Press, 1993). On Rangoon, see Chapter 7 in the present volume.

21 Pradip Kumar Datta, *Carving Blocs: Communal Ideology in Early Twentieth-Century Bengal* (Oxford: Oxford University Press, 1999).

22 Rosalind O'Hanlon, "Colonialism and Social Identities in Flux: Class, Caste, and Religious Community," in *India and the British Empire*, ed. Douglas M. Peers and Nandini (Oxford: Oxford University Press, 2012), 100–34; C. A. Bayly, *Indian Society and the Making of the British Empire* (Cambridge: Cambridge University Press, 1988), 14–66; Radhika Singha, "Settle, Mobilise, Verify: Identification Practices in Colonial India," *Studies in History* 16 (2000), 151–98; Dirks, *Castes*, 125–228; S. Bayly, *Caste, Society and Politics in India from the Eighteenth Century to the Modern Age* (Cambridge: Cambridge University Press, 1999), 187–232; David Gilmartin, " 'Divine Displeasure' and Muslim Elections: The Shaping of Community in Twentieth-Century Punjab," in *The Political Inheritance of Pakistan*, ed. D. A. Low (New York: St. Martin's Press, 1991), 106–29.

23 Sir Edmund Charles Cox, *A Short History of the Bombay Presidency* (Bombay: Thacker, 1887), 398.

24 Deep Kanta Lahiri Choudhury, *Telegraphic Imperialism: Crisis and Panic in the Indian Empire, c. 1830* (London: Palgrave Macmillan, 2010), 85; A. Martin Wainwright, "Representing the Technology of the Raj in Britain's Victorian Periodical Press," in *Negotiating India in the Nineteenth-Century Media*, ed. David Finkelstein and Douglas M. Peers (New York: St. Martin's Press, 2000), 185–209.

25 Sir A. P. MacDonnell, *Selections from Speeches of Sir A. P. MacDonnell, G.C.S.I., Lieutenant-Governor, N.-W. P., and Chief Commissioner of Oudh, from 1895 to 1901* (Naini Tal: N.-W. Provinces and Oudh Government Camp Branch Press, 1901), 3.

26 Daniel Headrick, "A Double-Edged Sword: Communications and Imperial Control in British India," *Historical Social Research / Historicsche Sozialforschung* 35, 1 (2010), 51–65.

27 Daniel R. Headrick, *The Tentacles of Progress: Technology Transfer in the Age of Imperialism, 1850–1940* (New York: Oxford University Press, 1988), 87.

28 H. J. S. Cotton, chief secretary to the government of Bengal, to the secretary to the government of India, Home Dept., October 28, 1893, BL, IOR, L/P&J/6/267/257.

29 Choudhury, *Telegraphic Imperialism.*

30 *Report of the Commissioners of Inquiry, 1869, into the Riots and Disturbances in the City of Londonderry, with Minutes of Evidence and Appendix.* HC 1870 (C.5) XXXII, 17.

31 Doyle, *Fighting*, ch. 6. On occasion new technologies could themselves become a weapon. In September 1854 a train carrying Lord Enniskillen and several hundred Irish Protestants home from an Orange demonstration in Derry flew off the tracks, killing two men and injuring several others, after someone placed several large stones on the tracks in an unsuccessful bid to assassinate the Earl. In London a horrified *Morning Chronicle* noted the irony that an agent of civilization like the railroad should be used to perpetrate such violence. The "worst feature" of the episode, it said, "is that the great social advances of the age have been enlisted in the cause of wholesale murder. This is the first time that a railway has been perverted from its ennobling and civilizing purposes; and if this is to be the result of Irish improvement, we might almost welcome the happier days when Irishmen, in the sacred cause of religion, only cut single throats and shot solitary religious aliens from behind a hedge." *Morning Chronicle*, September 28, 1854.

32 In India in 1889, language scholar George Grierson observed, "there is now scarcely a town of importance which does not possess its printing-press or two. Every scribbler can now see his writings in type or lithographed for a few rupees, and too often he avails himself of the power and the opportunity." G. A. Grierson, *The Modern Vernacular Literature of Hindustan* (Calcutta: Asiatic Society of Bengal, 1889), 145, quoted in C. A. Bayly, *Empire and Information: Intelligence Gathering and Social Communication in India, 1780–1870* (Cambridge: Cambridge University Press, 1996), 343. There is a large and growing literature on the imperial press, focusing especially on its role in identity formation among both settlers and natives. See Simon J. Potter, "Webs, Networks, and Systems: Globalization and the Mass Media in the Nineteenth- and Twentieth-Century British Empire," *Journal of British Studies* (July 2007), 621–46.

33 Su Lin Lewis, "Colonial Penang's 'Indigenous' English Press," in *Media and the British Empire*, ed. Chandrika Kaul (New York: Palgrave Macmillan, 2006), 233–47 (234).

34 Thomas Larcom, report to Queen Victoria, n.d., Larcom Papers, NLI, 7626/59.

35 Note from Charles Lyall, October. 6, 1893, written on riot report from Northwest Provinces and Oudh, "Recent riots between Muhammadans and Hindus in the Azamgarh and Ballia Districts and in the City of Bombay," NAIn, Home Dept., Public Branch, November 1893, no. 169.

36 Cox, *Short History*, 289.

37 Potter, "Webs," 627. See also J. Don Vann and Rosemary T. VanArsdel, "Introduction," in *Periodicals of Queen Victoria's Empire*, ed. J. Don Vann and Rosemary T. VanArsdel (Toronto: University of Toronto Press, 1996), 3–16; S. Natarajan, *A History of the Press in India* (Bombay: Asia Publishing House, 1962); and Margarita Barns, *The Indian Press: A History of the Growth of Public Opinion in India* (London: George Allen & Unwin, 1940).

38 Quoted in Merrill Tilghman Boyce, *British Policy and the Evolution of the Vernacular Press in India, 1835–1878* (Delhi: Chanakya Publications, 1988), 40.

39 C. A. Bayly, *Empire and Information*, 340–1.

40 Within Britain the final measure that liberated the press from formal government control came with the repeal of the Stamp Act in 1855. For a history and critique of the struggle for press freedom in Britain, see James Curran, "Press History," in *Power Without Responsibility: The Press, Broadcasting and the Internet in Britain*, 7th ed., ed. James Curran and Jean Seaton (New York: Routledge, 2010), 1–99.

41 John M. MacKenzie, "'To Enlighten South Africa': The Creation of a Free Press at the Cape in the Early Nineteenth Century," in *Media and the British Empire*, ed. Chandrika Kaul (New York: Palgrave Macmillan, 2006), 20–36.

42 Myles Dungan, *Mr Parnell's Rottweiler: Censorship and the United Ireland Newspaper, 1881–1891* (Sallins, Co. Kildare: Irish Academic Press, 2014).

43 Robert Darnton, "Literary Surveillance in the British Raj: The Contradictions of Liberal Imperialism," *Book History* 4 (2001), 133–76; Boyce, *British Policy*, 91–119; Paul R. Brumpton, *Security and Progress: Lord Salisbury at the India Office* (Westport, CT: Greenwood Press, 2002), 22–7; Barns, *Indian Press*, 280–95; Natarajan, *History*, 94–6. On press censorship in twentieth-century India, see N. Gerald Barrier, *Banned: Controversial Literature and Political Control in British India, 1907–1947* (Columbia, MO: University of Missouri Press, 1974).

44 Lord Kimberley to Lord Lansdowne, October 26, 1893, Lansdowne Papers, BL, IOR, Mss. Eur D558/6, no. 66 (to viceroy).

45 Lord Kimberley to Lord Lansdowne, September 8, 1893, Lansdowne Papers, BL, IOR, Mss. Eur D558/6, no. 56 (to viceroy); Lord Lansdowne to D. Fitzpatrick, August 22, 1893, Lansdowne Papers, BL, IOR, Mss. Eur D558/25, no. 119 (from viceroy). In another part of his note quoted above, Charles Lyall wrote, "This rapid dissemination of news is of course a thing with which it is impossible to interfere." Note from Charles Lyall, October 6, 1893, written on riot report from Northwest Provinces and Oudh, "Recent riots between Muhammadans and Hindus in the Azamgarh and Ballia Districts and in the City of Bombay," NAIn, Home Dept., Public Branch, November 1893, no. 169.

46 Thursby, *Hindu-Muslim Relations*, 23.

47 Peter Van Der Veer, *Imperial Encounters: Religion and Modernity in India and Britain* (Princeton: Princeton University Press, 2001), 23; David Gilmartin, *Empire*

and Islam: Punjab and the Making of Pakistan (Berkeley: University of California Press, 1988); Thursby, *Hindu-Muslim Relations*, 174.

48 On the importance of communications technology to South Asian Islam, in particular, see Francis Robinson, "Technology and Religious Change: Islam and the Impact of Print," *Modern Asian Studies* 27, 1 (February 1993), 229–51.

49 K. H. M. Sumathipala, "The Kotahena Riots and their Repercussions," *The Ceylon Historical Journal* (1969–70), 65–81; Kitsiri Malalgoda, *Buddhism in Sinhalese Society: A Study of Religious Revival and Change* (Berkeley: University of California Press, 1976), 220–8; Tessa Bartholomeusz, "Catholics, Buddhists, and the Church of England: The 1883 Sri Lankan Riots," *Buddhist-Christian Studies* 15 (1995), 89–103.

50 Emmet Larkin, "The Devotional Revolution in Ireland, 1850–75," *The American Historical Review* 77 (June 1972), 625–52.

51 Howard Brown, *Ending the French Revolution: Violence, Justice, and Repression from the Terror to Napoleon* (Charlottesville: University of Virginia Press, 2006), ch. 10; Ali Parchami, *Hegemonic Peace and Empire: The* Pax Romana, Britannica, *and* Americana (London: Routledge, 2009), 100.

52 On the difficulties inherent in the impartiality principle as applied to India, see Mark Doyle, "The Perils of Impartiality: Policing Communal Violence in Victorian India," in *Policing Empires*, ed. Amandine Lauro, Emmanuel Blanchard, and Marieke Bloembergen (Berne: Peter Lang, forthcoming). I have drawn on this article for some of the following discussion.

53 Van Der Veer, *Imperial Encounters*, 23; Thomas Metcalf, *Ideologies of the Raj* (Cambridge: Cambridge University Press, 1994), 40.

54 Quoted in Dirks, *Castes*, 40.

55 Quoted in Thursby, *Hindu-Muslim Relations*, 116.

56 Religious neutrality did not always mean religious indifference, however. In 1875 Ceylon's governor, Sir William Gregory, praised the work of Christian missionaries while affirming his government's commitment to "thoroughly impartial action" in its treatment of the various competing Christian denominations. Sir William Gregory, *An Autobiography*, ed. Lady Gregory (London: John Murray, 1894), 335.

57 Keith Hunte, "Protestantism and Slavery in the British Caribbean," in *Christianity in the Caribbean: Essays on Church History*, ed. Armando Lampe (Kingston, Jamaica: The University of the West Indies Press, 2001), 115–17. For a narrative account of the disestablishment and disendowment of the Church of England in the West Indies, see Alfred Caldecott, *The Church in the West Indies* (London: Society for Promoting Christian Knowledge, 1898), 134–47.

58 Lord Eglinton, *HL Deb 19 April 1853, vol 126, cc14.*

59 R. Suntharalingam, "The Salem Riots, 1882: Judiciary versus Executive in the Mediation of a Communal Dispute," *Modern Asian Studies* 3, 3 (1969), 193–208 (196).

60 *Times of India*, October 4, 1882.

61 Suntharalingam, "Salem Riots," 198.

62 Ibid., 198–9.

63 *Madras Times*, July 6, 1882, in "Newspaper Reports and Petitions about the Salem Riots," NAIn, Home Dept., Judicial Branch, July 1882, nos. 350–1 (B).

64 Suntharalingam, "Salem Riots," 203.

65 Letter from a "European Correspondent," *Madras Times*, August 23, 1882.

66 Suntharalingam, "Salem Riots," 204.

67 *Times of India*, August 22, 1882. On August 29, the same paper called for European troops to be called out in the case of any future emergencies, since the native police were powerless and may have "secretly coalesced with their co-religionists."

68 Ibid.

69 *Times of India*, October 4, 1882.

70 Suntharalingam, "Salem Riots," 207.

71 On Ireland, see Mark Doyle, "Martyrs of Liberty: Open-Air Preaching and Popular Violence in Victorian Britain and Ireland," in *Faith, War, and Violence: Religion and Public Life*, vol. 39, ed. Gabriel Ricci (New Brunswick, NJ: Transaction Publishers, 2014), 149–64. On Ceylon, see K. H. M. Sumathipala, "The Kotahena Riots and Their Repercussions," *The Ceylon Historical Journal* (1969–70), 65–81. On Trinidad, see "Petition of Certain Immigrants with Reference to the Immigrants' Festivals Regulations" to John Scott Bushe, September 22, 1884, in *Correspondence Respecting the Recent Coolie Disturbances in Trinidad at the Mohurrum Festival, with the Report Thereon by Sir H. W. Norman, K. C. B., C. I. E.*, HC 1884–5 (C.4366) LIII, encl. 1 in no. 6, 8.

72 Memorial to Lord Ripon (governor-general), signed by Keshub Chunder Sen, NAIn, Home Dept., Public Branch, October 1882, nos. 201–2. On the Salvation Army's "invasion" of Bombay, and the public and official response, see Andrew M. Eason, "Religion versus the Raj: The Salvation Army's 'Invasion' of British India," *Mission Studies* 28 (2011), 71–90.

73 Eason, "Religion," 86. A similar clash with the state occurred when the Salvation Army arrived in Cape Town a few years later. See Andrew M. Eason, "'Desperate Fighting at the Cape': The Salvation Army's Arrival and Earliest Work in Late-Victorian Cape Town," *Journal of Religious History* 33, 3 (September 2009), 265–84.

74 Lord Chelmsford, speaking as viceroy in 1918, made this point in a letter to the India Office. Arguing that religious liberty was the "root cause" of recent cow-protection clashes between Hindus and Muslims, he wrote, "Disturbances do not take place in Native States because where the ruler is a Hindu the Moslems know better than to give trouble and cows are not slain. Conversely where a Moslem is ruler the Hindus know better than to raise the question and cows are slain with no objection taken." Lord Chelmsford to Edwin Montagu, May 30, 1918, Chelmsford Papers, BL, IOR, Mss. Eur. E264/4, no. 11 (from viceroy).

75 Extract from a letter from the government of India to the secretary of state, No. 84, dated 27th December 1893, Received 15th January 1894, *East India (religious disturbances). Copies or extracts of reports relating to the recent conflicts between Hindus and Muhammadans in India, and particularly to the causes which led to them*, HC 1893–4 (538) LXIII (hereafter, *1893–4 India Riots Reports*), 58.

76 Letter from "Observer," *Times of India*, February 26, 1894.

77 As John McLane has written of the cow-protection controversy in India, "One community adjusted or expanded its behavior toward the limit permitted by the law or the limit the community thought should be permitted, while the other community held that local custom and precedent should prevail. When local custom, municipal regulations, and civil law were in conflict with popular notions of fairness, the potential for trouble was considerable." John McLane, *Indian Nationalism and the Early Congress* (Princeton: Princeton University Press, 1977), 292.

78 Extract from a letter from the government of India to the secretary of state, No. 84, dated December 27, 1893, Received January 15, 1894, *1893–4 India Riots Reports*, 58.

79 *Glasgow Herald*, September 29, 1893.

80 The Indian railways are probably the best example of how private and public bodies sometimes worked together and sometimes independently to promote economic and technological change, but a similar dynamic was evident across the empire, as for instance with the laying of telegraph cables in southern and western Africa. See Headrick, *Tentacles*, 50–96 and 106–110.

Chapter 3

1 Peter Gordon, "Spencer, John Poyntz, fifth Earl Spencer (1835–1910)," in *Oxford Dictionary of National Biography*, ed. H. C. G. Matthew and Brian Harrison (Oxford: Oxford University Press, 2004), http://www.oxforddnb.com/view/36209 (accessed December 27, 2014).

2 Lord Spencer to Lord Dufferin, August 23, 1872, PRONI, Dufferin papers, D1071/H/B/S/476/28.

3 *Northern Whig*, August 9, 1872.

4 Spencer to Dufferin, August 23, 1872, PRONI, Dufferin papers, D1071/H/B/S/476/28.

5 Spencer to Viscount Halifax, August 19, 1872, Borthwick Institute of Historical Research, University of York HALIFAX/A4/110A.

6 Spencer to Dufferin, August 23, 1872, PRONI, Dufferin papers, D1071/H/B/S/476/28.

7 Mark Doyle, *Fighting like the Devil for the Sake of God: Protestants, Catholics, and the Origins of Violence in Victorian Belfast* (Manchester: Manchester University Press, 2009), ch. 6.

8 A postriot leader in the *Northern Star and Ulster Observer* (August 27, 1872) claimed that the Orangemen of Belfast had betrayed the good faith of Catholics, who had "united in returning Mr. Johnston as a member for the borough."

9 James Kennedy to Thomas O'Hagan, June 11, 1870, PRONI, James Kennedy Papers, D2777/9/59/3.

10 *Northern Star and Ulster Observer*, July 11, 1872; *Daily Examiner*, July 11, 1872.

11 *Northern Whig*, July 13, 1872.

12 *Northern Star and Ulster Observer*, July 13, 1872.

13 Ibid.; *Daily Examiner*, July 13, 1872; *Northern Whig*, July 13, 1872.

14 *Daily Examiner*, August 13, 1872.

15 Ibid.; *Northern Star and Ulster Observer*, August 17, 1872; *Northern Whig*, August 16, 1872.

16 *Daily Examiner*, August 16, 1872; RM of Lisburn (Major Percy) to Undersecretary of Dublin Castle, August 22, 1872, NAIr, CSORP 1872/12879.

17 *Northern Star and Ulster Observer*, August 17, 1872.

18 RM of Lisburn (Major Percy) to Undersecretary of Dublin Castle, August 22, 1872, NAIr, CSORP 1872/12879.

19 *Daily Examiner*, August 17, 1872.

20 *Daily Examiner*, August 16, 1872; *Northern Star and Ulster Observer*, August 17, 1872; *Belfast Newsletter*, August 17, 1872.

21 *Times* (London), August 17, 1872; *Northern Star and Ulster Observer*, August 17, 1872; *Daily Examiner*, August 16, 1872; *Northern Whig*, August 16, 1872.

22 *Northern Whig*, August 18, 1872.

23 *Northern Whig*, August 19, 1872.

24 Ibid.

25 *Daily Examiner*, August 19, 1872.

26 Ibid.

27 *Northern Star and Ulster Observer*, August 20, 1872.

28 *Daily Examiner*, August 21, 1872.

29 *Northern Star and Ulster Observer*, August 22, 1872.

30 *Northern Whig*, August 19, 1872.

31 *Belfast Newsletter*, August 19, 1872.

32 *Freeman's Journal*, August 19, 1872; *Daily Express*, August 19, 1872.

33 This was the case with Protestants leaving Albert Street and Catholics leaving Willow Street. *Northern Star and Ulster Observer*, August 20, 1872.

34 *Northern Whig*, August 21, 1872.

35 Letter from the Marquis of Hartington to Sir John Savage, January 6, 1873, printed in *Freeman's Journal*, January 14, 1873.

36 If the average family size was five, for instance, then this would mean 4,185 men, women, and children became refugees.

37 *Northern Star and Ulster Observer*, August 20, 1872.

38 *Daily Examiner*, August 20, 1872.

39 Doyle, *Fighting*, 107–9 and 175.

40 *Daily Examiner*, August 20, 1872.

41 See, for example, letters in the *Daily Examiner* from "M" (Aug. 27, 1872); "Scrutator" (September 26, 1872); "Breffni" (September 28, 1872); "W" and "Catholica" (October 5, 1872).

42 *Northern Star and Ulster Observer*, August 22, 1872; *Daily Examiner*, September 4, 1872.

43 *Northern Star and Ulster Observer*, August 27, 1872.

44 *Daily Express*, August 22, 1872.

45 Report of Assistant Inspector General Duncan on the Belfast Riots, November 5, 1872, NAIr, CSORP 1872/17338; letter from "A Kildare Sub-Constable," *Northern Star and Ulster Observer*, August 31, 1872.

46 *Daily Examiner*, August 23, 1872; *Northern Star and Ulster Observer*, August 24, 1872; *Belfast Newsletter*, August 20, 1872.

47 *Northern Whig*, August 23, 1872; *Daily Examiner*, August 23, 1872; *Belfast Newsletter*, August 23, 1872.

48 *Belfast Newsletter*, August 22, 1872.

49 Marquis of Hartington to Sir John Savage, January 6, 1873, printed in *Freeman's Journal*, January 14, 1873. Report of Assistant Inspector General Duncan on the Belfast Riots, November 5, 1872, NAIr, CSORP 1872/17338.

50 *Northern Whig*, August 19, 1872.

51 Report of Assistant Inspector General Duncan on the Belfast Riots November 5, 1872, NAIr, CSORP 1873/1022; *Daily News*, August 22, 1872; *Daily Express*, August 23, 1872; Spencer to Halifax, August 26, 1872, Borthwick Institute of Historical Research, University of York HALIFAX/A4/110A.

52 *Northern Whig*, August 19, 1872. See also the leader of August 19, 1872 in the *Freeman's Journal*.

53 *Northern Star and Ulster Observer*, August 22, 1872. This was the attitude of many British papers as well. An editorial leader in the *Hampshire Telegraph and Sussex Chronicle* (August 24, 1872) maintained, "The best and, indeed, the only way to terminate the yearly interval of civil war in Belfast is to peremptorily put down the mutual provocations to breaches of the peace, to render the possession of firearms under certain circumstances penal, and to make terrible examples of those who are caught inciting others to commit disturbances." The *Pall Mall Gazette* (August 29,

1872) made the same suggestion: "Nothing could so effectually have shielded Belfast from the danger of another riot as an exhibition of severity which would have taught the rioters that every man who showed himself in the disturbed streets did so at the risk of his life."

54 *Northern Star and Ulster Observer*, August 20, 1872.

55 Report of Police Court, *Daily Examiner*, August 28, 1872.

56 Report of Town Council meeting, *Daily Examiner*, September 3, 1872.

57 Ibid.

58 *Daily Telegraph*, August 22, 1872. The man who had recommended the "trail of a six-pounder" was R. George Dundas, MP for Linlithgowshire, who had suggested in 1855 that the Metropolitan Police should have dealt more harshly with rioters in Hyde Park who opposed the Sunday Trading Bill.

59 *Preston Guardian*, August 24, 1872.

60 *Daily Telegraph*, August 22, 1872.

61 *Times* (London), August 21, 1872.

62 *Pall Mall Gazette*, August 20, 1872.

63 *Times* (London), August 21, 1872.

64 *Daily Examiner*, August 22, 1872.

65 "The Belfast Riots," *The Spectator*, August 24, 1872, 1065–1066. See also leaders in the *Daily Telegraph* (August 22, 1872) and *Examiner* (August 24, 1872).

66 H. G. Thompson to Lord Dufferin, August 20, 1872, Dufferin Papers, PRONI D1071/H/B/T/138/3.

67 Spencer to Halifax, August 26, 1872, Borthwick Institute of Historical Research, University of York HALIFAX/A4/110A.

68 Sandhurst (1819–1876) had long experience in India generally and in Bombay specifically. He was army chief of staff during the 1857 Indian "Mutiny," taking part in the second relief of Lucknow, and from 1860 to 1865 he commanded the military of the Bombay Presidency. Between 1865 and 1870 he was commander-in-chief of the British army in India. His son, the second Baron Sandhurst, served as governor of Bombay from 1895 to 1900.

69 Minute by the Right Honorable Lord Sandhurst, G.C.B., G.C.S.I., Commander of the Forces. *Belfast Riots—Means for Suppression.* NLI, IR 32341 pp. 49, 2.

70 Draft letter from Lord Justices to Inspector General of Constabulary, September 30, 1872, NAIr, CSORP 1872/15087; Marquis of Hartington to Sir John Savage, January 6, 1873, printed in *Freeman's Journal*, January 14, 1873.

71 Minute by the Right Honorable Lord Sandhurst, G.C.B., G.C.S.I., Commander of the Forces. *Belfast Riots—Means for Suppression.* NLI, IR 32341 pp. 49, 1.

72 Mark Radford, *The Policing of Belfast, 1870–1914* (London: Bloomsbury, 2015), ch. 5.

73 Minute Book of the Belfast Town Council, Feb 1, 1874, PRONI LA/7/2/EA/10.

74 W. J. Lowe and E. L. Malcolm, "The Domestication of the Royal Irish Constabulary, 1836–1922," *Irish Economic and Social History* 19 (1992), 27–48.

75 Spencer to Dufferin, August 23, 1872, Dufferin Papers, PRONI D1071/H/B/S/476/28.

76 "Circular to the Resident Magistrates Sent to the North of Ireland for the 12th July, 1873," NAGB, CO904/182/A.

77 Papers on Party Processions in Ireland, NAGB, CO904/182/A.

78 James Lowther, note dated May 30, 1878, NAGB, CO904/182/A.

Chapter 4

1 Gyanendra Pandey, *The Construction of Communalism in Colonial North India* (Delhi: Oxford University Press, 1990), 24.

2 Ibid., 45.

3 *Northern Echo*, March 16, 1874.

4 *The Era*, March 20, 1859. Here one might also observe, following Nicholas Dirks, that caste, like communalism, was at least in part a modern construct. See Nicholas Dirks, *Castes of Mind: Colonialism and the Making of Modern India* (Princeton: Princeton University Press, 2001).

5 Pandey, *Construction*, 62.

6 This tendency persists in more recent discussions of the conflict in Northern Ireland. See, for example, Andrew Boyd, *Holy War in Belfast* (Tralee: Anvil Books, 1969); and A. T. Q. Stewart, *The Narrow Ground: Aspects of Ulster, 1609–1969* (Belfast: The Blackstaff Press, 1997), 143–54.

7 We might also refer to the *Pall Mall Gazette's* opinion that the 1872 riots demonstrated Ireland's unfitness for self-governance, since "the ancient hostility of old Irish families and factions is not dead, but only sleeping, and wants but little to revive it to its old murderous activity." *Pall Mall Gazette*, August 20, 1872.

8 *Times* (London), August 24, 1864.

9 John, Viscount Morley, *Recollections* (New York: The Macmillan Company, 1917), vol. 1, 344.

10 Sir Alfred C. Lyall, *Asiatic Studies: Religious and Social* (London: John Murray, 1899), 303.

11 Ibid., 309–10.

12 HL Deb June 7, 1858, vol. 150, cc1595.

13 Letter from "A Visitor" to the *Times* (London) dated August 19, 1864, extracted in *Belfast Newsletter*, August 22, 1864.

14 Thomas Larcom to Lord Carlisle, August 29, 1864, Larcom Papers, NLI, 7626/64. See also the *Bristol Mercury*, July 21, 1860: "Let us, however, hope that, in the rapid

advancement which Ireland is making, she will in time assimilate herself to the political and social condition of this country. Happily there are Irishmen who, in spite of hereditary animosities, are working for the practical improvement of their native land; and a reasonable trust may be indulged in, that if the Government rules with a steady hand, the last embers of faction will die out in a few years, and that Irishmen will direct their pugnacious impulses only against the enemies of their island and of the empire of which it forms a part."

15 HL Deb June 7, 1858, vol. 150 cc1595.

16 *Daily Telegraph*, August 19, 1864. The previous day the *Telegraph* had made a similar point: "Belfast, the prosperous and populous capital of Ulster, is not at this moment one of the cities of Queen Victoria. It has to its disgrace allowed itself to fall out of her Majesty's hands into the possession of a brutal and ferocious mob, who use it for a fighting-ring." See also the *Saturday Review* of August 20, 1864: "Day after day, the streets of thriving, prosperous, and educated Belfast (the 'Irish Athens' we believe it calls itself) have been in the occupation of ferocious mobs"; and the letter appearing in the *Times* (London) on August 19, 1864, from the correspondent quoted above: "I am in the town of Belfast; trade flourishing, weather beautiful, employment for all who wish work, operatives enjoying their annual holiday in some of the demesnes within easy reach of the town, noblemen's parks thrown open, Providence gladdening earth; and yet within a stonethrow are hussars, soldiers, constabulary mounted and on foot, crowds of police, magistrates plenty as blackberries, shops shut, crowds running hither and thither, the crack of musket or pistol reverberating, ladies flying in terror; and all this in one of the most prosperous towns in the empire, and at twelve o'clock in flaming noonday."

17 Morley, *Recollections*, 222.

18 *Times* (London), August 10, 1874.

19 *Glasgow Herald*, August 14, 1893.

20 Lyall, *Asiatic Studies*, 304.

21 *Pall Mall Gazette*, August 14, 1893.

22 *Daily Examiner* (Belfast), August 22, 1872.

23 Letter from "A Creole" in *The Creole*, December 20, 1856.

24 *Ceylon Examiner*, March 28 and 30, 1883, in G. P. V. Somaratna, *Kotahena Riot 1883: A Religious Riot in Sri Lanka* (Gangodawila, Sri Lanka: Deepanee, 1991), 116 and 122.

25 Alberto Toscano, *Fanaticism: On the Uses of an Idea* (London: Verso, 2010), xi.

26 Ibid., xix.

27 Ibid., 14.

28 *The Era*, March 20, 1859.

29 *Bristol Mercury*, September 27, 1862.

30 *Birmingham Daily Post*, August 16, 1864.

31 *Daily News*, August 22, 1872.
32 *Pall Mall Gazette*, August 13, 1874; *Daily News*, May 27, 1874; *Northern Echo*, March 16 and June 15, 1874; *Glasgow Herald*, March 28, 1874; *Times* (London), March 18, 1874.
33 It should be noted that the epithet was occasionally redirected at the colonizers themselves. Thus the nationalist Belfast newspaper the *Ulsterman* (August 31, 1857) blamed the "coarse, harsh, fanaticism of England's imbecile officers" for the Indian revolt of 1857.
34 William Tracy to Lord Naas, June 7, 1858. NAIr, CSORP (1858) 14919.
35 Alfred C. Lyall, March 23, 1874, notes on preliminary report by Bombay government to the India Office, "Riots Which Occurred in the Town of Bombay in February last," NAIn, Home Dept., Police Branch, April 1874, nos. 30–41, pp. 43–46.
36 G. C. Paul to A. C. Lyall, undated memorandum, "State of the law relating to the suppression of riots," NAIn, Home Dept., Police Branch, January 1875, no. 18, p. 3.
37 S. M. Edwardes, *The Bombay City Police: A Historical Sketch, 1672–1916* (London: Oxford University Press, 1923), 103 and 197.
38 Richard I. Cashman, *The Myth of the* Lokmanya*: Tilak and Mass Politics in Maharashtra* (Berkeley: University of California Press, 1975), 73.
39 Antony MacDonnell to A. Forbes, September 13, 1893, Bodleian Library, MacDonnell Papers, fol. 39.
40 Lord Harris to Lord Kimberley, August 15, 1893, Bodleian Library, Kimberley Papers, Ms. Eng. c.4323.
41 *Liverpool Mercury*, July 18, 1851.
42 Anthony Trollope, *The West Indies and the Spanish Main* (London: Chapman and Hall, 1860), 189.
43 Sir H. W. Norman to the Earl of Derby, January 13, 1885, *Correspondence Respecting the Recent Coolie Disturbances in Trinidad, with the Report by Sir H. W. Norman Thereon*, HL 1885 (C.4366) XXII, 39–49.
44 Edwardes, *Bombay City Police*, 181.
45 *Aberdeen Journal*, November 21, 1860.
46 Francis Robinson, "The British Empire and the Muslim World," in *Oxford History of the British Empire*, vol. iv, ed. Judith Brown and Wm. Roger Louis (Oxford: Oxford University Press, 1999), 398–420 (405). The *Times of India*, for instance, repeatedly used the term "fanatic" to describe Muslim rioters during the Bombay riots of 1874, as did the correspondents whose letters they published, but the term was rarely used when describing Parsis.
47 Sir Bampfylde Fuller, *Studies of Indian Life and Sentiment* (London: John Murray, 1910), 130; Sir John Strachey, *India: Its Administration and Progress*, 4th ed. (London: Macmillan, 1911), 333.

48 Strachey, *India*, 336–7.

49 Winston Churchill, *The Story of the Malakand Field Force: An Episode of Frontier War* (London: Thomas Nelson, 1916), 58–9.

50 In fact, Muslim elites in India frequently tried to restrain lower-class Muslims, positioning themselves as mediators between the state and the "mob." Subho Basu, "Strikes and 'Communal' Riots in Calcutta in the 1890s: Industrial Workers, Bhadralok Nationalist Leadership and the Colonial State," *Modern Asian Studies* 32, 4 (1998), 949–83.

51 *Times* (London), March 18, 1874 and August 14, 1893. Lord Harris to Lord Kimberley, August 31, 1893, Bodleian Library, Kimberley Papers, Ms. Eng. c.4323.

52 *Glasgow Herald*, March 28, 1874.

53 Basu, "Strikes."

54 George Campbell, *Memoirs of My Indian Career* (London: Macmillan, 1893), vol. 1, 26.

55 See, for example, Fuller, *Studies*, 118: "The foundations of the Hindu religion are lost in the maze of speculations with which men endeavour to account for the unreasonableness of life's circumstances. The origin of Muhammadanism—of the faith of Islam—is altogether clear."

56 Strachey, *India*, 317.

57 Sir Bampfylde Fuller, *The Empire of India* (London: Sir Isaac Pitman, 1913), 126.

58 Fuller, *Studies*, 140.

59 Edmund C. Cox, *A Short History of the Bombay Presidency* (Bombay: Thacker, 1887), 18–19.

60 Charles Crosthwaite to Lord Lansdowne, September 26, 1893, BL, IOR, Lansdowne Papers, Mss. Eur D558/25, no. 298 (to viceroy).

61 *Birmingham Daily Post*, May 16, 1894.

62 Thomas Metcalf, *Ideologies of the Raj* (Cambridge: Cambridge University Press, 1994), 135. Muslims, meanwhile, might just as readily be compared to Protestants (especially Puritans). See Fuller, *Studies*, 120–1.

63 This letter was published in the *Times* (London) on November 7, 1850.

64 Cox, *Short History*, 19.

65 *Belfast Weekly News*, September 5, 1857.

66 Palmerston memo written on Thomas Larcom's letter to the Home Office, August 23, 1853, NAGB, HO45/5129A.

67 *Preston Guardian*, August 24, 1872.

68 *Saturday Review*, August 20, 1864.

69 Lord Carlisle to Sir George Grey, October 1857, NAGB, HO45/6464; *Liverpool Mercury*, July 18, 1851.

70 *Aberdeen Journal*, November 21, 1860.

71 *Times* (London), October 11, 1886.

72 John David Rees, *The Real India* (London: Methuen, 1908), 180.
73 *Daily News*, May 27, 1874; W. H. Holmes, *Free Cotton: How and Where to Grow It* (London: Chapman and Hall, 1862), extracted in George W. Bennett, *An Illustrated History of British Guiana* (Georgetown, Demerara: Richardson, 1866), 102–4.
74 *The Ceylon Examiner*, April 3, 1883, in Somaratna, *Kotahena Riot*, 123.
75 P. E. Wodehouse to H. Labouchere, March 10, 1856, *British Guiana. Copies or extracts of correspondence between the Governor of British Guiana and the Secretary of State for the Colonies, on the subject of the recent disturbances in that colony*, HC 1856 (432) XLIV, no. 3, 37.
76 Charles J. Lyall to Col. Ardagh, November 9, 1893, BL, IOR, Lansdowne Papers, Mss. Eur. D558/25, no. 473d (to viceroy). See also Lord Lansdowne to Lord Kimberley, August 22, 1893, BL, IOR, Lansdowne Papers, Mss. Eur. D558/6 no. 52 (from viceroy); and Lord Lansdowne to Lord Harris, August 25, 1893, BL, IOR, Lansdowne Papers, Mss. Eur. D558/25, no. 130 (from viceroy). Newspapers and their correspondents also drew comparisons between Irish nationalists and Asian revivalists. After the Colombo riot of 1883, for instance, the *Ceylon Observer* (March 29, 1883) argued that Catholic priests who rang bells to signal the start of the riot should be held responsible for the actions of their followers, just as "Messrs Parnell & Co. are told in the House of Commons that they are responsible for the acts and deeds of their co-Land Leaguers," in Somaratna, *Kotahena Riot*, 142.
77 W. W. Hunter, *The Indian Musalmans: Are They Bound in Conscience to Rebel against the Queen?* (London: Trübner, 1871), 146. The *Glasgow Herald* (September 2, 1874) concurred, arguing that one reason for the 1874 Bombay riots was that, "The Mohammedans of India, like the Roman Catholics of Ireland, are indignant at the manner in which their religious theories have been excluded from the programme of education in the country."
78 Lord Elgin to Lord George Hamilton, September 16, 1897, BL, IOR, The Earl of Elgin and Kincardine papers, F84/15, no. 42 (from viceroy).
79 Campbell, *Memoirs*, 205.
80 Their Irish experience certainly influenced their Indian careers in other ways. Mayo's policy of ameliorating Muslim grievances in order to weaken Muslim militants echoed his policy toward Irish nationalists in the 1860s, and MacDonnell's interest in Indian land reform stemmed partly from his experience of the problematic land system in Ireland. See W. W. Hunter, *A Life of the Earl of Mayo: Fourth Viceroy of India*, vol. 2 (London: Smith, Elder, 1875), 306–11; and Andrew Gailey, *Ireland and the Death of Kindness: The Experience of Constructive Unionism, 1890–1905* (Cork: Cork University Press, 1987), 184–5.
81 *Birmingham Daily Post*, October 8, 1886.
82 *Daily Telegraph*, August 22, 1872.
83 *Leeds Mercury*, August 17, 1864; *Bristol Mercury*, April 1, 1865.

84 See Susan Thorne, "'The Conversion of the Englishmen and the Conversion of the World Inseparable': Missionary Imperialism and the Language of Class in Early Industrial Britain," in *Tensions of Empire: Colonial Cultures in a Bourgeois World*, ed. Frederick Cooper and Ann Laura Stoler (Berkeley: University of California Press, 1997), 238–62; and John Marriott, *The Other Empire: Metropolis, India and Progress in the Colonial Imagination* (Manchester: Manchester University Press, 2009).

85 *Daily Telegraph*, August 22, 1872.

86 For a thoughtful discussion of the tension between abstract liberalism and the practicalities of rule in the case of press freedom in India, see Merrill Tilghman Boyce, *British Policy and the Evolution of the Vernacular Press in India, 1835–1878* (Delhi: Chanakya Publications, 1988).

87 John Stuart Mill, *On Liberty*, 2nd ed. (London: John W. Parker, 1859), 23.

88 *Times* (London), August 24, 1864.

89 *Madras Times*, July 6, 1882.

90 *Saturday Review*, August 20, 1864.

91 Ibid., April 1, 1865.

92 *Pall Mall Gazette*, August 20, 1872; *Preston Guardian*, August 24, 1872

93 *Ipswich Journal*, January 4, 1884; *The Graphic*, July 19, 1884.

94 *Times* (London), June 15, 1886.

95 P. E. Wodehouse to H. Labouchere, March 10, 1856, *British Guiana. Copies or extracts of correspondence between the Governor of British Guiana and the Secretary of State for the Colonies, on the subject of the recent disturbances in that colony*, HC 1856 (432) XLIV, no. 3, 37.

96 *Glasgow Herald*, September 29, 1893. The *Manchester Times* (September 2, 1882) made a similar point following the Salem riots of 1882: "Race antagonism cannot fail to prove in many parts of India an insurmountable obstacle for years to come, at all events, to a successful experiment in self-government. It will simply resolve itself into race and religious tyranny to be exercised by that class which finds itself, for the time being, supported by a numerical majority, and will necessarily tend greatly to exacerbate existing feuds and increase religious animosities between Hindoos and Mahometans."

97 Charles Crosthwaite to Lord Lansdowne, September 26, 1893, BL, IOR, Lansdowne Papers, Mss. Eur D558/25, no. 298 (to viceroy).

98 Lord Wodehouse to Sir George Grey, July 30, 1865, Bodleian Library, Kimberley Papers, Ms. Eng. c.4029.

99 *Times* (London), March 18, 1874.

100 Quoted in Ali Parchami, *Hegemonic Peace and Empire: The* Pax Romana, Britannica, *and* Americana (London: Routledge, 2009), 102.

101 *Daily News*, September 5, 1893.

102 *Leeds Mercury*, July 16, 1864.

103 *Daily Examiner*, August 22, 1872. The *Northern Star and Ulster Observer* (August 24, 1872) made a similar point, attacking "the antiquated politicians who dilate on the blessings of English rule, and tell us to be thankful that we are not left to govern ourselves!"

104 *Pall Mall Gazette*, August 14, 1893.

105 *Bristol Daily Mercury*, July 15, 1886.

106 *Times* (London), October 11, 1886.

Chapter 5

1 S. M. Edwardes, *The Bombay City Police: A Historical Sketch, 1672–1916* (London: Oxford University Press, 1923), 54; *Kaye's and Malleson's History of the Indian Mutiny of 1857–8*, vol. 5, ed. Sir John William Kaye and George Bruce Malleson (London: W. H. Allen, 1889), 171.

2 *The Bombay Riots of 1874* (Bombay: Bombay Gazette, 1874), 1–2; Edwardes, *Police*, 36.

3 Report of Frank Souter to C. Gonne, Secretary to the Government of Bombay, Judicial Department (No. 464), February 28, 1874, 1874 (305) *East India (Bombay Riots). Despatches from India Office in reference to Riots at Bombay; Reports by Coms. of Police at Bombay; Memorial from Parsee Community to Secretary of State for India*, HC 1874 (305) XLVII (hereafter, *1874 Bombay Riots Reports*), 12.

4 Ibid.; *The Bombay Riots of 1874*, 4. "Memorial of the Parsee Inhabitants of the City of Bombay, in the East Indies" to Lord Salisbury, Secretary of State of India, April 13, 1874, *1874 Bombay Riots Reports*, 56.

5 Edwardes, *Police*, 68; P. B. Vachha, *Famous Judges, Lawyers and Cases of Bombay: A Judicial History of Bombay during the British Period* (Bombay: N. M. Tripathi, 1962), 247–52.

6 See, for example, Dosabhoy Framjee, *The Parsees: Their History, Manners, Customs, and Religion* (London: Smith, Elder., 1858), 4–5: "Toleration in religion is unknown to the haughty, uncivilized barbarian believers in the Koran. Bigotry is the highest virtue demanded of the Mahomedan, and one which secures for him favour in the eyes of his prophet and his God, and takes him by the shortest route to a place in heaven."

7 Jesse Palsetia, "The Parsis of India and the Opium Trade in China," *Contemporary Drug Problems* 35 (Winter 2008), 647–78.

8 *Times of India*, March 3, 1874. In London the *Spectator* (March 21, 1874) struck a similar tone about the Parsis after the riots had broken out, describing them as having an "exasperatingly gratifying confidence in British Rule."

9 Marianne Young, *The Moslem Noble: His Land and People, with Some Notices of the Parsees, or Ancient Persians* (London: Saunders and Otley, 1857), 106.

10 Some 44,091 Parsis lived in Bombay in the early 1870s, greatly outnumbering Europeans (who numbered 7,253) and other minority groups like the Chinese and Jews, but at roughly 7 percent of the population the Parsi community was dwarfed by the Hindus (408,680, or 63.42%) and Muslims (137,644, or 21.36%). S. M. Edwardes, *The Rise of Bombay: A Retrospect* (Bombay: Times of India Press, 1902), 299.

11 Nile Green, *Bombay Islam: The Religious Economy of the West Indian Ocean, 1840–1915* (Cambridge: Cambridge University Press, 2011), 6.

12 *The Gazetteer of Bombay City and Island,* vol. 1 (Bombay: Times Press, 1909), 177–81 and 207; Jim Masselos, *The City in Action: Bombay Struggles for Power* (New Delhi: Oxford University Press, 2007), 64–5; Young, *Moslem Noble*, 71–8.

13 Following a cotton boom in the early 1860s Bombay's population dropped dramatically (from over 816,000 in 1864 to 645,000 in 1872) as Muslim and Hindu migrants lost work and returned home, and as late as 1891 it was estimated that only a quarter of the city's inhabitants had been born there. Prashant Kidambi, *The Making of an Indian Metropolis: Colonial Governance and Public Culture in Bombay, 1890–1920* (Aldershot: Ashgate, 2007), 22.

14 *The Gazetteer of Bombay City*, 209, n.1.

15 Ibid., 210–13.

16 Qeymuddin Ahmad, *The Wahabi Movement in India* (Calcutta: Firma K. L. Mukhopadhyay, 1966), 232–53.

17 W. W. Hunter, *The Indian Musalmans: Are They Bound in Conscience to Rebel against the Queen?* (London: Trübner, 1871), 84–104; Helen James, "The Assassination of Lord Mayo: The 'First' Jihad?," *International Journal of Asia Pacific Studies* 5, 2 (2009), 1–19. Ahmad, *Wahabi Movement*, 301, notes that neither of the assassins were Wahhabis, but British officials certainly believed that they were, and it is this perception that matters most for the present argument.

18 Hunter, *Indian Musalmans*, 75.

19 On fanaticism and Islam in the British imagination, see Francis Robinson, "The British Empire and the Muslim World," in *The Oxford History of the British Empire,* vol. 4, ed. Judith Brown and Wm. Roger Louis (Oxford: Oxford University Press, 1999), 398–420 (405). For a sample of negative British attitudes toward Muslim political and social practices (alongside more sympathetic attitudes toward Islam's theology), see the works of the influential scholar and administrator James Muir, especially J. Murray Mitchell and Sir William Muir, *Two Old Faiths: Essays on the Religions of the Hindus and the Mohammedans* (New York: Chautauqua Press, 1891).

20 C. Forjett, *Our Real Danger in India* (London, Paris, and New York: Cassell Petter & Galpin, 1877), 131; Ahmad, *Wahabi Movement*, 283–4; James Mackenzie Maclean, *Guide to Bombay: Historical, Statistical, and Descriptive*, 14th ed. (Bombay: Bombay Gazette, 1889), 95.
21 Report of Frank Souter to C. Gonne, Secretary to the Government of Bombay, Judicial Department (No. 464), February 28, 1874, *1874 Bombay Riots Reports*, 12.
22 *Times of India*, February 14, 1874.
23 Report of Frank Souter to C. Gonne, Secretary to the Government of Bombay, Judicial Department (No. 464), February 28, 1874, *1874 Bombay Riots Reports*, 12–13.
24 Ibid., 15.
25 "Memorial of the Parsee Inhabitants of the City of Bombay, in the East Indies" to Lord Salisbury, Secretary of State of India, April 13, 1874," Appendix A, *1874 Bombay Riots Reports*, 64.
26 Ibid., Appendix C and D, 65–6.
27 Ibid., Appendix G, 67–8.
28 *The Bombay Riots of 1874*, 6; Report of Frank Souter to C. Gonne, Secretary to the Government of Bombay, Judicial Department (No. 464), February 28, 1874, *1874 Bombay Riots Reports*, 12–13.
29 "Memorial of the Parsee Inhabitants of the City of Bombay, in the East Indies" to Lord Salisbury, Secretary of State of India, April 13, 1874," Appendix F, *1874 Bombay Riots Reports*, 67.
30 *The Bombay Riots of 1874*, 6.
31 Muslim memorial to P. E. Wodehouse, February 23, 1874, NAIn, Home Department, Police Branch, April 1874, no. 32, 11–12.
32 Report on Native Newspapers (hereafter, RNN) (Bombay) for the week ending February 21, 1874, 8–9.
33 *Times of India*, February 14, 1874; *The Bombay Riots of 1874*, 6–7.
34 Ibid.
35 Ibid.; Report of Frank Souter to C. Gonne, Secretary to the Government of Bombay, Judicial Department (No. 464), February 28, 1874, *1874 Bombay Riots Reports*, 13.
36 Report of Frank Souter to the C. Gonne, Secretary to the Government of Bombay, Judicial Department (No. 464), February 28, 1874, *1874 Bombay Riots Reports*, 13, 20.
37 *The Bombay Riots of 1874*, 8.
38 Ibid., 11–12.
39 Donald Horowitz, *The Deadly Ethnic Riot* (Berkeley: University of California Press, 2001), 75.
40 Letter from "A Friend," dated February 27, 1874 in *Times of India*, March 5, 1874. Other sources corroborate this picture. Within a few days of the initial outbreak

Rast Goftar, a newspaper belonging to the prominent Parsi and future nationalist politician Dadabhai Naoroji, advised the men in charge of the fire temples to hire private guards to protect their properties (Extracted in *Times of India*, February 17, 1874). A few days later "D. E. M." wrote to the *Times of India* (February 20, 1874) to suggest that Parsis form their own "vigilance committees" to sniff out the source of such riots and to prevent "other future plots and traps against them," since the police were unable to do so.

41 *The Bombay Riots of 1874*, 12.

42 "Memorial of the Parsee Inhabitants of the City of Bombay, in the East Indies" to Lord Salisbury, Secretary of State of India, April 13, 1874, *1874 Bombay Riots Reports*, 59.

43 *The Bombay Riots of 1874*, 28.

44 Report of Frank Souter to C. Gonne, Secretary to the Government of Bombay, Judicial Department (No. 464 of 1874), February 28, 1874, *1874 Bombay Riots Reports*, 13.

45 Frank Souter to the Secretary to the Government, Judicial Department, Bombay (No. 1025 of 1874), April 29, 1874, *1874 Bombay Riots Reports*, 54.

46 Extracted in *Times of India*, February 28, 1874.

47 *Times of India*, February 21, 1874.

48 Extracted in *Times of India*, February 21, 1874.

49 *The Bombay Riots of 1874*, 33. Another Parsi, Nowrozjee Furdoonjee wrote to the London *Times* (extracted in *Times of India*, May 1, 1874) that Bombay's "Mahomedan fanatics" were part of a much broader Muslim threat that encompassed, among other outbreaks of "Mahomedan frenzy," the assassination of Lord Mayo in 1872.

50 Report of Frank Souter to C. Gonne, Secretary to the Government of Bombay, Judicial Department (No. 464 of 1874), February 28, 1874, and Deposition of Thomas Mills, Superintendent of Police (C Division), February 18, 1874, *1874 Bombay Riots Reports*, 13–14 and 23–4; *The Bombay Riots of 1874*, 12–13.

51 *The Bombay Riots of 1874*, 20.

52 Report of Frank Souter to C. Gonne, Secretary to the Government of Bombay, Judicial Department (No. 464), February 28, 1874, *1874 Bombay Riots Reports*, 14.

53 *The Bombay Riots of 1874*, 13–15; "Memorial of the Parsee Inhabitants of the City of Bombay, in the East Indies" to Lord Salisbury, Secretary of State of India, April 13, 1874, Appendix H, *1874 Bombay Riots Reports*, 68–9.

54 Ibid.

55 *The Bombay Riots of 1874*, 21.

56 Ibid., 22.

57 Ibid., 35.

58 Ibid., 47–50.

59 Ibid., 27.

60 "Memorial of the Parsee Inhabitants of the City of Bombay, in the East Indies" to Lord Salisbury, Secretary of State of India, April 13, 1874, Appendix M, *1874 Bombay Riots Reports*, 72–4.

61 *The Bombay Riots of 1874*, 24–7.

62 Ibid., 35.

63 Decorative model tombs symbolizing the seventh-century martyrdom of Hussayn ibn Ali, Muhammad's grandson.

64 Government of Bombay to Her Majesty's Principal Secretary of State for India in Council, London (no. 3 of 1874—Judicial Department), March 2, 1874, *1874 Bombay Riots Reports*, 4.

65 *The Bombay Riots of 1874*, 35–6.

66 Ibid., 36; Muslim Petition to Sir Philip Wodehouse, February 25, 1874, *1874 Bombay Riots Reports*, 8.

67 *The Bombay Riots of 1874*, 36.

68 According to *The Bombay Gazette*, "not one single newspaper, European or Native, of any importance in India, hesitated to condemn the Government of Bombay" after Wodehouse's remarks. *The Bombay Riots of 1874*, 46. See also extracts from Indian newspapers in the *Times of India*, February 23 and 24, 1874, as well as the *Times of India* itself on February 19, 1874.

69 *North-West Herald*, February 21, 1874, extracted in *Times of India*, February 24, 1874.

70 *The Bombay Riots of 1874*, 39.

71 Ibid., 52; "Memorial of the Parsee Inhabitants of the City of Bombay, in the East Indies" to Lord Salisbury, Secretary of State of India, April 13, 1874, *1874 Bombay Riots Reports*, 60.

72 *The Bombay Riots of 1874*, 53–7; Report of Frank Souter to C. Gonne, Secretary to the Government of Bombay, Judicial Department (No. 464), February 28, 1874, *1874 Bombay Riots Reports*, 15.

73 *Times of India*, February 16, 1874. The government's Reports on Native Papers for the weeks ending February 21 and 28 and March 3 and 17 show the general tone of the Parsi press to have been uniformly hostile to Souter as well as Wodehouse and suggest that these feelings were widespread among the Parsi population.

74 "Memorial of the Parsee Inhabitants of the City of Bombay, in the East Indies" to Lord Salisbury, Secretary of State of India, April 13, 1874, *1874 Bombay Riots Reports*, 57.

75 Extracted in *Times of India* February 26, 1874.

76 *Times of India*, March 10, 1874.

77 *The Bombay Riots of 1874*, 32.

78 *Times of India*, February 14, 1874.

79 "The Mahomedan Riots in Bombay," *The Oriental*, April 1874, extracted in *Times of India*, May 25, 1874.
80 After the 1857 revolt there was severe anxiety in British circles about the "acute failure in intelligence-gathering and analysis," which had permitted the rebellion to take them mostly by surprise. This anxiety undoubtedly fueled British criticism of Souter in 1874. See C. A. Bayly, *Empire and Information: Intelligence Gathering and Social Communication in India, 1780–1870* (Cambridge: Cambridge University Press, 1996), 315–37.
81 Forjett, *Our Real Danger*, 131–2. See also, Edmund C. Cox, *A Short History of the Bombay Presidency* (Bombay: Thacker, 1887), 367.
82 Forjett, *Our Real Danger*, 137–43; Maclean, *Guide*, 64.
83 *The Bombay Riots of 1874*, 38. *The Oriental* also suggested that Souter should have followed the example of Forjett, who, in addition to blowing conspirators from the mouths of cannons, had also pointed a cannon "at the same Jumma Musjid, where the rioters of 1851 and 1874 had met immediately before they entered on their career of destruction." Extracted in *Times of India*, May 25, 1874.
84 Muslim memorial to P. E. Wodehouse, February 23, 1874, NAIn, Home Department, Police Branch, April 1874, no. 32, 11–12.
85 Report of Frank Souter to C. Gonne, Secretary to the Government of Bombay, Judicial Department (No. 464), February 28, 1874, *1874 Bombay Riots Reports*, 12–13, 15.
86 Ibid., 16.
87 The Bombay Government subsequently blamed the inadequate police force on the lack of money coming from the central government in Calcutta. Calcutta, in turn, promised to look into the matter. *1874 Bombay Riots Reports*, 15–16, 26, 30.
88 Memo from Alfred C. Lyall on preliminary riot report from Bombay, March 23, 1874, NAIn, Home Department, Police Branch, April 1874, no. 30–41, 43–6.
89 NAIn, Home Department, Police Branch, April 1874, no. 30–41.
90 *The Bombay Riots of 1874*, 71–2.
91 Report of the Government of Bombay to Her Majesty's Principal Secretary of State for India in Council, May 8, 1874 (No. 6 of 1784—Judicial Department) and Frank Souter to the Secretary of Government, Judicial Department, Bombay (No. 760 of 1874), April 7, 1874, *1874 Bombay Riots Reports*, 30 and 48–50.
92 "Memorial of the Parsee Inhabitants of the City of Bombay, in the East Indies" to Lord Salisbury, Secretary of State of India, April 13, 1874, ibid., 64–8.
93 *Pall Mall Gazette*, August 13, 1874; *Glasgow Herald*, March 28, 1874.
94 *Times* (London), March 18, 1874; *Daily News*, May 27, 1874. See also the *Spectator* of March 14, 1874: "The Parsees in Bombay, who occupy much the position of the Jews in London, are very much aggrieved.… The Parsees are not the kind of people to be oppressed with impunity. You might as well oppress Scotchmen."
95 *Glasgow Herald*, September 12, 1874.

96 *The Northern Echo*, March 16, 1874.

97 Andrew Roberts, *Salisbury: Victorian Titan* (London: Phoenix, 1999), 139. See also Paul R. Brumpton, *Security and Progress: Lord Salisbury at the India Office* (Westport, CT: Greenwood Press, 2002).

98 Quoted in Roberts, *Salisbury*, 139.

99 Report of the Government of Bombay to Her Majesty's Principal Secretary of State for India in Council, May 8, 1874 (No. 6 of 1784—Judicial Department), *1874 Bombay Riots Reports*, 28.

100 Report of the Government of India to the Marquis of Salisbury, June 2, 1874 (Home Department—Judicial—Police—No. 18 of 1874), ibid., 76.

101 Lord Salisbury to Lord Northbrook, July 9, 1874 (Judicial, No. 31), ibid., 78–9. Salisbury did recognize that Wodehouse might have a legitimate legal concern about the extent of his powers, however. To alleviate those concerns he announced that Sections 480 and 488 of the Code of Criminal Procedure (which granted governors the power to call on the military in aid of the civil power) would be extended to Bombay and other Presidency towns.

102 Arthur Howell, Offg. Secretary to the Govt. of India, to the Secretary to the Govt. of Bombay, January 6, 1875, NAIn, Home Dept, Police Branch, January 1875, no. 19, 11–12.

103 Lord Salisbury to Lord Northbrook, July 9, 1874 (Judicial, No. 31), *1874 Bombay Riots Reports*, 77.

104 Edwardes, *Police*, 77.

105 *Times of India*, August 21, 1874.

Chapter 6

1 Here I am departing from David Arnold's argument that the value of the police lay in their willingness to act outside of the law—that is, in their "unlicensed petty tyranny, their corruption and brutality," which was "sanctioned" by the British state. This may have been true with respect to the policing of political sedition, but, as I will show, it was not the norm during moments of communal crisis. David Arnold, *Police Power and Colonial Rule: Madras 1859–1947* (Delhi: Oxford University Press, 1986), 3.

2 As David Gilmartin has written of India, "there is little doubt that the colonial state increasingly justified its authority in the late nineteenth century as the regulator and protector of a society of innumerable communities, bound together by the British in a larger, rationalized structure." David Gilmartin, "'Divine Displeasure' and Muslim Elections: The Shaping of Community in Twentieth-Century Punjab," in *The Political Inheritance of Pakistan*, ed. D. A. Low (New York: St. Martin's Press, 1991), 106–29 (109–10).

3 Katherine Prior, “Making History: The State’s Intervention in Urban Religious Disputes in the North-Western Provinces in the Early Nineteenth Century,” *Modern Asian Studies* 27, 1 (1993), 179–203. There was a similar dynamic among mill workers in Calcutta. See Subho Basu, “Strikes and ‘Communal’ Riots in Calcutta in the 1890s: Industrial Workers, Bhadralok Nationalist Leadership and the Colonial State,” *Modern Asian Studies* 32, 4 (1998), 949–83 (964–5).

4 Michael Roberts, “Noise as Cultural Struggle: Tom-Tom Beating, the British, and Communal Disturbances in Sri Lanka, 1880s–1930s,” in *Mirrors of Violence: Communities, Violence, and Survivors in South Asia*, ed. Veena Das (Delhi: Oxford University Press, 1990), 240–85.

5 Resolution of the Government of Bengal, December 16, 1863, NAIn, Home Dept., Public Branch, January 31, 1865, nos. 99–101.

6 “Memorial of the undersigned inhabitants of Hooghly, Chinsurah, Bally, Bansbariah, &c., in the District of Hooghly, to His Excellency the Viceroy and Governor General in Council,” December 14, 1864, NAIn, Home Dept., Public Branch, January 31, 1865, nos. 99–101.

7 A. Eden, Secretary to Government of Bengal, to Secretary to the Government of India, Home Department, Jan. 17, 1865. NAIn, Home Dept., Public Branch, January 31, 1865, nos. 99–101.

8 At other times Muslims might feel a similar sense of grievance. As Subho Basu has shown, during labor and communal disturbances in 1890s Calcutta policemen tended to act on the assumption that Muslim millworkers were inherently “turbulent and disorderly,” singling them out for repression even when the blame for a disturbance (especially in Muslim minds) lay equally with Hindus. Basu, “Strikes.”

9 Letter from “Creole,” *The Creole*, Novemer 13, 1860.

10 Sir H. W. Norman to the Earl of Derby, January 13, 1885, *Correspondence Respecting the Recent Coolie Disturbances in Trinidad, with the Report by Sir H. W. Norman Thereon*, HL 1884–5 (C.4366) XXII, 39–49. Norman also pointed out that the regulation of Muharram processions was in no way inconsistent with religious liberty, and that similar regulations were common in India itself.

11 Prabhu P. Mohapatra, “The Hosay Massacre of 1884: Class and Community among Indian Immigrant Labourers in Trinidad,” in *Work and Social Change in Asia: Essays in Honour of Jan Breman*, ed. Arvind N. Das and Marcel Van Der Linden (New Delhi: Manohar, 2003), 187–230 (195). See also Kelvin Singh, *Bloodstained Tombs: The Mohurrum Massacre, 1884* (Basingstoke: Macmillan Caribbean, 1988); and Madhavi Kale, “Projecting Identities: Indentured Labor Migration from India to Trinidad and British Guiana, 1836–1885,” in *Nation and Migration: The Politics of Space in the South Asian Diaspora*, ed. Peter van der Veer (Philadelphia: University of Pennsylvania Press, 1995), 73–92.

12 On concurrent attempts to regulate carnival processions in Trinidad, see Bridget Brereton, "The Trinidad Carnival in the Late Nineteenth Century," in *Carnival: Culture in Action: the Trinidad Experience*, ed. Milla Cozart Riggio (New York: Routledge, 2004), 53–63.

13 Sometimes the state only began reaching out to local leaders after violence had already broken out. Thus the Indian viceroy, Lord Lansdowne, addressed the Municipal Board of Agra in 1893 in the following terms: "I appeal then earnestly to those gentlemen whose position in the Indian community enables them to exercise influence over their neighbours, and I would implore them to impress upon those who are less well informed than themselves the folly and the disastrous consequences of such acts as those which have lately taken place in these Provinces and elsewhere." Lansdowne's speech to Municipal Board of Agra, November 10, 1893, Lansdowne Papers, BL, IOR, D558/60, 600.

14 Sandria B. Freitag, *Collective Action and Community: Public Arenas and the Emergence of Communalism in North India* (Berkeley: University of California Press, 1989), 56–7.

15 Sir A. P. MacDonnell, Speech to Municipal Board of Ballia and Ballia Institute, November 23, 1895, in *Selections from Speeches of Sir A. P. MacDonnell, G.C.S.I., Lieutenant-Governor, N.-W. P., and Chief Commissioner of Oudh, from 1895 to 1901.* (Naini Tal: N.-W. Provinces and Oudh Government Camp Branch Press, 1901), 5.

16 *Report of the Belfast Riots Commissioners. Minutes of Evidence and Appendices*, HC 1887 (4925-I) XVIII (hereafter, *1886 Belfast Riots Inquiry*), 11: "We are of opinion that the comparative good conduct of the Catholics must be largely attributed to the zealous exertions of the Catholic Bishop and clergy, who, during the riots, laboured persistently in the cause of peace, and who exercised over their people a great and beneficial influence."

17 Palmerston memo written on Thomas Larcom's letter to the Home Office, August 23, 1853, NAGB, HO45/5129A; *Times of India*, February 17, 1874; James Longden to Lord Derby, June 26, 1883, No. 306, Misc., in G. P. V. Somaratna, *Kotahena Riot 1883: A Religious Riot in Sri Lanka* (Gangodawila, Sri Lanka: Deepanee, 1991), 43–5.

18 Freitag, *Collective Action*, 73.

19 *Belfast Daily Mercury*, September 8, 1857.

20 Lord Naas to William Tracy, June 3, 1858, NAIr, CSORP (1858) 14915.

21 *Belfast Morning News*, June 7, 1858.

22 *Northern Whig*, August 18, 1864; *Report of the Commissioners of Inquiry, 1864, Respecting the Magisterial and Police Jurisdiction Arrangements and Establishment of the Borough of Belfast*, HC 1865 (3466) XXVIII (hereafter, *1864 Belfast Riots Inquiry*) Appendix B, tables C & D, 362. "Report on the Military Measures taken

in aid of the Civil Power during the Riots in Bombay, on the 11th August 1893 and following days," *East India (religious disturbances). Copies or extracts of reports relating to the recent conflicts between Hindus and Muhammadans in India, particularly to the causes which led to them*, HC 1893–4 (538) LXIII, 41–7; "The Recent Bombay Riots," letter from H. E. Barrell, August 18, 1893, in *The Missionary Herald of the Baptist Missionary Society*, October 1, 1893.

23 Report to Lord Advocate from R. Bell, Sheriff Substitute of Ayrshire at Kilmarnock, July 12, 1848, NAS, Lord Advocate's Papers, AD58/70.

24 Lord Minto to Lord Morley, May 28, 1908, quoted in Mary, Countess of Minto, *India Minto and Morley, 1905–1910* (London: Macmillan, 1934), 235.

25 Charles Crosthwaite to Lord Lansdowne, September 26, 1893, Lansdowne Papers, BL, IOR, Mss. Eur. D558/25, no. 298 (to viceroy).

26 J. Lambert to the Chief Secretary to the Government of Bengal, May 18, 1891, NAIn, Home Dept., Public Branch, June 1891, no. 63.

27 The discussion that follows is derived from an earlier article of mine focusing on riot control in Britain and India: Mark Doyle, "Massacre by the Book: Amritsar and the Rules of Public-Order Policing in Britain and India," *Britain and the World* 4, 2 (September 2011), 247–68.

28 In Britain, regulations governing riot control were primarily articulated by judicial decisions and parliamentary inquiries into police conduct following specific riots. These were often reiterated and refined by the government's law advisors. Most of the nineteenth-century regulations are collected in the Home Office records at the National Archives of Great Britain, HO317/40, which contain rulings and correspondence relating to the Bristol riots of 1831, the Fenian disturbances of 1867, the Trafalgar Square riots of 1887, and the Salvation Army disturbances of 1890. Additional regulations emerged from a parliamentary inquiry into the Featherstone Riots of 1893, *Featherstone inquiry. Report of the committee appointed to inquire into the circumstances connected with the disturbances at Featherstone on the 7th of September 1893*. HC 1893–4 (C.7234), XVII (hereafter, *Featherstone Inquiry*). The evolution of riot control regulations in the empire was less linear, but they were usually articulated in police manuals. As early as 1837 the Irish Constabulary had written instructions for policing riots, although in India most police manuals did not contain specific instructions on riot policing until after 1900.

29 Quoted in Elizabeth Malcolm, *The Irish Policeman, 1822–1922: A Life* (Dublin: Four Courts Press, 2006), 112.

30 Adrian Randall, *Riotous Assemblies: Popular Protest in Hanoverian England* (Oxford: Oxford University Press, 2006), 26. Richard Vogler calls the Riot Act "a law to abolish law; a kind of modified martial law." Richard Vogler, *Reading the Riot Act: The Magistracy, the Police and the Army in Civil Disorder* (Milton Keynes: Open University Press, 1991), 2.

31 George Rudé, "The Gordon Riots: A Study of the Rioters and Their Victims," *Transactions of the Royal Historical Society*, Fifth Series 6 (1956), 93–114 (99).

32 "Unlawful and Riotous Meetings. Provisions of the Law and the Powers and Duties of Persons in regard thereto," NAGB HO317/30/3.

33 D. Philips, "Riots and Public Order in the Black Country, 1835–1860," in *Popular Protest and Public Order: Six Studies in British History, 1790–1920*, ed. R. Quinault and J. Stevenson (London: George Allen and Unwin, 1974), 141–80 (151). These changing attitudes toward state violence coincided with a broader shift away from retributive justice in the Victorian period (especially with regard to capital punishment), as public sentiment began to regard lethal action by state forces as inappropriate within Britain itself. See Christopher Herbert, *War of No Pity: The Indian Mutiny and Victorian Trauma* (Princeton: Princeton University Press, 2008), 113–15. Thomas Mockaitis dates these "changing attitudes in Britain toward violence" to a somewhat later period, following the controversies over state violence during the Boer War, the Anglo-Irish War, and the Punjab disturbances after the First World War. It is probably more accurate to say that these events helped change British attitudes toward *colonial* violence; attitudes toward state violence within Britain began shifting considerably earlier. Thomas R. Mockaitis, *British Counterinsurgency, 1919–60* (New York: St. Martin's Press, 1990), 18.

34 "Memorandum on Law of Riots and Insurrections," February 26, 1867, NAGB, HO317/30/4. This principle was reiterated by parliamentary committees in 1893 and 1908. See *Featherstone Inquiry*; and *Report of the Select Committee on Employment of Military in Cases of Disturbances*, HC 1908 (C.236) VII (hereafter, *Report on Employment of Military*).

35 Walter Arnstein, "The Murphy Riots: A Victorian Dilemma," *Victorian Studies*, no. 19 (September 1975), 51–70; Donald Richter, *Riotous Victorians* (Athens: Ohio University Press, 1981).

36 Charles Townshend, *Britain's Civil Wars: Counterinsurgency in the Twentieth Century* (London: Faber and Faber, 1986), 18–19.

37 "Public Meetings in the Metropolis," by Mr. Davis, July 12, 1887, NAGB, HO317/30/12, 23–4.

38 *Featherstone Inquiry*, 396; *Report on Employment of Military*, 368.

39 Townshend, *Britain's Civil Wars*, 43.

40 *Proceedings of the Government of Bengal, Political Department*, April 1909, BL, IOR, P/8145, no. 15, 173.

41 Sir Andrew Reed, *The Irish Constable's Guide*, 3rd ed. (Dublin: Alex Thom, 1895), 287–93. See also Thomas Fennell, *The Royal Irish Constabulary: A History and Personal Memoir*, ed. Rosemary Fennell (Dublin: University College Dublin Press, 2003), 36.

42 *Report on Employment of Military*.

43 Report of the Administration of the N.W. Provinces for the Year 1871–72 (Allahabad: North-Western Provinces Government Press, 1873), BL, IOR, V/10/135, 5.

44 The military in India was similarly constrained. In 1872, for instance, the Bengal Army adopted the Queen's Regulations and Orders for the Army (already applicable elsewhere), which directed that soldiers must not fire upon rioters unless directed to do so by a magistrate, and that they must then act with "coolness and steadiness, and in such manner as to be able to discontinue their fire at the instant at which it shall be found that there is no longer occasion for it." NAIn, Home Dept., Judicial Branch, June 1872, nos. 235–45 (A).

45 Extracts from R. P. Wilson, *Memories of Bihar*, unpublished memoir, Police Files on Pre-1947 Communal Disturbances, BL, IOR Mss. Eur F161/142, 39.

46 A fine example of the hatred that these shootings inspired among Belfast Protestants toward the Royal Irish Constabulary can be found in Arthur Patton and George Foy, *Reports Submitted to the Executive Committee of the Irish Loyal and Patriotic Union on the Subject of the Belfast Riots* (Dublin: Humphrey and Armour, 1886). In 1887 an officer of the constabulary was also convicted of murder during a nationalist disturbance at Mitchelstown, but the conviction was overturned on a technicality. See Fennell, *Royal Irish Constabulary*, 34–6.

47 R. Quinault, "The Warwickshire County Magistracy and Public Order, c.1830–1870," in Quinault and Stevenson, *Popular Protest*, 181–214.

48 On the military nature of the Irish Constabulary, see W. J. Lowe and E. L. Malcolm, "The Domestication of the Royal Irish Constabulary, 1836–1922," *Irish Economic and Social History* 19 (1992), 27–48; Charles Townshend, *Political Violence in Ireland: Government and Resistance since 1848* (Oxford: Clarendon Press, 1983), 71–84; and Virginia Crossman, *Politics, Law and Order in Nineteenth-Century Ireland* (Dublin: Gill & Macmillan, 1996), 94–8. For a general comparison of policing in Ireland and Britain, see Stanley H. Palmer, *Police and Protest in England and Ireland, 1780–1850* (Cambridge: Cambridge University Press, 1988).

49 David M. Anderson and David Killingray, *Policing the Empire: Government, Authority, and Control, 1830–1940* (Manchester: Manchester University Press, 1991).

50 Ranajit Guha, *Dominance without Hegemony: History and Power in Colonial India* (Cambridge, MA: Harvard University Press, 1997); Elizabeth A. Muenger, *The British Military Dilemma in Ireland: Occupation Politics, 1886–1914* (Lawrence, KS: University Press of Kansas, 1991).

51 On the pre-1850 outbreaks, see George Rudé, "Protest and Punishment in Nineteenth-Century Britain," *Albion* 5, 1 (Spring 1973), 1–23. On the Mold riots, see NAGB, HO45/8240. On Trafalgar Square, see Richter, *Riotous Victorians*, 133–62. On Featherstone, see *Featherstone Inquiry*.

52 *Report of the Belfast Riots Commissioners. Minutes of Evidence and Appendices,* British Parliamentary Papers, HC 1887 (4925-I) XVIII. In addition to Belfast, police shootings occurred during riots or disturbances in Limerick (1853), Portadown (1869), Mitchelstown (1887), Leitrim (1887), Youghal (1887), and Lurgan (1887). Most incidents resulted in a handful of injuries and one or two (or no) deaths.

53 Fennell, *Royal Irish Constabulary*, 36.

54 *East India (Religious Disturbances). Copies or extracts of reports relating to the recent conflicts between Hindus and Muhammadans in India, and particularly to the causes which led to them*, British Parliamentary Papers, HC 1893–4 (538) LXII, 24.

55 There does seem to have been a shift toward more lethal policing around the period of the 1893 riots, however. In the four years immediately preceding the 1893 riots, there were no reported police shootings during some forty-seven reported riots. "Hindu-Muhammadan Riots, 1889–1893," BL, IOR, L/PJ/6/382/1795. We will explore this shift in Chapter 8.

56 Mohapatra, "Hosay Massacre," 190; "Alarming Negro Riot in Georgetown," *Liverpool Daily Post*, March 21, 1856; Frank Cundall, *Political and Social Disturbances in the West Indies: A Brief Account and Bibliography* (Kingston: The Institute of Jamaica, 1906), 21–2.

57 BL, IOR, L/P&J/1544/3810; P. T. M. Fernando, "The Post Riots Campaign for Justice," *The Journal of Asian Studies* 29, 2 (February 1970), 255–66 (255).

58 Lowe and Malcolm, "Domestication," 35; Townshend, *Political Violence*, 71–84; Crossman, *Politics*, 94–8; Anderson and Killingray, *Policing*; Das and Verma, "Armed Police," 354–67; P. J. Stead, *The Police of Britain* (Basingstoke: Macmillan, 1985); Sir C. J. Jeffries, *The Colonial Police* (London: M. Parrish, 1952); S. Breathnach, *The Irish Police* (Dublin: Anvil Books, 1974).

59 *Times* (London), August 19, 1879.

60 Report on the Administration of the N.W. Provinces and Oudh for the year ending March 31, 1894, BL, IOR, V/10/163, 18.

61 This was the case in Belfast in 1858, when the Protestant preacher Thomas Drew warned the Irish Executive that the heavy military presence in town, designed to deter violence, was in fact attracting large crowds onto the streets. Thomas Drew to the Lord Chancellor, June 1, 1858, Larcom Papers, NLI, 7624/94.

62 Lord Harris to Lord Lansdowne, August 20, 1893, Lansdowne Papers, BL, IOR, Mss. Eur D558/25, no. 154 (to viceroy).

63 P. E. Wodehouse to H. Labouchere, March 10, 1856, *British Guiana. Copies or extracts of correspondence between the Governor of British Guiana and the Secretary of State for the Colonies, on the subject of the recent disturbances in that colony*, HC 1856 (432) XLIV (hereafter, *1856 British Guiana Riots Correspondence*), nos. 3, 38.

64 HC Deb *21 March 1887 vol. 312 c1117.*
65 Fennell, *Royal Irish Constabulary*, 78.
66 William Forster, *HC Deb 26 August 1880 vol. 256 cc147-8; William Forster,* HC Deb 08 April 1881 vol. 260 cc1013.
67 *HC Deb 26 August 1880* vol. 256 cc142-3.
68 Ibid., *cc161.*
69 Ibid., *cc147.*
70 Ibid., *cc150.*
71 *HC Deb 03 May 1881* vol. 260 cc1659.
72 See Thomas Scanlon, *HC Deb 05 November 1918 vol. 110 cc2017.*
73 *HC Deb 29 August 1887 vol. 320 cc403-4.*
74 *HC Deb 29 March 1904 vol. 132 cc983-4.*
75 *Featherstone Inquiry.*
76 BL, IOR L/P&J/6/379/1498.
77 J. F. Price, Chief Secretary to the Government of Madras, Judicial Department, to Secretary to the Government of India, Home Department, May 3, 1894, ibid.
78 W. Lee Warner, Secretary to Government of Bombay, to Secretary to the Government of India, Home Department, June 7, 1894, ibid.
79 E. Younghusband, Officiating Junior Secretary to the Government of Punjab, Police Department, to the Secretary to the Government of India, Home Department, February 8, 1894, ibid.
80 A. L. Saunders, Officiating Secretary to the Chief Commissioner of the Central Provinces, to the Secretary to the Government of India, Home Department, February 16, 1894, ibid.
81 Secretary to Government of North-West Provinces to Secretary to the Government of India, Home Department, May 7, 1894, ibid.
82 Lord Elgin to H. H. Fowler, July 24, 1894, Earl of Elgin and Kincardine papers, BL, IOR, Mss Eur F84/12, no. 27 (to viceroy).
83 Report on the Administration of Bengal, 1893–4, BL, IOR, V/10/65; C. A. Elliot to Lord Elgin, July 28, 1894, Earl of Elgin and Kincardine papers, BL, IOR, Mss Eur F84/64, no. 35 (to viceroy).
84 C. A. Elliot to Lord Elgin, June 19, 1894, Earl of Elgin and Kincardine papers, BL, IOR, Mss Eur F84/64, no. 236 (to viceroy).
85 Sir Herbert Thirkell White, *A Civil Servant in Burma* (London: Edward Arnold, 1913), 238.
86 F. W. Duke, Chief Secretary to the Government of Bengal, to all Commissioners and Divisions, April 19, 1909, Proceedings of the Government of Bengal, Political Department, April 1909, BL, IOR, P/8145/15, 173.
87 "Unlawful and Riotous Meetings. Provisions of the Law and the Powers and Duties of Persons in Regard Thereto" and "Memorandum on Law of Riots and

Insurrections" (compiled by Henry Thring, February 26, 1867), NAGB, HO317/30/3–4.

88 Carolyn Steedman, *Policing the Victorian Community: The Formation of English Provincial Police Forces, 1856–80* (London: Routledge & Kegan Paul, 1984), 34; NAGB, HO45/7991.

89 During an 1841 election riot in Liverpool, specials who became too "excited" were imprisoned overnight in a market by the regular police. Anne Bryson, "Riotous Liverpool, 1815–1860," in *Popular Politics, Riot and Labour: Essays in Liverpool History, 1790–1940*, ed. John Belchem (Liverpool: Liverpool University Press, 1992), 98–134 (115).

90 R. E. Swift, "Anti-Catholicism and Irish Disturbances: Public Order in Mid-Victorian Wolverhampton," *Midland History* 9 (1984), 87–108 (102–3).

91 W. T. B. Lyons' evidence, *1864 Belfast Riots Inquiry*, 105–6. According to resolutions adopted at an Orange meeting shortly after the riots, a number of Orange lodges had enlisted their members as special constables. See *Ulster Observer*, August 30, 1864. When Orangemen tried a similar thing in Glasgow during an Irish nationalist celebration in 1875, however, the authorities refused. See Ian Wood, "Irish Immigrants and Scottish Radicalism, 1880–1906," in *Essays in Scottish Labour History*, ed. Ian MacDougall (Edinburgh: John Donald, 1978), 65–89 (69).

92 Lord Spencer to Lord Halifax, August 26, 1872, Borthwick Institute, University of York, HALIFAX/A4/110A; *1886 Belfast Riots Inquiry*, 18–19; Lord Naas to Lord Abercorn, December 3, 1866, Abercorn Papers, PRONI, D623/A/304/4; Minute by the Right Honorable Lord Sandhurst, G.C.B., G.C.S.I., Commander of the Forces, &c., &c. *Belfast Riots—Means for Suppression, &c., &c.*, NLI, Ir 32341 p49, 4.

93 "Memorial of the Parsee Inhabitants of the City of Bombay, in the East Indies" to Lord Salisbury, Secretary of State of India, April 13, 1874, *East India (Bombay Riots). Despatches from India Office in reference to Riots at Bombay; Reports by Coms. of Police at Bombay; Memorial from Parsee Community to Secretary of State for India*, HC 1874 (305) XLVII, 59; *Times of India*, July 14, 1874; *Glasgow Herald*, September 2, 1874.

94 Antony MacDonnell to Lord Lansdowne, September 18, 1893, MacDonnell Papers, Bodleian Library, fol. 40. By 1902 this suggestion had found its way into the Bengal police regulations, which directed magistrates only to appoint special constables when absolutely necessary and to ensure that these were the most influential members of the relevant communities. Government Circulars and Orders in Force in Bengal, vol. 1, BL, IOR, V/27/242/35.

95 Report on native newspapers (hereafter, RNN) (Bengal) for the week ending July 15, 1893, 550.

96 Antony MacDonnell to Lord Lansdowne, September 18, 1893, Bodleian Library, fol. 40.

97 Samuel T. Sheppard, *The Bombay Volunteer Rifles: A History* (Bombay: The Times Press, 1919), 81–5.

98 *The Bombay Riots of 1874* (Bombay: Bombay Gazette, 1874), 21.

99 *Belfast Daily Mercury*, July 18, 1857.

100 Report from *Demerara Royal Gazette*, extracted in *Hereford Times*, March 29, 1856.

101 "Alarming Negro Riot in Georgetown," *Liverpool Daily Post*, March 21, 1856.

102 C. C. Stevens to Lord Elgin, July 8, 1897, The Earl of Elgin and Kincardine Papers, BL, IOR, F84/71, no. 24 (to viceroy).

103 Robert N. Kearney, "The 1915 Riots in Ceylon: A Symposium," *The Journal of Asian Studies* 29, 2 (February 1970), 219–22; P. T. M. Fernando, "The British Raj and the 1915 Communal Riots in Ceylon," *Modern Asian Studies* 3, 3 (1969), 245–55.

104 Thomas MacKnight, *Ulster as It Is: or, Twenty-Eight Years' Experience as an Irish Editor*, vol. 1 (London: Macmillan, 1896), 35.

105 *Papers Relating to the Donaghmore Riot, with Report of the Commissioners appointed to inquire into the conduct of the justices of the peace presiding at a court of petty sessions held at Dungannon, on 1st October, 1866; and Copy of Letter from the Secretary of the Lord Chancellor to the Justices who formed the bench at the Dungannon Petty Sessions, held at Dungannon on the 1st October, 1866* HC 1867 (3906) LIX, 3–4.

106 *Glasgow Free Press*, October 10, 1857.

107 Report of the Administration of the N.W. Provinces for the Year 1871–72, BL, IOR, V/10/135.

108 *Times of India*, October 25, 1882.

109 P. E. Wodehouse to H. Labouchere, February 24, 1856, *1856 British Guiana Riots Correspondence*, no. 1, 5–6; P. T. M. Fernando, "British Raj," 247.

110 James McLean to R. M. O'Donnell, November 15, 1872, NAIr, CSORP 1872/17919. His request was refused.

111 Grand Orange Lodge of Ireland, *Report of the Proceedings of the Grand Orange Lodge of Ireland, at the Half-Yearly Meeting, Held at Newry, on Wednesday, the 26th, and Thursday, the 27th, days of May, 1858* (Downpatrick: Printed for the Grand Lodge of Ireland, at the "Downshire Protestant" office, 1858), 10.

112 See, for example, the *Banner of Ulster's* response (November 10, 1864) to the prospect of an inquiry after the 1864 Belfast riots: "To fritter away three months—to allow the angry feelings engendered by the riots to subside—to wait until excited animosities on both sides had cooled down, and then to commence an officious inquiry that must necessarily have the effect of reviving party and religious antipathies, while it must seriously interfere with the peaceable industry of the town—to pursue such a course was quite worthy of the jobbing cliques that rule in Dublin Castle."

113 Mark Radford, *The Policing of Belfast, 1870–1914* (London: Bloomsbury, 2015).

114 The armed reserves were to be picked from among the existing ranks and would mostly be Malays, a group whom the British regarded as good fighters; they would live in barracks and act as guards most of the time, but when disturbances broke out they would be summoned by bugle to the scene of the trouble. Longden to Derby, June 26, 1883, National Archives of Sri Lanka, Lot 5/60 (no. 306), in Somaratna, *Kotahena Riot*, 48; A. C. Dep, *A History of the Ceylon Police*. Vol. II, 1866–1913 (N. p.: n. p., 1969), 207–12.

115 Dep, *History*, 211; Report of Police Inspector Goneratna, May 31, 1883, National Archives of Sri Lanka, lot 33/991, no. 233, and Riots Commission Report, in Somaratna, *Kotahena Riot*, 19 and 50–62.

116 These were Antony MacDonnell's goals after the 1893 riots in Bengal when he decided not only to station punitive police "in the offending villages" but also to prosecute "all landholders who were party to, or cognizant of, or who did not report" cow-protection demonstrations to the authorities. Antony MacDonnell to Lord Lansdowne, September 18, 1893, Bodleian Library, MacDonnell Papers, fol. 40.

117 In 1858 Col. Fitzstephen French, MP for Roscommon, complained that the cost of policing riots in Belfast was being borne by the Exchequer, but, "When a riot occurred elsewhere the constabulary was poured into the district, and the inhabitants were assessed to pay for them." HC Deb 04 June 1858 vol. 150 c1538. Following the Belfast riots of 1864 the *Telegraph* (August 30, 1864) called for the stationing of punitive police on the grounds that, "If the chief men of Belfast suffered severely in their pockets, and were required to make ample compensation for the injuries inflicted by their townsmen, the public spirit of the borough would be effectually enlisted in the cause of peace." The following year, however, the lord lieutenant rejected the idea that Belfast should pay more for constabulary forces sent in during a riot, since localities always paid a fixed amount toward the constabulary and any overages were normally covered by the imperial government. Lord Wodehouse to Sir George Grey, May 7, 1865, Kimberley Papers, Bodleian Library, Ms. Eng. c.4025.

118 *Times of India*, March 17, 1894.

119 RNN (Bombay) for the week ending August 5, 1893, p. 13.

Chapter 7

1 Ramachandra Guha, *A Corner of a Foreign Field: The Indian History of a British Sport* (London: Picador, 2002), 54.

2 Lord Harris, "Recreation and 'Cricket,'" in *Cricket*, ed. T. C. Collings (London: T. Fisher Unwin, 1900), 111–19 (113). On the alcohol consumption at the governor's residence during Harris's first year on the job, which totaled 5,399 bottles of wine and spirits, see Guha, *Corner*, 67.

3 Lord Harris, *A Few Short Runs* (London: John Murray, 1921), 231–2. Harris felt his cricket playing might set a positive example to young Indians, who might see the game as "a counter-attraction to pice and politics."

4 James D. Coldham, *Lord Harris* (London: George Allen & Unwin, 1983), 86–7.

5 Harris, *Few Short Runs*, 242.

6 B. Majumdar, "Cricket in Colonial Bombay: 1850–1940," *The International Journal of the History of Sport* 23, 6 (September 2006), 1014–32.

7 *Proceedings of the Council of the Governor of Bombay, Assembled for the Purpose of Making Laws and Regulations 1893*, vol. XXXI, August 12, 1893, 57–8.

8 Guha, *Corner*, 68. See, for example, Tilak's *Mahrátta* of August 20, 1893: "His Excellency was expected in Bombay when the disturbances broke out, but enquiries were made by him if his presence was absolutely necessary in Bombay at that time, and the Police Commissioner, who could never be expected to give any other reply, humbly reported that His Excellency need not undergo the trouble of going down to Bombay. We do not know if Government officials really think that the public are not intelligent enough to read these facts aright; but if they do, we assure them that they are greatly mistaken. Lord Harris has, we are sorry to observe, shown singular weakness in dealing with the question of the recent disturbances in Junágad between the Hindus and the Muhammadans from the beginning." Report on Native Newspapers (hereafter, RNN) (Bombay) for the week ending August 26, 1893, 9–10.

9 Ibid., 12.

10 Ibid., 9–10.

11 Sandria B. Freitag, *Collective Action and Community: Public Arenas and the Emergence of Communalism in North India* (Berkeley: University of California Press, 1989), 55.

12 Note from Charles Lyall, October 6, 1893, NAIn, Home Dept, Public Branch, November 1893, nos. 169, 5.

13 As Richard Cashman observes, "The cow protection movement was a fundamentalist and revivalist movement, an attempt to cleave to one of the basic symbols of Hinduism at a time when many traditional ideas and customs were under attack." Richard I. Cashman, *The Myth of the* Lokmanya*: Tilak and Mass Politics in Maharashtra* (Berkeley: University of California Press, 1975), 67. See also Peter Robb, "The Challenge of Gau Mata: British Policy and Religious Change in India, 1880–1916," *Modern Asian Studies* 20, 2 (1986), 285–319.

14 The Indian Government's official report to the India Office, to which Lyall likely contributed, made this point directly. "The rapid dissemination of news" and the cow-protection controversies promoted through the press, public meetings, and itinerant preachers were relatively new features in Indian life, it said. Education, which "has made the most progress among the Hindu portion of the community," was emboldening Hindus politically as well as giving them a virtual monopoly over

the higher professions, which caused resentment among Muslims. And religious revivalism was evidently "a reaction against the influx of Western ideas and habits" among a naturally conservative people. Britain's reluctance to interfere with either the press or with religious expression gave oxygen to these flammable materials, with calamitous results. Extract from a Letter from the Government of India to the Secretary of State, No. 84; dated December 24, 1893, received January 15, 1894, *East India (religious disturbances). Copies or Extracts of Reports Relating to the Recent Conflicts between Hindus and Muhammadans in India, Particularly to the Causes which Led to Them*, HC 1893–4 (538) LXIII (hereafter, *1893–4 India Riots Reports*), 58.

15 Edmund C. Cox, *My Thirty Years in India* (London: Mills & Boon, 1909), 208.

16 In fact, the first cow-protection societies originated with Sikh Kukas, a reformist group dedicated to purifying Sikhism. For a comprehensive discussion of the background of the cow-protection movement and the violence it engendered, see John McLane, *Indian Nationalism and the Early Congress* (Princeton: Princeton University Press, 1977), 271–331.

17 H. E. Barrell, "The Recent Bombay Riots," *The Missionary Herald of the Baptist Missionary Society*, October 1, 1893; Report by A. Forbes, Commissioner of the Patna Division, to the Government of Bengal, October 27, 1893, Dharampal Archives, CPS-CPM-03.

18 For an excellent bottom-up examination of the riots in this area, see Gyanendra Pandey, "Rallying Round the Cow: Sectarian Strife in the Bhojpuri Region, c. 1888–1917," in *Subaltern Studies II: Writings on South Asian History and Society*, ed. Ranajit Guha (Delhi: Oxford University Press, 1983), 60–129.

19 McLane, *Indian Nationalism*, 273.

20 Ibid.; Chief Secretary to the Government, North-Western Provinces and Oudh, to the Secretary to the Government of India, Home Department, August 28, 1893, *1893–4 India Riots Reports*.

21 *Report on the Disturbances which Occurred at the End of June 1893 in the Gházipur District in Connection with the Cow-Protection Movement*, NAIr, Home Dept, Public Branch, December 1893, nos. 155–7.

22 Chief Secretary to the Government, North-West Provinces and Oudh, to the Secretary to the Government of India, Home Department, August 28, 1893, *1893–4 India Riots Reports*, 21–2.

23 *1893–4 India Riots Reports*, 3–16; Sir Herbert Thirkell White, *A Civil Servant in Burma* (London: Edward Arnold, 1913), 235–9.

24 For a full account of the cow-protection riots in Bombay, see Jim Masselos, *The City in Action: Bombay Struggles for Power* (New Delhi: Oxford University Press, 2007), 105–24.

25 Cashman, *Myth*, 67.

26 Report of R. H. Vincent to Bombay Government, September 9, 1893, *1893–4 India Riots Reports*, 27.
27 SM Edwardes, *The Bombay City Police: A Historical Sketch, 1672–1916* (London: Oxford University Press, 1923), 100.
28 Report of R. H. Vincent to Bombay Government, September 9, 1893, *1893–4 India Riots Reports*, 28.
29 Ibid., 28–9; Barrell, "Recent Bombay Riots."
30 Report of R. H. Vincent to Bombay Government, September 9, 1893, *1893–4 India Riots Reports*, 29–30. The trope of the fanatical and bigoted Julai, or Julaha, was well established by this time. See Gyanendra Pandey, *The Construction of Communalism in Colonial North India* (New Delhi: Oxford University Press, 2006), 6–108.
31 Report of R. H. Vincent to Bombay Government, September 9, 1893, *1893–4 India Riots Reports*, 30–2.
32 "Report on the Military Measures Taken in Aid of the Civil Power during the Riots in Bombay, on the 11th August 1893 and following days," *1893–4 India Riots Reports*, 41–7; Edwardes, *Police*, 101–2.
33 Samuel T. Sheppard, *The Bombay Volunteer Rifles: A History* (Bombay: The Times Press, 1919), 83.
34 Cox, *Thirty Years*, 208.
35 Barrell, "Recent Bombay Riots."
36 Ibid.
37 Ibid.
38 RNN (Bombay) for the week ending August 19, 1893, p. 18.
39 Report of R. H. Vincent to Bombay Government, September 9, 1893, *1893–4 India Riots Reports*, 32–3.
40 H. A. Acworth, Municipal Commissioner of the City of Bombay, to G. C. Whitworth, Secretary to Government, Judicial Department, September 21, 1893, *1893–4 India Riots Reports*, 47–9.
41 Prashant Kidambi, *The Making of an Indian Metropolis: Colonial Governance and Public Culture in Bombay, 1890–1920* (Aldershot: Ashgate, 2007), 119.
42 Barrell, "Recent Bombay Riots."
43 Cox, *Thirty Years*, 209; Lord Harris to Lord Kimberley, September 29, 1893, Kimberley Papers, Bodleian Library, Mss. Eng. c.4323.
44 Report of R. H. Vincent to Bombay Government, September 9, 1893, *1893–4 India Riots Reports*, 35, 40; Edwardes, *Police*, 102.
45 Thomas Fennell, *The Royal Irish Constabulary: A History and Personal Memoir*, ed. Rosemary Fennell (Dublin: University College Dublin Press, 2003), 74.
46 Antony MacDonnell to Lord Lansdowne, August 4, 1893, MacDonnell Papers, Bodleian Library, Ms. Eng. his. d.235.

47 MacDonnell to Lansdowne, August 8, 1893, MacDonnell Papers, Bodleian Library, Ms. Eng. his. d.235.

48 Michael Brillman, "Bengal Tiger, Celtic Tiger: The Life of Sir Antony Patrick MacDonnell, 1844–1925," vol. 1 (PhD diss., University of Chicago, 2009), 93.

49 Antony MacDonnell to A. Forbes, September 13, 1893, MacDonnell Papers, Bodleian Library, d.235 fol. 39.

50 Report by A. Forbes to the Government of Bengal, October 27, 1893, Dharampal Archives, CPS-CPM-03.

51 Report of Bengal Legislative Council, November 11, 1893, Proceedings of Police Department, Bengal, March 1894, BL, IOR, P/4544 (nos. 36–7). Indeed, most of his district officers felt such an initiative was likely to do more harm than good. When asked, they reported that, since the ultimate goal of Hindus was to ban all cow killing, and the Muslims were determined to retain their right to eat beef, there was no real middle ground; the committees would, they feared, simply create another point of conflict. Report by A. Forbes, October 27, 1893, Dharampal Archives, CPS-CPM-03.

52 Reports by A. Forbes, October 27, 1893; D. J. Macpherson, Magistrate of Gaya, to A. Forbes, October 8, 1893; and H. N. Harris to D. J. Macpherson September 27, 1893, Dharampal Archives, CPS-CPM-03.

53 Report by A. Forbes, October 27, 1893, Dharampal Archives, CPS-CPM-03.

54 MacDonnell to Lansdowne, September 18, 1893, MacDonnell Papers, Bodleian Library, Ms. Eng. his. d.235 (fol. 40); Report on the Administration of Bengal, 1893–4, BL, IOR V/10/65, 11–12.

55 McLane, *Indian Nationalism*, 318.

56 See, for example, "Report on Vernacular Press, Punjab, for 1893," NAIn, Home Dept., Public Branch, May 1894, nos. 98–9.

57 D. F. McCracken, "Note on the Agitation Against Cow-Killing," August 9, 1893, BL, IOR, L/P&J/254/1894, 11.

58 RNN (Bengal) for the week ending July 8, 1893, 531.

59 See, for example, report of *Dnyán Chakshu* in RNN (Bombay) for the week ending August 26, 1893, 20.

60 Report of *Sanjivani* in RNN (Bengal) for the week ending August 5, 1893, 623.

61 This was the position of the Maradabad (NWP) *Sitáfa-i-Hind* of July 20, as rendered in the government précis of vernacular newspapers, Dharampal Archives, CPS-CPM-04, 18.

62 RNN (Bombay) for the week ending August 19, 1893, 18.

63 Ibid., 20.

64 RNN (Bengal) for the week ending July 8, 1893, 616.

65 Lansdowne to Crosthwaite, July 6, 1893, Lansdowne Papers, BL, IOR, Mss. Eur. D558/25, no. 8 (from viceroy).

66 Crosthwaite to Lansdowne, July 20, 1893, Lansdowne Papers, BL, IOR, Mss. Eur D558/25, no. 35 (to viceroy).
67 Crosthwaite to Lansdowne, August 18, 1893, Lansdowne Papers, BL, IOR, Mss. Eur D558/25, no. 139 (to viceroy).
68 Crosthwaite to Lansdowne, July 20, 1893, Lansdowne Papers, BL, IOR Mss. Eur D558/25, no. 35 (to viceroy).
69 Report by D. F. McCracken, August 9, 1893, Government of India Political and Judicial files for 1894, BL, IOR, L/P&J/6/267/257.
70 Chief Secretary to Government, N.W. Provinces and Oudh, to Secretary to the Government of India, Home Department, September 18, 1893, Dharampal Archives, CPS-CPM-05.
71 Kimberley to Lansdowne, October 26, 1893, Lansdowne Papers, BL, IOR, Mss. Eur D558/6, no. 61 (from viceroy).
72 Kimberley to Lansdowne, August 25, 1893, Lansdowne Papers, BL, IOR, Mss. Eur D558/25, no. 53 (to viceroy).
73 Lansdowne to Kimberley, September 29, 1893, Lansdowne Papers,IOR, BL, IOR, Mss. Eur D558/6, no. 61 (from viceroy).
74 Lansdowne to Kimberley, August 15, 1893, Lansdowne Papers, BL, IOR, Mss. Eur D558/6, no. 50 (from viceroy).
75 That the agitation was inherently dangerous to Britain's position, insofar as it promoted Hindu solidarity and placed the British in the unpopular position of interfering with Hindu religious activity, seems clear enough. What is doubtful is whether undermining British power was an explicit goal of the agitation or merely a necessary side effect. See Robb, "Challenge."
76 Cashman, *Myth*, 69–70.
77 Harris to Kimberley, August 31, 1893, Kimberley Papers, Bodleian Library, Mss. Eng. c.4323. This was a danger to which others were alive as well. Reflecting on these riots in 1911, Sir John Strachey observed, "This question of cow-killing has been a cause of frequent trouble throughout a great part of India, and while Hindu agitation has been primarily directed against Muhammadans, it has obviously a serious significance for ourselves," since the holiness of the cow was almost the only thing about which India's 230 million Hindus agreed. Sir John Strachey, *India: Its Administration and Progress*, 4th ed. (London: Macmillan, 1911), 340–1.
78 Harris to Kimberley, October 4, 1893, Kimberley Papers, Bodleian Library, Mss. Eng. c.4323.
79 Kimberley to Harris, October 26, 1893, Kimberley Papers, Bodleian Library, Mss. Eng. c.4323.
80 Report by A. Forbes, October 27, 1893, Dharampal Archives, CPS-CPM-03.
81 MacDonnell to Lansdowne, October 6, 1893, Lansdowne Papers, BL, IOR, Mss. Eur. D558/25, no. 336 (to viceroy).
82 MacDonnell to Lansdowne, September 18, 1893, MacDonnell Papers, Bodleian Library, Ms. Eng. his. d.235 (fol. 40).

83 MacDonnell to Forbes, October 17, 1897, MacDonnell Papers, Bodleian Library, Ms. Eng. his. d.235.

84 In October 1893 the Bengal government issued a report warning, "The Hindu's reverence for the cow is one of the 'magazines of physical force' on which, it has been said, the forward party in Indian politics might rely in their contest with the Government; and it would be unwise in existing circumstances to ignore this aspect of the case." H. J. S. Cotton, Chief Secretary to the Government of Bengal, to the Secretary to the Government of India, Home Department, October 28, 1893, Dharampal Archives, CPS-CPM-08.

85 Ibid. A. Forbes, commissioner of Bihar, agreed that legislation targeting the *sabhas* specifically was not only dangerous but also impractical, although he did maintain that surveillance and registration of the groups might be increased under existing law and that some restrictions on inflammatory publications and speech might be imposed. Upholding the rights of Muslims, while respecting the sensitivities of the Hindus, was the government's duty, he said; giving in to one side or the other would be to "acknowledge ourselves unequal to the fulfillment of our mission here any longer." Confidential memorandum from A. Forbes on Government of India, no. 1462, October 4, 1893, Dharampal Archives, CPS-CPM-08.

86 T. M. Gibbon to A Forbes, September 1, 1893, Dharampal Archives, CPS-CPM-03.

87 H. C. Williams to A. Forbes, October 18, 1893, Dharampal Archives, CPS-CPM-03.

88 Ibid.

89 C. J. Lyall to Col. Ardagh, November 9, 1893, Lansdowne Papers, BL, IOR, Mss. Eur D/558/25, no. 473d (to viceroy).

90 Lansdowne to Kimberley, August 22, 1893, Lansdowne Papers, BL, IOR, Mss. Eur D558/6, no. 52 (from viceroy). Lansdowne made the same point in a subsequent letter to Lord Harris, arguing that the "parallel" between the two cases was "exact and ominous." Lansdowne to Harris, August 25, 1893, Lansdowne Papers, BL, IOR, Mss. Eur D558/25, no. 130 (from viceroy).

91 RNN (Bombay) for the week ending August 26, 1893, 17.

92 MacDonnell to Lansdowne, September 18, 1893, MacDonnell Papers, Bodleian Library, Ms. Eng. his. d.235 (fol. 40).

93 A few years later, as cow-protection violence continued in some places, a letter from Sir Charles Ollivant, municipal commissioner of Bombay, seems to have convinced India Secretary Lord George Hamilton that (in Ollivant's words) the *sabhas* were trying "to imitate Irish Nationalist methods as closely as possible," right down to convincing peasants not to pay their rents ("This was the 'No Rent Manifesto' ") and conducting political assassinations (the recent "murders of [plague officers] Rand and Ayerst were the equivalent of the Phoenix Park tragedy."). Lord George Hamilton to Lord Elgin, Jan. 21, 1898, with enclosure of letter from E. C. K Ollivant to Sir J. Peile, November 3, 1897, Earl of Elgin and Kincardine papers, BL, IOR, F84/16, no. iii, confidential appendix (to viceroy)

94 For a full consideration of postriot policies at the local and central level, including an examination of how those efforts developed in the next century, see Robb, "Challenge."

95 Circular from C. J. Lyall to governments of Madras, Bombay, Punjab, and Central Provinces, Jan. 17, 1894, Dharampal Archives, CPS-CPM-09.

96 Cox, *Thirty Years*, 208–9.

97 Kidambi, *Making*, 117.

98 Ibid., 136–8.

99 Robert Darnton, "Literary Surveillance in the British Raj: The Contradictions of Liberal Imperialism," *Book History* 4 (2001), 133–76; Janaki Bakhle, "Savarkar (1883–1966), Sedition and Surveillance: The Rule of Law in a Colonial Situation," *Social History* 35, 1 (February 2010), 51–75.

100 Shabnum Tejani, *Indian Secularism: A Social and Intellectual History, 1890–1950* (Bloomington: Indiana University Press, 2008), 70–1.

101 Harris to Elgin, March 7, 1894, Earl of Elgin and Kincardine Papers, BL, IOR, Mss. Eur F84/64, no. 47 (to viceroy).

102 *Times of India*, September 14, 1894.

103 Queen Victoria to Lord Elgin, September 20, 1894, Earl of Elgin and Kincardine Papers, BL, IOR, Mss. Eur F84/1, no. 11 (from queen).

104 Elgin to H. H. Fowler, September 19, 1894, Earl of Elgin and Kincardine Papers, BL, IOR, Mss. Eur F84/12, no. 35 (from viceroy); Harris to Elgin, October 1, 1894, Earl of Elgin and Kincardine Papers, BL, IOR, Mss. Eur F84/65, no. 164b (from India).

105 McLane, *Indian Nationalism*, 321–7.

Chapter 8

1 R. L. Stirrat, "Constructing Identities in Nineteenth-Century Colombo," in *Identity and Affect: Experiences of Identity in a Globalizing World*, ed. John R. Campbell and Alan Rew (London: Pluto Press, 1999), 39–63 (57).

2 *The Bombay Riots of 1874* (Bombay: Bombay Gazette, 1874); letter from F. M. B., *Times of India*, February 14, 1874; *North-West Herald*, February 21, 1874, extracted in *Times of India*, February 24, 1874.

3 Hugh Hanna to the Lord Lieutenant, September 9, 1857, printed in *Banner of Ulster*, September 10, 1857.

4 *The Bombay Riots of 1874* (Bombay: Bombay Gazette, 1874), 21; *Belfast Daily Mercury*, July 18, 1857.

5 *The Economist*, Aug. 20, 1864.

6 *Friend of India and Statesman*, September 9, 1882.

7 *Ceylon Observer*, March 26, 1883; *Ceylon Examiner*, March 28 and 30, 1883.

8 Letter from "A Lover of Peace," dated February 14, 1874, *Times of India*, February 16, 1874.

9 *Irish People*, August 20, 1864.

10 Report on Native Newspapers (hereafter, RNN) (Bengal) for the week ending August 5, 1893; "Report on vernacular press, Punjab, for 1893," NAIn, Home Dept., Public Branch, May 1894, nos. 98–9.

11 Lord Naas to Thomas Larcom, September 9, 1864, Larcom Papers, NLI, 7626.

12 D. Fitzpatrick to Lord Lansdowne, August 14, 1893, Lansdowne Papers, BL, IOR, Mss. Eur D558/25, no. 119 (to viceroy).

13 Antony MacDonnell to Lord Lansdowne, August 4, 1893, Lansdowne Papers, BL, IOR, Mss. Eur D558/25, no. 86 (to viceroy). On the Hindu press, see the report on the *Dainik-o-Samachar Chandrika* in RNN (Bengal) for the week ending July 8, 1893, 531. See also the reports on *Poona Vaibhav, Mahrátta, Sudhárak, Native Opinion*, and *Dnyán Chakshu* in RNN (Bombay) for the week ending August 26, 1893, 15–20.

14 Sir Alfred C. Lyall, *Asiatic Studies: Religious and Social*, first series, vol. 1 (London: John Murray, 1899), 290.

15 See, for example, Philip Wodehouse's report to the Colonial Office following the 1856 Guiana riots: "we have been enabled gradually to bring about the restoration of tranquility, and partially to revive confidence." P. E. Wodehouse to H. Labouchere, March 10, 1856, *British Guiana. Copies or Extracts of Correspondence between the Governor of British Guiana and the Secretary of State for the Colonies, on the Subject of the Recent Disturbances in That Colony*, HC 1856 (432) XLIV (hereafter, *1856 British Guiana Riots Correspondence*), no. 3, p. 34. By the same token, official bungling or heavy-handedness could also shake "the confidence of the public in the wisdom and courage of our rulers," as Guiana's *Creole* put it (December 13, 1856).

16 Sir Bampfylde Fuller, *Studies of Indian Life and Sentiment* (London: John Murray, 1910), 347.

17 Lord Minto to Lord Morley, May 28, 1906, quoted in Mary, Countess of Minto, *India Minto and Morley, 1905–1910* (London: Macmillan, 1934), 29.

18 The following discussion is derived from a separately published article of mine: Mark Doyle, "The Perils of Impartiality: Policing Communal Violence in Victorian India," in *Policing Empires*, ed. Amandine Lauro, Emmanuel Blanchard, and Marieke Bloembergen (Berne: Peter Lang, forthcoming).

19 Evidence of John Rice, Samuel Donaldson, and John McClean, *Report of the Commissioners of Inquiry into the Origin and Character of the Riots in Belfast, in July and September, 1857; together with Minutes of Evidence and Appendix*, HC 1857–58 (2309) XXVI, 130–2 and 244–7. There were also the Beers brothers, magistrates in County Down who in 1849 led an Orange procession that ended with

a vicious rampage against Catholic bystanders. *Papers Relating to an Investigation Held at Castlewellan into the Occurrences at Dolly's Brae, on the 12th July, 1849*, HC 1850 (C.331) LI, 11–12.

20 Report of the government of the North-West Provinces and Oudh, Dec. 6, 1893, NAIn, Home Dept, Public Branch, December 1893, no. 156.

21 Subho Basu, "Strikes and 'Communal' Riots in Calcutta in the 1890s: Industrial Workers, Bhadralok Nationalist Leadership and the Colonial State," *Modern Asian Studies* 32, 4 (1998), 949–83 (961–72).

22 Report of Inspector of Police Goneratna, May 31, 1883, National Archives of Sri Lanka, lot 6/6664 (no. 233), in G. P. V. Somaratna, *Kotahena Riot 1883: A Religious Riot in Sri Lanka* (Gangodawila, Sri Lanka: Deepanee, 1991), 50–62; A. C. Dep, *A History of the Ceylon Police (1866–1913)*, vol. II (N.p.: n.p., 1969), 211.

23 Perceived and actual state partiality has, of course, been crucial in creating conditions for many riots around the world, especially in the postcolonial multiethnic states of the twentieth century. See Donald Horowitz, *The Deadly Ethnic Riot* (Berkeley: University of California Press, 2001), 352–9.

24 Mark Doyle, *Fighting like the Devil for the Sake of God: Protestants, Catholics, and the Origins of Violence in Victorian Belfast* (Manchester: Manchester University Press, 2009), ch. 5; Virginia Crossman, *Politics, Law and Order in Nineteenth-Century Ireland* (Dublin: Gill & Macmillan, 1996); Elizabeth A. Muenger, *The British Military Dilemma in Ireland: Occupation Politics, 1886–1914* (Lawrence, KS: University Press of Kansas, 1991); Brian Griffin, *The Bulkies: Police and Crime in Belfast, 1800–1865* (Dublin: Irish Academic Press, 1997), 139–41; R. B. McDowell, *The Irish Administration, 1801–1914* (London: Routledge & Kegan Paul, 1964), 114–15.

25 Saunders to Derby, March 31, 1883, National Archives of Sri Lanka, lot 33/991, in Somaratna, *Kotahena Riot*, 312.

26 The role of "authoritative tolerance, acquiescence, or condonation" in creating the conditions for communal riots is discussed in Horowitz, *Deadly*, 343–52.

27 Somaratna, *Kotahena Riot*, 401–2.

28 L. G. Tucker to R. G. Butts, Inspector General of Police, February 24, 1856, *1856 British Guiana Riots Correspondence*, encl. 6 in no. 1, p. 21; *Demerara Royal Gazette*, no date, extracted in *Hereford Times*, March 29, 1856.

29 On the unique potency of rumors as methods of transmitting popular mentalitès in a colonial setting, see Anand A. Yang, "A Conversation of Rumors: The Language of Popular 'Mentalitès' in Late Nineteenth-Century Colonial India," *Journal of Social History* 20, 3 (1987), 485–505. On rumors as precipitating events for ethnic riots, see Horowitz, *Deadly*, 74–88.

30 Frank Wright refers to this process, in which nonviolent actors gravitate toward communal entrepreneurs for protection from rival groups, as "communal

deterrence." See Frank Wright, "Communal Deterrence and the Threat of Violence in the North of Ireland in the Nineteenth Century," in *Political Violence: Ireland in a Comparative Perspective*, ed. John Darby, Nicholas Dodge, and A. C. Hepburn (Belfast: Appletree Press, 1990), 11–28.

31 General Random to John Wodehouse, July 30, 1865, Bodleian Library, Kimberley Papers, c.4029.

32 John Wodehouse to General Random, August 1, 1865, Bodleian Library, Kimberley Papers, c.4029.

33 "The Battle of the Navvies," Larcom Papers, NLI, 7626/106; Doyle, *Fighting*, 170–7.

34 Doyle, *Fighting*, 107–9.

35 *Bombay Samachar*, February 27, 1874, translated extract printed in *Times of India*, February 28, 1874.

36 For good overviews, see Alvin Jackson, *Ireland 1798–1998: Politics and War* (Oxford: Oxford University Press, 2005); and Paul Bew, *Ireland: The Politics of Enmity, 1789–2006* (Oxford: Oxford University Press, 2007).

37 On the violence in Belfast during this period, see Alan F. Parkinson, *Belfast's Unholy War: The Troubles of the 1920s* (Dublin: Four Courts Press, 2004).

38 William Gould points out that the many "Associations," "Societies," and "Committees" of late nineteenth-century India (of which the cow-protection *sabhas* were examples) were themselves adaptations of British forms of social organizations. William Gould, *Religion and Conflict in Modern South Asia* (Cambridge: Cambridge University Press, 2012), 51.

39 John McLane, *Indian Nationalism and the Early Congress* (Princeton: Princeton University Press, 1977), 294.

40 Ibid., 322.

41 Barbara D. Metcalf and Thomas R. Metcalf, *A Concise History of India* (Cambridge: Cambridge University Press, 2002), 152.

42 Richard I. Cashman, *The Myth of the* Lokmanya*: Tilak and Mass Politics in Maharashtra* (Berkeley: University of California Press, 1975), 73–4.

43 S. M. Edwardes, *The Bombay City Police: A Historical Sketch, 1672–1916* (London: Oxford University Press, 1923), 104–5. On the emergence of the Ganapati festival as a mass nationalist movement, see Cashman, *Myth*, 75–97.

44 Cashman, *Myth*, 80–1 and 92–3.

45 Ibid., 75.

46 Ibid., 88.

47 On Hindu–Muslim relations during this period, see Sumit Sarkar, *The Swadeshi Movement in Bengal* (New Delhi: People's Publishing House, 1973), 404–64.

48 It is also worth noting the impact of the 1893 riots on Vanayak Damodar Savarkar, future disciple of Tilak and father of modern Hindu nationalism. As a young boy in Maharashtra, Tilak and a group of friends responded to the news of rioting in

Azamgarh by throwing stones at the village mosque. Amalendu Misra, "Savarkar and the Discourse on Islam in Pre-Independent India," *Journal of Asian History* 33, 2 (1999), 142–84, n.6.

49 Stephen Prothero, *The White Buddhist: The Asian Odyssey of Henry Steel Olcott* (Bloomington, IN: Indiana University Press, 1996), 95.

50 K. H. M. Sumathipala, "The Kotahena Riots and their Repercussions," *The Ceylon Historical Journal* (1969–70), 65–81 (77).

51 K. M. De Silva, "Religion and Nationalism in Nineteenth-Century Sri Lanka: Christian Missionaries and their Critics," *Ethnic Studies Report* 16, 1 (Jan. 1998), 103–39 (130–1); K. M. de Silva, "The Government and Religion: Problems and Policies, c. 1832 to c. 1910," in *History of Ceylon*, vol. 3, ed. K. M. de Silva (Colombo: The Colombo Apothecaries, 1973), 187–212 (204).

52 Rod Thornton, "The British Army and the Origins of its Moral Force Philosophy," *Small Wars and Insurgencies* 15, 1 (Spring 2004), 83–106 (95–6).

53 Sandria B. Freitag, *Collective Action and Community: Public Arenas and the Emergence of Communalism in North India* (Berkeley: University of California Press, 1989), 56, 66–78.

54 Arun Mukherjee, *Crime and Public Disorder in Colonial Bengal, 1861–1912* (Calcutta: K P Bagchi, 1995), 229.

55 Prashant Kidambi, *The Making of an Indian Metropolis: Colonial Governance and Public Culture in Bombay, 1890–1920* (Aldershot: Ashgate, 2007), 133.

56 Ibid., 136–8.

57 Ibid., 138.

58 On the evolution of surveillance techniques and sedition law in early twentieth-century India, processes especially apparent in the state's handling of Hindu nationalist V. D. Savarkar, see Janaki Bakhle, "Savarkar (1883–1966), Sedition and Surveillance: The Rule of Law in a Colonial Situation," *Social History* 35, 1 (February 2010), 51–75.

59 Letter from "Observer," *Times of India*, February 26, 1894.

60 Mukherjee, *Crime*, 229–30.

61 *India. Police Commission. Report of the Indian Police Commission And Resolution of the Government of India* (London: Printed for H. M. Stationery Off., by Darling, 1905).

62 Bridget Brereton, "The Trinidad Carnival in the Late Nineteenth Century," in *Carnival: Culture in Action: The Trinidad Experience*, ed. Milla Cozart Riggio (New York: Routledge, 2004), 53–63; Kelvin Singh, *Bloodstained Tombs: The Muharram Massacre of 1884* (Basingstoke: Macmillan Caribbean, 1988), 14–16.

63 In much of the West Indies the increasing frequency of state violence was visible not during riots but during labor strikes (often called riots by the authorities), many of which involved East Indian laborers. British Guiana, for instance, saw numerous

police shootings of striking workers in the late nineteenth and early twentieth centuries, with thirteen killed and eighteen wounded during a plantation dispute as late as 1924. Particularly brutal was the repression of a strike in Georgetown and surrounding areas in 1905, during which police fired on unarmed protestors and the authorities dispatched two warships to preserve order. Joan Mars, *Deadly Force, Colonialism, and the Rule of Law: Police Violence in Guyana* (Westport, CT: Greenwood Press, 2002), 75–83.

64 Sir H. W. Norman to Lord Derby, January 14, 1885, in *Correspondence Respecting the Recent Coolie Disturbances in Trinidad, with the Report by Sir H. W. Norman Thereon*, HL 1884–5 (C.4366) XXII, 46. See also Prabhu P. Mohapatra, "The Hosay Massacre of 1884: Class and Community among Indian Immigrant Labourers in Trinidad," in *Work and Social Change in Asia: Essays in Honour of Jan Breman*, ed. Arvind N. Das and Marcel Van Der Linden (New Delhi: Manohar, 2003), 187–230; and Singh, *Bloodstained Tombs*.

65 On the evolution of police violence in Guyana, see Mars, *Deadly Force*.

66 *Report of the Belfast Riots Commissioners. Minutes of Evidence and Appendices*, HC 1887 (4925-I) XVIII.

67 On the crisis of the Royal Irish Constabulary during the Anglo-Irish War, see D. M. Leeson, *The Black and Tans: British Police Auxiliaries in the Irish War of Independence* (Oxford: Oxford University Press, 2011). The most comprehensive study of the force is Elizabeth Malcolm, *The Irish Policeman, 1822–1922: A Life* (Dublin: Four Courts Press, 2006).

68 P. T. M. Fernando, "The British Raj and the 1915 Communal Riots in Ceylon," *Modern Asian Studies* 3, 3 (1969), 245–55.

69 A. P. Kannangara, "The Riots of 1915 in Sri Lanka: A Study in the Roots of Communal Violence," *Past and Present* 102 (February 1984), 130–65.

70 Charles S. Blackton. "The Action Phase of the 1915 Riots," *The Journal of Asian Studies* 29, 2 (February 1970), 235–54 (235). See also additional articles in the same issue of *The Journal of Asian Studies*, which was devoted to these riots.

Bibliography

Manuscripts

Bodleian Library, Oxford University
Kimberley Papers
MacDonnell Papers
Borthwick Institute of Historical Research, University of York
Halifax Papers
Center for Policy Studies, Chennai
Dharampal Archives: Cow Protection Movement
India Office Records, British Library
Chelmsford Papers
Earl of Elgin and Kincardine Papers
Government of India Political and Judicial Files
Lansdowne Papers
Official Publications (Administration Reports and Monographs)
Police files on pre-1947 Communal Disturbances
Proceedings of the Government of Bengal
National Archives of Great Britain, Kew
Colonial Office: Ireland, Dublin Castle Records
Home Office: Private Office Papers
Home Office: Registered Papers
National Archives of India, New Delhi
Home Department Records
Reports on Native Newspapers
National Archives of Ireland, Dublin
Chief Secretary's Office Registered Papers
National Archives of Scotland, Edinburgh
Lord Advocate's Papers
National Library of Ireland, Dublin
Larcom Papers
Public Record Office of Northern Ireland, Belfast
Abercorn Papers

Dufferin Papers
James Kennedy Papers
Minute Book of the Belfast Town Council

Newspapers and periodicals

Aberdeen Journal
Banner of Ulster
Belfast Daily Mercury
Belfast Newsletter
Belfast Weekly News
Berkshire Chronicle
Birmingham Daily Post
Bristol Mercury
Ceylon Examiner
Ceylon Observer
Chambers's Journal
The Colonist (British Guiana)
The Creole
Daily Examiner (Belfast)
Daily Express
Daily News
Daily Telegraph
Devizes and Wiltshire Gazette
Dumfries and Galloway Standard
The Economist
The Era
Freeman's Journal
Friend of India and Statesman
Glasgow Courier
Glasgow Free Press
Glasgow Herald
The Graphic
Hampshire Telegraph and Sussex Chronicle
Hereford Times
Ipswich Journal
Irish People
Leeds Mercury
Liverpool Daily Post

Liverpool Mercury
Madras Times
Manchester Times
Missionary Herald of the Baptist Missionary Society
Morning Chronicle
Morning Post
Northern Echo
Northern Star and Ulster Observer
Northern Whig
Paisley Herald and Renfrewshire Advertiser
Pall Mall Gazette
Preston Guardian
Saturday Review
Spectator
Times (London)
Times of India
Ulsterman

Parliamentary papers

British Guiana. Copies or Extracts of Correspondence between the Governor of British Guiana and the Secretary of State for the Colonies, on the Subject of the Recent Disturbances in That Colony, HC 1856 (432) XLIV.

Correspondence Respecting the Recent Coolie Disturbances in Trinidad at the Mohurrum Festival, with the Report Thereon by Sir H. W. Norman, K. C. B., C. I. E., HC 1884–5 (C.4366) LIII.

East India (Bombay Riots). Despatches from India Office in Reference to Riots at Bombay; Reports by Coms. of Police at Bombay; Memorial from Parsee Community to Secretary of State for India, HC 1874 (305) XLVII.

East India (Religious Disturbances). Copies or Extracts of Reports Relating to the Recent Conflicts between Hindus and Muhammadans in India, and Particularly to the Causes Which Led to Them, HC 1893–94 (538) LXIII.

Featherstone Inquiry. Report of the Committee Appointed to Inquire into the Circumstances Connected with the Disturbances at Featherstone on the 7th of September 1893, HC 1893–94 (C.7234) XVII.

House of Commons Debates

House of Lords Debates

India. Police Commission. Report of the Indian Police Commission and Resolution of the Government of India. London: Printed for H. M. Stationery Off., by Darling, 1905.

Papers Relating to an Investigation Held at Castlewellan into the Occurrences at Dolly's Brae, on the 12th July, 1849, HC 1850 (C.331) LI.

Papers Relating to the Donaghmore Riot, with Report of the Commissioners Appointed to Inquire into the Conduct of the Justices of the Peace Presiding at a Court of Petty Sessions Held at Dungannon, on 1st October 1866; and Copy of Letter from the Secretary of the Lord Chancellor to the Justices Who Formed the Bench at the Dungannon Petty Sessions, Held at Dungannon on the 1st October 1866, HC 1867 (3906) LIX.

Report of the Belfast Riots Commissioners. Minutes of Evidence and Appendices, HC 1887 (4925-I) XVIII.

Report of the Commissioners of Inquiry into the Origin and Character of the Riots in Belfast, in July and September 1857; together with Minutes of Evidence and Appendix, HC 1857–58 (2309) XXVI.

Report of the Commissioners of Inquiry, 1864, Respecting the Magisterial and Police Jurisdiction Arrangements and Establishment of the Borough of Belfast, HC 1865 (3466) XXVIII.

Report of the Commissioners of Inquiry, 1869, into the Riots and Disturbances in the City of Londonderry, with Minutes of Evidence and Appendix, HC 1870 (C.5) XXXII.

Report of the Select Committee on Employment of Military in Cases of Disturbances, HC 1908 (C.236) VII.

Published primary sources

Bennett, George W. *An Illustrated History of British Guiana*. Georgetown, Demerara: Richardson, 1866.

Boddam-Whetham, J. W. *Roraima and British Guiana, with a Glance at Bermuda, the West Indies, and the Spanish Main*. London: Hurst and Blackett, 1879.

The Bombay Riots of 1874. Bombay: Bombay Gazette, 1874.

Caldecott, Alfred. *The Church in the West Indies.* London: Society for Promoting Christian Knowledge, 1898.

Campbell, George. *Memoirs of My Indian Career.* London: Macmillan, 1893.

Churchill, Winston. *The Story of the Malakand Field Force: An Episode of Frontier War.* London: Thomas Nelson, 1916.

Connolly, James. "Labour and the Proposed Partition of Ireland," *Irish Worker* (March 14, 1914).

Cox, Edmund C. *My Thirty Years in India.* London: Mills & Boon, 1909.

Cox, Edmund C. *A Short History of the Bombay Presidency.* Bombay: Thacker, 1887.

Cundall, Frank. *Political and Social Disturbances in the West Indies: A Brief Account and Bibliography.* Kingston: The Institute of Jamaica, 1906.

de Silva, K. M., ed. *Letters on Ceylon 1846–50. The Administration of Viscount Torrington and the "Rebellion" of 1848. The Private Correspondence of the Third Earl Grey (Secretary of State for the Colonies 1846–52) and Viscount Torrington.* Kandy and Colombo: KVG de Silva, 1965.

Edwardes, S. M. *The Bombay City Police: A Historical Sketch, 1672–1916.* London: Oxford University Press, 1923.

Edwardes, S. M. *The Rise of Bombay: A Retrospect.* Bombay: Times of India Press, 1902.

Fennell, Thomas. *The Royal Irish Constabulary: A History and Personal Memoir,* edited by Rosemary Fennell. Dublin: University College Dublin Press, 2003.

Forjett, Charles. *Our Real Danger in India.* London, Paris, and New York: Cassell Petter & Galpin, 1877.

Framjee, Dosabhoy. *The Parsees: Their History, Manners, Customs, and Religion.* London: Smith, Elder, 1858.

Fuller, Sir Bampfylde. *Studies of Indian Life and Sentiment.* London: John Murray, 1910.

The Gazetteer of Bombay City and Island. 3 Vols. Bombay: Times Press, 1909.

Grand Orange Lodge of Ireland. *Report of the Proceedings of the Grand Orange Lodge of Ireland, at the Half-Yearly Meeting, Held at Newry, on Wednesday, the 26th, and Thursday, the 27th, Days of May, 1858.* Downpatrick: Downshire Protestant office, 1858.

Gregory, Sir William. *An Autobiography,* edited by Lady Gregory. London: John Murray, 1894.

Harris, Lord. "Recreation and 'Cricket.'" In *Cricket,* edited by T. C. Collings, 111–19. London: T. Fisher Unwin, 1900.

Harris, Lord. *A Few Short Runs.* London: John Murray, 1921.

Hunter, W. W. *A Life of the Earl of Mayo: Fourth Viceroy of India.* 2 Vols. London: Smith, Elder, 1875.

Hunter, W. W. *The Indian Musalmans: Are They Bound in Conscience to Rebel against the Queen?* London: Trübner, 1871.

Kalyvas, Stathis. *The Logic of Violence in Civil War*. Cambridge: Cambridge University Press, 2006.

Karaka, Dosabhai Framji. *History of the Parsis*. 2 Vols. London: Macmillan, 1884.

Kaye, Sir John and George Bruce, eds. *Kaye's and Malleson's History of the Indian Mutiny of 1857–8*. 6 Vols. London: W. H. Allen, 1889.

Kirke, Henry. *Twenty-Five Years in British Guiana*. London: Sampson Low, Marston, 1898.

Lyall, Sir Alfred C. *Asiatic Studies: Religious and Social*. London: John Murray, 1899.

MacDonnell, Sir A. P. *Selections from Speeches of Sir A. P. MacDonnell, G.C.S.I., Lieutenant-Governor, N.-W. P., and Chief Commissioner of Oudh, from 1895 to 1901*. Naini Tal: N.-W. Provinces and Oudh Government Camp Branch Press, 1901.

MacKnight, Thomas. *Ulster as It Is: Or, Twenty-Eight Years' Experience as an Irish Editor*. 2 Vols. London: Macmillan, 1896.

Maclean, James Mackenzie. *Guide to Bombay: Historical, Statistical, and Descriptive*. 14th ed. Bombay: Bombay Gazette, 1889.

Mill, John Stuart. *On Liberty*. 2nd ed. London: John W. Parker, 1859.

Minto, Mary, Countess of. *India Minto and Morley, 1905–1910*. London: Macmillan, 1934.

Minute by the Right Honorable Lord Sandhurst, G.C.B., G.C.S.I., Commander of the Forces. *Belfast Riots—Means for Suppression*.

Mitchell, J. Murray and Sir William Muir. *Two Old Faiths: Essays on the Religions of the Hindus and the Mohammedans*. New York: Chautauqua Press, 1891.

Morley, John, Viscount. *Recollections*. 2 Vols. New York: The Macmillan Company, 1917.

The New Local Guide of British Guiana. Demerara: "Royal Gazette" Office, 1862.

Patton, Arthur and George Foy. *Reports Submitted to the Executive Committee of the Irish Loyal and Patriotic Union on the Subject of the Belfast Riots*. Dublin: Humphrey and Armour, 1886.

Proceedings of the Council of the Governor of Bombay, Assembled for the Purpose of Making Laws and Regulations 1893. Vol. XXXI. August 12, 1893.

Reed, Sir Andrew. *The Irish Constable's Guide*. 3rd ed. Dublin: Alex Thom, 1895.

Rees, John David. *The Real India*. London: Methuen, 1908.

Strachey, Sir John. *India*. London: K. Paul, Trench, Trübner, 1888.

Strachey, Sir John. *India*. 2nd ed. London: K. Paul, Trench, Trübner, 1894.

Strachey, Sir John. *India*. 4th ed. London: Macmillan, 1911.

Trollope, Anthony. *The West Indies and the Spanish Main*. London: Chapman and Hall, 1860.

White, Sir Herbert Thirkell. *A Civil Servant in Burma*. London: Edward Arnold, 1913.

Young, Marianne. *The Moslem Noble: His Land and People, with Some Notices of the Parsees, or Ancient Persians*. London: Saunders and Otley, 1857.

Secondary sources

Adamson, Alan H. "Monoculture and Village Decay in British Guiana: 1854–1872," *Journal of Social History* 3, 4 (Summer 1970), 386–405.

Ahmad, Qeymuddin. *The Wahabi Movement in India*. Calcutta: Firma K. L. Mukhopadhyay, 1966.

Anderson, David M. and David Killingray. *Policing the Empire: Government, Authority, and Control, 1830–1940*. Manchester: Manchester University Press, 1991.

Arnold, David. *Police Power and Colonial Rule: Madras 1859–1947*. Delhi: Oxford University Press, 1986.

Arnstein, Walter. "The Murphy Riots: A Victorian Dilemma," *Victorian Studies* 19 (September 1975), 51–70.

Baker, Sybil. "Orange and Green: Belfast, 1832–1912." In *The Victorian City: Images and Realities*, vol. 2, edited by H. J. Dyos and M. Wolff, 787–815. London: Routledge & Kegan Paul, 1973.

Bakhle, Janaki. "Savarkar (1883–1966), Sedition and Surveillance: The Rule of Law in a Colonial Situation," *Social History* 35, 1 (February 2010), 51–75.

Barns, Margarita. *The Indian Press: A History of the Growth of Public Opinion in India*. London: George Allen & Unwin, 1940.

Barrier, N. Gerald. *Banned: Controversial Literature and Political Control in British India, 1907–1947*. Columbia, MO: University of Missouri Press, 1974.

Bartholomeusz, Tessa. "Catholics, Buddhists, and the Church of England: The 1883 Sri Lankan Riots," *Buddhist-Christian Studies* 15 (1995), 89–103.

Basu, Subho. "Strikes and 'Communal' Riots in Calcutta in the 1890s: Industrial Workers, Bhadralok Nationalist Leadership and the Colonial State," *Modern Asian Studies* 32, 4 (1998), 949–83.

Bayly, C. A. *Empire and Information: Intelligence Gathering and Social Communication in India, 1780–1870*. Cambridge: Cambridge University Press, 1996.

Bayly, C. A. *Indian Society and the Making of the British Empire*. Cambridge: Cambridge University Press, 1988.

Bayly, C. A. "Ireland, India and the Empire: 1780–1914," *Transactions of the Royal Historical Society (Sixth Series)* 10 (2000), 377–97.

Bayly, S. *Caste, Society and Politics in India from the Eighteenth Century to the Modern Age*. Cambridge: Cambridge University Press, 1999. 187–232.

Bender, Jill. "The Imperial Politics of Famine: The 1873–74 Bengal Famine and Irish Parliamentary Nationalism," *Eire-Ireland* 42 (Spring/Summer 2007), 132–56.

Bew, Paul. *Ireland: The Politics of Enmity, 1789–2006*. Oxford: Oxford University Press, 2007.

Blackton, Charles S. "The Action Phase of the 1915 Riots," *The Journal of Asian Studies* 29, 2 (February 1970), 235–54.

Boyce, Merrill Tilghman. *British Policy and the Evolution of the Vernacular Press in India, 1835–1878*. Delhi: Chanakya Publications, 1988.

Boyd, Andrew. *Holy War in Belfast*. Tralee: Anvil Books, 1969.

Breathnach, S. *The Irish Police*. Dublin: Anvil Books, 1974.

Brereton, Bridget. "The Trinidad Carnival in the Late Nineteenth Century." In *Carnival: Culture in Action: The Trinidad Experience*, edited by Milla Cozart Riggio, 53–63. New York: Routledge, 2004.

Brillman, Michael. "Bengal Tiger, Celtic Tiger: The Life of Sir Antony Patrick MacDonnell, 1844–1925," vol. 1. PhD diss., University of Chicago, 2009.

Brooke, David. "The 'Lawless' Navvy: A Study of the Crime Associated with Railway Building," *The Journal of Transport History* 10 (September 1989), 145–65.

Brooke, David. *The Railway Navvy: 'That Despicable Race of Men.'* Newton Abbot: David & Charles, 1983.

Brown, Howard. *Ending the French Revolution: Violence, Justice, and Repression from the Terror to Napoleon*. Charlottesville: University of Virginia Press, 2006.

Brumpton, Paul R. *Security and Progress: Lord Salisbury at the India Office*. Westport, CT: Greenwood Press, 2002.

Bryson, Anne. "Riotous Liverpool, 1815–1860." In *Popular Politics, Riot and Labour: Essays in Liverpool History, 1790–1940*, edited by John Belchem, 98–134. Liverpool: Liverpool University Press, 1992.

Cashman, Richard I. *The Myth of the* Lokmanya*: Tilak and Mass Politics in Maharashtra*. Berkeley: University of California Press, 1975.

Chakrabarty, Dipesh. "Communal Riots and Labour: Bengal's Jute Mill-Hands in the 1890s," *Past and Present* 91 (May 1981), 140–69.

Choudhury, Deep Kanta Lahiri. *Telegraphic Imperialism: Crisis and Panic in the Indian Empire, c. 1830*. London: Palgrave Macmillan, 2010.

Cohn, Bernard. "The Census, Social Structure and Objectification in South Asia." In *An Anthropologist Among the Historians and Other Essays*, edited by Bernard Cohn, 224–54. Delhi: Oxford University Press, 1987.

Cohn, Bernard. *Colonialism and its Forms of Knowledge: The British in India*. Princeton: Princeton University Press, 1996.

Coldham, James D. *Lord Harris*. London: George Allen & Unwin, 1983.

Crossman, Virginia. *Politics, Law and Order in Nineteenth-Century Ireland*. Dublin: Gill & Macmillan, 1996.

Curran, James and Jean Seaton. *Power Without Responsibility: The Press, Broadcasting and the Internet in Britain*. 7th ed. New York: Routledge, 2010.

Darnton, Robert. "Literary Surveillance in the British Raj: The Contradictions of Liberal Imperialism," *Book History* 4 (2001), 133–76.

Das, Dilip K. and Arvind Verma. "The Armed Police in the British Colonial Tradition: The Indian Perspective," *Policing: An International Journal of Police Strategies & Management* 21, 2 (1998), 354–67.

Das, Suranjan. *Communal Riots in Bengal, 1905–1947*. Oxford: Oxford University Press, 1991.

Datta, Pradip Kumar. *Carving Blocs: Communal Ideology in Early Twentieth-Century Bengal*. Oxford: Oxford University Press, 1999.

de Silva, K. M. "The Government and Religion: Problems and Policies, c. 1832 to c. 1910." In *History of Ceylon*, vol. 3, edited by K. M. de Silva, 187–212. Colombo: The Colombo Apothecaries' Company, 1973.

de Silva, K. M. "Religion and Nationalism in Nineteenth-Century Sri Lanka: Christian Missionaries and their Critics," *Ethnic Studies Report* 16, 1 (January 1998), 103–39.

Dep, A. C. *A History of the Ceylon Police*. Vol. 2, 1866–1913. N. p.: n. p., 1969.

Dirks, Nicholas. *Castes of Mind: Colonialism and the Making of Modern India*. Princeton: Princeton University Press, 2001.

Doyle, Mark. *Fighting like the Devil for the Sake of God: Protestants, Catholics, and the Origins of Violence in Victorian Belfast*. Manchester: Manchester University Press, 2009.

Doyle, Mark. "Martyrs of Liberty: Open-Air Preaching and Popular Violence in Victorian Britain and Ireland." In *Faith, War, and Violence: Religion and Public Life*, vol. 39, edited by Gabriel Ricci, 149–64. New Brunswick, NJ: Transaction Publishers, 2014.

Doyle, Mark. "Massacre by the Book: Amritsar and the Rules of Public-Order Policing in Britain and India," *Britain and the World* 4, 2 (September 2011), 247–68.

Doyle, Mark. "The Perils of Impartiality: Policing Communal Violence in Victorian India." In *Policing Empires*, edited by Amandine Lauro, Emmanuel Blanchard, and Marieke Bloembergen. Berne: Peter Lang, forthcoming.

Dungan, Myles. *Mr Parnell's Rottweiler: Censorship and the United Ireland Newspaper, 1881–1891*. Sallins, Co. Kildare: Irish Academic Press, 2014.

Eason, Andrew M. "'Desperate Fighting at the Cape': The Salvation Army's Arrival and Earliest Work in Late-Victorian Cape Town," *Journal of Religious History* 33, 3 (September 2009), 265–84.

Eason, Andrew M. "Religion versus the Raj: The Salvation Army's 'Invasion' of British India," *Mission Studies* 28 (2011), 71–90.

Farrell, Sean. *Rituals and Riots: Sectarian Violence and Political Culture in Ulster, 1784–1886*. Lexington, KY: University Press of Kentucky, 2000.

Farrell, Sean. "Ulster Sectarianism and the Lessons of South Asian Historiography," *History Compass* 8, 9 (September 2010), 1023–35.

Ferguson, Niall. *Empire: The Rise and Demise of the British World Order and the Lessons for Global Power*. New York: Basic Books, 2003.

Fernando, P. T. M. "The British Raj and the 1915 Communal Riots in Ceylon," *Modern Asian Studies* 3, 3 (1969), 245–55.

Fernando, P. T. M. "The Post Riots Campaign for Justice," *The Journal of Asian Studies* 29, 2 (February 1970), 255–66.

Foley, Tadhg and Maureen O'Connor, eds. *Ireland and India: Colonies, Culture, and Empire*. Dublin: Irish Academic Press, 2006.

Foynes, Mark. "Manchester's 'Disgraceful Riot,' July 3 and 4, 1854," *Horizons* 22 (Winter 2002). www.nhhistory.org/edu/support/nhimmigration/disgracefulriot.pdf, accessed December 26, 2014.

Freitag, Sandria B. *Collective Action and Community: Public Arenas and the Emergence of Communalism in North India*. Berkeley: University of California Press, 1989.

Gailey, Andrew. *Ireland and the Death of Kindness: The Experience of Constructive Unionism, 1890–1905*. Cork: Cork University Press, 1987.

Garner, Steve. "Atlantic Crossing: Whiteness as a Transatlantic Experience," *Atlantic Studies* 4, 1 (2007), 117–32.

Gilmartin, David. "'Divine Displeasure' and Muslim Elections: The Shaping of Community in Twentieth-Century Punjab." In *The Political Inheritance of Pakistan*, edited by D. A. Low, 106–29. New York: St. Martin's Press, 1991.

Gilmartin, David. *Empire and Islam: Punjab and the Making of Pakistan*. Berkeley: University of California Press, 1988.

Gordon, Michael A. *The Orange Riots: Irish Political Violence in New York City, 1870 and 1871*. Ithaca: Cornell University Press, 1993.

Gordon, Peter. "Spencer, John Poyntz, Fifth Earl Spencer (1835–1910)." In *Oxford Dictionary of National Biography*, edited by H. C. G. Matthew and Brian Harrison. Oxford: Oxford University Press, 2004. www.oxforddnb.com/view/36209, accessed December 27, 2014.

Gossman, Patricia A. *Riots and Victims: Violence and the Construction of Communal Identity among Bengali Muslims, 1905–1947*. Boulder, CO: Westview Press, 1999.

Gott, Richard. *Britain's Empire: Resistance, Repression and Revolt*. London: Verso, 2011.

Gough, Barry. *Pax Britannica: Ruling the Waves and Keeping the Peace before Armageddon*. New York: Palgrave, 2014.

Gould, William. *Religion and Conflict in Modern South Asia*. Cambridge: Cambridge University Press, 2012.

Gray, Peter. "Famine and Land in Ireland and India, 1845–1880: James Caird and the Political Economy of Hunger," *The Historical Journal* 49 (2006), 193–215.

Green, Nile. *Bombay Islam: The Religious Economy of the West Indian Ocean, 1840–1915*. Cambridge: Cambridge University Press, 2011.

Griffin, Brian. *The Bulkies: Police and Crime in Belfast, 1800–1865*. Dublin: Irish Academic Press, 1997.

Guha, Ramachandra. *A Corner of a Foreign Field: The Indian History of a British Sport*. London: Picador, 2002.

Guha, Ranajit. *Dominance without Hegemony: History and Power in Colonial India*. Cambridge, MA: Harvard University Press, 1997.

Handley, James E. *The Navvy in Scotland*. Cork: Cork University Press, 1970.

Headrick, Daniel. "A Double-Edged Sword: Communications and Imperial Control in British India," *Historical Social Research / Historicsche Sozialforschung* 35, 1 (2010), 51–65.

Headrick, Daniel. *The Tentacles of Progress: Technology Transfer in the Age of Imperialism, 1850–1940*. New York: Oxford University Press, 1988.

Heath, Deana. *Purifying Empire: Obscenity and the Politics of Moral Regulation in Britain, India and Australia*. Cambridge: Cambridge University Press, 2010.

Herbert, Christopher. *War of No Pity: The Indian Mutiny and Victorian Trauma*. Princeton: Princeton University Press, 2008.

Hirst, Catherine. *Religion, Politics, and Violence in Nineteenth-Century Belfast: The Pound and Sandy Row*. Dublin: Four Courts Press, 2002.

Horowitz, Donald. *The Deadly Ethnic Riot*. Berkeley: University of California Press, 2001.

Howe, Stephen. "Minding the Gaps: New Directions in the Study of Ireland and Empire," *Journal of Imperial and Commonwealth History* 37, 1 (2009), 134–49.

Howe, Stephen, ed. *New Imperial Histories Reader*. New York: Routledge, 2009.

Hunte, Keith. "Protestantism and Slavery in the British Caribbean." In *Christianity in the Caribbean: Essays on Church History*, edited by Armando Lampe, 86–125. Kingston, Jamaica: The University of the West Indies Press, 2001.

Hussain, Nasser. *The Jurisprudence of Emergency: Colonialism and the Rule of Law*. Ann Arbor: The University of Michigan Press, 2003.

Jackson, Alvin. *Ireland 1798–1998: Politics and War*. Oxford: Oxford University Press, 2005.

James, Helen. "The Assassination of Lord Mayo: The 'First' *Jihad?*," *International Journal of Asia Pacific Studies* 5, 2 (2009), 1–19.

Jeffries, Sir C. J. *The Colonial Police*. London: M. Parrish, 1952.

Kale, Madhavi. "Projecting Identities: Indentured Labor Migration from India to Trinidad and British Guiana, 1836–1885." In *Nation and Migration: The Politics of Space in the South Asian Diaspora*, edited by Peter van der Veer, 73–92. Philadelphia: University of Pennsylvania Press, 1995.

Kamra, Sukeshi. *The Indian Periodical Press and the Production of Nationalist Rhetoric*. New York: Palgrave Macmillan, 2011.

Kannangara, A. P. "The Riots of 1915 in Sri Lanka: A Study in the Roots of Communal Violence," *Past and Present* 102 (February 1984), 130–65.

Kearney, Robert N. "The 1915 Riots in Ceylon: A Symposium," *Journal of Asian Studies* 29, 2 (February 1970), 219–22.

Kidambi, Prashant. *The Making of an Indian Metropolis: Colonial Governance and Public Culture in Bombay, 1890–1920*. Aldershot: Ashgate, 2007.

Koditschek, Theodore. *Liberalism, Imperialism, and the Historical Imagination: Nineteenth-Century Visions of a Greater Britain*. Cambridge: Cambridge University Press, 2011.

Kolsky, Elizabeth. "Codification and the Rule of Colonial Difference: Criminal Procedure in British India," *Law and History Review* 23, 3 (Fall 2005), 631–84.

Kostal, R. W. "A Jurisprudence of Power: Martial Law and the Ceylon Controversy of 1848–51," *The Journal of Imperial and Commonwealth History* 28, 1 (2000), 1–34.

Kostal, R. W. *A Jurisprudence of Power: Victorian Empire and the Rule of Law*. Oxford: Oxford University Press, 2005.

Larkin, Emmet. "The Devotional Revolution in Ireland, 1850–75," *The American Historical Review* 77 (June 1972), 625–52.

Leeson, D. M. *The Black and Tans: British Police Auxiliaries in the Irish War of Independence*. Oxford: Oxford University Press, 2011.

Lewis, Su Lin. "Colonial Penang's 'Indigenous' English Press." In *Media and the British Empire*, edited by Chandrika Kaul, 233–427. New York: Palgrave Macmillan, 2006.

Lowe, W. J. and E. L. Malcolm, "The Domestication of the Royal Irish Constabulary, 1836–1922," *Irish Economic and Social History* 19 (1992), 27–48.

MacKenzie, John M. " 'To Enlighten South Africa': The Creation of a Free Press at the Cape in the Early Nineteenth Century." In *Media and the British Empire*, edited by Chandrika Kaul, 20–36. New York: Palgrave Macmillan, 2006.

Majumdar, B. "Cricket in Colonial Bombay: 1850–1940," *The International Journal of the History of Sport* 23, 6 (September 2006), 1014–32.

Malalgoda, Kitsiri. *Buddhism in Sinhalese Society: A Study of Religious Revival and Change*. Berkeley: University of California Press, 1976.

Malcolm, Elizabeth. *The Irish Policeman, 1822–1922; A Life*. Dublin: Four Courts Press, 2006.

Marriott, John. *The Other Empire: Metropolis, India and Progress in the Colonial Imagination*. Manchester: Manchester University Press, 2009.

Mars, Joan. *Deadly Force, Colonialism, and the Rule of Law: Police Violence in Guyana*. Westport, CT: Greenwood Press, 2002.

Masselos, Jim. *The City in Action: Bombay Struggles for Power*. New Delhi: Oxford University Press, 2007.

McDowell, R. B. *The Irish Administration, 1801–1914*. London: Routledge & Kegan Paul, 1964.

McLane, John. *Indian Nationalism and the Early Congress*. Princeton: Princeton University Press, 1977.

McMaster, John Bach. *A History of the People of the United States*, vol. VIII (1850–1861). New York and London: D. Appelton, 1913.

Mehta, Uday Singh. *Liberalism and Empire: A Study in Nineteenth-Century British Liberal Thought*. Chicago: University of Chicago Press, 1999.

Menezes, Mary Noel. *Scenes from the History of the Portuguese in Guyana*. London: Sister M. N. Menezes, 1986.

Metcalf, Barbara D. and Thomas R. Metcalf. *A Concise History of India*. Cambridge: Cambridge University Press, 2002.

Metcalf, Thomas. *Ideologies of the Raj*. Cambridge: Cambridge University Press, 1994.

Misra, Amalendu. "Savarkar and the Discourse on Islam in Pre-Independent India," *Journal of Asian History* 33, 2 (1999), 142–84.

Mockaitis, Thomas R. *British Counterinsurgency, 1919–60*. New York: St. Martin's Press, 1990.

Mohapatra, Prabhu P. "The Hosay Massacre of 1884: Class and Community among Indian Immigrant Labourers in Trinidad." In *Work and Social Change in Asia: Essays in Honour of Jan Breman*, edited by Arvind N. Das and Marcel Van Der Linden, 187–230. New Delhi: Manohar, 2003.

Moore, Brian L. "The Social Impact of Portuguese Immigration into British Guiana after Emancipation," *Boletín de Estudios Latinoamericanos y del Caribe* 19 (December 1975), 3–15.

Morris, Jan. *Pax Britannica: The Climax of an Empire*. New York: Harcourt, Brace, 1968.

Muenger, Elizabeth A. *The British Military Dilemma in Ireland: Occupation Politics, 1886–1914*. Lawrence, KS: University Press of Kansas, 1991.

Mukherjee, Arun. *Crime and Public Disorder in Colonial Bengal, 1861–1912*. K P Bagchi: Calcutta, 1995.

Natarajan, S. *A History of the Press in India*. Bombay: Asia Publishing House, 1962.

Neal, Frank. *Sectarian Violence: The Liverpool Experience, 1819–1914: An Aspect of Anglo-Irish History*. Manchester: Manchester University Press, 1988.

O'Hanlon, Rosalind. "Colonialism and Social Identities in Flux: Class, Caste, and Religious Community." In *India and the British Empire*, edited by Douglas M. Peers and Nandini, 100–34. Oxford: Oxford University Press, 2012.

O'Malley, Kate. *Ireland, India and Empire: Indo-Irish radical Connections, 1919–64*. Manchester: Manchester University Press, 2008.

Palmer, Stanley H. *Police and Protest in England and Ireland, 1780–1850*. Cambridge: Cambridge University Press, 1988.

Palsetia, Jesse. "The Parsis of India and the Opium Trade in China," *Contemporary Drug Problems* 35 (Winter 2008), 647–78.

Pandey, Gyanendra. *The Construction of Communalism in Colonial North India*. Delhi: Oxford University Press, 1990.

Pandey, Gyanendra. "Rallying Round the Cow: Sectarian Strife in the Bhojpuri Region, c. 1888–1917." In *Subaltern Studies II: Writings on South Asian History and Society*, edited by Ranajit Guha, 60–129. Delhi: Oxford University Press, 1983.

Parchami, Ali. *Hegemonic Peace and Empire: The* Pax Romana, Britannica, *and* Americana. London: Routledge, 2009.

Parkinson, Alan F. *Belfast's Unholy War: The Troubles of the 1920s*. Dublin: Four Courts Press, 2004.

Philips, D. "Riots and Public Order in the Black Country, 1835–1860." In *Popular Protest and Public Order: Six Studies in British History, 1790–1920*, edited by R. Quinault and J. Stevenson, 141–80. London: George Allen and Unwin, 1974.

Pitts, Jennifer. *A Turn to Empire: The Rise of Imperial Liberalism in Britain and France*. Princeton: Princeton University Press, 2006.

Potter, Simon J. "Webs, Networks, and Systems: Globalization and the Mass Media in the Nineteenth- and Twentieth-Century British Empire," *Journal of British Studies* (July 2007), 621–46.

Price, Richard. "One Big Thing: Britain, Its Empire, and Their Imperial Culture," *Journal of British Studies* 45, 3 (July 2006), 602–27.

Prior, Katherine. "Making History: The State's Intervention in Urban Religious Disputes in the North-Western Provinces in the Early Nineteenth Century," *Modern Asian Studies* 27, 1 (1993), 179–203.

Prothero, Stephen. *The White Buddhist: The Asian Odyssey of Henry Steel Olcott.* Bloomington, IN: Indiana University Press, 1996.

Quinault, R. "The Warwickshire County Magistracy and Public Order, c.1830–1870." In *Popular Protest and Public Order: Six Studies in British History, 1790–1920*, edited by R. Quinault and J. Stevenson, 181–214. London: George Allen and Unwin, 1974.

Radford, Mark. *The Policing of Belfast, 1870–1914.* London: Bloomsbury, 2015.

Radford, Mark. "The 'Social Volcano': Policing Victorian Belfast." In *Politics and Power in Victorian Ireland*, edited by Roger Swift and Christine Kinealy, 166–77. Dublin: Four Courts Press, 2006.

Randall, Adrian. *Riotous Assemblies: Popular Protest in Hanoverian England.* Oxford: Oxford University Press, 2006.

Richter, Donald. *Riotous Victorians.* Athens, OH: Ohio University Press, 1981.

Robb, Peter. "The Challenge of Gau Mata: British Policy and Religious Change in India, 1880–1916," *Modern Asian Studies* 20, 2 (1986), 285–319.

Roberts, Andrew. *Salisbury: Victorian Titan.* London: Phoenix, 1999.

Roberts, Michael. "Noise as Cultural Struggle: Tom-Tom Beating, the British, and Communal Disturbances in Sri Lanka, 1880s–1930s." In *Mirrors of Violence: Communities, Violence, and Survivors in South Asia*, edited by Veena Das, 240–85. Delhi: Oxford University Press, 1990.

Robinson, Francis. "The British Empire and the Muslim World." In *Oxford History of the British Empire*, edited by Judith Brown and Wm. Roger Louis. Vol. 4: The Twentieth Century, 398–420. Oxford: Oxford University Press, 1999.

Robinson, Francis. "Technology and Religious Change: Islam and the Impact of Print," *Modern Asian Studies* 27, 1 (February 1993), 229–51.

Rudé, George. "The Gordon Riots: A Study of the Rioters and Their Victims," *Transactions of the Royal Historical Society*, Fifth Series, 6 (1956), 93–114.

Rudé, George. "Protest and Punishment in Nineteenth-Century Britain," *Albion* 5, 1 (Spring 1973), 1–23.

Sarkar, Sumit. *The Swadeshi Movement in Bengal.* New Delhi: People's Publishing House, 1973.

Schuler, Monica. "Liberated Africans in Nineteenth-Century Guyana." In *Slavery, Freedom and Gender: The Dynamics of Caribbean Society*, edited by Brian L. Moore, B. W. Higman, Carl Campbell, and Patrick Bryan, 133–57. Kingston, Jamaica: University of the West Indies Press, 2001.

Senior, Hereward. *Orangeism in Ireland and Britain, 1795–1836.* London: Routledge and Kegan Paul, 1966.

Senior, Hereward. *Orangeism: The Canadian Phase.* Toronto: McGraw-Hill Ryerson, 1972.

Sheppard, Samuel T. *The Bombay Volunteer Rifles: A History.* Bombay: The Times Press, 1919.

Silvestri, Michael. *Ireland and India: Nationalism, Empire and Memory*. Houndmills, Basingstoke: Palgrave Macmillan, 2009.

Singh, Kelvin. *Bloodstained Tombs: The Mohurrum Massacre, 1884*. Basingstoke: Macmillan Caribbean, 1988.

Singha, Radhika. "Settle, Mobilise, Verify: Identification Practices in Colonial India," *Studies in History* 16 (2000), 151–98.

Smyth, William J. *Toronto, the Belfast of Canada: The Orange Order and the Shaping of Municipal Culture*. Toronto: University of Toronto Press, 2015.

Somaratna, G. P. V. *Kotahena Riot 1883: A Religious Riot in Sri Lanka*. Gangodawila, Sri Lanka: Deepanee, 1991.

St. Pierre, Maurice. "The Nature and Development of Social Conflict in Guyana." In *Governance, Conflict Analysis, and Conflict Resolution*, edited by Cedric H. Grant and R. Mark Kirton, 177–93. Kingston, Jamaica: Ian Randle, 2007.

Stead, P. J. *The Police of Britain*. Basingstoke: Macmillan, 1985.

Steedman, Carolyn. *Policing the Victorian Community: The Formation of English Provincial Police Forces, 1856–80*. London: Routledge & Kegan Paul, 1984.

Stewart, A. T. Q. *The Narrow Ground: Aspects of Ulster, 1609–1969*. Belfast: The Blackstaff Press, 1997.

Stirrat, R. L. "Constructing Identities in Nineteenth-Century Colombo." In *Identity and Affect: Experiences of Identity in a Globalizing World*, edited by John R. Campbell and Alan Rew, 39–63. London: Pluto Press, 1999.

Streets, Heather. *Martial Races: The Military, Race and Masculinity in British Imperial Culture, 1857–1914*. Manchester: Manchester University Press, 2004.

Sumathipala, K. H. M. "The Kotahena Riots and their Repercussions," *The Ceylon Historical Journal* 19 (1969–70), 65–81.

Suntharalingam, R. "The Salem Riots, 1882: Judiciary versus Executive in the Mediation of a Communal Dispute," *Modern Asian Studies* 3, 3 (1969), 193–208.

Swift, R. E. "Anti-Catholicism and Irish Disturbances: Public Order in Mid-Victorian Wolverhampton," *Midland History* 9 (1984), 87–108.

Tager, Jack. *Boston Riots: Three Centuries of Social Violence*. Boston: Northeastern University Press, 2001.

Tejani, Shabnum. *Indian Secularism: A Social and Intellectual History, 1890–1950*. Bloomington: Indiana University Press, 2008.

Thorne, Susan. "'The Conversion of the Englishmen and the Conversion of the World Inseparable': Missionary Imperialism and the Language of Class in Early Industrial Britain." In *Tensions of Empire: Colonial Cultures in a Bourgeois World*, edited by Frederick Cooper and Ann Laura Stoler, 238–92. Berkeley: University of California Press, 1997.

Thornton, Rod. "The British Army and the Origins of its Moral Force Philosophy," *Small Wars and Insurgencies* 15, 1 (Spring 2004), 83–106

Thursby, G. R. *Hindu-Muslim Relations in British India: A Study of Controversy, Conflict, and Communal Movements in Northern India, 1923–1928*. Leiden: E. J. Brill, 1975.

Toscano, Alberto. *Fanaticism: On the Uses of an Idea*. London: Verso, 2010.

Townshend, Charles. *Britain's Civil Wars: Counterinsurgency in the Twentieth Century*. London: Faber and Faber, 1986.

Townshend, Charles. *Making the Peace: Public Order and Security in Modern Britain*. Oxford: Oxford University Press, 1993.

Townshend, Charles. *Political Violence in Ireland: Government and Resistance since 1848*. Oxford: Clarendon Press, 1983.

Vaccha, P. B. *Famous Judges, Lawyers and Cases of Bombay: A Judicial History of Bombay During the British Period*. Bombay: N. M. Tripathi, 1962.

Van Der Veer, Peter. *Imperial Encounters: Religion and Modernity in India and Britain*. Princeton: Princeton University Press, 2001.

Vann, J. Don and Rosemary T. VanArsdel. *Periodicals of Queen Victoria's Empire: An Exploration*. Toronto: University of Toronto Press, 1996.

Vogler, Richard. *Reading the Riot Act: The Magistracy, the Police and the Army in Civil Disorder*. Milton Keynes: Open University Press, 1991.

Wadia, Jal H. *The Life of Sir Jamsetjee Jejeebhoy, First Baronet, and the Lives of the Members of his Family, and a Short History of Sir J. J. P. B. Institution*. Bombay: Mody Printing Press, 1950.

Wainwright, A. Martin. "Representing the Technology of the Raj in Britain's Victorian Periodical Press." In *Negotiating India in the Nineteenth-Century Media*, edited by David Finkelstein and Douglas M. Peers, 185–209. New York: St. Martin's Press, 2000.

Webber, A. R. F. *Centenary History and Handbook of British Guiana*. British Guiana: The Argosy, 1931.

Wiener, Martin J. *An Empire on Trial: Race, Murder, and Justice under British Rule, 1870–1935*. Cambridge: Cambridge University Press, 2009.

Wilson, Kathleen, ed. *A New Imperial History: Culture, Identity and Modernity in Britain and the Empire, 1660–1840*. Cambridge: Cambridge University Press, 2004.

Wolffe, John. "North Atlantic Anti-Catholicism in the Nineteenth Century: A Comparative Overview," *European Studies* 31 (2013), 25–31.

Wood, Ian. "Irish Immigrants and Scottish Radicalism, 1880–1906." In *Essays in Scottish Labour History*, edited by Ian MacDougall, 65–89. Edinburgh: John Donald, 1978.

Wright, Frank. "Communal Deterrence and the Threat of Violence in the North of Ireland in the Nineteenth Century." In *Political Violence: Ireland in a Comparative Perspective*, edited by John Darby, Nicholas Dodge, and A. C. Hepburn, 11–28. Belfast: Appletree Press, 1990.

Wright, Julia M. *Ireland, India and Nationalism in Nineteenth-Century Literature*. Cambridge: Cambridge University Press, 2007.

Yang, Anand A. "A Conversation of Rumors: The Language of Popular 'Mentalitès' in Late Nineteenth-Century Colonial India," *Journal of Social History* 20, 3 (1987), 485–505.

Yong, Tan Tai. *The Garrison State: The Military, Government and Society in Colonial Punjab, 1849–1947.* New Delhi: Sage, 2005.

Index